INSTRUCTOR'S MANUAL TO ACCOMPANY
FUNDAMENTALS OF
PHYSIOLOGY
A HUMAN PERSPECTIVE

SECOND EDITION

LAURALEE SHERWOOD

DEPARTMENT OF PHYSIOLOGY
SCHOOL OF MEDICINE
WEST VIRGINIA UNIVERSITY

WEST PUBLISHING COMPANY

MINNEAPOLIS/ST. PAUL   NEW YORK   SAN FRANCISCO   LOS ANGELES

WEST'S COMMITMENT TO THE ENVIRONMENT

In 1906, West Publishing Company began recycling materials left over from the production of books. This began a tradition of efficient and responsible use of resources. Today, up to 95% of our legal books and 70% of our college texts and school texts are printed on recycled, acid-free stock. West also recycles nearly 22 million pounds of scrap paper annually—the equivalent of 181,717 trees. Since the 1960s, West has devised ways to capture and recycle waste inks, solvents, oils, and vapors created in the printing process. We also recycle plastics of all kinds, wood, glass, corrugated cardboard, and batteries, and have eliminated the use of Styrofoam book packaging. We at West are proud of the longevity and the scope of our commitment to the environment.

Production, Prepress, Printing and Binding by West Publishing Company.

 TEXT IS PRINTED ON 10% POST CONSUMER RECYCLED PAPER

Table of Contents

Preface

This manual, designed to accompany Sherwood, <u>Fundamentals of Physiology: A Human Perspective, second edition,</u> offers the following features to aid faculty members using the text.

DETAILED CONTENTS OF MAIN TEXT

By providing the faculty member with a quick overview of the content within each section of a chapter, this feature can be used to facilitate lecture planning and assignment of text reading.

LECTURE HINTS AND SUGGESTIONS

This feature offers a range of classroom activities to supplement lectures. Suggested sources of materials are provided as an added convenience to the instructor.

CHAPTER TEST QUESTIONS

A large pool of test questions generated by the text author is provided for each chapter to facilitate exam preparation. The pool can be used to prepare multiple exams on a given topic because of the large number, format variety, and varying degree of difficulty of questions available. The majority of the questions have been classroom-tested by the author over a period of years. All questions are compatible with the text and have been updated as necessary.

West Publishing Company provides a computerized testing service based on the pool of questions in this manual. Questions used are of the instructor's choice. For further information, contact your local West sales representative. If you do not know who your representative is, you can find out by contacting the St. Paul headquarters of the company.

AUDIOVISUAL AIDS

Films suitable to accompany this textbook are available from **West's Life Science Video Library** as well as some selections from **West's Health, Nutrition, and Fitness Video Library.** A list and description of these films plus an explanation of West's policy for loaning films at no charge to adopters of the text is presented in Appendix A

A list of other relevant films and software that may be ordered to complement lectures is presented for each chapter. Sources for these learning aids, designated by abbreviation in the lists, are prvided in Appendix B. These materials represent a consolidated guide to available audiovisual resources that can be further explored by the instructor for appropriateness for the class involved. They have not been previewed or rated by the text author or preparer of these lists.

APPENDIXES

Appendix A, as mentioned, consists of a list of films available from West's Video Libraries. Appendix B is an alphabetized list of sources for audiovisual and software materials. Also included in Appendix A is a roster of biological supply houses that may be explored for classroom aids and supplies. Appendix C of this manual contains short explanations of "Points to Ponder" questions from the textbook's review exercises. Appendix D contains a list of figures from the text available as full color acetate transparencies. The transparency package may be ordered free of charge through your local West sales representative.

ACKNOWLEDGEMENTS

I wish to thank the following individuals for their invaluable contributions in preparing this manual. First, a heartfelt expression of gratitude and love is extended to my daughter, Melinda Marple for preparing the camera-ready copy for this manual. Her conscientiousness, diligence, and excellent word-processing skills were invaluable in getting this manual to production within tight time constraints so that it would be available for use by instructors at the time of publication of the main text. Second, John Harley, Eastern Kentucky University, deserves a special recognition for preparing the thoughtful "Lecture Hints and Suggestions." Third, a special thank you is extended to David Shepard, Southeastern Louisiana University, for updating the helpful list of "Audiovisual Aids." Finally, my sincere appreciation goes to Betsy Friedman, a highly organized and understanding developmental editor for West Publishing Company, who oversaw the development of this manual.

Chapter 1
Homeostasis: The Foundation of Physiology

CONTENTS
(All page references are to the main text.)

Chapter in Perspective: **Focus on Homeostasis**, p.11

Chapter Summary, p.12

LECTURE HINTS AND SUGGESTIONS

1. Have students provide some characteristics of living versus nonliving entities.

2. Use a laboratory animal (e.g., rat, mouse, rabbit) to illustrate the various organ systems. William C. Brown Company, Dubuque, IA, has the following dissection manuals: cat, pig, frog, mink, perch, pigeon, rat, rabbit, shark, and turtle.

3. Use a mechanical clock as an example of nonhomeostasis as it progressively "winds down" and stops. Ask the students for examples of homeostasis within the body and elsewhere in the environment (e.g., a see-saw, insulin versus glucagon, temperature control in a room).

4. Use a series of steps (staircase) to illustrate the increasing level of organizational complexity.

5. Have students give their reasons why homeostasis is important.

6. Use an anatomical model to illustrate the organs that comprise each body system. A good source is Carolina Biological Supply Company, Burlington, NC.

7. Use models and/or slides to illustrate the basic tissue types. A good source is Carolina Biological Supply Company.

CHAPTER TEST QUESTIONS

Multiple Choice

1. Which of the following is (are) basic functions carried out by each cell for its own survival?

    (a) Obtaining oxygen and nutrients.
    (b) Eliminating wastes.
    (c) Producing digestive enzymes.
    (d) Both (a) and (b) above are correct.
    (e) All of the above are correct.

ANSWER: d

2. Which of the following is **not** a primary tissue type?

   (a) Lung tissue.
   (b) Muscle tissue.
   (c) Nervous tissue.
   (d) Epithelial tissue.
   (e) Connective tissue.

ANSWER: a

3. Which of the following factors of the internal environment
    is not homeostatically maintained?

   (a) Its concentration of nutrient molecules.
   (b) Its concentration of nitrogen gas, of which 80% of
        the atmospheric air is composed.
   (c) Its concentration of oxygen and carbon dioxide.
   (d) Its pH.
   (e) Its temperature.

ANSWER: b

4. The respiratory system

   (a) obtains oxygen from and eliminates carbon dioxide to
        the external environment.
   (b) consists of the nose, pharynx, larynx, trachea,
        bronchi, and lungs.
   (c) plays an important role in maintaining the proper pH
        of the internal environment by adjusting the rate of
        removal of acid-forming carbon dioxide.
   (d) Both (a) and (b) above are correct.
   (e) All of the above are correct.

ANSWER: e

5. Which of the following statements regarding extrinsic
    controls is **incorrect**?

   (a) Extrinsic controls are inherent to an organ.
   (b) Extrinsic controls are regulatory mechanisms initi-
        ated outside of an organ that alter the activity of
        the organ.
   (c) Extrinsic controls are accomplished by the nervous
        and endocrine systems.
   (d) Extrinsic controls permit coordinated regulation of
        several organs toward a common goal.
   (e) Extrinsic controls generally operate on the princi-
        ple of negative feedback.

ANSWER: a

6. At least part of the activities of which of the following body systems is **not** directed toward maintaining homeostasis?

    (a) Reproductive system.
    (b) Muscular system.
    (c) Nervous system.
    (d) Both (a) and (b) above are correct.
    (e) All of the above are correct.

ANSWER: e

7. The internal environment

    (a) is in direct contact with the body's cells.
    (b) consists of the extracellular fluid.
    (c) must be maintained at absolutely unchanging composi-
         tion, temperature and volume for survival of the
         body.
    (d) Both (a) and (b) above are correct.
    (e) All of the above are correct.

ANSWER: d

8. Extracellular fluid

    (a) is the internal environment of the body
    (b) is outside the cells but inside the body
    (c) consists of the plasma and interstitial fluid
    (d) Two of the above are correct
    (e) All of the above are correct

ANSWER: e

9. Which of the following statements concerning negative feedback is **incorrect**?

    (a) Negative feedback exists when a change in a regulated
         variable triggers a response that opposes the change.
    (b) Negative feedback exists when the input to a system
         increases the output and the output limits its own
         production by inhibiting the input.
    (c) With negative feedback, a control system's input and
         output continue to enhance each other.
    (d) Most of the body's homeostatic control mechanisms
         operate on the principle of negative feedback.

ANSWER: c

10. Endocrine glands

     (a) lack ducts.
     (b) secrete hormones internally into the blood.
     (c) are derived from epithelial tissue.
     (d) Both (a) and (b) above are correct.
     (e) All of the above are correct.

ANSWER: e

11. Which of the following is (are) a type of connective
    tissue?

     (a) exocrine glands
     (b) bone
     (c) blood
     (d) Both (b) and (c) above are correct
     (e) None of the above are correct.

ANSWER: d

12. The hormone insulin enhances the transport of glucose
    (sugar) from the blood into most of the body's cells. Its
    secretion is controlled by a negative-feedback system
    between the concentration of glucose in the blood and the
    insulin-secreting cells. Therefore, which of the following
    statements is correct?

     (a) A decrease in blood glucose concentration stimulates
          insulin secretion, which in turn further lowers the
          blood glucose concentration.
     (b) An increase in blood glucose concentration stimulates
          insulin secretion, which in turn lowers the blood
          glucose concentration.
     (c) A decrease in blood glucose concentration stimulates
          insulin secretion, which in turn increases the blood
          glucose concentration.
     (d) An increase in blood glucose concentration stimulates
          insulin secretion, which in turn further increases the
          blood glucose concentration.
     (e) None of the above are correct.

ANSWER: b

13. Sweating is initiated in response to a rise in body temperature that occurs on exposure to a hot environment. Evaporation of the sweat from the surface of the skin cool the body. This is an example of

    (a) negative feedback
    (b) positive feedback
    (c) a feedforward mechanism
    (d) an intrinsic (local) control mechanism

ANSWER: a

True/False

14. All cells are capable of reproducing.

ANSWER: False

15. Nerve and muscle cells are not capable of reproducing.

ANSWER: True

16. Tissues are composed of two or more types of cells organized to perform a particular function or functions.

ANSWER: False

17. Blood is a type of connective tissue.

ANSWER: True

18. Exocrine glands secrete hormones through ducts into the blood.

ANSWER: False

19. Cells are progressively organized into tissues, organs, systems, and, finally, the whole body.

ANSWER: True

20. Factors that are homeostatically regulated are maintained at a constant, fixed level unless disease is present.

ANSWER: False

21. To sustain life, the internal environment must be maintained in an absolutely unchanging state.

ANSWER: False

22. Not all activities performed by the muscular and nervous systems are directed toward maintaining homeostasis.

ANSWER: True

23. The plasma surrounds and bathes all of the body's cells.

ANSWER: False

24. Exocrine glands are the only structures in the body capable of secretion.

ANSWER: False

25. Secretion refers to the release from a cell, in response to appropriate stimulation, of specific products that have in large part been synthesized by the cell.

ANSWER: True

26. The muscular and integumentary systems are both important in regulation of body temperature.

ANSWER: True

27. Some organs, such as the heart, skin, and intestine, belong to more than one body system.

ANSWER: True

28. The digestive system eliminates waste products other than carbon dioxide from the body.

ANSWER: False

29. Negative feedback operates to maintain a controlled factor in a relatively steady state, whereas positive feedback moves a controlled factor even further from a steady state.

ANSWER: True

30. With positive feedback, a control system's input and output continue to enhance each other.

ANSWER: True

31. Feedforward mechanisms bring about a response in reaction to a change in a regulated variable.

ANSWER: False

8   Chapter 1

32. Most homeostatic mechanisms operate on the principle of positive feedback.

ANSWER: False

Fill-in-the-blanks

33. The smallest unit capable of carrying out the processes associated with life is the _____.

ANSWER: cell

34. _____ are composed of two or more types of primary tissue organized to perform a particular function or functions.

ANSWER: Organs

35. A _____ is a collection of organs that perform related functions and interact to accomplish a common activity that is essential for survival of the whole body.

ANSWER: body system

36. The internal environment consists of the _____, which is made up of _____, the fluid portion of the blood, and _____, which surrounds and bathes all cells.

ANSWER: extracellular fluid, plasma, interstitial fluid

37. The body cells are in direct contact with and make life-sustaining exchanges with the _____.

ANSWER: internal environment (extracellular fluid)

38. _____ refers to maintenance of a relatively stable internal environment.

ANSWER: Homeostasis

39. _____ are epithelial-tissue derivatives that are specialized for secretion.

ANSWER: Glands

40. _____ tissue is composed of cells specialized for contraction and force generation.

ANSWER: Muscle

41. The _____ system consists of all hormone-secreting tissues.

ANSWER: endocrine

42. The two major control systems of the body are the _____ and the _____.

ANSWERS: nervous system, endocrine system

43. The _____ system is the transport system of the body.

ANSWER: circulatory

44. The _____ system eliminates waste products other than carbon dioxide and plays a key role in regulating the volume, electrolyte composition and acidity of the extracellular fluid.

ANSWER: urinary

45. The _____ system controls and coordinates bodily activities that require swift responses, especially to changes in the external environment.

ANSWER: nervous

46. _____ refers to the abnormal functioning of the body associated with disease.

ANSWER: Pathophysiology

Short Answer

47. State the relationship among cells, body systems, and homeostasis that serves as the foundation for modern-day physiology.

ANSWER: Homeostasis is essential for cell survival, body systems maintain homeostasis, and cells make up body systems.

48. List the eleven major body systems and describe how each contributes to homeostasis.

ANSWER: See text pages 6 through 7 and Figure 1-4 on pages 8 and 9.

49. List the factors that must be homeostatically maintained.

ANSWER: See text page 6.

Matching

50. Use the following answer code to indicate which tissue is being identified.

> (a) = nervous tissue
> (b) = epithelial tissue
> (c) = muscle tissue
> (d) = connective tissue

_____composed of cells specialized for contraction and force generation

_____consists of cells specialized for initiation and transmission of electrical signals, sometimes over long distances

_____made up of cells specialized in the exchange of materials between the cell and its environment

_____connects, supports, and anchors various body parts

_____the heart is primarily composed of this tissue type

_____bone is this tissue type

_____the lining of the digestive tract is this tissue type

_____glands are this tissue type

_____the brain is primarily composed of this tissue type

_____the blood is this tissue type

_____this tissue is distinguished by relatively few cells dispersed within an abundance of extracellular material

_____the skin is this tissue type

ANSWERS: c, a, b, d, c, d, b, b, a, d, d, b

51. Temperature-sensitive nerve cells monitor the body temperature and provide information about its status to a temperature-control center in the hypothalamus, a part of the brain. The hypothalamus can bring about adjustments in body temperature by inducing shivering or sweating, among other things.

    Indicate the roles served by each component of this control system using the following answer code.

    > (a) = controlled variable
    > (b) = integrator
    > (c) = sensor
    > (d) = effector

    _____ body temperature

    _____ temperature-sensitive nerve cells

    _____ skeletal muscles and sweat glands

    _____ hypothalamus

ANSWER: a, c, d, b

AUDIOVISUAL AIDS

Films

A list of films available from West Publishing Company is presented in Appendix A.   Following are other films that may be suitable. The sources for these films, which are coded by abbreviation, are provided in Appendix B.

Biochemical Balances, FHS, 10 min.

Biology: Form and Function (VCR), MG, 24 min.

Coping with Change, FHS, 10 min.

Cybernetics, MH, 22 min.

Design for Living, FM, 26 min.

From Atoms to Organisms, NET, 29 min.

Functions of the Body, UC, 15 min.

Homeostasis, IM, 60 min.

Homeostasis: Maintaining the Body's Environment, IM, 30 min.

Homeostasis: Maintaining the Stability of Life, EI

Incredible Voyage, MH, 26 min.

Man: The Incredible Machine, NG, 28 min.

Nature of Science, (4-part series), COR, 56 min.

Osmoregulation, FHS, 10 min.

Patterns of Life: Living vs Nonliving, NET, 29 min.

Search for Life, TLV, 30 min.

The Feedback Cycle, FHS, 10 min.

The Nature of Life, NET, 28 min.

The Sea Within, FHS, 10 min.

Software

Homeostasis, PLP.   Covers homeostasis as central framework of physiology.

The Human Body: An Overview, CBS. Seven lessons introduce students to six human body systems.

Your Body (Series I, II), CBS. Covers all body systems.

Chapter 2
Cellular Physiology

CONTENTS
(All page references are to the main text.)

Cytosol and Cytoskeleton, p.29
  -The cytosol is important in intermediary metabolism,
  ribosomal protein synthesis, and storage of fat and glycogen.
  p.30
  -The cytoskeleton supports and organizes the intracellular
  components and controls their movements. p. 30

Chapter in Perspective: Focus on Homeostasis, p.34

Chapter Summary, p.34

LECTURE HINTS AND SUGGESTIONS

1. The utilization of slides, transparencies, and electron
    micrographs are very useful for pointing out the major
    features of cells and organelles. These can be obtained from
    Carolina Biological Supply Company, Burlington, NC.

2. Demonstrate a model of a cell and the organelles. These can
    be obtained from Carolina Biological Supply Company.

3. Students enjoy the "Cell Game" available from Carolina
    Biological Supply Company.

CHAPTER TEST QUESTIONS

Multiple Choice

1. The plasma membrane

    (a) serves as a mechanical barrier to hold in the contents
         of the cell.
    (b) selectively controls movement of molecules between the
         ECF and ICF.
    (c) is the barrier that surrounds the blood vessels and
         separates the blood plasma from the interstitial fluid.
    (d) Both (a) and (b) above are correct.
    (e) None of the above are correct.

ANSWER: d

2. The rough endoplasmic reticulum

    (a) is studded with ribosomes.
    (b) synthesizes proteins for export from the cell or for use
         in construction of new cellular membrane.
    (c) is continuous with the smooth endoplasmic reticulum.
    (d) Both (a) and (b) above are correct.
    (e) All of the above are correct.

ANSWER: e

3.   The smooth endoplasmic reticulum

(a)   is most abundant in cells specialized for protein secretion.
(b)   gives rise to transport vesicles containing newly synthesized molecules wrapped in a layer of smooth-ER membrane.
(c)   consists of stacks of relatively flattened sacs.
(d)   Both (a) and (b) above are correct.
(e)   All of the above are correct.

ANSWER: b

4.   Which of the following <u>does not</u> apply to lysosomes?

(a)   Contain powerful hydrolytic enzymes.
(b)   Detoxify various wastes produced within the cell or foreign compounds that have entered the cell.
(c)   Remove useless parts of the cell.
(d)   Attack material engulfed by the cell by means of endocytosis.
(e)   After completing their digestive activities are known as residual bodies.

ANSWER: b

5.   In an anaerobic condition,

(a)   oxygen is not present.
(b)   the degradation of glucose cannot proceed beyond glycolysis.
(c)   mitochondrial processing of nutrient molecules takes place.
(d)   Both (a) and (b) above are correct.
(e)   Both (a) and (c) above are correct.

ANSWER: d

6.   _____ provides the greatest yield of ATP molecules for each molecule of glucose processed.

(a)   Glycolysis
(b)   The citric-acid cycle
(c)   The electron-transport chain

ANSWER: c

7.   Microtubules

    (a)   serve as a mechanical stiffener for microvilli.
    (b)   are specialized to detect sound and positional changes
          in the ear.
    (c)   form nonmuscle contractile assemblies.
    (d)   play a structural role in parts of the cell subject to
          mechanical stress.
    (e)   None of the above are correct.

ANSWER: e

8.   Which of the following organelles contains oxidative
     enzymes?

    (a)   peroxisomes
    (b)   mitochondria
    (c)   lysosomes
    (d)   Both (a) and (b) above are correct.
    (e)   All of the above are correct.

ANSWER: d

9.   Glycolysis

    (a)   yields two molecules of ATP for each molecule of
          glucose processed
    (b)   requires oxygen
    (c)   takes place in the mitochondrial matrix
    (d)   Both (a) and (b) above are correct.
    (e)   All of the above are correct.

ANSWER: a

10.   Nicotimamide adenine dinucleotide (NAD)

    (a)   converts ADP + P_i to ATP
    (b)   is found in the cytosol
    (c)   is a hydrogen carrier molecule
    (d)   Both (b) and (c) above are correct.
    (e)   All of the above are correct.

ANSWER: c

11. Which of the following is not associated with the cytosol?

    (a) synthesis of proteins for export from the cell
    (b) enzymatic regulation of intermediary metabolism
    (c) storage of fat and glycogen
    (d) synthesis of proteins for use in the cytosol
    (e) presence of cytoskeletal elements

ANSWER: a

12. Which of the following is <u>not</u> characteristic of the cytoskeleton?

    (a) The cytoskeleton supports the plasma membrane and is responsible for the particular shape, rigidity, and spatial geometry of each different cell type.
    (b) The cytoskeleton probably plays a role in regulating cell growth and division.
    (c) The cytoskeletal elements are all rigid, permanent structures.
    (d) The cytoskeleton is responsible for cell contraction and cell movements.
    (e) The cytoskeleton supports and organizes the ribosomes, mitochondria, and lysosomes.

ANSWER: c

True/False

13. "Life" is due to the complex organization and interaction of chemical molecules within the cells.

ANSWER: True

14. The average human cell is about one hundred times smaller than the smallest particle visible by the unaided eye.

ANSWER: False

15. The three major subdivisions of a cell are plasma membrane, the nucleus, and the cytoplasm.

ANSWER: True

16. The nucleus is typically the largest single organized cellular component.

ANSWER: True

17. The nucleus indirectly governs most cellular activities by directing the kinds and amounts of various enzymes and other proteins that are produced by the cell.

ANSWER: True

18. Rough endoplasmic reticulum is most abundant in cells specialized for protein secretion, whereas smooth endoplasmic reticulum is abundant in cells that specialize in lipid metabolism.

ANSWER: True

19. Proteins synthesized by the endoplasmic reticulum become permanently separated from the cytosol as soon as they have been synthesized.

ANSWER: True

20. The endoplasmic reticulum is one continuous organelle consisting of many tubules and cisternae.

ANSWER: True

21. Secretory vesicles are released to the exterior of the cell by means of the process of phagocytosis.

ANSWER: False

22. ATP synthetase is located in the flattened sacs of the Golgi complex.

ANSWER: False

23. Most intermediary metabolism is accomplished in the cytosol.

ANSWER: True

24. The protective, waterproof outer layer of skin is formed by the tough skeleton of the microtrabecular lattice that persists after the surface skin cells die.

ANSWER: False

Fill-in-the-blanks

25. The three major subdivisions of a cell are the _____, the _____, and the _____.

ANSWERS: plasma membrane, nucleus, cytoplasm

26. The fluid contained within all of the cells of the body is known collectively as _____, and the fluid outside of the cells is referred to as _____.

ANSWERS: intracellular fluid, extracellular fluid

27. The two major parts of the cell's interior are the _____ and the _____.

ANSWERS: nucleus, cytoplasm

28. The _____ ER is the central packaging and discharge site for molecules to be transported from the ER.

ANSWER: smooth

29. The ribosomes of the rough ER synthesize _____, whereas its membranous walls contain enzymes essential for the synthesis of _____.

ANSWER: proteins, lipids

30. _____ refers to the process of an intracellular vesicle fusing with the plasma membrane, then opening and emptying its contents to the exterior.

ANSWER: exocytosis

31. Foreign material to be attacked by lysosomal enzymes is brought into the cell by the process of _____.

ANSWER: endocytosis

32. Lysosomes contain (what type of) _____ enzymes.

ANSWER: hydrolytic

33. Lysosomes that have completed their digestive activities are known as _____.

ANSWER: residual bodies

34. _____ is the universal energy carrier.

ANSWER: adenosine triphosphate, ATP

35. _____ refers collectively to the large set of intra-cellular chemical reactions that involve the degradation, synthesis, and transformation of small organic molecules.

ANSWER: intermediary metabolism

36. _____ are the dominant structural and functional components of cilia and flagella.

ANSWER: microtubules

Short Answer

37. State the advantage of compartmentalization of specific sets of chemicals within organelles.

ANSWER: on text page 16

38. List and state the functions of each of the six types of organelles.

ANSWER: summarized in chart on text page 18

39. State the three main categories of cellular activities that require energy expenditure.

ANSWER: synthesis of new chemical compounds, membrane transport, mechanical work

Matching

40. Indicate which of the properties listed applies to each of the chemical activities by circling the appropriate letters using the answer code below.

    (a) = directly uses inspired oxygen
    (b) = does not directly use inspired oxygen
    (c) = takes place in the cytosol
    (d) = takes place in the mitochondrial matrix
    (e) = takes place on the inner mitochondrial membrane
    (f) = low yield of ATP
    (g) = rich yield of ATP

    Glycolysis: a, b, c, d, e, f, g
    Citric-acid cycle: a, b, c, d, e, f, g
    Electron-transport chain: a, b, c, d, e, f, g

ANSWERS: Glycolysis: b, c, f; Citric-acid cycle: b, d, f; Electron-transport chain: a, e, g

41. _____ houses the cell's DNA
_____ responsible for cell shape and movement
_____ highly organized membrane-bound intracellular structures
_____ selectively controls movement of molecules between the intracellular fluid and extracellular fluid
_____ consists of organelles and cytosol
_____ site of intermediary metabolism
_____ presence of this (these) structure(s) permits incompatible chemical reactions to occur simultaneously in the cell
_____ separates contents of the cell from its surroundings
_____ site of fat and glycogen storage

(a) plasma membrane
(b) nucleus
(c) cytoplasm
(d) cytosol
(e) organelles
(f) cytoskeleton

ANSWERS: b, f, e, a, c, d, e, a, d

42 _____ largest of cytoskeletal elements
_____ present in parts of the cell subject to mechanical stress
_____ smallest element(s) visible with a conventional electron microscope
_____ consist(s) of actin
_____ organize(s) the glycolytic enzymes in a sequential alignment
_____ form(s) the mitotic spindle
_____ essential for creating and maintaining an asymmetrical cell shape
_____ composed of tubulin
_____ form "highways" that transport secretory vesicles from one region of the cell to another
_____ visible only with a high voltage electron microscope
_____ play(s) a key role in muscle contraction
_____ responsible for ciliary bending and whiplike motion of flagella

(a) microtubules
(b) microfilaments
(c) intermediate filaments
(d) microtrabecular lattice

ANSWERS: a, c, b, b, d, a, a, a, a, d, b, a

43. ____ modifies newly synthesized proteins into their final form

____ contains powerful oxidative enzymes important in detoxifying various wastes

____ important components of cilia and flagella

____ one continuous extensive organelle consisting of a network of tubules and flattened sacs

____ removes unwanted cellular debris and foreign material

____ energy organelle

____ acts as a mechanical stiffener

____ responsible for sorting and segregating molecules destined for secretion or to various intracellular sites

____ synthesizes proteins for use in the cytosol

____ consists of stacks of flattened sacs

____ organizes cytosolic enzymes into a sequential alignment

____ shaped like octagonal barrel

____ contains powerful hydrolytic enzymes

____ contains cristae projecting into a matrix

____ forms mitotic spindle

____ structurally important in parts of cell subject to mechanical stress

____ synthesizes proteins destined for construction of new cellular membrane or secretion out of the cell

____ three-dimensional meshwork of exceedingly fine interlinked filaments

____ believed to carry messenger RNA from the nucleus to sites of protein synthesis within the cytoplasm

____ plays vital role in various cellular contractile systems

____ surface partially studded with ribosomes

(a) endoplasmic reticulum
(b) Golgi complex
(c) lysosome
(d) peroxisome
(e) mitochondria
(f) vault
(g) free ribosome
(h) microtubule
(i) microfilament
(j) intermediate filament
(k) microtrabecular lattice

ANSWERS: b, d, h, a, c, e, i, b, g, b, k, f, c, e, h, j, a, k, f, i, a

44. ____ hairlike motile protrusions

____ found in hair cells of inner ear

____ sweep mucus and debris out of respiratory airways

____ increase the surface area of intestine and kidney cells

____ enable sperm to move

____ whiplike appendage

____ guide egg to oviduct

(a) flagella
(b) cilia
(c) microvilli

ANSWERS: b, c, b, c, a, a, b

AUDIOVISUAL AIDS

Films

A list of films available from West Publishing Company is presented in Appendix A.   Following are other films that may be suitable.   The sources for these films, which are coded by abbreviation, are provided in Appendix B.

An Introduction to Cells, EI, 30 min.

Bags of Life, PS, 54 min.

Biological Membranes, PS, 17 min.

Cell Biology: Life Functions, COR, 20 min.

Cell Biology: Structure and Composition, COR, 13 min.

Cell Motility, EI

Cell Motility and Microtubules, FHS, 30 min.

Cell Structure (VCR), MG, 24 min.

Cell Structure, PS, 25 min.

Cell-Unit of Life, PLP, 15 min.

Inside the Cell, IM, 45 min.

Introduction to Cell Structure, IM, 34 min.

Introduction to Living Cells, PLP, 18 min.

Learning About Cells, EBE, 16 min.

The Building Blocks of Life, CBS, 60 min.

The Cell: Parts I and II, MH, 16 min.

The Cell, A Functioning Structure, Parts I and II, CCM, 30 min.

The Cell: Structural Unit of Life, COR, 11 min.

The Embattled Cell, WFL, 20 min.

The Life and Death of a Cell, UC, 27 min.

The Living Cell: An Introduction, EBE, 20 min.

<u>The Unit of Life</u>, MH, 28 min.

Software

<u>Cells</u>, CBS. Covers the cell theory and differences between plant and animal cells.

<u>Cell Structure and Function</u>, EI. Presents an overview of the animal cell.

Chapter 3
Membrane and Neuronal Physiology

CONTENTS
(All page references are to the main text.)

Membrane Structure and Composition, p.38

Beyond the Basics - Cystic Fibrosis: A Fatal Defect in Membrane Transport, p.41

Membrane Receptors and Postreceptor Events, p.42

Cell-to-Cell Adhesions, p.43

Chapter Summary, p.78

LECTURE HINTS AND SUGGESTIONS

1.   There are many excellent slides and overlays on the plasma membrane that can be shown. A good source is Carolina Biological Supply Company, Burlington, NC.

2.   Electron micrographs of cell-to-cell adhesions are very informative. See <u>Tissues and Organs</u> by Kessel & Kardon, W.H. Freeman & Company.

3.   Set up a carrot osmometer at the beginning of the period to illustrate osmosis. Fill the carrot with maple syrup and place in distilled water. The water will cause the syrup to rise in the tube. Ask the class to observe it from time to time and explain what is happening.

4.   Demonstrate the membrane potential and an action potential on an oscilloscope. See a physiology lab manual, e.g., Fox, <u>Laboratory Experiments in Physiology</u>, William C. Brown Company, Dubuque, IA, for details.

5.   Use models of neurons to illustrate their function. A good source is Carolina Biological Supply Company, Burlington, NC.

6.   Use an anatomical chart or torso or full-body manikin to illustrate the major parts of the nervous system.

7.   Set up microscope slides of histological preparations of neurons. Carolina Biological Supply Company has many to choose from.

8.   Use a nerve model to demonstrate a neuron's anatomical parts.

CHAPTER TEST QUESTIONS

Multiple Choice

1.   The plasma membrane

    (a)   is composed primarily of phospholipids and proteins arranged in a fluid mosaic structure.
    (b)   has a trilaminar appearance under an electron microscope.
    (c)   can be permeated only by substances that are less than 0.8 nm in diameter.
    (d)   Both (a) and (b) above are correct.
    (e)   All of the above are correct.

ANSWER: d

2.   Which of the following statements concerning the plasma membrane is correct?

   (a)   The plasma membrane appears as a trilaminar structure under a light microscope.
   (b)   The carbohydrates on the outer surface of the membrane serve as receptor sites for binding chemical messengers in the environment of the cell.
   (c)   The lipid bilayer serves as a barrier to passage of H_2O-soluble substances through the membrane.
   (d)   Carrier proteins shuttle back and forth across the membrane as they carry passenger molecules from one side to the other.
   (e)   The plasma membrane is impermeable to any substance that is not lipid soluble or is greater than 0.8 nm in diameter.

ANSWER: c

3.   The plasma membrane

   (a)   appears as a double dark line with a light space between under an electron microscope.
   (b)   is composed primarily of a double layer of phospholipid molecules with proteins interspersed throughout the phospholipids in a mosaic pattern.
   (c)   separates the intracellular and extracellular fluid.
   (d)   Two of the above are correct.
   (e)   All of the above are correct.

ANSWER: e

4.   The plasma membrane

   (a)   appears as a double dark line with a light space between under an electron microscope.
   (b)   is composed primarily of a lipid bilayer with proteins interspersed throughout the phospholipids in a mosaic fashion.
   (c   is more permeable to K^+ than to Na^+ at resting potential.
   (d)   Both (a) and (b) above are correct.
   (e)   All of the above are correct.

ANSWER: e

5. Which of the following is **not** a function of membrane proteins?

    (a) Serve as channels.
    (b) Determine fluidity of the membrane.
    (c) Serve as carriers.
    (d) Serve as receptor sites.
    (e) Serve as membrane-bound enzymes.

ANSWER: b

6. The phospholipids within the plasma membrane

    (a) form a bilayer with the nonpolar tails buried in the center and the hydrophilic heads lined up on the outer and inner surfaces.
    (b) serve as a barrier to passage of water-soluble substances between the ICF and ECF.
    (c) form channels for passage of small ions.
    (d) Both (a) and (b) above are correct.
    (e) All of the above are correct.

ANSWER: d

7. Phospholipids

    (a) consist of a polar, hydrophilic, phosphate-bearing, head and two nonpolar hydrophobic, fatty-acid tails
    (b) are aligned in a lipid bilayer in the plasma membrane
    (c) serve as carrier molecules for lipid-soluble substances
    (d) Both (a) and (b) above are correct.
    (e) All of the above are correct.

ANSWER: d

8. Which of the following is **not** involved in the cyclic AMP second messenger system?

    (a) Adenylate cyclase.
    (b) ATP.
    (c) Protein kinase.
    (d) Ca^{2+}
    (e) Phosphorylated intracellular protein.

ANSWER: d

9.   Which of the following are common means by which binding of
     an extracellular chemical messenger with a cell's receptor
     brings about a desired intracellular response?

     (a)   Opening or closing of specific channels to regulate
           ionic movement across the plasma membrane.
     (b)   Activation of an intracellular second messenger system.
     (c)   Turning on genes that code for the synthesis of new
           cellular proteins.
     (d)   Both (a) and (b) above are correct.
     (e)   All of the above are correct.

ANSWER: e

10.   Which of the following are known to be second messengers?

     (a)   Cyclic AMP.
     (b)   Calcium.
     (c)   ATP.
     (d)   Both (a) and (b) above are correct.
     (e)   All of the above are correct.

ANSWER: d

11.   The cellular component that, once activated by the binding
      of an extracellular messenger to a surface receptor, in turn
      activates cyclic AMP is

     (a)   phospholipase C.
     (b)   adenylate cyclase.
     (c)   calmodulin.
     (d)   calcium.
     (e)   cyclic guanosine monophosphate.

ANSWER: b

12.   Collagen

     (a)   provides tensile strength.
     (b)   is most abundant in tissues that must be capable of
           easily stretching and then recoiling.
     (c)   promotes cell adhesion.
     (d)   is a rubberlike protein fiber.
     (e)   forms the intercellular filaments of a desmosome.

ANSWER: a

13. Which of the following is not part of the extracellular matrix?

    (a) Watery, gel-like ground substance.
    (b) Connexons.
    (c) Collagen.
    (d) Elastin.
    (e) Fibronectin.

ANSWER: b

14. Which of the following statements concerning gap junctions is incorrect?

    (a) Gap junctions are communicating junctions.
    (b) At a gap junction, filaments of unknown composition extend between the plasma membranes of two closely adjacent but not touching cells, acting as "spot rivets" to anchor the cells together.
    (c) Gap junctions are formed by small connecting tunnels that link two adjacent cells and permit exchange of small water-soluble particles between the cells.
    (d) Gap junctions play an important role in transmission of electrical activity throughout an entire muscle mass.
    (e) Connexons are an important structural component of gap junctions.

ANSWER: b

15. In the cyclic AMP second messenger system, binding of the first messenger to a surface receptor leads to activation of _____, which induces the conversion of intracellular _____ to cyclic AMP.

    (a) adenylate cyclase, ATP
    (b) adenylate cyclase, ADP
    (c) phospholipase C, ATP
    (d) phospholipase C, ADP
    (e) protein kinase, ATP

ANSWER: a

16.   _____ are adhering junctions, _____ are impermeable junctions, and _____ are communicating junctions.

   (a) Tight junctions, gap junctions, desmosomes
   (b) Desmosomes, gap junctions, tight junctions
   (c) Desmosomes, tight junctions, gap junctions
   (d) Gap junctions, tight junctions, desmosomes
   (e) None of the above are correct.

ANSWER: c

17.   Carrier-mediated transport

   (a) involves a specific membrane protein that serves as a carrier molecule.
   (b) always moves substances against a concentration gradient.
   (c) always requires energy expenditure.
   (d) Two of the above are correct.
   (e) All of the above are correct.

ANSWER: a

18.   Facilitated diffusion

   (a) involves a carrier molecule.
   (b) requires energy expenditure.
   (c) is the means by which glucose enters the cells.
   (d) Both (a) and (c) above are correct.
   (e) All of the above are correct.

ANSWER: d

19.   Which of the following statements concerning endocytosis is correct?

   (a) Phagocytosis refers to the endocytosis of large multi-molecular particles such as bacteria or cellular debris.
   (b) By means of endocytosis, a particle can gain entry to the interior of the cell without actually passing through the plasma membrane.
   (c) The endocytotic vesicle may be degraded by lysosomes within the cell.
   (d) Both (a) and (b) above are correct
   (e) All of the above are correct.

ANSWER: a

20. Which of the following descriptions of movement of molecules across the plasma membrane is correct?

    (a) If two similar molecules can both combine with the same carrier, the presence of one of these molecules decreases the rate of entry of the other.
    (b) In simple diffusion, the rate of transport of a molecule into the cell is directly proportional to the molecule's extracellular concentration.
    (c) When a carrier becomes saturated, the maximum rate of transport across the membrane is reached.
    (d) Two of the above are correct.
    (e) All of the above are correct.

ANSWER: e

21. Which of the following substances is most likely to passively diffuse across the plasma membrane by dissolving in the membrane?

    (a) A cation.
    (b) An anion.
    (c) A nonpolar or nonionized molecule.
    (d) A polar molecule.
    (e) A molecule less than 0.8 nm in diameter.

ANSWER: c

22. The electrical gradient for K^+

    (a) favors its movement out of the cell at resting potential.
    (b) favors its movement into the cell at resting potential.
    (c) opposes the concentration gradient for K^+ at the equilibrium potential for K^+.
    (d) Both (a) and (c) above are correct.
    (e) Both (b) and (c) above are correct.

ANSWER: e

23. The concentration gradient for Na^+

    (a) favors its movement into the cell at resting potential.
    (b) favors its movement out of the cell at resting potential.
    (c) is maintained by the Na^+ - K^+ pump.
    (d) Both (a) and (c) above are correct.
    (e) Both (b) and (c) above are correct.

ANSWER: d

24. During osmosis,

    (a) water moves down its own concentration gradient.
    (b) water moves to an area of higher solute concentration.
    (c) the solute moves against its concentration gradient.
    (d) Both (a) and (b) above are correct.
    (e) All of the above are correct.

ANSWER: d

25. Which of the following does **not** require energy expenditure?

    (a) Net potassium movement into the cell.
    (b) Net sodium movement into the cell.
    (c) Iodine uptake by thyroid gland cell.
    (d) All of the above require energy expenditure.

ANSWER: b

26. According to Fick's law of diffusion, which of the following changes would **decrease** the rate of net diffusion of a substance across a membrane?

    (a) An increase in the substance's concentration gradient.
    (b) An increase in the permeability of the membrane to the substance.
    (c) An increase in the surface area of the membrane.
    (d) An increase in the thickness of the membrane.
    (e) None of the above are correct.

ANSWER: d

27. If pure water and a solution containing a nonpenetrating solute are separated by a membrane,

    (a) water will diffuse by osmosis until the concentrations between the two compartments become equal.
    (b) both water and the solute will diffuse across the membrane down their concentration gradients until a state of equilibrium is established.
    (c) water will diffuse by osmosis until stopped by an opposing hydrostatic pressure.
    (d) no movement will take place across the membrane.
    (e) it is impossible to predict what will happen.

ANSWER: c

28. Exocytosis of secretory products is triggered by the entry
     of ____ into the cell in response to a specific neural or
     hormonal stimulus.

     (a) K^+
     (b) Na^+
     (c) Ca^{2+}
     (d) ATP
     (e) A^-

ANSWER: c

29. Which of the following statements concerning the Na^+-K^+
     pump is **incorrect**?

     (a) The phosphorylated conformation of the Na^+-K^+ pump has
          high affinity for K^+ when exposed to the ICF.
     (b) The Na^+-K^+ pump has ATPase activity.
     (c) The Na^+-K^+ pump establishes Na^+ and K^+ concentration
          gradients across the plasma membrane; these gradients
          are critically important in the ability of nerve and
          muscle cells to generate electrical impulses essential
          to their functioning.
     (d) The Na^+-K^+ pump helps regulate cell volume by
          controlling the concentration of solutes inside the cell
          to minimize osmotic effects that would induce swelling
          or shrinking of the cell.

ANSWER: a

30. The Na^+-K^+ pump

     (a) pumps Na^+ into the cell.
     (b) pumps K^+ into the cell.
     (c) pumps K^+ out of the cell.
     (d) has a higher affinity for K^+ when the carrier is
          phosphorylated.
     (e) More than one of the above are correct.

ANSWER: b

31. The large, negatively charged intracellular proteins
     (A^-) cannot permeate the cell membrane because

     (a) they are greater than 0.8 nm in diameter and are not
          lipid soluble.
     (b) there are no carriers for them.
     (c) no concentration or electrical gradient exists for them.
     (d) Both (a) and (b) above are correct.
     (e) All of the above are correct.

ANSWER: d

32.   Membrane potential

    (a)   refers to a separation of charges across the membrane or to a difference in the relative number of + and - charges in the ECF and ICF.
    (b)   is measured in units of millivolts with the sign always designating the charge on the outside.
    (c)   is less at the equilibrium potential for K^+ than at resting membrane potential.
    (d)   Both (a) and (b) above are correct.
    (e)   All of the above are correct.

ANSWER: a

33.   Assume that a membrane that is permeable to Na^+ but not to Cl^- separates two solutions. The concentration of sodium chloride on side 1 is much higher than on side 2. Which of the following ionic movements will take place?

    (a) Na^+ will move until its concentration gradient is dissipated (i.e., until the concentration of Na^+ on side 2 is the same as the concentration of Na^+ on side 1).
    (b) Cl^- will move down its concentration gradient from side 1 to side 2.
    (c)   A membrane potential, negative on side 1, will develop.
    (d)   A membrane potential, positive on side 1, will develop.
    (e)   More than one of the above are correct.

ANSWER: c

34 .   The resting membrane potential

    (a)   is much closer to the equilibrium potential for Na^+ than to the equilibrium potential for K^+.
    (b)   is much closer to the equilibrium potential for K^+ than to the equilibrium potential for Na^+.
    (c)   is halfway between the equilibrium potential for Na^+ and the equilibrium potential for K^+.

ANSWER: b

35.   At resting membrane potential

    (a)   the membrane is more permeable to K^+ than to Na^+
    (b)   the membrane is more permeable to Na^+ than to K^+
    (c)   the membrane is equally permeable to K^+ and Na^+

ANSWER: a

36. Graded potentials

   (a) are local changes in membrane potential that occur in
        varying degrees of magnitude.
   (b) serve as short-distance signals.
   (c) serve as long-distance signals.
   (d) Both (a) and (b) above are correct.
   (e) Both (a) and (c) above are correct.

ANSWER: d

37. The cells of excitable and nonexcitable tissues share which
     of the following properties?

   (a) A threshold potential.
   (b) A resting membrane potential.
   (c) An ability to open the Na^+ gates.
   (d) All of the above are correct.
   (e) None of the above are correct.

ANSWER: b

38. Threshold potential

   (a) is the potential achieved when two opposing forces
        acting upon an ion (concentration and electrical
        gradients) achieve a state of equilibrium.
   (b) is the peak potential achieved during an action
        potential.
   (c) is the point at which there is an explosive increase in
        Na^+ permeability.
   (d) is the potential at which PK^+ increases.
   (e) is always a positive potential.

ANSWER: c

39. During the rising phase of the action potential,

   (a) PK^+ is much greater than PNa^+.
   (b) PNa^+ is much greater than PK^+.
   (c) PK^+ is the same as PNa^+.
   (d) Na^+ efflux occurs.
   (e) Two of the above are correct.

ANSWER: b

40. At the peak of an action potential

   (a) the electrical gradient for K^+ tends to move this ion
        outward.
   (b) the concentration gradient for K^+ tends to move this ion
        outward.
   (c) K^+ permeability greatly increases.
   (d) Two of the above are correct.
   (e) All of the above are correct.

ANSWER: e

41. Which of the following is responsible for the falling phase
     of an action potential?

   (a) Opening of Na^+ gates.
   (b) Na^+ -K^+ pump restoring the ions to their original
        locations.
   (c) Greatly increased permeability to Na^+.
   (d) ATP-ase destroying the energy supply that was main-
        taining the action potential at its peak.
   (e) None of the above are correct.

ANSWER: e

42. The membrane is more permeable to K^+ than to Na^+

   (a) at resting potential.
   (b) during the rising phase of an action potential.
   (c) during the falling phase of an action potential.
   (d) Both (a) and (b) above are correct.
   (e) Both (a) and (c) above are correct.

ANSWER: e

43. A recording electrode is placed into a nerve cell to measure
     the membrane potential at a particular point. When the
     physiologist glances at the recording and sees that the
     membrane at that instant has a potential of +15 mV, s/he
     knows that the portion of the membrane being recorded is

   (a) in the normal resting state.
   (b) in the reversal phase of an action potential when the
        inside of the cell becomes more positive than the
        outside.
   (c) hyperpolarized
   (d) Two of the above are correct.

ANSWER: b

44. Conduction by local current flow

(a) occurs in unmyelinated fibers.
(b) is faster than propagation of an action potential in myelinated fibers because myelin acts as an insulator to slow down the impulse.
(c) involves current flowing locally between the active and adjacent inactive areas, thereby bringing the inactive areas to threshold so that they too become active (i.e., have an action potential).
(d) Both (a) and (c) above are correct.
(e) All of the above are correct.

ANSWER: d

45. Saltatory conduction

(a) occurs in unmyelinated nerve fibers.
(b) is slower than conduction by local current flow because the myelin acts as an insulator to slow the impulse down.
(c) involves the impulse jumping from one node of Ranvier to the adjacent node.
(d) refers to the action potential spreading from one myelin-forming cell to the adjacent myelin-forming cell.
(e) More than one of the above are correct.

ANSWER: c

46. Which of the following statements concerning propagation of action potentials is **incorrect**?

(a) Saltatory conduction occurs in myelinated nerve fibers.
(b) During conduction by local current flow, current flows between the active and adjacent inactive area of the cell membrane, thereby decreasing the potential in the inactive area to threshold.
(c) The action potential jumps from one myelin-forming cell to the adjacent myelin-forming cell in a myelinated fiber.
(d) Saltatory conduction is faster than conduction by local current flow.
(e) Conduction by local current flow is the method of propagation in unmyelinated fibers.

ANSWER: c

47. If an action potential were initiated in the center of an axon, in what direction would it travel?

    (a) Toward the cell body.
    (b) Away from the cell body.
    (c) In both directions.

ANSWER: c

48. If a neuron were experimentally stimulated at both ends simultaneously,

    (a) the action potentials would pass in the middle and travel to the opposite ends.
    (b) the action potentials would meet in the middle and then be propagated back to their starting positions.
    (c) the action potentials would stop as they met in the middle.
    (d) the strongest action potential would override the weaker action potential.
    (e) summation would occur when the action potentials met in the middle, resulting in a larger action potential.

ANSWER: c

49. Which of the following statements concerning the refractory period is (are) correct?

    (a) The absolute refractory period refers to the period of time during which another action potential cannot be initiated in a patch of membrane that has just undergone an action potential, no matter how strong the stimulus.
    (b) The absolute refractory period corresponds to the time period during which the Na^+ gates are first opened and then closed and inactivated.
    (c) The absolute and relative refractory periods assure the unidirectional spread of the action potential down the nerve fiber away from the initial site of activation.
    (d) Two of the above are correct.
    (e) All of the above are correct.

ANSWER: e

50.   The refractory period

    (a)   prevents action potentials from spreading both forward and backward, assuring the unidirectional propagation of the action potential away from the initial site of activation.

    (b)   refers to the time period during which a portion of the membrane that has just undergone an action potential cannot undergo another action potential in response to normal triggering events because the channels opened during the action potential have not been restored to their "closed but capable of opening" conformation.

    (c)   places an upper limit on the frequency with which a nerve cell can conduct action potentials.

    (d)   Both (a) and (b) above are correct.

    (e)   All of the above are correct.

ANSWER: e

51.   The period of time following an action potential during which a membrane cannot be restimulated no matter how strong the stimulus

    (a)   is known as the absolute refractory period.

    (b)   occurs during the time after the Na^+ gates have opened until they are restored to their "closed but capable of opening" conformation.

    (c)   prevents the action potential from spreading back over the part of the membrane where the impulse has just passed.

    (d)   Two of the above are correct.

    (e)   All of the above are correct.

ANSWER: e

52.   Which of the following is **not** a graded potential?

    (a)   action potential

    (b)   excitatory postsynaptic potential

    (c)   inhibitory postsynaptic potential

    (d)   grand postsynaptic potential

ANSWER: a

53.   Temporal summation

   (a)   takes place when two EPSPs from the same presynaptic input occur so closely together in time that they add together or sum.
   (b)   takes place when an EPSP and an IPSP occur simultaneously in time and cancel each other out.
   (c)   takes place when two EPSPs that occur simultaneously from different presynaptic inputs add together or sum.
   (d)   takes place when action potentials occurring in two presynaptic inputs simultaneously converge upon the postsynaptic cell, initiating two different action potentials in the postsynaptic cell.
   (e)   None of the above are correct.

ANSWER: a

54.   Spatial summation occurs in a postsynaptic neuron

   (a)   when several EPSPs from a single presynaptic input sum to reach threshold.
   (b)   when EPSPs from several presynaptic inputs sum to reach threshold.
   (c)   upon simultaneous interaction of an EPSP and an IPSP.
   (d)   when several IPSPs from a single presynaptic input sum to hyperpolarize the membrane.
   (e)   None of the above are correct.

ANSWER: b

55.   At an excitatory synapse

   (a)   an action potential in the postsynaptic neuron depolarizes the presynaptic cell membrane.
   (b)   an action potential in the presynaptic neuron increases the permeability of the subsynaptic membrane of the postsynaptic cell to both Na^+ and K^+.
   (c)   an action potential in the presynaptic neuron increases the permeability of the subsynaptic membrane of the postsynaptic cell to K^+ only.
   (d)   Both (a) and (b) above are correct.
   (e)   Both (a) and (c) above are correct.

ANSWER: b

56. At an excitatory synapse

   (a) there is increased permeability of the subsynaptic
        membrane to both Na^+ and K^+.
   (b) a small hyperpolarization occurs.
   (c) an action potential in the presynaptic neuron always
        causes an action potential in the postsynaptic neuron.
   (d) Two of the above are correct.
   (e) All of the above are correct.

ANSWER: a

57. An IPSP

   (a) is produced by increased PNa^+ and PK^+.
   (b) is produced by increased PK^+ or increased PCl^-.
   (c) is a small depolarization of the postsynaptic cell.
   (d) Both (a) and (c) above are correct.
   (e) Both (b) and (c) above are correct.

ANSWER: b

58. Two adjacent presynaptic knobs, one from neuron A, the
     other from neuron B, synapse on a third neuron C. The two
     presynaptic knobs simultaneously release transmitter, as a
     result of which an action potential is initiated in neuron
     C.

     This is an example of

   (a) temporal summation.
   (b) spatial summation.
   (c) convergence.
   (d) Both (a) and (c) above are correct.
   (e) Both (b) and (c) above are correct.

ANSWER: e

59. Assume a hypothetical postsynaptic neuron has three
     presynaptic inputs--"X," "Y," and "Z." When presynaptic
     neuron "X" and "Y" are stimulated simultaneously, the
     postsynaptic neuron reaches threshold and undergoes an action
     potential, yet when presynaptic neuron "X" and "Z" are
     stimulated simultaneously, there is no change in potential
     of the postsynaptic neuron. What can you tell about
     presynaptic neurons "Y" and "Z?"

     (a) Presynaptic neurons "Y" and "Z" are both excitatory.
     (b) Presynaptic neurons "Y" and "Z" are both inhibitory.
     (c) Presynaptic neuron "Y" is excitatory and presynaptic
          neuron "Z" is inhibitory.
     (d) Presynaptic neuron "Y" is inhibitory and presynaptic
          neuron "Z" is excitatory.
     (e) There is too little information provided to determine
          what type of neurons "Y" and "Z" might be.

ANSWER: c

60. In convergence

     (a) thousands of synapses from many different presynaptic
          cells end upon a single postsynaptic cell.
     (b) the axon of a nerve cell branches so that the activity
          in one neuron influences many other cells.
     (c) the dendrites all converge upon the cell body.
     (d) None of the above are correct.

ANSWER: a

61. In divergence

     (a) thousands of synapses from many presynaptic neurons end
          upon a single postsynaptic cell.
     (b) the dendrites diverge from the cell body to contact as
          many presynaptic neurons as possible.
     (c) the action potential initiated in the axon diminishes
          as it diverges into the axon terminals.
     (d) the axon of a nerve cell branches to synapse with many
          other cells so that activity in one neuron influences
          the excitability of many other cells.

ANSWER: d

62. Tetanus toxin

(a   causes hyperpolarization of the neurons that supply skeletal muscles

(b) destroys dopamine in the region of the brain involved in controlling complex movements

(c) prevents the release of gamma-aminobutyric acid from presynaptic inputs terminating on neurons that supply skeletal muscles

(d) acts as a neurotransmitter at excitatory synapses.

ANSWER: c

True/False

63. Under an ordinary light microscope, the plasma membrane appears as a trilaminar structure consisting of two dark layers separated by a light middle layer.

ANSWER: False

64. According to the fluid mosaic model of membrane structure, the plasma membrane consists primarily of a bilayer of mobile phospholipid molecules studded with an ever-changing mosaic pattern of proteins.

ANSWER: True

65. The surface carbohydrates within the plasma membrane serve as cell adhesion molecules (CAMs) that cells use to grip ahold of each other and to surrounding connective-tissue fibers.

ANSWER: False

66. The primary barrier to passage of water-soluble substances across the plasma membrane is the outer layer of carbohydrates.

ANSWER: False

67. The carbohydrate found in plasma membranes is believed to be involved in the aggregation of cells to form tissue.

ANSWER: True

68.   The two dark lines in the trilaminar appearance of the plasma membrane are believed to be caused by the preferential staining of the hydrophilic polar regions of the membrane constituents.

ANSWER: True

69.   A first messenger is an intracellular chemical messenger that triggers a preprogrammed series of biochemical events within a cell to bring about a desired response.

ANSWER: False

70.   The only means by which an extracellular chemical messenger can bring about a desired intracellular response is to activate a second messenger system.

ANSWER: False

71.   The extracellular matrix and the local cells that secrete it are collectively known as connective tissue.

ANSWER: True

72.   Because of the presence of tight junctions, passage of materials across an epithelial barrier must take place through the cells, not between them.

ANSWER: True

73.   Fibronectin is the extracellular matrix component that provides tensile strength.

ANSWER: False

74.   Because a solution of lower solute concentration has a higher concentration of water, it exerts a greater osmotic pressure than does a solution with a higher solute concentration.

ANSWER: False

75.   Carrier molecules always require energy to accomplish transport of a substance across the membrane.

ANSWER: False

76.   Phosphorylation of a carrier can alter the affinity of its binding sites, accompanied by a change in its conformation.

ANSWER: True

77. The carrier molecule actually moves from side to side
     through the membrane as it transports material across.

ANSWER: False

78. All molecules greater than 0.8 nm in diameter are unable to
     penetrate the plasma membrane unless there is a carrier for
     the molecule.

ANSWER: False

79. Uncharged or nonpolar molecules tend to be lipid soluble.

ANSWER: True

80. If two similar molecules can both combine with the same
     carrier, the presence of one of these molecules decreases the
     rate of entry of the other.

 ANSWER: True

81. Pinocytosis, or "cell drinking," refers to the process of a
     cell engulfing a small volume of fluid and bringing it within
     the contents of the cell.

ANSWER: True

82. Phagocytosis refers to the process of a cell engulfing a
     large, multimolecular particle and bringing the particle
     within the contents of the cell.

ANSWER: True

83. The predominant cation in the intracellular fluid is
     potassium.

ANSWER: True

84. Anions are attracted toward a more positively charged area
     along an electrical gradient.

ANSWER: True

85. Cations are attracted to a more positively charged area
     along an electrical gradient.

ANSWER: False

86. If a concentration or electrical gradient is present for a given substance, the substance will always passively permeate the membrane.

ANSWER: False

87. At the equilibrium potential for K^+, the concentration and electrical gradients for K^+ are in opposition to each other and exactly balance each other so there is no net movement of K^+.

ANSWER: True

88. The equilibrium potential for K^+ is less than the resting membrane potential.

ANSWER: False

89. Net movement of K^+ into the cell requires energy expenditure, whereas movement of Na^+ into the cell does not.

ANSWER: True

90. Net potassium movement into cells always requires energy expenditure.

ANSWER: True

91. At resting membrane potential, no ionic fluxes are taking place across the membrane.

ANSWER: False

92. When equilibrium is achieved and no net diffusion is taking place, there is no movement of molecules.

ANSWER: False

93. At resting membrane potential, passive and active forces exactly balance each other so there is no net movement of ions across the membrane.

ANSWER: True

94. Net sodium movement into the cell occurs passively, whereas net sodium movement out of the cell occurs actively.

ANSWER: True

95. At resting potential, the inside of the cell is negative compared to the extracellular fluid.

ANSWER: True

96. The large protein anion does not leave the cell because there is no concentration or electrical gradient to drive it outward.

ANSWER: False

97. A potential of +30 mV is larger than a potential of -70 mV.

ANSWER: False

98. With active transport, ATP energy is used in the phosphorylation-dephosphorylation cycle of the carrier.

ANSWER: True

99. All tissues of the body can have action potentials.

ANSWER: False

100. The Na^+ and K^+ channels that open and close during an action potential are voltage-gated channels.

ANSWER: True

101. Threshold potential is the peak potential achieved during an action potential.

ANSWER: False

102. After an action potential has occurred, there is more Na^+ inside the cell than outside the cell (before any Na^+ -K^+ pump activity has taken place).

ANSWER: False

103. The Na^+-K^+ pump returns the membrane potential to resting after it reaches the peak of an action potential.

ANSWER: False

104. During conduction by local current flow, current flows locally between the active and adjacent inactive area of the cell membrane, thereby decreasing the potential in the inactive area to threshold.

ANSWER: True

105. The nodes of Ranvier are formed by seperate cells
that wrap themselves "jelly roll fashion"around the axon.

ANSWER: False

106. The conduction velocity of a nerve impulse is slower in
myelinated fibers than in unmyelinated fibers, because myelin
acts as an insulator that slows down the flow of current.

ANSWER: False

107. The height of the action potential diminishes as it is
propagated away from the site where the action potential was
initiated.

ANSWER: False

108. The stronger the stimulus, the greater the frequency of
action potentials generated in a neuron.

ANSWER: True

109. The period of time following an action potential during
which a membrane cannot be restimulated, no matter how strong
the stimulus, is known as the subminimal response period.

ANSWER: False

110. The refractory period prevents action potentials from
spreading back over the part of the membrane where the
impulse has just passed.

ANSWER: True

111. During the absolute refractory period, the Na^+ gates are
not capable of opening again in response to another
triggering event.

ANSWER: True

112. A stimulus that is too weak to depolarize the membrane to
threshold produces an action potential smaller than normal.

ANSWER: False

113. A stimulus stronger than that necessary to bring the
membrane to threshold produces a larger action potential than
one produced by a stimulus that just brings the membrane to
threshold.

ANSWER: False

114. A postsynaptic neuron can either excite or inhibit a presynaptic neuron.

ANSWER: False

115. A single neuron may be presynaptic to one group of neurons and be postsynaptic to another group of neurons.

ANSWER: True

116. Increased permeability of the postsynaptic cell to Cl- lessens the likelihood that the postsynaptic cell will undergo an action potential because the membrane potential is moved farther away from threshold.

ANSWER: True

117. Increased permeability of the subsynaptic membrane to K^+ produces the same change in membrane potential of the post-synaptic cell as does increased permeability of the subsynaptic membrane to Cl^-.

ANSWER: True

118. A single synaptic knob contains two different transmitters - one that produces EPSPs and one that produces IPSPs.

ANSWER: False

119. A given synapse may produce EPSPs at one time and IPSPs at another time.

ANSWER: False

120. A balance of IPSPs and EPSPs will negate each other so that the grand postsynaptic potential is essentially unaltered.

ANSWER: True

121. Temporal summation occurs when EPSPs from several different excitatory presynaptic inputs occur simultaneously.

ANSWER: False

122. The grand postsynaptic potential depends on the sum of activity of the presynaptic inputs.

ANSWER: True

123. Presynaptic neurons converging upon a postsynaptic cell will either be all excitatory or all inhibitory.

ANSWER: False

124. Divergence refers to the neuronal arrangement wherein the dendrites diverge to synapse with as many presynaptic inputs as possible.

ANSWER: False

Fill-in-the-blanks

125. The model of the plasma membrane as a lipid bilayer studded and penetrated by proteins is known as the _____ model of membrane structure.

ANSWER: fluid mosaic

126. Of the lipids in the plasma membrane, _____ are most abundant, with lesser amounts of _____.

ANSWER: phospholipids, cholesterol

127. _____ refers to the transfer of a phosphate group from ATP to a protein, thereby bringing about a change in the shape and function of the protein.

ANSWER: Phosphorylation

128. The two major second messengers are _____ and _____.

ANSWER: cAMP and Ca^{2+}

129. The extracellular matrix plus the cells that secrete it are collectively known as _____.

ANSWER: connective tissue

130. _____ join the lateral edges of epithelial cells together near their luminal borders, thus preventing passage of materials between the cells.

ANSWER: Tight junctions

131. A rise in the cytosolic concentration of _____ induces fusion of an exocytotic vesicle with the plasma membrane.

ANSWER: Ca^{2+}

132. Net diffusion of water down its own concentration gradient toward an area of higher solute concentration is known as _____.

ANSWER: osmosis

133. The _____ refers to the maximum amount of a substance that can be transported across the plasma membrane via a carrier in a given time.

ANSWER: transport maximum (Tm)

134. _____ refers to carrier-mediated transport of a substance against its concentration gradient.

ANSWER: Active transport

135. Vesicular transport into the cells is known as _____, of which there are two types, _____ (engulfment of a large multimolecular particle) and _____ (internalization of fluid), whereas vesicular transport of the cell is called _____.

ANSWER: endocytosis, phagocytosis, pinocytosis, exocytosis

136. The membrane potential that exists when the concentration and electrical gradients for a given ion exactly counter-balance each other is known as the _____.

ANSWER: equilibrium potential

137. _____ refers to a separation of opposite charges across the membrane.

ANSWER: Membrane potential

138. At the equilibrium potential for an ion, its_____ gradient is exactly counterbalanced by its electrical gradient.

ANSWER: concentration

139. A single nerve cell or _____ typically consists of the following three basic parts: _____, _____, and _____.

ANSWERS: neuron, cell body, dendrites, axon

140. The _____ or _____ of a nerve cell is a single, elongated tubular process that conducts action potentials away from the cell body and eventually terminates at other cells.

ANSWERS: axon, nerve fiber

141. The junction between two neurons is known as a _____.

ANSWER: synapse

142. An action potential in a presynaptic neuron induces opening of voltage-gated _____ channels in the synaptic knob, which triggers exocytosis of synaptic vesicles.

ANSWER: Calcium (Ca^{2+})

143. When EPSPs occurring simultaneously from two different presynaptic inputs add together or sum to bring the postsynaptic cell to threshold it is called _____.

ANSWER: spatial summation

144. When EPSPs originating from a single presynaptic input occur so close together in time that they add together or sum, thereby bringing the postsynaptic cell to threshold, it is called _____.

ANSWER: temporal summation

145. The neuronal relationship where a single presynaptic cell branches to terminate on many other cells is called _____.

ANSWER: divergence

146. The neuronal relationship where many presynaptic cells terminate on a single postsynaptic cell is called _____.

ANSWER: convergence

Short Answer

147. State the all-or-none law.

ANSWER: in text, page 69

148. List the two methods of propagation of an action potential. Mark an * by the fastest method.

ANSWER: Conduction by local current flow.
        *Saltatory conduction.

Matching

149. ____ provides tensile strength   (a) collagen
     ____ provides a pathway for   (b) elastin
           diffusion of water soluble   (c) fibronectin
           particles between cells   (d) watery gel
     ____ promotes cell adhesion
     ____ enables tissue to stretch
           and recoil

ANSWER: a, d, c, b

150. Indicate which constituent of the plasma membrane is responsible for performing the function in question by filling in the appropriate blank using the answer code below.

     (a) = protein
     (b) = carbohydrate
     (c) = lipid bilayer

____ Serves as carrier to transport particles across the membrane.
____ Determinant of degree of fluidity of the membrane.
____ Important in the aggregation of cells to form tissues.
____ Forms channels through the membrane.
____ Serves as membrane-bound enzymes.
____ Apparently involved in limiting tissue growth within normal confines.
____ Found only on the outer surface of the membrane.
____ Provides receptor sites for combining with molecules in the cell's environment that modify cell function.
____ Serves as a barrier to diffusion of water-soluble substances through the membrane.
____ Forms the basic structure of the membrane.

ANSWERS: a, c, b, a, a, b, b, a, c, c

151. Indicate which characteristic of a mediated-transport system is referred to in each item by filling in the blank using the following answer code:

> (a) = specificity
> (b) = saturation
> (c) = competition

_____ If a carrier can handle substance X but not substance Y, what characteristic is being exemplified?

_____ If in the presence of substance Z there is a decreased rate of entry of substance X, what characteristic is being exemplified?

_____ If the concentration of substance X outside the cell continues to increase but the rate of substance X's transport into the cell remains constant, what characteristic is being exemplified?

ANSWERS: a, c, b

152. Indicate whether the force in question tends to move the involved ion in or out of the cell by filling in the blank using the following answer code.

(a) = Ion tends to be moved <u>into</u> the cell by this force.
(b) = Ion tends to be moved <u>out of</u> the cell by this force.

_____ concentration gradient for K^+ at resting potential

_____ electrical gradient for K^+ at resting potential

_____ electrical gradient for $_K$ at E_{K+}

_____ concentration gradient for Na^+ at resting potential

_____ electrical gradient for Na^+ at resting potential

_____ electrical gradient for Na^+ at E_{Na}^+

_____ Na^+-K^+ pump for Na^+

_____ Na^+-K^+ pump for K^+

_____ Concentration gradient for Na^+ at threshold potential.

_____ Electrical gradient for Na^+ at threshold potential.

_____ Concentration gradient for K^+ at the peak of an action potential.

_____ Electrical gradient for K^+ at the peak of an action potential.

_____ Concentration gradient for Na^+ at the end of an action potential.

_____ Concentration gradient for K^+ at the end of an action potential.

ANSWERS: b, a, a, a, a, b, b, a, a, a, b, b, a, b

153. Indicate the various roles of the following ions using the answer in the right column:

_____ cation in greatest concentration in the ICF   (a) Na^+

_____ cation in greatest concentration in the ECF   (b) K^+

(c) A^-

(d) Cl^-

_____ anion in greatest concentration in the ICF

_____ anion in greatest concentration in the ECF

_____ cation whose equilibrium potential is greater than the resting membrane potential

_____ cation whose equilibrium potential is opposite in charge of the resting membrane potential

_____ cation to which the membrane is most permeable under resting conditions

_____ anion to which the membrane is impermeable

_____ ion that has the predominant influence on the resting membrane potential

_____ ion that is actively transported out of the cell

_____ ion that is actively transported into the cell

ANSWER: b, a, c, d, b, a, b, c, b, a, b,

154. The following question refers to comparative concentrations, permeabilities, and potentials under various circumstances. Indicate the relationship between the two items listed in each situation by filling the appropriate letter in the blank using the following answer code.

        (a) = A is greater than B
        (b) = B is greater than A
        (c) = A and B are equal

_____ A. concentration of K^+ in the extracellular fluid
     B. concentration of K^+ in intracellular fluid of a resting nerve cell

_____ A. concentration of Na^+ in the extracellular fluid
     B. concentration of Na^+ in intracellular fluid of a resting nerve cell

_____ A. concentration of A^- in the extracellular fluid
     B. concentration of A^- in intracellular fluid of a resting nerve cell

_____ A. permeability of a resting nerve cell membrane to K^+
     B. permeability of a resting nerve cell membrane to A^-

_____ A. permeability of a resting nerve cell membrane to K^+
     B. permeability of a resting nerve cell membrane to Na^+

154. (cont.)

_____ A. concentration gradient for K^+ at the equilibrium potential for K^+
       B. electrical gradient for K^+ at the equilibrium potential for K^+

_____ A. resting membrane potential in a typical nerve cell
       B. equilibrium potential for K^+

_____ A. amount of Na^+ transported out of the cell by the Na^+ - K^+ pump
       B. amount of K^+ transported into the cell by the Na^+ -K^+ pump

_____ A. magnitude of membrane potential recorded at +30mV
       B. magnitude of membrane potential recorded at -30mV

_____ A. permeability of a nerve cell membrane to Na^+ during the rising phase of an action potential
       B. permeability of a nerve cell membrane to K^+ during the rising phase of an action potential

_____ A. permeability of a resting nerve cell membrane to Na^+
       B. permeability of a nerve cell membrane to Na^+ during the rising phase of an action potential

_____ A. permeability of a resting nerve cell membrane to K^+
       B. permeability of a nerve cell membrane to K^+ during the falling phase of an action potential

_____ A. permeability of a nerve cell membrane to Na^+ during the falling phase of an action potential
       B. permeability of a nerve cell membrane to K^+ during the falling phase of an action potential

_____ A. concentration of Na^+ in the intracellular fluid of a nerve cell immediately before an action potential
       B. concentration of Na^+ in the intracellular fluid of a nerve cell immediately following an action potential (assume that the Na^+ -K^+ pump has not yet acted)

_____ A. concentration of K^+ in the intracellular fluid of a nerve cell immediately before an action potential
       B. concentration of K^+ in the intracellular fluid of a nerve cell immediately following an action potential (assume that the Na^+ -K^+ pump has not yet acted)

154. (cont.)

_____ A.   concentration of Na$^+$ in the extracellular fluid
       B.   concentration of Na$^+$ in the intracellular fluid of a
            nerve cell immediately following an action potential
            (assume that the Na$^+$-K$^+$ pump has not yet acted)

_____ A.   membrane potential at rest
       B.   the potential of the same membrane when it is hyper-
            polarized

_____ A.   membrane potential at rest
       B.   the potential of the same membrane when it is
            depolarized

ANSWERS: b, a, b, a, a, c, b, a, c, a, b, b, b, b, a, a, b, a

155. Indicate whether the membrane is more permeable to K$^+$ or to
     Na$^+$ or equally permeable to these ions under the stated
     conditions by writing the appropriate letter in the blank
     using the following answer code:

     (a) = The membrane is more permeable to K$^+$ than to Na$^+$.
     (b) = The membrane is more permeable to Na$^+$ than to K$^+$.
     (c) = The membrane is about equally permeable to Na$^+$ and
           K$^+$.

     _____ During the rising phase of an action potential
     _____ During the falling phase of an action potential
     _____ At resting potential
     _____ During an EPSP
     _____ During an IPSP

ANSWERS: b, a, a, c, a

156. Indicate the ionic fluxes that are **primarily** responsible
     for each factor listed by writing the appropriate letter(s)
     in the blank, using the following answer code:

         (a) = associated with Na$^+$ influx
         (b) = associated with Na$^+$ efflux
         (c) = associated with K$^+$ influx
         (d) = associated with K$^+$ efflux
         (e) = associated with Cl$^-$ influx

     _____ rising phase of an action potential
     _____ falling phase of an action potential
     _____ an EPSP
     _____ an IPSP

ANSWERS: a, d, a, d/e

157. Use the answer code on the right to answer the questions in this section:

    _____ permeability change that occurs at threshold

    _____ two permeability changes that occur at the peak of an action potential

    _____ ion movement responsible for the rising phase of the action potential

    _____ ion movement responsible for the falling phase of the action potential

(a) increased P Na$^+$
(b) decreased P Na$^+$
(c) increased P K$^+$
(d) decreased P K$^+$
(e) Na$^+$ influx
(f) Na$^+$ efflux
(g) K$^+$ influx
(h) K$^+$ efflux

ANSWER: a, b/c, e, h

158. Indicate whether an excitatory or inhibitory synapse is being described by filling in the blank using the following answer code:

    (a) associated with an excitatory synapse
    (b) associated with an inhibitory synapse

    _____ a small hyperpolarization of the postsynaptic neuron
    _____ a small depolarization of the postsynaptic neuron
    _____ increased PNa$^+$ and increased PK$^+$ of the subsynaptic membrane
    _____ increased PCl$^-$ of the subsynaptic membrane
    _____ increased PK$^+$ of the subsynaptic membrane (no change in PNa$^+$)

ANSWERS: b, a, a, b, b

159. Assume that a hypothetical neuron has three presynaptic inputs converging upon it. Presynaptic inputs A and B are excitatory and C is inhibitory. Indicate which of the following changes will take place by writing the appropriate letter in the blank using the answer code below:

    (a) = There will be no change in potential of the postsynaptic cell.
    (b) = Spatial summation will occur.
    (c) = Temporal summation will occur.

    _____ What would occur if presynaptic neuron B is fired rapidly?
    _____ What would occur if both presynaptic neurons A and B were fired simultaneously?
    _____ What would occur if both presynaptic neurons A and C were fired simultaneously?

ANSWERS: c, b, a

For questions 160-166 assume a hypothetical postsynaptic neuron has three presynaptic inputs - "X," "Y" and "Z." Also assume that presynaptic neuron Z is excitatory. For each question indicate the best answer by circling the appropriate response.

160. If presynaptic neuron "X" is stimulated, the postsynaptic cell membrane becomes slightly hyperpolarized. What kind of a synapse is involved between presynaptic neuron "X" and the postsynaptic neuron?

    (a) excitatory synapse
    (b) inhibitory synapse
    (c) It could be either an excitatory or an inhibitory synapse.
    (d) Not sufficient information is given to know what kind of synapse is involved.

ANSWER: b

161. What permeability changes would you expect to occur at the postsynaptic neuron when presynaptic neuron "X" is stimulated? (Remember that the postsynaptic neuron becomes hyperpolarized by presynaptic neuron "X.")

    (a) increased PNa^+ and PK^+
    (b) increased PK^+ or PCl^-
    (c) increased PA^-
    (d) increased PCa^{2+}
    (e) Not sufficient information is provided to know what permeability change would be expected.

ANSWER: b

162. If presynaptic neuron "Y" is stimulated, the postsynaptic cell membrane becomes slightly depolarized. What kind of synapse is involved between presynaptic neuron "Y" and the postsynaptic neuron?

    (a)   excitatory synapse
    (b)   inhibitory synapse
    (c)   It could be either an excitatory or an inhibitory synapse.
    (d)   Not sufficient information is given to know what kind of synapse is involved.

ANSWER: a

163. What permeability changes would you expect to occur at the postsynaptic neuron when presynaptic neuron "Y" is stimulated? (Remember that the postsynaptic neuron becomes depolarized by presynaptic neuron "Y.")

    (a)   increased PNa^+ and PK^+
    (b)   increased PK^+ or PCl^-
    (c)   increased PA^-
    (d)   increased PCa^{2+}
    (e)   Not sufficient information is provided to know what permeability change would be expected.

ANSWER: a

164. If presynaptic neurons "Y" and "Z" are stimulated simultaneously, what change would you expect to occur in the postsynaptic neuron?

    (a)   a single EPSP
    (b)   a single IPSP
    (c)   temporal summation of EPSPs
    (d)   spatial summation of EPSPs
    (e)   An IPSP and EPSP would cancel each other out so there would be essentially no change in potential in the postsynaptic neuron.

ANSWER: d

165. If presynaptic neurons "X" and "Z" are stimulated
     simultaneously, what change would you expect to occur in the
     postsynaptic neuron?

     (a)   a single EPSP
     (b)   a single IPSP
     (c)   temporal summation of EPSPs
     (d)   spatial summation of EPSPs
     (e)   An IPSP and EPSP would cancel each other out, so there
           would be essentially no change in potential in the
           postsynaptic neuron.

ANSWER: e

166. If presynaptic neuron "Z" is repetitively stimulated very
     rapidly, what change would you expect to occur in the
     postsynaptic neuron?

     (a)   a single EPSP
     (b)   a single IPSP
     (c)   temporal summation of EPSPs
     (d)   spatial summation of EPSPs
     (e)   An IPSP and EPSP would cancel each other out, so there
           would be essentially no change in potential in the
           postsynaptic neuron.

ANSWER: c

AUDIOVISUAL AIDS

Films

A list of films available from West Publishing Company is
presented in Appendix A.   Following are other films that may be
suitable.   The sources for these films, which are coded by
abbreviation, are provided in Appendix B.

   Active Transport, FHS, 15 min.

   Biological Membranes, PS, 17 min.

   Brain Triggers: Biochemistry and Human Behavior, EI

   Cell Membrane and Cellular Communication (VCR), VA, 15 min.

   Diffusion and Osmosis, COR, 10 min.

   Diffusion and Osmosis, EBE, 14 min.

   Dynamic Aspects of the Neuron in Tissue Culture, UI,
   27 min.

<u>Impulse Propagation in a Nerve Fiber</u>, NM, 12 min.

<u>Introduction to the Nerve Cell and Brain Membranes</u>, SV, 27 min.

<u>Membranes</u> (VCR), MG, 24 min.

<u>Membranes</u>, EI

<u>Nerve Impulse: Use of the Cathode Ray Oscilloscope in Physiology</u>, UI, 19 min.

<u>Neurobiology I: Excitatory Membranes</u>, EI

<u>Neurobiology II: Neural Function</u>, EI

<u>Osmoregulation</u>, FHS, 10 min.

<u>Physiology: The Nerve Impulse</u>, UI, 22 min.

<u>System and Workings of a Nerve</u>, IP, 14 min.

<u>The Ionic Basis of the Action Potential</u>, USNAC, 11 min.

<u>The Keys of Paradise</u>, TLV, 57 min.

<u>The Nerve Impulse</u>, EBE, 22 min.

<u>The Nervous System</u>, IM, 29 min.

<u>The Outer Envelope</u>, PLP, 15 min.

<u>Transfer of Materials</u>, MH, 25 min.

Software

<u>Dynamics of the Human Nervous System</u>, EI. Examines nerve impulse transmission.

<u>Flash: Neurons</u>, PLP. Covers electrical potentials, synapses, and neurotransmitters.

<u>Membrane Potentials</u>, PLP. Uses animated graphics to explain membrane potentials.

<u>Nerve Impulse</u>: I and II, SOV. A <u>VCR</u> program that covers the origin of electrical potentials, diphasic action potentials, refractory period, summation, and monophasic action potentials.

<u>Nervous System</u>, CBS. Covers the nature of the nerve impulse, nerve impulses in simple organisms, and chemical transmitters.

<u>Osmo: Osmotic Conditions in Red Blood Cells</u>, BM. Uses a RBC to teach the principles of permeability, diffusion, osmosis, and tonicity.

<u>Osmosis</u>, CBS. Uses color graphics to examine and simulate the flow of matter across a semipermeable membrane.

<u>Osmosis and Diffusion</u>, EI. Examines the flow of matter across membranes.

<u>Osmosis and Diffusion</u>, PLP. Demonstrates flow across membranes.

<u>Osmosis and Diffusion</u>, SSS. Covers the principles of osmosis and osmotic pressure.

<u>Passive Transport</u>, PLP. Illustrates the processes of diffusion and osmosis.

<u>The Human Brain: Neurons</u>, PLP. Examines neurotransmitters, generation of action potential and function of neurons.

Chapter 4
Central Nervous System

CONTENTS

(All page references are to the main text.)

Spinal Cord, p.109
  - The spinal cord extends through the vertebral canal and is connected to the spinal nerves. p.109
  - The spinal cord is responsible for the integration of many basic reflexes. p.111

Chapter in Perspective: Focus on Homeostasis, p.113

Chapter Summary, p.114

LECTURE HINTS AND SUGGESTIONS

1. Point out the major anatomical structures on a preserved sheep brain or fresh calf's brain, and compare with a human brain.

2. Preserved specimens of brains from representative vertebrates illustrate the differences in size and complexity of various parts. A good source is Delta Biologicals, Tucson, AZ.

3. Use a "break-down" model of the brain to illustrate its anatomy. This is available from Carolina Biological Supply Company, Burlington, NC.

4. X-ray films of the brain are very informative. These can be obtained from local hospitals.

5. Point out the major motor and sensory regions of the cerebrum on a Carolina Biological Supply Company model of the brain.

6. Illustrate the ventricles of the brain on a Carolina Biological Supply Company model.

7. Obtain a fresh spinal cord from a steer for demonstration of the various anatomical parts. Local slaughter houses are a good source.

8. Prepare a demonstration of the cranial and spinal nerves of a cat. See Laboratory Anatomy of the Cat, Chaisson, William C. Brown Company, for dissection procedures.

9. Various charts and models can be used for the central nervous system. These can be obtained from Carolina Biological Supply Company.

10. Reference texts and atlases are very helpful. For example, Kieffer & Heitzman, <u>An Atlas of Cross-Sectional Anatomy</u>, Harper and Row, NY, 1979: Gluhbegovic & Williams, <u>The Human Brain: A Photographic Guide</u>, Harper & Row, NY.

11.   Demonstrate an EEG recording. See any general physiology lab manual for explanation of various wave forms.

12.   Use an articulated skeleton to illustrate the openings through which the various spinal nerves pass. Carolina Biological Supply Company is an excellent source.

13.   Use a model of the spinal cord to illustrate its structure.

14.   If available, demonstrate a human spinal cord. These are obtainable from Carolina Biological Supply Company.

15.   Have students examine a histological slide of a cross section through a nerve.

16.   Discuss some characteristics of life, death, and brain death.

CHAPTER TEST QUESTIONS

Multiple Choice

1.   Which of the following is (are) **not** part of the peripheral nervous system?

     (a)   Motor neurons.
     (b)   Sympathetic nervous system.
     (c)   Spinal cord.
     (d)   Afferent division.
     (e)   Autonomic nervous system.

ANSWER: c

2.   The most abundant type of neuron in the body is the

     (a)   Motor neurons.
     (b)   Efferent neurons.
     (c)   Afferent neurons.
     (d)   Interneurons.
     (e)   Sympathetic and parasympathetic neurons.

ANSWER: d

3.   Afferent neurons

     (a)   carry information to effector organs.
     (b)   have a sensory receptor at their peripheral ending.
     (c)   enter the spinal cord through the dorsal root.
     (d)   Two of the above are correct.
     (e)   All of the above are correct.

ANSWER: d

4.   Efferent neurons

(a)   carry information to the CNS.
(b)   have cell bodies that originate in the CNS.
(c)   lie entirely within the CNS.
(d)   Two of the above are correct.
(e)   All of the above are correct.

ANSWER: b

5.   Which of the following statements concerning glial cells is **incorrect**?

(a)   The vast majority of cells in the CNS are glial cells.
(b)   Glial cells include astrocytes, oligodendrocytes, ependymal cells, and microglia.
(c)   Glial cells do not have the ability to undergo cell division.
(d)   Glial cells do not initiate or conduct nerve impulses.
(e)   Glial cells serve as the connective tissue of the CNS and help support the neurons both physically and metabolically.

ANSWER: c

6.   Astrocytes

(a)   hold neurons together in proper spatial relationships.
(b)   are important in the repair of brain injuries and in neural scar formation.
(c)   take up excess K^+ from the brain ECF.
(d)   Two of the above are correct.
(e)   All of the above are correct.

ANSWER: e

7.   Which of the following is **not** a function of astrocytes? Astrocytes

(a)   hold the neurons together in proper spatial relationship.
(b)   line the internal cavities of the brain and spinal cord.
(c)   induce the formation of the blood-brain barrier.
(d)   take up excess K^+ to help maintain proper brain ECF ion concentration.
(e)   form neural scar tissue.

ANSWER: b

8.   Which type of glial cell lines the ventricles of the brain?

    (a)   Astrocytes.
    (b)   Neurons.
    (c)   Oligodendrocytes.
    (d)   Ependymal cells.
    (e)   Microglia.

ANSWER: d

9.   Which cell type signals the brain capillary cells to form tight junctions?

    (a)   Astrocytes.
    (b)   Ependymal cells.
    (c)   Neurons.
    (d)   Microglia.
    (e)   Oligodendrocytes.

ANSWER: a

10.   Neural damage following a cerebrospinal accident (stroke) is due to

    (a)   reduced O_2 and glucose delivery to the region of the brain deprived of its blood supply
    (b)   toxic release from damaged brain cells of glutamate, which overexcites and subsequently destroys surrounding brain cells
    (c)   a loss of the blood-brain barrier in the affected area of the brain as a result of rupture or occlusion of a cerebral vessel
    (d)   Both (a) and (b) above are correct.
    (e)   All of the above are correct.

ANSWER: d

11.   The brain

    (a)   consists of 90% interneurons and 10% glial cells.
    (b)   can perform anaerobic metabolism when oxygen supplies are low.
    (c)   normally uses only glucose as a fuel for energy production.
    (d)   Two of the above are correct.
    (e)   All of the above are correct.

ANSWER: c

12. The region of the brain that is smallest and oldest in evolutionary development is the

(a) cerebellum.
(b) brain stem.
(c) hypothalamus.
(d) forebrain.
(e) basal nuclei.

ANSWER: b

13. Which of the following is **not** accomplished by the cerebral cortex?

(a) Voluntary initiation of movement.
(b) Control of breathing, circulation, and digestion.
(c) Final sensory perception.
(d) Language ability.
(e) Personality traits.

ANSWER: b

14. Somesthetic sensation

(a) is initially processed by the frontal lobes of the cerebral cortex.
(b) is initially processed by the parietal lobes of the cerebral cortex
(c) is the awareness of body position.
(d) Both (a) and (c) above are correct
(e) Both (b) and (c) above are correct

ANSWER: b

15. The primary motor cortex

(a) is located in the parietal lobes.
(b) in the left cerebral hemisphere controls the skeletal muscles on the right side of the body.
(c) is the only region of the brain involved with motor control.
(d) develops motor programs for specific voluntary tasks.
(e) More than one of the above are correct.

ANSWER: b

16. Which of the following does **not** participate in control of skeletal muscle activity?

    (a)   Limbic system.
    (b)   Cerebellum.
    (c)   Supplementary motor area.
    (d)   Premotor cortex.
    (e)   Posterior parietal cortex.

ANSWER: a

17. Language ability is usually associated with

    (a)   the hypothalamus.
    (b)   the right cerebral hemisphere.
    (c)   the left cerebral hemisphere.
    (d)   the limbic system.
    (e)   the prefrontal association cortex.

ANSWER: c

18. Which of the following does **not** apply to Wernicke's area?

    (a)   Usually developed only in the left cerebral hemisphere.
    (b)   Responsible for controlling the muscles necessary for speaking ability.
    (c)   Concerned with language comprehension.
    (d)   Plays a critical role in understanding both spoken and written messages.
    (e)   Responsible for formulating coherent patterns of speech.

ANSWER: b

19. The prefrontal association cortex

    (a)   is concerned primarily with motivation and emotion.
    (b)   integrates somatic, auditory, and visual sensations.
    (c)   plays an important role in personality traits.
    (d)   localizes the source of sensory input and perceives the level of intensity of the stimulus.
    (e)   when damaged results in aphasia.

ANSWER: c

20. If a person suffers a severe blow to the upper back portion of the head, which of the following symptoms is most likely to occur?

    (a) Hearing problems.
    (b) Speech problems.
    (c) Problems with specific voluntary motor movement.
    (d) Visual problems.
    (e) Problems with specific somatic sensations.

ANSWER: d

21. The left cerebral hemisphere normally excels in all of the following **except**

    (a) musical ability.
    (b) verbal tasks.
    (c) math skills.
    (d) logical and analytical tasks.
    (e) language ability.

ANSWER: a

22. An electroencephalogram

    (a) is a record of action potential activity in the cerebral cortex.
    (b) represents the momentary collective postsynaptic activity in the cerebral cortex.
    (c) displays larger brain waves when the eyes are open than when the eyes are closed.
    (d) Both (a) and (c) above are correct.
    (e) Both (b) and (c) above are correct.

ANSWER: b

23. Parkinson's disease

    (a) is associated with a deficiency of serotonin.
    (b) is characterized by an intention tremor.
    (c) is characterized by a resting tremor.
    (d) Both (a) and (b) above are correct.
    (e) Both (a) and (c) above are correct.

ANSWER: c

24.   The thalamus

(a)   performs preliminary processing of all sensory input on its way to the cortex.
(b)   inhibits muscle tone throughout the body.
(c)   controls thirst, urine output, and food intake.
(d)   plays a role in emotional and behavioral patterns.
(e)   selects and maintains purposeful motor activity while suppressing useless or unwanted patterns of movement.

ANSWER: a

25.   Which of the following functions is not associated with the hypothalamus?

(a)   Control of respiration and circulatory function.
(b)   Control of thirst and urine output.
(c)   Control of body temperature.
(d)   Control of food intake.
(e)   Extensively involved with emotion and behavioral patterns.

ANSWER: a

26.   Which part of the brain controls thirst and urine output, food intake, and body temperature among other things?

(a)   Cerebral cortex.
(b)   Hypothalamus.
(c)   Basal nuclei.
(d)   Thalamus.
(e)   Pons.

ANSWER: b

27.   The limbic system

(a)   is a ring of forebrain structures that surround the brain stem.
(b)   plays a key role in emotion.
(c)   contains regions designated as reward and punishment centers.
(d)   Two of the above are correct.
(e)   All of the above are correct.

ANSWER: e

28. A deficiency of the neurotransmitter dopamine in the basal
     nuclei causes

     (a) schizophrenia.
     (b) epilepsy.
     (c) Parkinson's disease.
     (d) depression.
     (e) aphasia.

ANSWER: c

29. Procedural memories

     (a) are associated with the temporal lobes and closely
          associated limbic structures.
     (b) are associated with the cerebellum.
     (c) involve acquisition of motor skills gained via
          repetitive training.
     (d) Both (a) and (c) above are correct.
     (e) Both (b) and (c) above are correct.

ANSWER: e

30. Short-term memory

     (a) has a larger storage capacity than long-term memory.
     (b) takes longer to retrieve than long-term memory.
     (c) involves transient modifications in the function of
          preexisting synapses, such as channel modification.
     (d) Two of the above are correct.
     (e) All of the above are correct.

ANSWER: c

31. _____ memories are memories of facts that often result
     after only one experience, whereas _____ memories
     involve motor skills gained via repetitive training.

     (a) Declarative, procedural
     (b) Procedural, declarative
     (c) Short-term, long-term
     (d) Long-term, short-term
     (e) None of the above are correct.

ANSWER: a

32. What part of the brain plays a vital role in short-term memory involving the integration of various related stimuli and is also crucial for consolidation into long-term memory?

    (a) hippocampus
    (b) basal nuclei
    (c) cerebellum
    (d) cerebral cortex
    (e) hypothalamus

ANSWER: a

33. The cerebellum

    (a) is concerned primarily with motor activity, yet does not have any direct influence on efferent motor neurons.
    (b) is part of the subcortical region of the brain.
    (c) when diseased gives rise to resting tremors.
    (d) contains the reticular activating system.
    (e) is associated with declarative memories.

ANSWER: a

34. The cerebellum

    (a) is important for the maintenance of balance.
    (b) compares the intentions of the higher motor centers with the performance of the muscles and corrects any deviations from the intended movement.
    (c) inhibits muscle tone.
    (d) Both (a) and (b) above are correct.
    (e) All of the above are correct.

ANSWER: d

35. Which of the following statements concerning the brain stem is **incorrect**?

    (a) The medulla is part of the brain stem.
    (b) The brain stem is a critical connecting link through which all fibers traversing between the periphery and higher brain centers must pass.
    (c) The brain stem controls sociosexual behaviors conducive to mating.
    (d) The brain stem contains the reticular activating system.
    (e) The brain stem contains centers that control respiration, blood vessel and heart function, and digestive activities.

ANSWER: c

36. Which of the following statements concerning paradoxical
     sleep is **incorrect**?

     (a) The EEG pattern is similar to that of an alert, awake
          person.
     (b) Dreaming occurs.
     (c) Considerable muscle tone is present.
     (d) Respiration and heart rate are irregular.
     (e) Rapid eye movements occur.

ANSWER: c

37. Which of the following statements concerning paradoxical
     sleep is **incorrect**?

     (a) Paradoxical sleep is characterized by rapid eye
          movements.
     (b) A person normally passes through paradoxical sleep
          before entering slow-wave sleep.
     (c) Dreaming occurs only during paradoxical sleep.
     (d) The EEG pattern during paradoxical sleep is similar to
          that of an alert, awake person.
     (e) A specified amount of paradoxical sleep appears to be
          required.

ANSWER: b

38. Which of the following can activate the arousal system?

     (a) Motor activity.
     (b) Afferent sensory input.
     (c) Intense excitement.
     (d) Two of the above are correct.
     (e) All of the above are correct.

ANSWER: e

39. What region of the brain houses the centers that control
     the sleep-wake cycle?

     (a) Hypothalamus.
     (b) Thalamus.
     (c) Brain stem.
     (d) Cerebral cortex.
     (e) None of the above are correct.

ANSWER: c

40. Slow-wave sleep

    (a) occupies a greater percentage of sleeping time than
         paradoxical sleep.
    (b) is harder to arouse sleepers from than paradoxical
         sleep.
    (c) is characterized by frequent shifts in body position.
    (d) Both (a) and (c) above are correct.
    (e) All of the above are correct.

ANSWER: d

41. Ascending tracts

    (a) relay messages down the spinal cord from the brain to
         efferent neurons.
    (b) carry impulses from the periphery to the CNS.
    (c) carry impulses from the CNS to the periphery.
    (d) are part of the peripheral nervous system.
    (e) transmit signals derived from afferent input up the
         spinal cord to the brain.

ANSWER: e

42. Nerves

    (a) contain both afferent and efferent fibers traversing
         between a particular region of the body and the central
         nervous system.
    (b) do not contain complete nerve cells.
    (c) are not present within the central nervous system.
    (d) Both (a) and (b) above are correct.
    (e) All of the above are correct.

ANSWER: e

43. The peripheral nervous system

    (a) consists of the thirty-one pairs of spinal nerves and
         the twelve pairs of cranial nerves.
    (b) consists of nerve fibers that carry information between
         the CNS and other parts of the body.
    (c) includes afferent and efferent divisions
    (d) Both (a) and (b) above are correct.
    (e) All of the above are correct.

ANSWER: d

44. Information is carried up the spinal cord to the brain via

      (a) afferent pathways.
      (b) efferent pathways.
      (c) ascending tracts.
      (d) descending tracts.
      (e) the dorsal root ganglion.

ANSWER: c

45. Which of the following is **not** a component of the reflex arc?

      (a) Stimulus.
      (b) Afferent pathway.
      (c) Integrating center.
      (d) Efferent pathway.
      (e) Effector organ.

ANSWER: a

46. Which of the following is a monosynaptic reflex?

      (a) Stretch reflex.
      (b) Withdrawal reflex.
      (c) Brain stem reflexes.
      (d) Both (a) and (b) above are correct.
      (e) All of the above are correct.

ANSWER: a

47. Which of the following statements concerning the spinal
     cord is **incorrect**?

      (a) Afferent fibers enter the spinal cord through the
           ventral root.
      (b) The dorsal and ventral roots at each level of the spinal
           cord join to form a spinal nerve.
      (c) The spinal cord is not as long as the vertebral column.
      (d) The gray matter contains neuronal cell bodies and their
           dendrites, short interneurons and glial cells.
      (e) The white matter of the spinal cord is organized into
           ascending and descending tracts.

ANSWER: a

True/False

48. If neuronal pathways present at birth are not used during
     sensitive developmental periods, they may be eliminated.

ANSWER: True

49. Interneurons lie entirely within the central nervous
     system.

ANSWER: True

50. Afferent neurons have a long peripheral axon and a short
     central axon.

ANSWER: True

51. The cell bodies of afferent and efferent neurons both
     originate in the CNS.

ANSWER: False

52. Efferent neurons are the most abundant type of neuron.

ANSWER: False

53. Ninety percent of the cells within the CNS are neurons.

ANSWER: False

54. Microglia are phagocytic cells delivered by the blood to
     the central nervous system.

ANSWER: True

55. Most brain tumors of neural origin consist of glial cells.

ANSWER: True

56. The brain cannot produce ATP in the absence of oxygen.

ANSWER: True

57. Gray matter refers to regions of the central nervous system
     composed primarily of densely packed cell bodies, whereas
     white matter consists of bundles of myelinated nerve fibers.

ANSWER: True

58. An electroencephalogram is a record of action potential
     activity in the cerebral cortex.

ANSWER: False

59. The two regions of gray matter within the cerebrum are the
     cerebral cortex and the basal nuclei.

ANSWER: True

60. Different parts of the body are not equally represented in the somatosensory cortex and in the primary motor cortex.

ANSWER: True

61. White matter consists primarily of myelinated nerve fibers.

ANSWER: True

62. Gray matter consists predominantly of neuron cell bodies and dendrites.

ANSWER: True

63. Sound sensation is initially received by the parietal lobes.

ANSWER: False

64. The amount of cortical space in the primary motor cortex devoted to a given body part is proportional to the size of the part.

ANSWER: False

65. The right hemisphere is usually dominant in right-handed persons.

ANSWER: False

66. Stimulation of the frontal lobe produces changes in personality and social behavior.

ANSWER: False

67. The right and left cerebral hemispheres perform identical functions except for controlling opposite sides of the body.

ANSWER: False

68. The basal nuclei are part of the cerebrum.

ANSWER: True

69. Resting tremors are associated with diseases of the basal nuclei.

ANSWER: True

70. Centers for the control of respiration and circulatory function are located in the hypothalamus.

ANSWER: False

71. Reward centers are found most abundantly in regions involved in mediating the highly motivated behavioral activities of eating, drinking, and sexual activity.

ANSWER: True

72. Anterograde amnesia is the inability to recall recent past events.

ANSWER: False

73. Working memory involves comparing current sensory data with relevant stored knowledge and manipulating that information.

ANSWER: True

74. The recycling of newly acquired information through short-term memory increases the likelihood of long-term memory consolidation.

ANSWER: True

75. Disorders of the cerebellum are characterized by an intention tremor.

ANSWER: True

76. The majority of the twelve pairs of cranial nerves arise from the brain stem.

ANSWER: True

77. Consciousness refers to subjective awareness of the external world and self.

ANSWER: True

78. Sleep is accompanied by a reduction in neural activity.

ANSWER: False

79. The outer layer of the brain is gray matter but the outer layer of the spinal cord is white matter.

ANSWER: True

80.   There are no nerves in the CNS.

ANSWER: True

81.   The cell bodies in the spinal cord are located primarily in the white matter.

ANSWER: False

82.   Ascending tracts carry information from the periphery to the CNS.

ANSWER: False

83.   Reciprocal innervation refers to the dual innervation of organs by the autonomic nervous system.

ANSWER: False

84.   Efferent neurons leave the spinal cord through the dorsal root.

ANSWER: False

85.   A central bundle of interneuronal axons is known as a tract, whereas a peripheral bundle of afferent and efferent neuronal axons is called a nerve.

ANSWER: True

86.   Information as to whether a finger was touching an ice cube or being hit by a hammer would be carried to the brain in different ascending tracts within the spinal cord.

ANSWER: True

87.   The withdrawal reflex is a monosynaptic reflex.

ANSWER: False

88.   The stretch reflex is a polysynaptic reflex.

ANSWER: False

Fill-in-the-blanks

89. The nervous system is organized into the _____,
     consisting of the brain and _____, and the _____,
     consisting of nerve fibers that carry information between the
     CNS and other parts of the body.

ANSWERS: central nervous system, spinal cord, peripheral
           nervous system

90. The _____ system coordinates rapid responses of the
     body, whereas the _____ system is responsible for
     regulating metabolic functions and activities that require
     duration rather than speed.

ANSWERS: nervous, endocrine

91. The _____ division of the peripheral nervous system
     carries information to the CNS. Instructions from the CNS
     are transmitted via the _____ division of the
     peripheral nervous system to the _____ organs.

ANSWERS: afferent, efferent, effector

92. The efferent division of the peripheral nervous system is
     divided into the _____, which consists of _____
     that supply the skeletal muscles, and the _____, which
     innervates smooth muscle, cardiac muscle, and glands.

ANSWERS: somatic nervous system, motor neurons, autonomic
           nervous system

93. The two subdivisions of the autonomic nervous system are
     the _____ and the _____.

ANSWERS: sympathetic nervous system, parasympathetic
           nervous system

94. The four major types of glial cells are _____,
     _____, _____, and _____.

ANSWERS: astrocytes, oligodendrocytes, ependymal cells,
           microglia

95. The _____ is a special cushioning fluid that
     surrounds the brain and spinal cord.

ANSWER: cerebrospinal fluid

96. The brain normally uses only _____ as a source of fuel for energy production, yet does not store any of this nutrient.

ANSWER: glucose

97. The largest portion of the human brain is the _____, which is divided into two halves.

ANSWER: cerebrum

98. _____ matter consists predominantly of densely packaged cell bodies and dendrites, whereas _____ matter consists of bundles of myelinated nerve fibers.

ANSWERS: gray, white

99. The _____ lobes of the cerebral cortex are responsible for initial processing of visual input.

ANSWER: occipital

100. The _____ cortex, the site for initial cortical processing of somesthetic and proprioceptive input, is located in the _____ lobes.

ANSWERS: somatosensory, parietal

101. _____ area is responsible for speaking ability, whereas _____ area is concerned with language comprehension.

ANSWERS: Broca's, Wernicke's

102. _____ refers to the ability of the brain to be functionally remolded in response to the demands placed on it.

ANSWER: Plasticity

103. The _____ hemisphere excels in performance of logical, analytical, sequential and verbal tasks, whereas the _____ hemisphere excels in nonlanguage skills such as spatial perception and artistic and musical endeavors.

ANSWERS: left, right

104. The _____ consist of several masses of gray matter located deep within the cerebral white matter.

ANSWER: basal nuclei

105. The _____ serves as a relay station and synaptic integrating center for preliminary processing of all sensory input on its way to the cortex.

ANSWER: thalamus

106. The _____ is the area of the brain most notably involved in the direct regulation of the internal environment.

ANSWER: hypothalamus

107. _____ refers to the ability to direct behavior toward specific goals.

ANSWER: Motivation

108. _____ is the acquisition of knowledge as a consequence of experience.

ANSWER: Learning

109. _____ represent the subjective urges associated with specific bodily needs that motivate appropriate behavior to satisfy those needs.

ANSWER: homeostatic drives

110. The neural change responsible for retention or storage of knowledge is known as the _____.

ANSWER: memory trace

111. The inability to recall recent past events following a traumatic event is known as _____, whereas the inability to store new memories for later retrieval is called _____.

ANSWERS: retrograde amnesia, anterograde amnesia

112. An _____ tremor characterizes cerebellar disease.

ANSWER: intention

113. _____ refers to subjective awareness of surroundings and self.

ANSWER: consciousness

114. A _____ is a bundle of peripheral neuronal axons, some afferent and some efferent, which are enclosed by a connective tissue covering and follow the same pathway.

ANSWER: nerve

115. A _____ is a bundle of neuronal axons of similar function within the CNS.

ANSWER: tract

116. Stimulation of the nerve supply to one muscle and simultaneous inhibition of the nerves to its antagonistic muscle is known as _____.

ANSWER: reciprocal innervation

117. A collection of neuronal cell bodies located outside of the CNS is called a _____, whereas a functional collection of cell bodies within the CNS is referred to as a _____ or a _____.

ANSWERS: ganglion, center, nucleus

118. The cell bodies of afferent neurons are located in the _____.

ANSWER: dorsal root ganglion

119. A _____ is any response that occurs automatically without conscious effort.

ANSWER: reflex

Matching

120. Indicate which brain structure is associated with each function by writing the appropriate letter in the blank using the following answer code:

> (a) = cerebellum
> (b) = hypothalamus
> (c) = brain stem
> (d) = basal nuclei
> (e) = cerebral cortex

_____ Controls anterior pituitary hormone secretion.
_____ Structure that initiates all voluntary movement.
_____ Inhibits muscle tone throughout the body.
_____ Damage to this structure associated with a resting tremor.
_____ Controls thirst, urine output, food intake, and body temperature.
_____ Contains centers for respiration, heart and blood vessel function, and many digestive activities.
_____ Helps monitor and coordinate slow, sustained contractions, especially those related to balance and posture.
_____ Contains the autonomic nervous system coordinating center.
_____ Disorder of this structure characterized by an intention tremor.
_____ Plays a role in emotion and behavioral patterns.
_____ Concerned with the coordination of motor activity initiated by higher brain centers; compares the "intentions" of the higher centers with the "performance" of the muscles, and corrects any "errors."
_____ Structure that accomplishes final sensory perception.
_____ Consists of the medulla, pons, and midbrain.

ANSWERS: b, e, d, d, b, c, d, b, a, b, a, e, c

121. Indicate whether the characteristic pertains to the nervous system or endocrine system by writing the appropriate letter in the blanks using the following answer code:

> (a) = applies to the nervous system
> (b) = applies to the endocrine system
> (c) = applies to both the nervous system and endocrine system

_____ Coordinates rapid activities of the body.
_____ Secretes hormones.
_____ Primarily controls metabolic activities and other activities that require duration rather than speed.
_____ Alters target cells by release of chemical messengers that interact with specific receptors of the target cells.
_____ Chemical messengers travel long distances.
_____ Chemical messengers travel short distances.
_____ Chemical messengers released only in response to an action potential.

ANSWERS: a, b, b, c, b, a, a

122. _____ Initially process sound input
_____ Initially process visual input
_____ Initially process somesthetic sensation and proprioception
_____ Contain primary motor cortex.
_____ Contain the region responsible for personality traits.
_____ Contain the limbic association cortex.
_____ Located on the sides of the head.
_____ Located at the back of the head.
_____ Located in front of the central sulcus.
_____ Located to the rear of the central sulcus.

a. occipital lobes
b. temporal lobes
c. parietal lobes
d. frontal lobes

ANSWERS: b, a, c, d, d, b, b, a, d, c

123. _____ Storage of acquired knowledge   a. memory trace
           for later recall   b. learning
     _____ Neural change responsible for   c. memory
           retention or storage of   d. remembering
           knowledge   e. motivation
     _____ Acquisition of knowledge or   f. amnesia
           skills as a consequence of ex-   g. consolidation
           perience, instruction, or both
     _____ Ability to direct behavior
           toward specific goals.
     _____ Lack of memory that involves
           whole portions of time.
     _____ Process of retrieving specific
           information from memory stores.
     _____ Transfer and fixation of short-
           term memory traces into long-term
           memory stores.

ANSWERS: c, a, b, e, f, d, g

124. Indicate which nervous pathway is being described by
     writing the appropriate letter in the blanks using the
     following answer code:

                    (a) = ascending tracts
                    (b) = descending tracts
                    (c) = afferent neurons
                    (d) = efferent neurons

     _____ Carry information from the periphery to the CNS.
     _____ Carry information up the spinal cord to the
           brain.
     _____ Carry information from the brain down the spinal
           cord.
     _____ Carry information from the CNS to the effector
           organs.

ANSWERS: c, a, b, d

125. _____ brain phagocytes   a. astrocytes
     _____ line the brain ventricles   b. oligodendrocytes
     _____ form the insulative   c. ependymal cells
           myelin sheaths around axons   d. microglia
           in the CNS
     _____ main brain "glue"

ANSWERS: d, c, b, a

126. ____ Afferent fibers enter the spinal cord through this structure
____ Efferent fibers leave the spinal cord through this structure.
____ Location of cell bodies of afferent neurons.
____ Location of cell bodies of the efferent neurons.
____ Location of ascending and descending tracts
____ Location of short interneurons involved in integration of spinal reflexes
____ Outer portion of spinal cord
____ Inner portion of spinal cord

a. dorsal root
b. dorsal root ganglion
c. ventral root
d. gray matter of spinal cord
e. white matter of spinal cord

ANSWERS: a, c, b, d, e, d, e, d

127. ____ initial cortical processing for vision
____ initial cortical processing for hearing
____ initial cortical processing for sensations arising from the surface of the body
____ important in orienting the body and arms towards a specific target
____ triggers voluntary movement by activating motor neurons
____ responsible for speaking ability
____ responsible for comprehension and formulation of coherent patterns of speech
____ primarily concerned with motivation and emotion
____ lesions in this area result in changes in personality and social behavior

a. temporal lobe
b. Wernicke's area
c. somatosensory cortex
d. limbic association cortex
e. primary motor cortex
f. occipital lobe
g. Broca's area
h. premotor cortex
i. prefrontal association cortex

ANSWERS: f, a, c, h, e, g, b, d, i

128. Indicate which characteristic applies to which type of memory using the following answer code:

        (a) = short-term memory
        (b) = long-term memory

_____ very large storage capacity
_____ limited-storage capacity
_____ site for initial deposition of new information
_____ takes longer to retrieve information from this store
_____ involves transient modifications in function of preexisting synapses
_____ involves relatively permanent functional or structural changes between existing neurons

ANSWERS: b, a, a, b, a, b

129. Indicate which characteristics apply to each type of sleep using the following answer code:

        (a) = slow-wave sleep
        (b) = paradoxical sleep

_____ rapid eye movements occur
_____ has four stages
_____ must go through this type of sleep first before entering the other type
_____ EEG pattern similar to a wide-awake, alert person
_____ dreaming occurs
_____ mental activity similar to waking-time thoughts
_____ inhibition of muscle tone
_____ frequent shifting of body position
_____ spend greatest percentage of time in this type of sleep
_____ heart and respiratory rate irregular
_____ hardest from which to arouse
_____ most apt to awaken from on own

ANSWERS: b, a, a, b, b, a, b, a, a, b, b, b

AUDIOVISUAL AIDS

Films

A list of films available from West Publishing Company is presented in Appendix A. Following are other films that may be suitable. The sources for these films, which are coded by abbreviation, are provided in Appendix B.

Acupuncture, FI, 27 min.

Alzheimer's Disease: The Long Nightmare, FHS, 19 min.

Brain and Behavior, UC, 22 min.

Cerebral Cortex (VCR), WHS, 58 min.

Cerebrospinal Fluid, IOWA

Cerebrovascular Disease, WX, 30 min.

Convulsions, EFL, 20 min.

Decision, FM, 26 min.

Dreams: Theater of the Night, FHS, 28 min.

Dream Voyage, FM, 26 min.

Drugs and the Nervous System, CH, 18 min.

Exploring the Human Brain, BFA, 18 min.

Exploring the Human Nervous System, CH, 23 min.

Frontiers of the Mind, EBE, 25 min.

Fundamentals of the Nervous System, EBE, 17 min.

Inside Information: The Brain and How It Works, FHS, 58 min.

How the Mind Begins, UI, 24 min.

Human Body: Nervous System, COR, 16 min.

Human Body: The Brain, COR, 16 min.

Human Brain, TLV, 20 min.

Left Brain, Right Brain, FI, 56 min.

Marvels of the Mind, NG, 23 min.

Memory: Fabric of the Mind, FHS, 28 min.

Miracle of the Mind, MH, 26 min.

Modern Concepts of Epilepsy, EFL, 20 min.

Multiple Sclerosis, FHS, 26 min.

Mysteries of the Mind, NG, 59 min.

Nerves and Brain, TLF, 20 min.

Nervous System, MH, 28 min.

Nervous System in Animals, IU, 17 min.

Nervous System in Man, IU, 18 min.

Our Talented Brain, FM, 26 min.

Parkinson's Disease, FHS, 19 min.

Performance of Skills - The Pyramidal System, AVC, 18 min.

Psychoactive, PYR, 30 min.

Sleepwatchers, MH, 25 min.

The Addicted Brain, FHS, 26 min.

The Enlightened Machine, EBC, 58 min.

The Hidden Universe: The Brain, MH, 48 min. The Human Brain,
EBE, 11 min.

The Human Brain: A Dynamic View of Its Structure and
Organization, WX, 28 min.

The Mind of Man, UI, 25 min.

The Nervous System in Man, IU, 18 min.

The Sexual Brain, FHS, 28 min.

The Split Brain and Conscious Experience, HR, 17 min.

Software

Flash: The EEG, PLP. Covers physiological basis and EEG
frequencies.

Flash: The Human Brain, PLP. Functionally surveys the major
areas of the brain.

Flash: Nerves, PLP. Explores cervical, brachial, lumbar,
sacral, and cranial nerves.

Nervous System, PLP. Two part program that covers the human
nervous system.

The Human Brain: Neurons, PLP. Designed to provide mastery
of neuron anatomy and physiology.

<u>Thinking and Learning</u>, SSS. Three programs on how we think, evaluate, and reach reasonable conclusions.

<u>Your Body</u>: Series II, SSS. Covers the nervous system and brain.

Chapter 5
Peripheral Nervous System

CONTENTS
(All page references are to the main text.)

Eye: Vision, p.125
- -The eye is a fluid-filled sphere enclosed by three specialized tissue layers. p.125
- -The amount of light entering the eye is controlled by the iris. p.127
- -The eye refracts the entering light to focus the image on the retina. p.127
- -Accommodation increases the strength of the lens for near vision. p.129
- -Light must pass through several retinal layers before reaching the photoreceptors. p.130
- -Phototransduction by retinal cells converts light stimuli into neural signals that are perceived by the visual cortex. p.131
- -Rods provide indistinct gray vision at night whereas cones provide sharp color vision during the day. p.135
- -The sensitivity of the eyes can vary markedly through dark and light adaptation. p.135
- -Color vision is dependent on the ratios of stimulation of the three cone types. p.136
- -Visual information is separated and modified within the visual pathway before it is integrated into a perceptual image of the visual field by the cortex. p.137
- -Protective mechanisms help prevent eye injuries. p.137

Ear: Hearing and Equilibrium, p.138
- -Sound waves consist of alternate regions of compression and rarefaction of air molecules. p.140
- -The external and middle ear convert airborne sound waves into fluid vibrations in the inner ear. p.141
- -Hair cells in the organ of Corti transduce fluid movements into neural signals. p.143
- -Pitch discrimination depends on the region of the basilar membrane that vibrates; loudness discrimination depends on the amplitude of the vibration. p.143
- -Deafness is caused by defects either in conduction or neural processing of sound waves. p.145
- -The vestibular apparatus detects position and motion of the head and is important for equilibrium and coordination of head, eye, and body movements. p.145

Chemical Senses: Taste and Smell, p.149
- -Taste sensation is coded by patterns of activity in various taste bud receptors. p.150
- -Smell is the least understood of the special senses. p.151

Introduction: Efferent Output, p.152

Autonomic Nervous System, p.153

-An autonomic nerve pathway consists of a two-neuron chain, with the terminal neurotransmitter differing between sympathetic and parasympathetic nerves. p.153
-The autonomic nervous system controls involuntary visceral organ activities. p.155
-The sympathetic and parasympathetic nervous systems dually innervate most visceral organs. p.157
-The adrenal medulla, an endocrine gland, is a modified part of the sympathetic nervous system. p.157
-There are several different types of membrane receptor proteins for each autonomic neurotransmitter. p.158
-Many regions of the central nervous system are involved in the control of autonomic activities. p.158

Somatic Nervous System, p.159

-Motor neurons supply skeletal muscle. p.159
-Acetylcholine chemically links electrical activity in motor neurons with electrical activity in skeletal-muscle cells. p.159
-Acetylcholinesterase terminates acetylcholine activity at the neuromuscular junction. p.161
-The neuromuscular junction is vulnerable to several chemical agents and diseases. p.161

Chapter in Perspective: Focus on Homeostasis, p.163

Chapter Summary, p.164

LECTURE HINTS AND SUGGESTIONS

1. Use preserved specimens of beef or sheep eyes that can be dissected for demonstration purposes. Local slaughter houses are a good source.

2. The shark's vestibular apparatus and the middle ear bones of mammals are excellent demonstration materials. A good source is Delta Biologicals, P.O. Box 26666, Tucson, AZ. See any general physiology lab manual for techniques and supplies.

3. Have students localize receptors in their skin for touch, pressure, pain, and temperature. See any general physiology lab manual for techniques and supplies.

4. Use models of the eye and ear to illustrate their structure. These can be obtained from Carolina Biological Supply Company.

5. To demonstrate the interactions of the senses of taste and smell, have students try to detect the difference between the tastes of two foods (e.g., an apple and an onion) while holding their noses.

6. Demonstrate the test for color blindness. See any general physiology lab manual for techniques and supplies.

7. Have students examine their own eyes in a mirror and with an ophthalmoscope. See any general physiology lab manual for techniques and supplies.

8. To demonstrate sensory adaptation, aerosol some perfume into the air and measure how long it takes for students to lose the ability to detect its presence.

9. Use tuning forks to illustrate pitch and frequency. These can be obtained from Wards Biology, Rochester, NY.

10. The discussion of the autonomic nervous system can best be supported by the use of the tables and illustrations that summarize the key concepts. Have students compare observable differences in body function when they are in a stressful situation (sympathetic domination) (e.g., increased heart rate) and in a quiet, relaxed situation (parasympathetic domination) (e.g., slow heart rate).

11. Demonstrate the concept of biofeedback. Carolina Biological Supply Company has a feedback kit that demonstrates four psychophysiological parameters: galvanic skin resistance, heart rate/blood volume pulse, skin temperature, and muscle tension (EMG or electromyogram).

12. Use 2 x 2 slides of the anatomy and physiology of the neuromuscular junction. These can be obtained from Carolina Biological Supply Company.

13. Show some pathological slides of the influence of specific chemical agents and diseases (e.g., pesticides, drugs and x-rays). These can be obtained from Delta Biologicals, P.O. Box 26666, Tucson, AZ.

CHAPTER TEST QUESTIONS

Multiple Choice

1. Receptors

    (a) respond to various physical or chemical changes in their environment.
    (b) change other forms of energy into electrical energy.
    (c) respond more readily to their adequate stimulus.
    (d) are found at the peripheral endings of afferent neurons.
    (e) All of the above are correct.

ANSWER: e

2. Receptors

    (a) generate action potentials in afferent fibers in response to stimuli.
    (b) change other forms of energy into electrical energy.
    (c) are located in the dorsal root ganglion.
    (d) Both (a) and (b) above are correct.
    (e) All of the above are correct.

ANSWER: d

3. Which of the following statements concerning receptor potentials is correct? Receptor potentials

    (a) are usually depolarizations of receptors in response to adequate stimuli.
    (b) are graded potentials.
    (c) occur in neuronal cell bodies upon summation of pre-synaptic input.
    (d) Both (a) and (b) above are correct
    (e) All of the above are correct.

 ANSWER: d

4. Which of the following statements concerning receptors is correct?

    (a) The larger the receptor potential, the greater the frequency of action potentials initiated in the afferent neuron.
    (b) Tonic receptors often exhibit an "off-response."
    (c) Phasic receptors are important in situations where maintained information about a stimulus is valuable.
    (d) Receptor adaptation results from nerve fatigue.
    (e) Receptors are part of efferent neurons.

ANSWER: a

5.   Phasic receptors

     (a)   exhibit an "off-response."
     (b)   signal a change in stimulus intensity.
     (c)   are rapidly adapting receptors.
     (d)   All of the above are correct.
     (e)   None of the above are correct.

ANSWER: d

6.   Tonic receptors

     (a)   adapt rapidly.
     (b)   frequently exhibit an "off-response."
     (c)   are useful to signal a change in stimulus intensity
           rather than providing status quo information.
     (d)   All of the above are correct.
     (e)   None of the above are correct.

ANSWER: e

7.   Which of the following receptors is (are) rapidly adapting?

     (a)   Muscle stretch receptor.
     (b)   Tonic receptor.
     (c)   Phasic receptor.
     (d)   Both (a) and (b) above are correct.
     (e)   All of the above are correct.

ANSWER: c

8.   The smaller the receptive fields in a region,

     (a)   the greater the density of receptors in the region.
     (b)   the greater the acuity in the region.
     (c)   the more cortical space allotted for sensory reception
           from the region.
     (d)   Both (a) and (b) above are correct.
     (e)   All of the above are correct.

ANSWER: e

9.   Polymodal nociceptors

     (a)   respond only to mechanical damage such as cutting,
           crushing, or pinching.
     (b)   activate the slow pain pathway.
     (c)   activate the slow pain pathway.
     (d)   Both (a) and (b) above are correct.
     (e)   None of the above are correct.

ANSWER: b

10. The slow pain pathway

   (a) is activated by stimulation of mechanical or thermal nociceptors.
   (b) is activated by stimulation of polymodal nociceptors.
   (c) is activated by chemicals released into the ECF from damaged tissue.
   (d) Both (a) and (c) above are correct.
   (e) Both (b) and (c) above are correct.

ANSWER: e

11. Endorphins and enkephalins

   (a) are endogenous morphinelike substances.
   (b) are important in the body's natural analgesic system.
   (c) stimulate the release of substance P by binding with opiate receptors.
   (d) Both (a) and (b) above are correct.
   (e) All of the above are correct.

ANSWER: d

12. Which of the following is **not** a special sense?

   (a) Vision.
   (b) Hearing.
   (c) Gustation.
   (d) Olfaction.
   (e) Proprioception.

ANSWER: e

13. Which of the following structures normally controls the amount of light entering the eye?

   (a) Ciliary muscle.
   (b) Suspensory ligaments.
   (c) Iris.
   (d) Cornea.
   (e) Lens.

ANSWER: c

14. The retina

    (a)   is the middle layer of the eye.
    (b)   contains the photoreceptors.
    (c)   becomes specialized anteriorly to form the cornea.
    (d)   secretes the aqueous humor.
    (e)   None of the above are correct.

ANSWER: b

15. Which of the following help reduce internal reflection
     (scattering of light within the eye)?

    (a)   Sclera.
    (b)   Choroid.
    (c)   Blind spot.
    (d)   Lens.
    (e)   Iris.

ANSWER: b

16. Which of the following structures contributes the most to
     the total refractive ability of the eye?

    (a)   Lens.
    (b)   Cornea.
    (c)   Ciliary muscle.
    (d)   Retina.
    (e)   Iris.

ANSWER: b

17. The lens of the eye

    (a)   has convex surfaces.
    (b)   is stronger when it is flatter.
    (c)   contributes   most   extensively   to   the   eye's   total
          refractive ability.
    (d)   Two of the above are correct.
    (e)   All of the above are correct.

ANSWER: a

18. During accommodation for near vision

    (a) the ciliary muscle contracts.
    (b) the lens increases in strength.
    (c) the suspensory ligaments become taut.
    (d) Both (a) and (b) above are correct.
    (e) All of the above are correct.

ANSWER: d

19. In hyperopia

    (a) the eyeball is too short or the lens is too weak.
    (b) a near object is focused behind the retina, even with
         accommodation.
    (c) a far source of light is focused ahead of the retina.
    (d) Both (a) and (b) above are correct.
    (e) Both (a) and (c) above are correct.

ANSWER: d

20. Which of the following statements concerning myopia is
     correct?

    (a) The curvature of the lens is uneven.
    (b) A near source of light is focused on the retina without
         accommodation.
    (c) A convex lens is used to correct the condition.
    (d) The images from the two eyes are not fused within the
         cortex.
    (e) There is increased intraocular pressure.

ANSWER: b

21. The fovea

    (a) is located in the exact center of the retina.
    (b) contains a greater abundance of rods than cones.
    (c) is the point on the retina at which the optic nerve
         leaves and blood vessels pass through.
    (d) Both (a) and (b) above are correct.
    (e) All of the above are correct.

ANSWER: a

22. The blind spot

(a) is the point on the retina at which the optic nerve leaves and blood vessels pass through.
(b) contains no rods or cones.
(c) is in the exact center of the retina.
(d) Both (a) and (b) above are correct.
(e) All of the above are correct.

ANSWER: d

23. Rhodopsin

(a) is the photopigment found in the red cones.
(b) consists of an opsin and retinene.
(c) is most highly concentrated in the fovea.
(d) is slowly broken down in the absence of light.
(e) contains a derivative of vitamin B_{12}.

ANSWER: b

24. Cones

(a) are most abundant in the periphery of the retina.
(b) are more numerous than rods.
(c) have high sensitivity to light.
(d) are responsible for color vison.
(e) More than one of the above are correct.

ANSWER: d

25. Which of the following statements concerning cones is **incorrect**?

(a) Cones are used for day vision.
(b) Cones are very sensitive to light.
(c) Cones exhibit high acuity.
(d) Cones are concentrated in the fovea.
(e) Cones provide color vison.

ANSWER: b

26. Rods

(a) are more sensitive to light than cones.
(b) have low acuity.
(c) provide vision in shades of gray.
(d) Both (b) and (c) above are correct.
(e) All of the above are correct.

ANSWER: e

27. During dark adaptation

(a) photopigments are gradually regenerated.
(b) rhodopsin is rapidly broken down.
(c) the cones for gray vision are stimulated more than the cones for color vision.
(d) the sensitivity of the photoreceptors is reduced so that the image appears dim.
(e) retinene and opsin dissociate

ANSWER: a

28. Color vision
(a) is accomplished by rods at night and cones during the day.
(b) depends on the three cone types' various ratios of stimulation in response to different wavelengths of light.
(c) is usually lost in vitamin A deficiency.
(d) depends on activation of a specific cone for each visible color.
(e) is made possible by convergence within the cone pathways.

ANSWER: b

29. Vitamin A deficiency causes

(a) poor night vision.
(b) poor color vision.
(c) astigmatism.
(d) presbyopia.
(e) color blindness.

ANSWER: a

30. Presbyopia is characterized by

(a) the lack of a cone type.
(b) pronounced visual difficulty in the early teenage years.
(c) a reduction in accommodative ability as a result of a loss of lens elasticity.
(d) retinal damage.
(e) excessive refractive power in the lens system of the eye.

ANSWER: c

31. The optic tract

    (a) carries information from the lateral half of the retina on the same side and the medial half of the retina on the opposite side.
    (b) carries information from the lateral halves of both retinae.
    (c) carries information from the medial halves of both retinae.
    (d) carries information from the lateral half of the retina on the opposite side and the medial half of the retina on the same side.
    (e) carries information from both the lateral and medial halves of the retina on the same side.

ANSWER: a

32. In the visual pathway,

    (a) the fibers from the medial halves of both retinae cross at the optic chiasm.
    (b) the optic nerve carries information from the lateral half of one retina and the medial half of the other retina.
    (c) the optic nerve carries information from both the lateral half and the medial half of the retina of the same eye.
    (d) Both (a) and (b) above are correct.
    (e) Both (a) and (c) above are correct.

ANSWER: e

33. Which of the following is the proper sequence of retinal processing?

    (a) Rods and cones → ganglion cells → bipolar neurons.
    (b) Rods and cones → bipolar neurons → ganglion cells.
    (c) Ganglion cells → bipolar neurons → rods and cones.
    (d) Ganglion cells → rods and cones → bipolar neurons.
    (e) Bipolar neurons → ganglion cells → rods and cones.

ANSWER: b

34. The pitch of a sound

    (a) is determined by the frequency of vibrations of air molecules.
    (b) depends on the amplitude of the sound waves.
    (c) is measured in units of decibels.
    (d) Both (a) and (b) above are correct.
    (e) All of the above are correct.

ANSWER: a

35. The human ear is most sensitive to sound frequencies within the range of

    (a) 0-20,000 cycles per second.
    (b) 20-20,000 cycles per second.
    (c) 10-100,000 cycles per second.
    (d) 100-15,000 cycles per second.
    (e) 1,000-4,000 cycles per second.

ANSWER: e

36. All of the following are true statements about sound waves **except**:

    (a) They are produced by a disturbance pattern in air molecules.
    (b) They gradually dissipate as they travel from the original sound source.
    (c) The average human ear can detect sound waves of frequencies between 20 cycles per second to 20,000 cycles per second.
    (d) The average human ear is most sensitive to sound waves with frequencies between 5,000 cycles per second to 10,000 cycles per second.
    (e) They consist of alternating regions of air compression and rarefaction.

ANSWER: d

37. The tympanic membrane

    (a) vibrates when struck by sound waves.
    (b) contains the organ of Corti.
    (c) produces earwax.
    (d) is connected to the stapes.
    (e) None of the above are correct.

ANSWER: a

38. The ossicular system of the ear

    (a) serves to keep the pressure on the two sides of the
        tympanic membrane equal.
    (b) increases the pressure of vibration as it transfers the
        sound wave from air in the outer ear to fluid in the
        inner ear.
    (c) assists in determining whether a sound comes from the
        front or rear.
    (d) is part of the vestibular apparatus.
    (e) is in direct contact with the tympanic membrane and the
        round window.

ANSWER: b

39. Transmission of sound through the middle ear results in

    (a) amplification of the pressure of the sound vibrations.
    (b) stimulation of middle ear receptor cells.
    (c) opening of the eustachian tube.
    (d) increased firing rate in sensory axons associated with
        the tympanic membrane.
    (e) None of the above are correct.

ANSWER: a

40. Actual conversion of sound vibrations to nerve impulses
    occurs in the

    (a) eardrum.
    (b) ossicular system.
    (c) eustachian tube.
    (d) cochlea.
    (e) oval window.

ANSWER: d

41. High and low frequency sounds are discriminated chiefly by

    (a) low frequencies producing stronger eardrum vibrations.
    (b) high frequencies producing larger action potentials.
    (c) the middle ear bones vibrating more vigorously for low
        frequencies.
    (d) low frequencies deflecting the basilar membrane at a
        greater distance from the oval window.
    (e) low frequencies setting up fluid vibrations in the
        cochlea and high frequencies setting up vibrations in
        the vestibular apparatus.

ANSWER: d

42.   The oval window

    (a)   attaches to the stapes.
    (b)   transfers the sound wave from the middle ear to the
          inner ear.
    (c)   vibrates to dissipate energy in response to fluid
          movements in the cochlea.
    (d)   Both (a) and (b) above are correct.
    (e)   All of the above are correct.

ANSWER: d

43.   In response to movement of the oval window,

    (a)   pressure waves are set up in the cochlea.
    (b)   a portion of the basilar membrane vibrates.
    (c)   certain hair cell receptors in the organ of Corti
          become excited.
    (d)   the round window is displaced.
    (e)   All of the above are correct.

ANSWER: e

44.   Fluid movement in the cochlea

    (a)   causes displacement of the round window, which dissipates
          pressure.
    (b)   causes deflection of the basilar membrane.
    (c)   causes the hairs of the receptor cells of the organ of
          Corti to be bent as they are moved in relation to the
          tectorial membrane.
    (d)   Two of the above are correct.
    (e)   All of the above are correct.

ANSWER: e

45.   The organ of Corti

    (a)   rests on top of the basilar membrane.
    (b)   is located in the vestibular apparatus.
    (c)   contains hair cells sensitive to mechanical
          deformation in association with fluid movements in the
          inner ear.
    (d)   Two of the above are correct.
    (e)   All of the above are correct.

ANSWER: d

46. Deflection of the basilar membrane

   (a) activates the sound receptors of the organ of Corti.
   (b) occurs in response to fluid movements in the cochlea.
   (c) results from displacement of the round window.
   (d) Both (a) and (b) above are correct.
   (e) All of the above are correct.

ANSWER: d

47. Which of the following abnormalities could give rise to
     sensorineural deafness?

   (a) Rupture of the tympanic membrane.
   (b) Disease or injury in the organ of Corti.
   (c) Restriction of ossicular movement because of adhesions
        between the bones.
   (d) Damage to the occipital lobes of the cortex.
   (e) Presbyopia.

ANSWER: b

48. The semicircular canals

   (a) detect the position of the head relative to gravity.
   (b) detect rotational or angular acceleration of the head.
   (c) contain otoliths.
   (d) Both (a) and (c) above are correct.
   (e) Both (b) and (c) above are correct.

ANSWER: b

49. The utricle

   (a) is an otolith organ.
   (b) is activated when a person bends the head to look down
        at the ground.
   (c) is activated when a person starts to walk.
   (d) Both (a) and (b) above are correct.
   (e) All of the above are correct.

ANSWER: e

50. Vestibular information is important for all of the
     following **except**

   (a) hearing.
   (b) maintenance of balance and desired posture.
   (c) control of eye movement.
   (d) perception of motion and orientation.

ANSWER: a

51.   Taste

   (a)   discrimination depends on the ratio of stimulation of the taste buds, which have a variation in relative sensitivity.

   (b)   buds are stimulated only by chemicals in solution.
   (c)   discrimination does not go beyond distinguishing between the four primary tastes - sweet, sour, salty, and bitter.
   (d)   Both (a) and (b) above are correct.
   (e)   All of the above are correct.

ANSWER: d

52.   Olfactory receptors

   (a)   are specialized endings of afferent neurons, not separate cells.
   (b)   when stimulated, send impulses both to the limbic system for coordination between smell and behavior and to the thalamus and cortex for perception of smell.
   (c)   are replaced about every two months.
   (d)   Both (a) and (b) above are correct.
   (e)   All of the above are correct.

ANSWER: e

53.   The basal cells of the olfactory mucosa

   (a)   secrete mucus
   (b)   possess long cilia that contain binding sites for attachment of odoriferous molecules
   (c)   are precursors for new olfactory receptor cells
   (d)   Two of the above are correct
   (e)   All of the above are correct

ANSWER: c

54.   The autonomic nervous system

   (a)   is part of the somatic nervous system.
   (b)   is considered to be the involuntary branch of the efferent division of the peripheral nervous system.
   (c)   innervates skeletal muscle.
   (d)   Two of the above are correct.
   (e)   All of the above are correct.

ANSWER: b

55. Parasympathetic postganglionic fibers

    (a)   arise from the ganglion chain located along either side of the spinal cord.
    (b)   are cholinergic.
    (c)   secrete norepinephrine.
    (d)   Both (a) and (b) above are correct.
    (e)   Both (a) and (c) above are correct.

ANSWER: b

56. All of the following release acetylcholine **except**

    (a)   sympathetic preganglionic fibers.
    (b)   parasympathetic preganglionic fibers.
    (c)   sympathetic postganglionic fibers.
    (d)   parasympathetic postganglionic fibers.
    (e)   motor neurons.

ANSWER: c

57. The sympathetic nervous system

    (a)   is always excitatory.
    (b)   innervates only tissues concerned with protecting the body against challenges from the outside environment.
    (c)   dominates in fight or flight situations.
    (d)   is part of the somatic nervous system.
    (e)   is part of the afferent division of the peripheral nervous system.

ANSWER: c

58. The sympathetic nervous system

    (a)   is part of the somatic nervous system.
    (b)   has cholinergic preganglionic and adrenergic postganglionic fibers.
    (c)   originates in the thoracic and lumbar regions of the spinal cord.
    (d)   Both (b) and (c) above are correct.
    (e)   All of the above are correct.

ANSWER: d

59. Which of the following does **not** characterize the sympathetic nervous system?

   (a) It promotes responses that prepare the body for strenuous physical activity.
   (b) It is part of the autonomic nervous system.
   (c) It has norepinephrine as its postganglionic neurotransmitter.
   (d) It is always excitatory (that is, it increases the activity in every tissue it innervates).
   (e) It is part of the efferent division of the peripheral nervous system.

ANSWER: d

60. The parasympathetic nervous system

   (a) has long preganglionic fibers that end on terminal ganglia, which lie in or near the effector organ.
   (b) dominates in quiet, relaxed situations.
   (c) releases a postganglionic neurotransmitter that binds with muscarinic receptors.
   (d) Both (a) and (b) above are correct.
   (e) All of the above are correct.

ANSWER: e

61. Nicotinic receptors

   (a) bind with acetylcholine released from parasympathetic postganglionic fibers.
   (b) respond to acetylcholine released from both sympathetic and parasympathetic preganglionic fibers.
   (c) are found primarily in the heart.
   (d) bind with norepinephrine released from sympathetic postganglionic fibers.
   (e) More than one of the above are correct.

ANSWER: b

62. Atropine _____ the effect of acetylcholine at _____ receptors and _____ _____ receptors.

   (a) blocks, muscarinic, does not affect, nicotinic
   (b) enhances, muscarinic, does not affect, nicotinic
   (c) blocks, nicotinic, does not affect, muscarinic
   (d) enhances, nicotinic, does not affect, muscarinic
   (e) blocks, muscarinic, enhances, nicotinic

ANSWER: a

63. Which of the following regions of the CNS does not regulate autonomic output?

   (a) Spinal cord.
   (b) Medulla within the brain stem.
   (c) Basal nuclei.
   (d) Hypothalamus.
   (e) Frontal cortex.

ANSWER: c

64. The chemical transmitter substance at the neuromuscular junction is

   (a) acetylcholine.
   (b) the same as the transmitter substance at parasympathetic postganglionic nerve endings.
   (c) inactivated by organophosphates.
   (d) Both (a) and (b) above are correct.
   (e) All of the above are correct.

ANSWER: d

65. Acetylcholinesterase

   (a) is stored in vesicles in the terminal button.
   (b) when combined with receptor sites on the motor end plate brings about an end-plate potential.
   (c) is inhibited by organophosphates.
   (d) More than one of the above are correct.
   (e) None of the above are correct.

ANSWER: c

66. The motor end plate

   (a) contains receptor sites that are capable of binding curare.
   (b) contains acetylcholinesterase.
   (c) experiences an increase in permeability to Na^+ and a smaller increase in permeability to K^+ when combined with acetylcholine.
   (d) Both (b) and (c) above are correct.
   (e) All of the above are correct.

ANSWER: e

67. The neuromuscular junction

   (a) is the junction between a motor neuron and a skeletal
        muscle fiber.
   (b) transmits an action potential between the nerve cell and
        muscle cell on a one-to-one basis.
   (c) may produce either an EPSP or an IPSP on the motor end
        plate.
   (d) Both (a) and (b) above are correct.
   (e) All of the above are correct.

ANSWER: d

68. Acetylcholinesterase

   (a) is released from the terminal button.
   (b) destroys acetylcholine.
   (c) is blocked by curare.
   (d) Both (a) and (b) above are correct.
   (e) All of the above are correct.

ANSWER: b

69. Acetylcholine

   (a) is released from the vesicles when an action potential
        is propagated to the terminal button of a motor neuron.
   (b) increases the permeability of the motor end plate
        especially to Na^+ and to a lesser extent to K^+ when
        combined with the receptor sites on the motor end
        plate.
   (c) is the chemical transmitter substance at the
        neuromuscular junction.
   (d) Two of the above are correct.
   (e) All of the above are correct.

ANSWER: e

70. An EPP

   (a) occurs because of Na^+ movement inward at the motor end
        plate region as a result of permeability changes induced
        by binding of acetylcholine with end-plate receptor
        sites.
   (b) is usually smaller in magnitude than an EPSP.
   (c) is terminated when Ca^+ inactivates acetylcholine.
   (d) Both (a) and (b) above are correct.
   (e) All of the above are correct.

ANSWER: a

71. Which of the following chemicals paralyzes skeletal muscle
     by binding to the acetylcholine receptor sites?

     (a) Black widow spider venom.
     (b) Curare.
     (c) Organophosphates.
     (d) DDT.
     (e) Local anesthetics.

ANSWER: b

72. Curare

     (a) strongly binds to acetylcholine receptor sites.
     (b) inhibits acetylcholinesterase.
     (c) is found in pesticides and military nerve gases.
     (d) Two of the above are correct.
     (e) All of the above are correct.

ANSWER: a

73. Myasthenia gravis

     (a) is an autoimmune disease.
     (b) occurs when the terminal-button vesicles are unable to
          release adequate amounts of acetylcholine.
     (c) can be treated with a drug that temporarily inhibits
          acetylcholinesterase.
     (d) Both (a) and (c) above are correct.
     (e) All of the above are correct.

ANSWER: d

True/False

74. Perception duplicates reality.

ANSWER: False

75. A given receptor can respond to stimuli of any type.

ANSWER: False

76. Receptors change other forms of energy into electrical
     energy.

ANSWER: True

77. Any stimulus can excite any excitable tissue.

ANSWER: False

78. Receptor potentials can be graded, with a stronger stimulus resulting in a larger receptor potential.

ANSWER: True

79. Receptors can respond only to electrical stimulation.

ANSWER: False

80. Proprioception is the awareness of the body's position in space.

ANSWER: True

81. The stronger the stimulus, the greater the frequency of action potentials generated and propagated in the afferent neuron.

ANSWER: True

82. The identical nerve pathway conveys information regarding pressure and temperature sensation of the thumb.

ANSWER: False

83. Activation of a sensory pathway at any point gives rise to the same sensation that would be produced by stimulation of the receptors in the body part itself.

ANSWER: True

84. Humans have receptors to detect all stimulus modalities in the environment.

ANSWER: False

85. All nociceptors are naked nerve endings.

ANSWER: True

86. There are naturally occurring morphine-like substances in the brain.

ANSWER: True

87. Prostaglandins suppress the sensitivity of nociceptors.

ANSWER: False

88. Descending analgesic pathways are believed to suppress transmission in the pain pathways as they enter the spinal cord by blocking the release of substance P.

ANSWER: True

89. The thalamus is responsible for pain inhibition.

ANSWER: False

90. Short wave lengths of light within the visible spectrum are sensed as violet or blue.

ANSWER: True

91. Light rays travel faster through water or glass than through air.

ANSWER: False

92. Light is the only stimulus capable of stimulating the photoreceptors of the eye.

ANSWER: False

93. A convex lens converges light rays or brings them closer together.

ANSWER: True

94. The greater the curvature of a lens, the stronger the lens.

ANSWER: True

95. The fovea is the point on the retina where the optic nerve leaves.

ANSWER: False

96. The strength of the lens must be adjusted to enable the eye to focus both near and far sources on the retina.

ANSWER: True

97. A cataract refers to the condition in which the lens becomes stiff and loses its elasticity.

ANSWER: False

98. A concave lens is used to correct for a myopic eye.

ANSWER: True

99. Retinene is found in the rods but not the cones.

ANSWER: False

100. Vision in bright light is chiefly due to cone activation.

ANSWER: True

101. Cone photoreceptors provide high visual acuity.

ANSWER: True

102. When an individual sees pure red, only the red cones are stimulated.

ANSWER: False

103. Color blindness is caused by Vitamin A deficiency.

ANSWER: False

104. Night blindness is due to a deficiency of Vitamin C.

ANSWER: False

105. Each cone contains three different photopigments for selectively responding to red, blue, or green wavelengths of light.

ANSWER: False

106. A photoreceptor generates action potentials when its photopigment is activated.

ANSWER: False

107. Depth perception comes about in large part because of binocular vision.

ANSWER: True

108. Each hemisphere normally receives information from the entire visual field of both eyes.

ANSWER: False

109. Axons from retinal ganglion cells form the optic nerve.

ANSWER: True

110. Short wavelengths of light are perceived in the red-orange color range.

ANSWER: False

111. Photoreceptors, bipolar cells, and ganglion cells all display action potentials.

ANSWER: False

112. Each half of the visual cortex receives information from the opposite half of the visual field as detected by both eyes.

ANSWER: True

113. Unlike the visual pathways, auditory signals from each ear are transmitted to both hemispheres.

ANSWER: True

114. The inner ear is involved only with hearing.

ANSWER: False

115. The cochlea is primarily concerned with equilibrium.

ANSWER: False

116. Sound waves consist of regions of high-pressure compression alternating with regions of low-pressure rarefaction of air molecules.

ANSWER: True

117. A 100 dB sound is 100 times louder than hearing threshold.

ANSWER: False

118. The function of the Eustachian tube is to provide a drainage path for the fluid in the middle ear.

ANSWER: False

119. The ossicular system transmits the vibrations of the tympanic membrane to the oval window, movement of which sets up pressure waves in the cochlear fluid.

ANSWER: True

120. The tectorial membrane secretes a special fluid required for the normal function of the sound-receptive hair cells.

ANSWER: False

121. In response to high frequency sounds, the segment of the basilar membrane closer to the oval window vibrates maximally.

ANSWER: True

122. Exposure to very loud noises can result in partial conductive deafness.

ANSWER: False

123. Hearing aids are more beneficial in conductive deafness than in sensorineural deafness.

ANSWER: True

124. The semicircular canals are activated as the head starts to rotate but cease responding if the head movement continues at the same rate in the same direction.

ANSWER: True

125. The semicircular canals contain calcium carbonate stones that respond to gravity.

ANSWER: False

126. Taste buds are chemoreceptors.

ANSWER: True

127. The cortical gustatory area is located adjacent to the "tongue" region of the somatosensory cortex.

ANSWER: True

128. Molecules of similar smell have a similar chemical composition.

ANSWER: False

129. Normal breathing patterns directly bring odoriferous molecules in contact with the olfactory mucosa.

ANSWER: False

130. The receptors for smell are located in the upper nasal cavity out of the normal path of air currents.

ANSWER: True

131. Visual and hearing receptors are irreplaceable, but taste and olfactory receptors are continuously renewed.

ANSWER: True

132. Rapid reduction in sensitivity to a new odor results from rapid adaptation of the olfactory receptors.

ANSWER: False

133. The olfactory mucosa contains enzymes that remove odoriferous molecules so that the sensation of smell doesn't linger after the source of the odor is removed.

ANSWER: True

134. The sympathetic nervous system is always excitatory to the organs it innervates.

ANSWER: False

135. Most innervated blood vessels receive only sympathetic nerve fibers.

ANSWER: True

136. By blocking the effect of acetylcholine at muscarinic but not nicotinic receptors, atropine is able to block parasympathetic effects while not influencing sympathetic activity at all.

ANSWER: True

137. The autonomic nervous system is the part of the peripheral nervous system that regulates smooth muscle, cardiac muscle, and glands.

ANSWER: True

138. The autonomic nervous system is part of the somatic nervous system.

ANSWER: False.

139. Dual innervation of organs by both branches of the autonomic nervous system allows a fine degree of control over these organs.

ANSWER: True

140. The parasympathetic nervous system dominates in fight-or-flight situations.

ANSWER: False

141. Sympathetic preganglionic fibers originate in the thoracic and lumbar segments of the spinal cord.

ANSWER: True

142. Action potentials are transmitted on a one-to-one basis at both a neuromuscular junction and a synapse.

ANSWER: False

143. The sympathetic branch of the autonomic nervous system has its cells of origin in the brain stem as well as the spinal cord.

ANSWER: False

144. Sympathetic postganglionic fibers are shorter than parasympathetic postganglionic fibers.

ANSWER: False

145. Atropine blocks all nicotinic receptor sites.

ANSWER: False

146. It is possible through the use of drugs to activate the receptors found in bronchiolar smooth muscle without influencing the receptors in the heart.

ANSWER: True

147. An EPP is similar to an EPSP, except that the magnitude of an EPSP is much larger.

ANSWER: False

148. Action potentials are initiated at the motor end plate region of skeletal muscle fibers.

ANSWER: False

149. Acetylcholinesterase is stored in secretory vesicles in the motor end plate of the muscle fiber.

ANSWER: False

150. Binding of ACh with receptor sites on the motor end plate opens chemical messenger-gated cation channels in the motor end plate, bringing about depolarization of the motor end plate.

ANSWER: True

151. Clostridium botulinum toxin inhibits acetylcholinesterase.

ANSWER: False

152. An EPP is a graded potential.

ANSWER: True

Fill-in-the-blanks

153. _____ is our conscious interpretation of the external world as created by the brain from a pattern of nerve impulses delivered to it from sensory receptors.

ANSWER: Perception

154. An incoming pathway for subconscious information derived from the internal viscera is called a _____, whereas an incoming pathway for information propagated to the conscious levels of the brain is called a _____.

ANSWERS: visceral afferent, sensory afferent

155. Each sensory neuron responds to stimulus information within its _____, which is a circumscribed region of the skin surface surrounding it.

ANSWER: receptive field

156. _____, a neurotransmitter unique to pain fibers, is released from afferent pain terminals.

ANSWER: Substance P

157. _____ receptors bind the endorphins, enkephalins, and morphine.

ANSWER: Opiate

158. Light is a form of electromagnetic radiation composed of particle-like individual packets of energy called _____ that travel in wave-like fashion.

ANSWER: photons

159. The _____ is the layer of the eye that contains the photoreceptor cells.

ANSWER: retina

160. The two major components of the ciliary body are the _____, which regulates the strength of the lens, and a capillary network that produces _____.

ANSWERS: ciliary muscle, aqueous humor

161. The point of the retina with the most distinct vision is the _____.

ANSWER: fovea

162. The primary structures responsible for the refractive ability of the eye are the _____ and _____.

ANSWER: Cornea and lens

163. The eye structure with the greatest refractive ability is the _____.

ANSWER: Cornea

164. The refractive structure of the eye that has the ability to change its strength is the _____.

ANSWER: Lens

165. _____ are traveling vibrations of air that consist of regions of high pressure caused by compression of air molecules alternating with regions of low pressure caused by rarefaction of the molecules.

ANSWER: Sound waves

166. The two components of the efferent division of the peripheral nervous system are the _____ nervous system, which supplies cardiac muscle, smooth muscle, and glands, and the _____ nervous system, which supplies skeletal muscle.

ANSWERS: autonomic, somatic

167. The two divisions of the autonomic nervous system are the _____ nervous system, which dominates in fight-or-flight situations, and the _____ nervous system, which dominates in quiet, relaxed situations.

ANSWERS: sympathetic, parasympathetic

168. Sympathetic postganglionic fibers secrete the neurotransmitter _____, whereas parasympathetic postganglionic fibers secrete the neurotransmitter _____.

ANSWERS: norepinephrine (noradrenaline), acetylcholine

169. The _____ is a modified sympathetic ganglion that does not give rise to postganglionic fibers but instead secretes hormones similar or identical to sympathetic postganglionic neurotransmitters into the blood.

ANSWER: adrenal medulla

Sequencing

170. Indicate the proper sequence of involvement in the visual pathway by writing the appropriate letter in the blank, using the answer code below.

                    a = bipolar neurons
                    b = optic nerve
                    c = optic chiasm
                    d = rods and cones
                    e = visual cortex
                    f = optic tracts
                    g = ganglion cells

        First   _____
        Second   _____
        Third   _____
        Fourth   _____
        Fifth   _____
        Sixth   _____
        Seventh _____

ANSWERS: d, a, g, b, f, c, e

171. Indicate the proper sequence of events at the neuromuscular junction by filling in the blank with the appropriate number from 2 through 7. Numbers 1 and 8 are already identified.

_____ ACh is released from the axon terminal by exocytosis.
_____ An EPP takes place, primarily as a result of Na⁺ influx.
__8_ Acetylcholinesterase inactivates ACh, terminating activity at the neuromuscular junction.
__1_ An action potential is propagated to an axon terminal of a motor neuron.
_____ Channels that permit passage primarily of Na⁺ and K⁺ are opened in the motor end plate.
_____ Ca²⁺ channels are opened in the axon terminal.
_____ Local current flow between the motor end plate and adjacent muscle cell membrane initiates an action potential that spreads throughout the muscle fiber.
_____ ACh binds with receptor sites on the motor end plate.

ANSWERS: 3, 6, 8, 1, 4, 2, 7, 5

Statement Completion

Complete the statement by circling the correct response.

172. For near vision, the ciliary muscle (contracts or relaxes) so that the suspensory ligaments become (taut or slack). This allows the lens to (flatten or round up), which (increases or decreases) the strength of the lens.

ANSWERS: contracts, slack, round up, increases

Matching

173. Indicate the properties associated with each type of nociceptor by using the answer code below: (more than one answer may apply)

>   (a) = mechanical nociceptor
>   (b) = thermal nociceptor
>   (c) = polymodal nociceptor

>   _____ respond(s) to cutting, crushing, pinching
>   _____ respond(s) to irritating chemicals
>   _____ respond(s) to temperature extremes
>   _____ activates slow pain pathway
>   _____ activates fast pain pathway

ANSWERS: a, c, b, c, a and b

174. Indicate the properties of rods and cones using the following answer code:

>   (a) = rods
>   (b) = cones
>   (c) = both rods and cones

>   _____ used for day vision
>   _____ used for night vision
>   _____ confer color vision
>   _____ confer vision in shades of gray
>   _____ high acuity
>   _____ low acuity
>   _____ contain opsin and retinene
>   _____ three different types as a result of difference in photopigment content

ANSWERS: b, a, b, a, b, a, c, b

175. _____ eyeball too long
_____ eyeball too short
_____ corrected by concave lens
_____ corrected by convex lens
_____ corneal surface uneven
_____ increased intraocular pressure
_____ opaque lens
_____ stiffened lens
_____ Vitamin A deficiency
_____ lack of a cone type

(a) color blindness
(b) night blindness
(c) glaucoma
(d) hyperopia
(e) presbyopia
(f) myopia
(g) cataract
(h) astigmatism

ANSWERS: f, d, f, d, h, c, g, e, b, a

176. _____ determined by the frequency of sound waves
_____ dependent on the overtones of a sound wave
_____ dependent on the amplitude of the sound wave
_____ measured in cycles per second
_____ measured in decibels

(a) timbre (quality)
(b) pitch (tone)
(c) intensity (loudness)

ANSWERS: b, a, c, b, c

177. _____ receptors in retina
_____ receptors in cochlea
_____ receptors in otolith organs
_____ receptors in semicircular canals
_____ receptors in taste buds
_____ receptors in olfactory mucosa

(a) chemoreceptors
(b) mechanoreceptors
(c) photoreceptors

ANSWERS: c, b, b, b, a, a

178. _____ taste(s) salty
_____ taste(s) sour
_____ taste(s) bitter

_____ taste(s) sweet

(a) alkaloids
(b) acids
(c) anything with chemical configuration similar to glucose
(d) NaCl

ANSWERS: d, b, a, c

179. Indicate the characteristics associated with each part of the ear using the answer code below: (more than one answer may apply)

    (a) = external ear
    (b) = middle ear
    (c) = cochlea in the inner ear
    (d) = semicircular canals in the inner ear
    (e) = utricle and saccule in the inner ear

_____ air-filled
_____ fluid-filled
_____ contain(s) receptive hair cells
_____ concerned with hearing
_____ concerned with sense of equilibrium
_____ contain(s) the tympanic membrane, which vibrates in synchrony with sound waves that strike it
_____ contain(s) the ossicular system, which contributes to the amplification of the sound wave
_____ contain(s) a cupula, which sways in the direction of fluid movement, bending the embedded hair cells
_____ provides information about the position of the head relative to gravity
_____ detect(s) rotational acceleration or deceleration of the head
_____ contain(s) otoliths in a gelatinous mass, movement of which bends the hair cells
_____ contain(s) the organ of Corti whose hair cells are bent during vibration of the basilar membrane
_____ is/are connected with the throat via the eustachian tube
_____ provide(s) information useful for keeping the eyes focused on a fixed object even when the head is moving
_____ part of the vestibular apparatus
_____ fluid-filled, snail shaped tubular system
_____ components aligned in each of three different planes all perpendicular to each other

ANSWERS: a and b; c, d, and e; c, d, and e; a, b, and c; d and e; b; b; d; e; d; e; c; b; d and e; d and e; c: d

180. Indicate which part of the autonomic nervous system is being described by writing the appropriate letter in the blank using the following answer code.

(a) = sympathetic nervous system
(b) = parasympathetic nervous system
(c) = both sympathetic and parasympathetic nervous system
(d) = neither sympathetic nor parasympathetic nervous system

_____ preganglionic fiber secretes acetylcholine
_____ preganglionic fiber secretes norepinephrine
_____ postganglionic fiber secretes acetylcholine
_____ postganglionic fiber secretes norepinephrine
_____ dominates in fight-or-flight situations
_____ dominates in relaxed situations
_____ has a long preganglionic fiber and a short postganglionic fiber
_____ has a short preganglionic fiber and a long postganglionic fiber
_____ originates in the cranial and sacral regions of CNS
_____ originates in the thoracic and lumbar regions of CNS
_____ innervates smooth muscle, cardiac muscle, and glands
_____ innervates skeletal muscle

ANSWERS: c, d, b, a, a, b, b, a, b, a, c, d

181. Indicate which type of neuron is associated with the characteristic by writing the appropriate letter in the blank using the answer code below.

(a) = all three types of neurons
(b) = both afferent and efferent
(c) = afferent neurons
(d) = efferent neurons
(e) = interneurons

_____ has a receptor at its peripheral ending
_____ autonomic nerves are this type of neuron
_____ lie primarily within the peripheral nervous system
_____ lie entirely within the central nervous system
_____ carry information from the central nervous system
_____ carry information to the central nervous system
_____ responsible for thoughts and other higher mental functions
_____ motor neurons are this type of neuron
_____ terminate on effector organs

ANSWERS: c, d, b, e, d, c, e, d, d

182. Indicate the characteristics of the types of autonomic receptors using the following answer code: (More than one answer may apply).

   (a) = characteristic of nicotinic receptors
   (b) = characteristic of muscarinic receptors
   (c) = characteristic of alpha receptors
   (d) = characteristic of beta$_1$ receptors
   (e) = characteristic of beta$_2$ receptors

   _____ bind with acetylcholine released from parasympathetic postganglionic fibers.
   _____ have equal affinity for epinephrine and norepinephrine.
   _____ adrenergic receptor found primarily in the heart.
   _____ response to activation of this type of adrenergic receptor is generally inhibitory.
   _____ bind with acetylcholine released from all autonomic preganglionic fibers.
   _____ response to activation of this type of adrenergic receptor is usually excitatory.
   _____ found in all autonomic ganglia.
   _____ found on effector cell membranes.
   _____ binds primarily with epinephrine.

ANSWERS: b; c and d; d; e; a; c and d; a; b, c, d, and e; e

183. _____ binds with ACh receptor   a. myasthenia gravis
         sites   b. black widow spider
      _____ causes explosive release   venom
         of ACh   .   c. curare
      _____ blocks release of ACh   d. Clostridium
      _____ inhibits acetyl-   botulinum toxin
         cholinesterase   e. organophosphates
      _____ antibodies inactivate
         ACh receptor sites

ANSWERS: c, b, d, e, a

AUDIOVISUAL AIDS

Films

A list of films available from West Publishing Company is presented in Appendix A.   Following are other films that may be suitable.   The sources for these films, which are coded by abbreviation, are provided in Appendix B.

   A Sense of Hearing, BTC, 10 min.

Autonomic Nervous System, IF, 17 min.

Colors and How We See Them: Color Vision, SSS, 20 min.

Ears and Hearing, EBE, 22 min.

Eye Dissection and Anatomy, IM, 16 min.

Eyes and Ears, FM, 26 min.

Eyes and Vision, EBE, 10 min.

Glaucoma, LPI, 15 min.

How Much Do You Smell? FI, 50 min.

Human Body: Sense Organs, COR, 19 min.

Information Processing, ASF, 25 min.

Inner Ear, FI, 11 min.

Mind Over Body, TL, 35 min.

More Than Meets the Eye, TLV, 30 min.

Parasympathetic and Sympathetic Innervation, TNF, 40 min.

Spinal Nerves, UT, 18 min.

The Autonomic Nervous System, PH, 6 min.

The Autonomic Nervous System - An Overview, USNAC, 17 min.

The Autonomic Nervous System, IM, 29 min.

Senses and Perception, UC, 18 min.

Signals and Receptors, PSU, 24 min.

Skin Deep, FHS, 26 min.

Smell and Taste, FHS, 30 min.

The Ear, IP, 14 min.

The Ears, NM, 17 min.

The Ears and Hearing, COR, 18 min.

The Enchanted Loom, FHS, 26 min.

The Eyes and Seeing, EBE, 20 min.

The Human Eye, ISC, 14 min.

The Incredible Seeing Machine, BL, 26 min.

The Mind's Eye, FI, 50 min.

The Neuromuscular Junction: Pharmacology, IM, 23 min.

The Neuromuscular Junction: Physiology, IM 23 min.

The Nose (Structure and Function), EBE, 11 min.

The Peripheral Nervous System, IFB, 19 min.

The Rod Cell, PSU, 25 min.

The Rod Cell (VCR), MG, 24 min.

The Senses, MH, 28 min.

The Senses of Man, IU, 18 min.

The Sensory World, MH, 32 min.

The Sixth Sense... and the Rest, FHS, 26 min.

The Skin as a Sense Organ, IF, 12 min.

The Structure of the Eye, CCM, 7 min.

The Sound of Silence, FHS, 26 min.

Survival and the Senses, PSU, 25 min.

Viva la Difference, FHS, 26 min.

What Smells?, FHS, 60 min.

What the Nose Knows, FHS, 26 min.

Software

Dynamics of the Human Ear, EI. Presents vocabulary and diagrams of ear.

Dynamics of the Human Eye, EI. Details the part of the eye, emphasizing retinal receptors.

<u>Dynamics of the Human Senses of Touch, Taste, and Smell</u>, EI.
Covers the structures relating to touch, taste, and smell.

<u>Nervous System</u>, CBS. Covers the nature of the nervous system
and chemical transmitters.

<u>Neuromuscular Concepts</u>, PLP. Covers skeletal muscle
contraction beginning with neuromuscular junction.

<u>Senses</u>, CBS. Covers the eye, ear, nose, tongue, and skin.

<u>Your Body</u>: Series II, SSS. Covers the nervous system and the
brain.

Chapter 6
Muscle Physiology

CONTENTS

(All page references are to the main text.)

LECTURE HINTS AND SUGGESTIONS

1.   This is a very good place to illustrate the structure-function relationship between the striated nature of skeletal muscle and its contractility.

2.   Electron micrographs of muscle fibers, myofibrils and myofilaments are particularly useful here. See <u>Tissues and Organs</u> by Kessel and Kardon, W.H. Freeman and Company.

3.   Use a Carolina Biological Supply Company model of a muscle fiber to illustrate its structure.

4.   Demonstrate isometric versus isotonic contraction. See any general physiology lab manual for procedures.

5.   Show and/or record various physiological muscle responses; e.g., tetanus and muscle twitch. The gastrocnemius muscle and sciatic nerve from a frog leg attached to a kymograph or physiograph is classical. See any general physiology lab manual for procedures.

6.   If available, have students use the muscle grip tester to demonstrate strength of contraction as well as muscle fatigue.

7.   Demonstration slides of the three types of muscle tissue provide an important dimension to understanding specific structural differences. These can be obtained from Carolina Biological Supply Company.

8.   A clinical dimension can be added by describing motor impairments resulting from trauma at various muscle innervation sites; e.g., polio and tetanus.

9.   The general functions of muscles need to be stated clearly so that students do not get the sole impression that all muscles do is contract. For example, posture, heat production, and glycogen storage are also functions of muscles.

CHAPTER TEST QUESTIONS

Multiple Choice

1. Myosin

    (a) is found in the A band.
    (b) is found in the I band.
    (c) is the primary protein found in the thin filaments.
    (d) contracts during muscle contraction because it is one of the contractile proteins.
    (e) More than one of the above are correct.

ANSWER: a

2. Myosin

    (a) is spherical shaped.
    (b) is the main structural component of the thin filaments.
    (c) is referred to as a regulatory protein.
    (d) More than one of the above are correct.
    (e) None of the above are correct.

ANSWER: e

3. Actin

    (a) has ATPase activity.
    (b) is spherical shaped.
    (c) forms a double helical chain that forms the main structural component of the thin filaments.
    (d) Two of the above are correct.
    (e) All of the above are correct.

ANSWER: d

4. Actin

    (a) is spherical shaped.
    (b) contains a globular head that forms the cross bridges between the thick and thin filaments.
    (c) is referred to as a regulatory protein.
    (d) binds with Ca^{2+} during muscle excitation.
    (e) More than one of the above are correct.

ANSWER: a

5.   Thick filaments in skeletal muscle are composed of

     (a)   actin.
     (b)   troponin and tropomyosin.
     (c)   myosin.
     (d)   Both (a) and (b) above are correct.
     (e)   All of the above are correct.

ANSWER: c

6.   Z lines

     (a)   are formed by the T tubules.
     (b)   extend down the middle of the I band.
     (c)   are formed by the cross bridges.
     (d)   are the thin filaments.
     (e)   extend down the middle of the sarcomere.

ANSWER: b

7.   Which of the following statements concerning cross bridges
     is **not** correct? Cross bridges

     (a)   bind to actin during muscle contraction.
     (b)   are formed by the globular heads of the myosin
           molecules.
     (c)   consist of troponin and tropomyosin protruding from
           the actin helix.
     (d)   bend during muscle contraction.
     (e)   protrude from the thick filaments.

ANSWER: c

8.   The striated appearance of skeletal muscle is due to

     (a)   the regular arrangement of the T tubules running
           transversely through the muscle fiber.
     (b)   the presence of the Z lines extending down the middle of
           the I bands.
     (c)   the presence of gap junctions.
     (d)   the regular arrangement of the motor units.
     (e)   None of the above are correct.

ANSWER: e

9. The striated appearance of skeletal muscle is due to

    (a) the regular orderly arrangement of the T tubules.
    (b) the regular orderly arrangement of the lateral sacs of
         the sarcoplasmic reticulum.
    (c) the regular orderly arrangement of the thick and thin
         filaments into A and I bands.
    (d) the regular orderly arrangement of the motor units.
    (e) the presence of white and red muscle fibers within the
         muscle.

ANSWER: c

10. Which of the following characteristics are shared by all
    three types of muscles?

    (a) Contains myosin and actin.
    (b) Is neurogenic.
    (c) Is striated.
    (d) Is considered to be under voluntary control.
    (e) More than one of the above are correct.

ANSWER: a

11. The functional unit of skeletal muscle is

    (a) the smallest contractile component of a muscle fiber.
    (b) the area between two Z lines.
    (c) the sarcomere.
    (d) Two of the above are correct.
    (e) All of the above are correct.

ANSWER: e

12. What is the smallest contractile unit within skeletal
    muscle?

    (a) Myofibril.
    (b) Muscle fiber.
    (c) Sarcomere.
    (d) Functional unit of muscle.
    (e) Both (c) and (d) above are correct.

ANSWER: e

13. According to the sliding-filament mechanism of muscle contraction,

    (a)   the A bands slide in closer between the I bands.
    (b)   the thin filaments slide inward toward the center of the A band.
    (c)   the Z lines slide in between the T tubules.
    (d)   the contractile proteins contract, thus shortening the sarcomere.
    (e)   the filaments slide into the lateral sacs of the sarcoplasmic reticulum.

ANSWER: b

14. During contraction of a skeletal muscle fiber,

    (a)   the contractile proteins contract.
    (b)   the thin filaments slide inward toward the A band's center as a result of cycles of cross-bridge binding and bending.
    (c)   the thick and thin filaments become tightly coiled, thus shortening the sarcomere.
    (d)   the I bands slide in between the A bands.
    (e)   the lateral sacs of the sarcoplasmic reticulum shrink, pulling the Z lines closer together.

ANSWER: b

15. During muscle contraction,

    (a)   the contractile proteins contract.
    (b)   the A band becomes shorter.
    (c)   the H zone becomes smaller or disappears.
    (d)   the I band remains unchanged.
    (e)   More than one of the above are correct.

ANSWER: c

16. The H zone

    (a)   is the area within the middle of the A band where the thin filaments do not reach.
    (b)   shortens or disappears during contraction.
    (c)   contains only thick filaments.
    (d)   Both (a) and (b) above are correct.
    (e)   All of the above are correct.

ANSWER: e

17. Which of the following changes in banding pattern occur during muscle contraction?

    (a) The A band gets shorter.
    (b) The I band gets shorter.
    (c) The H zone gets shorter.
    (d) Both (b) and (c) above are correct.
    (e) All of the above are correct.

ANSWER: d

18. The sarcoplasmic reticulum stores _____ when a muscle is relaxed and releases it for binding to _____ during contraction.

    (a) calcium, troponin
    (b) calcium, tropomyosin
    (c) sodium, tropomyosin
    (d) potassium, tropomyosin
    (e) sodium, troponin

ANSWER: a

19. The T tubules

    (a) store Ca^{2+}.
    (b) provide a means of rapidly transmitting the action potential from the surface into the central portions of the muscle fiber.
    (c) store ATP.
    (d) run longitudinally between the myofibrils.
    (e) have expanded lateral sacs.

ANSWER: b

20. The T tubules

    (a) form the Z lines.
    (b) store Ca^{2+}.
    (c) provide a means of rapidly transmitting the action potential to the central portions of the muscle fiber.
    (d) allow for nutrients to be carried into the cell.
    (e) More than one of the above are correct.

ANSWER: c

21. An action potential rapidly spreads to the central portions of a muscle cell by means of the

    (a) Z lines.
    (b) sarcoplasmic reticulum.
    (c) H zone.
    (d) pores in the membrane surface.
    (e) T tubules.

ANSWER: e

22. Binding of _____ to myosin permits cross-bridge _____ between actin and myosin.

    (a) ATP, binding
    (b) ATP, detachment
    (c) calcium, binding
    (d) calcium, detachment
    (e) None of the above are correct.

ANSWER: b

23. During excitation-contraction coupling

    (a) the action potential travels down the transverse tubules.
    (b) Ca^{2+} is released from the sarcoplasmic reticulum.
    (c) Ca^{2+} is taken up by the sarcoplasmic reticulum.
    (d) Both (a) and (b) above are correct.
    (e) All of the above are correct.

ANSWER: d

24. Which of the following statements concerning cross bridges is **incorrect**? Cross bridges

    (a) are formed by the globular heads of the myosin molecules as they protrude from the thick filaments.
    (b) bend during muscle contraction.
    (c) bind to actin during muscle contraction.
    (d) are not found in the I band.
    (e) bind with troponin and tropomyosin during muscle contraction to pull them away from the actin helical chain.

ANSWER: e

25. During a cross-bridge cycle in skeletal muscle

    (a) the cross bridge is energized as myosin ATPase activity
         hydrolyzes ATP.
    (b) the myosin cross bridge is able to bind with an actin
         molecule when Ca^{2+} pulls the troponin-tropomyosin
         complex aside.
    (c) the linkage between actin and the myosin cross bridge is
         broken at the end of the cross-bridge cycle as Mg^{2+} binds
         to the cross bridge.
    (d) Both (a) and (b) above are correct.
    (e) All of the above are correct.

ANSWER: d

26. Cross bridges

    (a) extend between the A and I bands and bend to pull the
         bands together during muscle contraction.
    (b) are formed by the globular heads of the myosin
         molecules.
    (c) link troponin and tropomyosin to actin to form the thin
         filament.
    (d) extend from the thick filaments and bind to actin, then
         bend to pull the thin filaments in closer together
         during muscle contraction.
    (e) Two of the above are correct.

ANSWER: e

27. Which of the following statements concerning cross bridges
    is **incorrect**?

    (a) Cross bridges are the globular heads of myosin
         molecules.
    (b) Cross bridges have actin binding sites that are
         normally covered by troponin and tropomyosin except
         during excitation-contraction coupling.
    (c) Cross bridges bind with actin and then bend to pull
         the thin filaments inward during contraction according
         to the sliding filament mechanism.
    (d) Mg^{2+} is necessary to bind ATP to the cross bridge.
    (e) A fresh molecule of ATP must be bound to the cross
         bridge to break the bond between actin and myosin.

ANSWER: b

28. Cross bridge interaction between actin and myosin in skeletal muscle is directly blocked by

    (a) acetylcholine.
    (b) the T tubules
    (c) Z lines.
    (d) calcium.
    (e) tropomyosin.

ANSWER: e

29. The energy for cross bridge cycling during muscle contraction is provided by

    (a) acetylcholine.
    (b) Ca^{2+}.
    (c) ATP.
    (d) myosin.
    (e) actin.

ANSWER: c

30. Which of the following is not involved in the relaxation of muscle?

    (a) When acetylcholine is destroyed by acetylcho - linesterase.
    (b) When there is no longer a local action potential.
    (c) When the T tubules actively take up the Ca^{2+} that had been released.
    (d) When the actin and myosin molecules are no longer bound together.
    (e) When the troponin-tropomyosin complex slips back into its blocking position.

ANSWER: c

31. Why are you able to repeatedly contract and relax your muscles of respiration, allowing you to breathe in and breathe out?

    (a)   As soon as all of the Ca^{2+} stored in the lateral sacs of the sarcoplasmic reticulum is used up, muscle relaxation occurs.
    (b)   After the muscle cell becomes excited, acetylcholinesterase rapidly destroys acetylcholine, allowing the muscle cell to return to resting potential.
    (c)   When there is no longer a local action potential in the muscle cell, Ca^{2+} is actively transported back into the lateral sacs of the sarcoplasmic reticulum and muscle relaxation occurs.
    (d)   Both (b) and (c) above are correct.
    (e)   All of the above are correct.

ANSWER: d

32. Which of the following is involved in the process of muscle relaxation

    (a)   Acetylcholinesterase destroys acetylcholine to allow the muscle membrane to return to resting potential.
    (b) Ca^{2+} is actively taken up by the lateral sacs of the sarcoplasmic reticulum when there is no longer a local action potential.
    (c)   The cross bridges from the thick filaments bind to the thin filaments and bend in such a way as to return the filaments to their original resting position.
    (d)   Both (a) and (b) above are correct.
    (e)   All of the above are correct.

ANSWER: d

33. Which of the following is **not** a determinant of whole muscle tension?

    (a)   The number of muscle fibers contracting.
    (b)   The tension produced by each contracting fiber.
    (c)   The extent of motor-unit recruitment.
    (d)   The frequency of stimulation.
    (e)   The proportion of each motor unit that is contracting at any given time.

ANSWER: e

34. Which of the following is **not** a method of gradation of skeletal muscle contraction?

    (a) Twitch summation.
    (b) Motor unit recruitment.
    (c) Stimulating variable portions of each motor unit.
    (d) Varying the number of motor units stimulated.
    (e) Varying the frequency at which a motor unit is stimulated.

ANSWER: c

35. Which of the following is (are) involved in the gradation of muscle contraction?

    (a) Variation in the number of motor units activated.
    (b) Variation in the frequency of action potentials initiated in each muscle fiber.
    (c) Variation in the size of the action potentials initiated in each muscle fiber.
    (d) Both (a) and (b) above are correct.
    (e) All of the above are correct.

ANSWER: d

36. A motor unit refers to

    (a) a single motor neuron plus all of the muscle fibers it innervates.
    (b) a single muscle fiber plus all of the motor neurons that innervate it.
    (c) all of the motor neurons supplying a single muscle.
    (d) a pair of antagonistic muscles.
    (e) a sheet of smooth muscle cells connected by gap junctions.

ANSWER: a

37. In twitch summation,

    (a) the muscle fiber is stimulated again before the action potential has returned to resting potential.
    (b) the muscle fiber is stimulated again before the filaments have completely returned to their resting position.
    (c) stronger muscle contractions occur but stronger action potentials do not occur.
    (d) Both (b) and (c) above are correct.
    (e) All of the above are correct.

ANSWER: d

38. Twitch summation

    (a)   is a means by which gradation of muscle contraction may
          be accomplished.
    (b)   results from increasing the number of motor units that
          are firing within a muscle.
    (c   results from increasing the frequency at which motor
          units are firing within a muscle.
    (d)   Both (a) and (b) above are correct.
    (e)   Both (a) and (c) above are correct.

ANSWER: e

39. If you wanted to pick up something heavier than your pencil
    (such as your book), you would need to have a stronger
    muscle contraction.   In what way might you accomplish this?

    (a)   Stimulate more motor units.
    (b)   Decrease the frequency of stimulation to allow a more
          prolonged contraction to occur.
    (c)   Decrease the refractory period.
    (d)   Block acetylcholinesterase at the neuromuscular
          junction to allow acetylcholine to function longer.
    (e)   None of the above would increase the strength of muscle
          contraction.

ANSWER: a

40. Which of the following statements concerning the
    length-tension relationship is **incorrect**?   The length-
    tension relationship

    (a)   refers to the relationship between the length of the
          muscle before the onset of contraction and the tetanic
          tension that each contracting fiber can subsequently
          develop at that length.
    (b)   is based on the amount of overlap of thick and thin
          filaments.
    (c)   allows no tension development if the whole muscle is
          stretched to 30% longer than its l_o.
    (d)   within the body is limited to a functional range because
          of limitations on muscle length imposed by attachment to
          the skeleton.

ANSWER: c

41. Which of the following statements concerning the length-tension relationship of skeletal muscle is **incorrect**?

    (a) When a muscle is maximally stretched, it can develop the most tension upon contraction because the thin filaments can slide in a maximal distance.
    (b) Maximum tension can be developed if the muscle is at its l_o at the onset of contraction.
    (c) In the body, the relaxed length of muscle is at its l_o.
    (d) When the initial length of muscle prior to contraction becomes very short, tension is decreased during contraction because of thin filament overlap and because the thick filaments are compressed against the Z lines.
    (e) The tension that can be achieved during a tetanic contraction is less when a muscle is shorter or longer than its optimal length at the onset of contraction.

ANSWER: a

42. Energy sources available to form ATP in muscle fibers are

    (1) phosphorylation of ADP by creatine phosphate.
    (2) oxidative phosphorylation of ADP in the mitochondria.
    (3) phosphorylation of ADP by the glycolytic pathway in the cytosol.

    (a) (1) and (2) above are correct.
    (b) (2) and (3) above are correct.
    (c) (1) and (3) above are correct.
    (d) (1), (2) and (3) above are correct.
    (e) None of the above are used as energy sources in muscle.

ANSWER: d

43. The first means by which ATP is produced at the onset of contractile activity is

    (a) transfer of energy and phosphate from creatine phosphate to ADP.
    (b) oxidative phosphorylation.
    (c) glycolysis.
    (d) degradation of myoglobin.
    (e) None of the above are correct.

ANSWER: a

44. Which of the following statements concerning the characteristics of different types of muscle fibers is **incorrect**?

    (a) The higher the ATPase activity, the faster the speed of contraction.
    (b) Muscles that have high glycolytic capacity and large glycogen stores are more resistant to fatigue.
    (c) Muscles with high ATP-synthesizing ability are more resistant to fatigue.
    (d) Oxidative types of muscle fibers contain myoglobin.
    (e) Muscle fibers containing large amounts of myoglobin have a dark red color in comparison to the paler fibers, which have little myoglobin.

ANSWER: b

45. Which of the following properties characterize fast-oxidative (type IIa) muscle fibers?

    (a) High myosin-ATPase activity.
    (b) Low myosin-ATPase activity.
    (c) Low oxidative capacity.
    (d) Both (a) and (c) above are correct.
    (e) Both (b) and (c) above are correct.

ANSWER: a

46. Fatigue is the failure of a muscle fiber to maintain _____ as a result of previous contractile activity.

    (a) excitability
    (b) muscle mass
    (c) tension
    (d) sarcomere number
    (e) mitochondria

ANSWER: c

47. To pick up a book,

    (a) muscle tension must exceed the load.
    (b) the muscle shortens during contraction.
    (c) the muscle undergoes an isotonic contraction.
    (d) muscle tension remains constant as the muscle changes length.
    (e) All of the above are correct.

ANSWER: e

48. When a muscle atrophies,

  (a) the muscle fibers split lengthwise.
  (b) it decreases in mass and becomes weaker.
  (c) its fibers increase in diameter.
  (d) its fibers undergo mitotic cell division.
  (e) the muscle fibers dissolve and are replaced by fibrous scar tissue.

ANSWER: b

49. Muscle tension

  (a) is created during muscle contraction as the tension generated by the contractile elements is transmitted via the connective tissue and tendons to the bones.
  (b) is the force exerted on a muscle by the weight of an object.
  (c) is greater than the load during an isometric contraction.
  (d) More than one of the above are correct.
  (e) None of the above are correct.

ANSWER: a

50. Muscle tension

  (a) is the force exerted on a muscle by the weight of an object.
  (b) exceeds the load during isotonic contractions.
  (c) must be greater than the load before the muscle can shorten.
  (d) Both (b) and (c) are correct.
  (e) All of the above are correct.

ANSWER: d

51. Which of the following is **not** characteristic of isotonic muscle contractions?

  (a) Occur at constant tension.
  (b) Muscle shortens.
  (c) Used for body movements.
  (d) Occur at constant length.
  (e) Muscle tension is greater than the load.

ANSWER: d

52. With eccentric muscle contractions,

    (a) the development of tension occurs at constant muscle length.
    (b) the muscle lengthens while contracting.
    (c) the muscle shortens while contracting.
    (d) muscle length and tension vary throughout a range of motion.
    (e) None of the above are correct.

ANSWER: b

53. Muscles developing tension while lengthening are performing _____ contractions.

    (a) concentric
    (b) eccentric
    (c) isometric
    (d) fatiguing
    (e) oscillating

ANSWER: b

54. In a muscle fiber undergoing maximal tetanic stimulation, the velocity of shortening _____ as the load _____.

    (a) decreases, decreases
    (b) decreases, increases
    (c) increases, increases
    (d) remains constant, increases
    (e) remains constant, decreases

ANSWER: b

55. Which of the following does not directly influence motor neurons?

    (a) Primary motor cortex.
    (b) Cerebellum.
    (c) Brain stem.
    (d) Afferent neurons (through intervening interneurons).
    (e) None of the above are correct.

ANSWER: b

56. The corticospinal system

   (a) consists of fibers that originate within the primary
        motor cortex and terminate on motor neurons.
   (b) involves the motor regions of the cortex, the
        cerebellum, the basal nuclei, and the thalamus.
   (c) is primarily concerned with regulation of overall body
        posture.
   (d) Both (a) and (c) above are correct.
   (e) Both (b) and (c) above are correct.

ANSWER: a

57. Spastic paralysis occurs when

   (a) descending excitatory pathways are destroyed.
   (b) excitatory inputs to motor neurons are unopposed because
        of disruption of an inhibitory system in the brain stem.
   (c) muscle spindles are destroyed.
   (d) the cerebellum is damaged.
   (e) the motor neurons are destroyed.

ANSWER: b

58. During coactivation

   (a) all of the muscle fibers in a skeletal muscle are
        activated simultaneously.
   (b) the gamma motor-neuron and alpha motor-neuron systems
        to a skeletal muscle are activated simultaneously.
   (c) all of the cross bridges within a single skeletal
        muscle are activated simultaneously.
   (d) the corticospinal and multineuronal systems.
   (e) None of the above are correct.

ANSWER: b

59. Intrafusal muscle fibers

   (a) are supplied by alpha motor neurons.
   (b) are found within muscle spindles.
   (c) contain sensory nerve endings that are activated by
        stretch.
   (d) Both (b) and (c) above are correct.
   (e) All of the above are correct.

ANSWER: d

60. The stretch receptors in the central portion of the muscle
     spindle can be activated by

     (a)   passive stretch of the whole muscle, including stretch
            of the muscle spindle.
     (b)   contraction of the end portions of the muscle spindle.
     (c)   gamma motor neuron stimulation of the muscle spindle.
     (d)   Two of the above are correct.
     (e)   All of the above are correct.

ANSWER: e

61. Calcium turns on cross bridges by physically repositioning
     the troponin-tropomyosin complex to uncover the actin
     cross-bridge binding sites in

     (a)   skeletal muscle.
     (b)   cardiac muscle.
     (c)   smooth muscle.
     (d)   Both (a) and (b) above are correct.
     (e)   All of the above are correct.

ANSWER: d

62. The regulation of smooth muscle contraction is mediated by
     the phosphorylation of _____ as a result of a chain of
     biochemical events triggered by a rise in cytosolic Ca^{2+}.

     (a)   myosin
     (b)   actin
     (c)   troponin
     (d)   tropomyosin
     (e)   ATP

ANSWER: a

63. Which of the following muscle types are myogenic?

     (a)   Cardiac muscle.
     (b)   Single-unit smooth muscle.
     (c)   Multiunit smooth muscle.
     (d)   Both (a) and (b) above are correct.
     (e)   All of the above are correct.

ANSWER: d

64.   Single-unit smooth muscle

    (a)   contains an abundance of gap junctions and forms
        functional syncytia.
    (b)   is self-excitable.
    (c)   is found in the walls of the digestive, reproductive,
        and urinary tracts and small blood vessels.
    (d)   Both (a) and (b) above are correct.
    (e)   All of the above are correct.

ANSWER: e

65.   A functional syncytium

    (a)   refers to a pair of antagonistic muscles that function
        together to move a joint in two opposite directions.
    (b)   can be excited to contract as a unit because action
        potentials can be conducted from one cell to adjacent
        cells through gap junctions.
    (c)   refers to the functional junction between a smooth
        muscle fiber and an autonomic nerve ending.
    (d)   More than one of the above are correct.
    (e)   None of the above are correct.

ANSWER: b

66.   Gap junctions

    (a)   allow action potentials to spread from cell to cell
        through these points of electric contact.
    (b)   are the junctions between the muscle fibers within a
        motor unit.
    (c)   are found only in smooth muscle.
    (d)   are the junctions between the autonomic nervous system
        and smooth muscle cells.
    (e)   None of the above are correct.

ANSWER: a

67.   What is responsible for initiating contraction of smooth
    muscle?

    (a)   Stimulation by motor neurons.
    (b)   Inhibition of acetylcholinesterase.
    (c)   Membrane potential drifting to threshold as a result of
        automatic changes in ion movement across the membrane.
    (d)   Excitation of the gap junctions by transmitter substance.
    (e)   Stimulation by the autonomic nervous system.

ANSWER: c

68. Pacemaker activity

(a) refers to spontaneous depolarizations of the membrane resulting from shifts in passive ionic fluxes accompanying automatic changes in channel permeability.
(b) refers to spontaneous depolarizations of the membrane due to cyclical changes in Na^+ -K^+ pump activity.
(c) is characteristic of single-unit smooth muscle but is not found in any other muscle type.
(d) Both (a) and (c) above are correct.
(e) Both (b) and (c) above are correct.

ANSWER: a

69. Which of the following statements concerning smooth muscle is **incorrect**?

(a) Smooth muscle can develop less tension per unit cross-sectional area compared to skeletal muscle.
(b) Smooth muscle can maintain tension with comparatively less ATP consumption than skeletal muscle.
(c) Smooth muscle lacks troponin and tropomyosin.
(d) The range of lengths over which smooth muscle is able to develop near maximal tension is much greater than for skeletal muscle.
(e) A hollow organ enclosed by smooth muscle can accommodate variable volumes of contents with little change in the pressure exerted on the contents.

ANSWER: a

70. Which of the following statements concerning cardiac muscle is **incorrect**? Cardiac muscle

(a) is found only in the heart.
(b) is innervated by motor neurons.
(c) is self-excitable.
(d) is striated.
(e) contains gap junctions.

ANSWER: b

True/False

71. A single muscle cell is known as a myofibril.

ANSWER: False

72. The M line is formed by a flattened disc-like cytoskeletal protein that connects the thin filaments of two adjoining sarcomeres.

ANSWER: False

73. Myosin contains globular heads that form the cross bridges.

ANSWER: True

74. Myosin and actin are found in striated muscle but not in smooth muscle.

ANSWER: False

75. The striated appearance of skeletal muscle is due to the presence of M and Z lines.

ANSWER: False

76. Myosin is considered to be a regulatory protein because it plays an important role in the regulation of muscle contraction.

ANSWER: False

77. The functional unit of skeletal muscle is the myofibril.

ANSWER: False

78. According to the sliding filament mechanism of muscle contraction, the thick filaments slide in closer together to shorten the sarcomere.

ANSWER: False

79. According to the sliding filament mechanism of muscle contraction, the muscle fibers of one motor unit slide in closer together between the muscle fibers of adjacent motor units.

ANSWER: False

80. Cross bridges have actin binding sites that are normally covered by troponin and tropomyosin except during excitation - contraction coupling.

ANSWER: False

81. During muscle contraction, the A band becomes shorter.

ANSWER: False

82. Muscle relaxation does not take place until all of the ATP is used up.

ANSWER: False

83. Rigor mortis occurs when Ca^{2+} links actin and the myosin globular head together in a rigor complex.

ANSWER: False

84. ATP expenditure is required for both contraction and relaxation of a muscle fiber.

ANSWER: True

85. More tension is developed during twitch summation than during a single twitch because the duration of elevated cytosolic Ca^{2+} concentration increases during summation, thus increasing the availability of cross-bridge binding sites.

ANSWER: True

86. Gradation of muscle contraction can be accomplished by stimulating variable portions of each motor unit.

ANSWER: False

87. According to the all-or-none law, all of the muscle fibers within a skeletal muscle must be stimulated or none of them will be.

ANSWER: False

88. A motor unit is a single muscle plus all of the motor neurons that innervate it.

ANSWER: False

89. Muscles that have a large number of muscle fibers supplied by each motor neuron produce powerful, coarsely graded contractions.

ANSWER: True

90. Muscles that have a fine degree of control have small motor units.

ANSWER: True

91. The larger the motor units within a muscle, the more precisely controlled the gradations of contraction.

ANSWER: False

92. With twitch summation, the muscle fiber is stimulated so rapidly that it does not have an opportunity to return to resting potential between stimuli.

ANSWER: False

93. Tetanus occurs when a muscle fiber is stimulated so rapidly that it is not allowed to relax between stimulations, resulting in a smooth, sustained contraction.

ANSWER: True

94. The shorter a muscle fiber is before the onset of a contraction, the greater the force that can be developed upon the subsequent contraction because the thin filaments are already partially slid inward.

ANSWER: False

95. At l_o, a muscle is maximally stretched so that it can develop the most tension upon contraction, because the thin filaments can slide in a maximal distance.

ANSWER: False

96. Denervated muscle fibers become progressively smaller and their content of actin and myosin decreases.

ANSWER: True

97. Muscle tension does not occur in isometric contractions.

ANSWER: False

98. Single-unit smooth muscle has no innervation.

ANSWER: False

99. Single-unit smooth muscle and cardiac muscle are both self-excitable.

ANSWER: True

100. All smooth muscle is myogenic.

ANSWER: False

101. The strength and rate of contraction of the heart can be influenced by the autonomic nervous system.

ANSWER: True

Fill-in-the-blanks

102. Thick filaments are made up of the protein _____, whereas thin filaments are composed of the three proteins _____, _____, and _____.

ANSWERS: myosin, actin, tropomyosin, troponin

103. _____ and _____ are referred to as contractile proteins, whereas _____ and _____ are referred to as regulatory proteins.

ANSWERS: Myosin, actin, tropomyosin, troponin

104. _____ refers to the series of events linking muscle excitation to muscle contraction.

ANSWER: Excitation-contraction coupling

105. The _____ is a modified endoplasmic reticulum within muscle.

ANSWER: sarcoplasmic reticulum

106. The functional unit of skeletal muscle is a _____.

ANSWER: sarcomere

107. The contractile response of a muscle fiber to a single action potential is called a _____.

ANSWER: twitch

108. The only energy source that can be used directly by the contractile machinery of a muscle fiber is _____.

ANSWER: ATP

109. The immediate source for supplying additional ATP at the onset of exercise is _____.

ANSWER: creatine phosphate

110. Which descending motor pathway mediates performance of fine, discrete voluntary movements of the hands?

_____.

ANSWER: corticospinal (pryamidal) system

111. Which descending pathway is primarily concerned with regulation of posture involving involuntary movements of the trunk and limbs?   _____

ANSWER: multineuronal (extrapyramidal) system

Matching

112. Indicate which of the muscle proteins in skeletal muscle is associated with the item in question by writing the appropriate letters in the blanks using the answer code below.

        (a) = actin only
        (b) = myosin only
        (c) = actin and myosin
        (d) = troponin-tropomyosin complex
        (e) = actin, troponin and tropomyosin
        (f) = actin, myosin, troponin and tropomyosin

_____ found in the A band
_____ found in the I band
_____ contractile protein(s)
_____ found in the H zone
_____ regulatory protein(s)
_____ protein(s) found in thin filaments
_____ spherical shaped
_____ possess(es) cross bridges
_____ shape consists of two globular heads attached to a tail
_____ proteins(s) found in thick filament
_____ has (have) ATPase capacity
_____ can bind with myosin during muscle contraction
_____ lie(s) near the groove of the thin filament helix
_____ found in the sarcomere
_____ can bind with calcium during muscle contraction
_____ form(s) a helical chain
_____ Mg^{2+} binds ATP to this structure

ANSWERS: f, e, c, b, d, e, a, b, b, b, b, a, d, f, d, a, b

113. Indicate which bands are being described in each statement by writing the appropriate letter(s) in the blank using the answer code below. Note that more than one answer may apply.

            (a) = A band
            (b) = I band
            (c) = H zone

    _____ Composed of thin filaments only.
    _____ Composed of thick filaments only.
    _____ Composed of both thick and thin filaments
    _____ Shortens during muscular contraction.
    _____ Remains the same size during muscle contraction.

ANSWERS: b, c, a, b-c, a

114. _____ dark band   a. Z line
     _____ light band   b. A band
     _____ contains only thick   c. I band
            filaments   d. H zone
     _____ contains only thin
            filaments
     _____ contains partially
            overlapping thick and
            think filaments
     _____ joins adjacent
            sarcomeres together
     _____ runs down the middle
            of the A band
     _____ runs down the middle of
            the I band

ANSWERS: b, c, d, c, b, a, d, a

115. Indicate which characteristic applies to which type of muscle contraction by using the following answer code:

            (a) = isometric contraction
            (b) = isotonic contraction

    _____ muscle tension exceeds the load
    _____ load exceeds muscle tension
    _____ length changes
    _____ length remains constant
    _____ tension remains constant
    _____ important in maintaining posture
    _____ used to accompany movement
    _____ does not accomplish any work

ANSWERS: b, a, b, a, b, a, b, a

116. Indicate which of the characteristics in question apply to each of the muscle fiber types by using the following answer code: (more than one answer may apply)

          (a) = slow-oxidative fiber
          (b) = fast-oxidative fiber
          (c) = fast-glycolytic fiber

_____ has high myosin ATPase activity
_____ most resistant to fatigue
_____ most readily fatigues
_____ contains considerable myoglobin
_____ found predominantly in muscles designed for endurance
_____ has abundant glycolytic enzymes
_____ most powerful fibers
_____ found predominantly in muscles adapted for short-duration, high intensity activities
_____ produces the most lactic acid
_____ hypertrophies in response to weight training
_____ uses up considerable glycogen
_____ requires a constant supply of O_2
_____ has high yield of ATP for each nutrient molecule processed

ANSWERS: b and c;   a;   c;   a and b;   a;   c;   c;   c;   c;   c;   c;   a and b;   a and b

117. Indicate the characteristics of the muscle-tension receptors using the following answer code:

          (a) = muscle spindle
          (b) = Golgi tendon organ
          (c) = both of these receptors

_____ monitors change in muscle length
_____ detects change in muscle tension
_____ activated by muscle stretch
_____ initiates a monosynaptic reflex when activated
_____ unless compensatory measures are taken, this receptor becomes slack
_____ involved in negative feedback
_____ provides information to motor regions of the brain

ANSWERS: a, b, c, a, a, c, c

118. Indicate which type(s) of muscle are associated with the property in question by writing the appropriate letter in the blank using the answer code below.

       (a) = skeletal muscle only
       (b) = single-unit smooth muscle only
       (c) = cardiac muscle only
       (d) = skeletal muscle and cardiac muscle
       (e) = skeletal muscle and single-unit smooth muscle
       (f) = single-unit smooth muscle and cardiac muscle
       (g) = skeletal, single-unit smooth, and cardiac muscles

_____ contains actin, myosin, troponin, and tropomyosin
_____ contains gap junctions
_____ innervated by motor neurons
_____ is self-excitable
_____ maintains a constant resting membrane potential unless stimulated
_____ innervated by the autonomic nervous system
_____ is attached to bones
_____ considered to be involuntary
_____ thick and thin filaments are highly organized into a banding pattern
_____ found in the heart
_____ can exist over a variety of lengths with little change in tension
_____ is striated
_____ is found in the walls of hollow organs such as the digestive tract, bladder, uterus, blood vessels, etc.
_____ behaves as a functional syncytium
_____ is under voluntary control
_____ has a clear-cut length-tension relationship
_____ basis of contraction is cross bridge interaction between actin and myosin
_____ contraction is triggered as Ca^{2+} physically pulls troponin and tropomyosin from its blocking position over actin's binding sites for the cross bridges
_____ myosin must be phosphorylated before it can bind with actin
_____ contains T tubules
_____ displays pacemaker potentials and slow-wave potentials
_____ is neurogenic

ANSWERS: d, f, a, f, a, f, a, f, d, c, b, d, b, f, a, d, g, d, b, d, b, a

119. Indicate the characteristics that cardiac muscle shares with skeletal muscle and single-unit smooth muscle by using the following answer code:

(a) = cardiac muscle shares this characteristic with skeletal muscle
(b) = cardiac muscle shares this characteristic with single-unit smooth muscle
(c) = cardiac muscle shares this characteristic with both skeletal muscle and single-unit smooth muscle
(d) = cardiac muscle does not exhibit this characteristic
(e) = cardiac muscle exhibits this characteristic, but neither skeletal muscle nor single-unit smooth muscle do

_____ contracts according to the sliding-filament mechanism of muscle contraction
_____ contains intercalated discs
_____ is striated
_____ contains myosin, actin, troponin, and tropomyosin
_____ is innervated by motor neurons
_____ is found in the heart
_____ is involuntary
_____ behaves as a functional syncytium
_____ is found in the walls of blood vessels
_____ has thick and think myofilaments arranged in an orderly fashion
_____ exhibits autorhythmicity
_____ maintains a constant resting potential unless stimulated
_____ is innervated by the autonomic nervous system
_____ Ca^{2+} switches on muscle contraction by activating calmodulin, which in turn activates myosin ATPase activity

ANSWERS: c, e, a, a, d, e, b, b, d, a, b, d, b, d

AUDIOVISUAL AIDS

Films

A list of films available from West Publishing Company is presented in Appendix A. Following are other films that may be suitable. The sources for these films, which are coded by abbreviation, are provided in Appendix B.

Human Body: Muscular System, COR, 13 min.

Human Facial Expression, FHS, 15 min.

Mechanics of Human Motions - Throwing, USC, 21 min.

Microelectrodes in Muscle, PS, 19 min.

Moving Parts, CBS, 26 min.

Muscle, MH, 30 min.

Muscle: A Study of Integration, MH, 25 min.

Muscle: Chemistry of Contraction, EBE, 15 min.

Muscle Contraction and Oxygen Debt, MH, 16 min.

Muscle: Dynamics of Contraction, EBE, 21 min.

Muscle: Electrical Activity of Contraction, EBE, 9 min.

Muscles and Exercise, IM, 29 min.

Muscles and Joints: Muscle Power (VCR), FM, 26 min.

Muscles and Power, FM, 26 min.

Muscular System, CFV, 11 min.

Myoglobin, SB, 10 min.

Physiology of Exercise, FHS, 15 min.

The Muscle Spindle, UI, 19 min.

The Physiology of Exercise (VCR), FM, 30 min.

Steroids: Crossing the Line, FHS, 54 min.

Steroids: Shortcut to Make-Believe Muscles, CBS, 32 min

What Can Go Wrong?, PLP, 40 min.

What Makes Muscles Pull, JW, 10 min.

Software

Biochemistry of Muscle, EI.   Covers   contraction and relaxation.

Dynamics of the Human Muscular System, EI. Presents muscle types with animals of muscle contraction.

Exercises in Muscle Contraction, EI. Animated exercises in muscle stimulation and contractions

Flash: Skeletal Muscles, PLP. Surveys more than 200 muscles.

Frog Skeletal Muscle, SOV. A VCR program that covers muscle threshold, twitch amplitude, duration, summation, tetanus, and fatigue.

Location, CBS. Reviews functions of bones and muscles and covers types of muscles and joints.

Muscular System, PLP. Three part program covering human muscular system.

Neuromuscular Concepts, PLP. Covers skeletal muscle contraction beginning with neuromuscular junction.

Skeletal Muscle Anatomy and Physiology, PLP. Covers three muscle types, lever systems and sliding filament theory.

Chapter 7
Cardiac Physiology

CONTENTS
(All page references are to the main text.)

175

LECTURE HINTS AND SUGGESTIONS

1. Use demonstrations of various vertebrate hearts. These are
    available from Delta Biologicals, P.O. Box 26666, Tucson, AZ.

2. Use a torso or full-body manikin to illustrate the location
    of the heart.

3. Demonstrate a dissectible Carolina Biological Supply Company model of the heart to illustrate its external and internal structures.

4. Play a tape or record recording of heart sounds. These can be obtained from your local chapter of the American Heart Association.

5. Demonstrate how an electrocardiogram is recorded. See any general physiology lab manual.

6. Display ECGs illustrating various cardiac arrhythmias. A good source is <u>Rapid Interpretation of EKG's</u>, Dubin, 1974, Cover Publishing Company, Tampa, FL.

7. X-ray films of normal and diseased hearts are of great interest to students. These can be obtained from local cardiologists.

8. Demonstrate the use of a stethoscope to listen to the various heart sounds. Indicate the best location for detecting each valve.

9. Demonstrate a frog heart in situ. Indicate differences to expect between frog heart and human heart.

10. Show slides of coronary artery disease. These are available from Carolina Biological Supply Company.

11. Selective x-ray films of angiograms are informative. These can be obtained from your local chapter of the American Heart Association or local cardiologists.

CHAPTER TEST QUESTIONS

Multiple Choice

1. The systemic circulation

    (a) receives more blood than the pulmonary circulation does.
    (b) receives blood from the left ventricle.
    (c) is a high pressure system compared to the pulmonary circulation.
    (d) Both (b) and (c) above are correct.
    (e) All of the above are correct.

ANSWER: d

2. The wall of the left ventricle is thicker than the wall of the right ventricle because

    (a)   the left ventricle must pump much more blood than the right ventricle so it must have stronger walls.
    (b)   the right ventricle must pump much more blood than the left ventricle so it has a larger chamber to accommodate the blood and a correspondingly thinner wall.
    (c)   the left ventricle must pump the same amount of blood into the high-resistance, high-pressure systemic system as does the right ventricle into the low-resistance, low-pressure pulmonary system.
    (d)   the right ventricle must create higher tension within its walls.
    (e)   the left ventricle must pump oxygenated blood, which requires more energy than pumping unoxygenated blood.

ANSWER: c

3. Adjacent cardiac muscle cells are joined together end-to-end in the ventricles by

    (a)   intercalated discs.
    (b)   sarcomeres.
    (c)   Purkinje fibers.
    (d)   sinoatrial nodes.
    (e)   atrioventricular nodes.

ANSWER: a

4. The primary function of the pericardial sac is to

    (a)   prevent excessive expansion of the heart as it fills with blood.
    (b)   secrete a fluid that reduces friction as the heart beats.
    (c)   serve as a reservoir for blood to be used during strenuous exercise.
    (d)   provide oxygen and nutrients to the heart muscle.
    (e)   catch and kill any bacteria in the blood flowing through the heart chambers.

ANSWER: b

5. Indicate which is the proper sequence of blood flow through the circulatory system.

    1. right atrium   6. pulmonary vein
    2. left atrium   7. lungs
    3. right ventricle   8. systemic tissues
    4. left ventricle   9. aorta
    5. pulmonary artery   10. venae cavae

    (a) 1 to 2 to 3 to 4 to 5 to 6 to 7 to 8 to 9 to 10
    (b) 10 to 2 to 4 to 5 to 7 to 6 to 1 to 3 to 9 to 8
    (c) 10 to 1 to 3 to 5 to 7 to 6 to 2 to 4 to 9 to 8
    (d) 10 to 1 to 2 to 3 to 4 to 5 to 7 to 6 to 9 to 8
    (e) None of the above are correct.

ANSWER: c

6. The heart chamber having the greatest work load is

    (a) the right ventricle.
    (b) the left ventricle.
    (c) the left atrium.
    (d) the right atrium.

ANSWER: b

7. The aortic valve

    (a) prevents the backflow of blood into the aorta during
         ventricular diastole.
    (b) prevents the backflow of blood into the left ventricle
         during ventricular diastole.
    (c) prevents the backflow of blood into the right ventricle
         during ventricular diastole.
    (d) closes when the first heart sound is heard.
    (e) Two of the above are correct.

ANSWER: b

8. The right half of the heart pumps blood through the _____
    circulation and the left half pumps blood through the _____
    circulation.

    (a) systolic, diastolic
    (b) diastolic, systolic
    (c) systemic, pulmonary
    (d) pulmonary, systemic

ANSWER: d

9. The chordae tendineae

    (a) keep the AV valves from opening in the opposite
         direction during ventricular contraction.
    (b) hold the AV valves open during diastole.
    (c) hold the right and left ventricles together.
    (d) transmit the electrical impulse from the atria to the
         ventricles.
    (e) contract when the ventricles contract.

ANSWER: a

10. The low electrical resistance pathway that allows action
    potentials to spread from one cardiac muscle cell to
    adjacent cells in myocardial tissue is the

    (a) desmosome.
    (b) septum.
    (c) gap junction.
    (d) t-tubule.
    (e) sarcoplasmic reticulum.

ANSWER: c

11. The pacemaker of the heart is normally the

    (a) SA node.
    (b) AV node.
    (c) bundle of His.
    (d) Purkinje system.
    (e) ventricular myocardium.

ANSWER: a

12. The plateau of the cardiac action potential results from
     the opening of voltage-gated slow _____ channels in the
     plasma membrane of the cardiac cell.

    (a) sodium
    (b) potassium
    (c) calcium
    (d) chloride
    (e) glucose

ANSWER: c

13. On a normal ECG, a wave for repolarization of the atria is
     not recorded.   Why?

     (a)   The leads are not placed in a position to pick up
           atrial repolarization.
     (b)   No repolarization of the atria occurs normally.
     (c)   Atrial repolarization occurs simultaneously with
           ventricular depolarization and is masked by the QRS
           complex.
     (d)   The atrial repolarization wave does not travel through
           body fluids.
     (e)   It is too small to be picked up by external recording
           electrodes.

ANSWER: c

14. Which of the following criteria must be met for the heart
     to function efficiently?

     (a)   Excitation and consequently contraction of the cardiac
           muscle fibers of each heart chamber should be
           coordinated to assure efficient pumping.
     (b)   The atria should be excited and contract before the
           onset of ventricular contraction to assure that
           ventricular filling is complete.
     (c)   The right side of the heart should contract first to
           assure that oxygenated blood is delivered to the heart
           before the left side contracts.
     (d)   Both (a) and (b) above are correct.
     (e)   All of the above are correct.

ANSWER: d

15. The AV nodal delay

     (a)   ensures that the atria contract and empty their
           contents into the ventricles prior to ventricular
           systole.
     (b)   ensures that the ventricles contract prior to atrial
           systole.
     (c)   ensures that tetanic contraction of cardiac muscle is
           impossible.
     (d)   is shortened by parasympathetic stimulation.
     (e)   More than one of the above are correct.

ANSWER: a

16.   The function of the atrioventricular node is to

      (a)   excite the left and right atrium.
      (b)   control the heart rate.
      (c)   provide a time delay for ventricular filling.
      (d)   repolarize the heart after systole.
      (e)   More than one of the above are correct.

ANSWER: c

17.   The QRS complex represents

      (a)   depolarization of the atria.
      (b)   depolarization of the ventricles.
      (c)   the AV nodal delay.
      (d)   repolarization of the ventricles.
      (e)   the time during which the heart is contracting.

ANSWER: b

18.   The impulse is passing through the AV node

      (a)   during the P wave.
      (b)   between the P wave and QRS complex.
      (c)   during the QRS complex.
      (d)   between the QRS complex and T wave.
      (e)   during the T wave.

ANSWER: b

19.   Which of the following ECG waves represents ventricular
      repolarization?

      (a)   P wave.
      (b)   QRS complex.
      (c)   T wave.
      (d)   PR segment.
      (e)   Ventricular repolarization occurs simultaneously with
            atrial   depolarization   and   consequently   cannot   be
            recorded.

ANSWER: c

20. Which is the normal sequence of the spread of cardiac excitation?

   1. AV node   4. Purkinje fibers
   2. SA node   5. Bundle of His
   3. Atria   6. Ventricular myocardium

   (a) 2 to 3 to 1 to 5 to 4 to 6
   (b) 3 to 2 to 1 to 4 to 5 to 6
   (c) 2 to 3 to 1 to 4 to 5 to 6
   (d) 1 to 2 to 3 to 4 to 5 to 6
   (e) None of the above are correct.

ANSWER: a

21. Which of the following is the proper sequence of cardiac excitation?

   (a) SA node → AV node → atrial myocardium → bundle of His → Purkinje fibers → ventricular myocardium.
   (b) SA node → atrial myocardium → AV node → bundle of His → ventricular myocardium → Purkinje fibers.
   (c) SA node → atrial myocardium → ventricular myocardium → AV node → bundle of His → Purkinje fibers.
   (d) SA node → atrial myocardium → AV node → bundle of His Purkinje fibers → ventricular myocardium.

ANSWER: d

22. The sinoatrial node is the heart's normal pacemaker because

   (a) it has the fastest natural rate of autorhythmicity.
   (b) it has both sympathetic and parasympathetic innervation.
   (c) it lies in the right atrium.
   (d) activation of K^+ channels occurs more rapidly in this region than elsewhere in the heart.
   (e) None of the above are correct.

ANSWER: a

23. The AV node

   (a) is the normal pacemaker of the heart.
   (b) is the only electrical connection between the atria and the ventricles.
   (c) rapidly conducts the impulse from the atria to the ventricles so that they contract simultaneously.
   (d) is not innervated by the vagus.
   (e) has the fastest rate of depolarization in the heart.

ANSWER: b

184   Chapter 7

24.   The electrocardiogram is most useful in determining which component of cardiac output?

   (a)   Stroke volume.
   (b)   Heart rate.
   (c)   Ejection fraction.
   (d)   End-diastolic volume.
   (e)   Murmurs.

ANSWER: b

25.   An ectopic focus is the place where

   (a)   an abnormally excitable area of the heart initiates a premature action potential.
   (b)   all of the electrical impulses of the heart normally terminate.
   (c)   an ECG lead is attached on the outside of the chest.
   (d)   a heart valve is attached.
   (e)   the chordae tendineae attach to a valve.

ANSWER: a

26.   The function of the ventricular conduction system of the heart is to

   (a)   expedite the spread of the action potential throughout the large ventricular mass to assure a single, coordinated contraction of the ventricles.
   (b)   spread the action potential in the absence of sympathetic stimulation.
   (c)   set the heart rate.
   (d)   spread the action potential throughout the atria and ventricles.
   (e)   slow down the original action potential so it has time to spread throughout the large ventricular mass.

ANSWER: a

27.   The refractory period of cardiac muscle

   (a)   lasts almost as long as the resultant period of contraction.
   (b)   is much longer than the refractory period in skeletal muscle.
   (c)   allows tetanic contraction of the heart to occur to assure smooth, coordinated ejection of blood from the ventricles.
   (d)   Both (a) and (b) above are correct.
   (e)   All of the above are correct.

ANSWER: d

28. Why is tetanic contraction of the heart impossible?

    (a) Because there are no distinct motor units in the heart.
    (b) Because there is inadequate oxygen supply via the coronary circulation to metabolically support a sustained contraction.
    (c) Because the refractory period in cardiac muscle lasts almost as long as the duration of the resultant contraction.
    (d) Because the heart contracts with maximal force every beat so it is impossible to increase the strength of cardiac contraction.
    (e) Because vagal stimulation slows down the heart rate to prevent summation of contractions.

ANSWER: c

29. What percentage of ventricular filling is normally accomplished before atrial contraction begins?

    (a) 0%
    (b) 20%
    (c) 80%
    (d) 50%
    (e) 100%

ANSWER: c

30. The second heart sound is produced by the

    (a) opening of the AV valves.
    (b) closing of the AV valves.
    (c) opening of the semilunar valves.
    (d) closing of the semilunar valves.
    (e) blood rushing through the AV valves during diastole, creating a turbulent flow.

ANSWER: d

31. The first heart sound

    (a) occurs when the AV valves close.
    (b) occurs when the semilunar valves close.
    (c) signals the onset of ventricular systole.
    (d) Both (a) and (c) above are correct.
    (e) Both (b) and (c) above are correct.

ANSWER: d

32. The aortic valve opens

(a) when ventricular pressure exceeds aortic pressure.
(b) at the start of systole.
(c) at the maximum ventricular pressure.
(d) immediately after atrial contraction.
(e) None of the above are correct.

ANSWER: a

33. During isovolumetric ventricular contraction,

(a) rapid filling of the ventricles occurs.
(b) no blood enters or leaves the ventricles.
(c) the maximum volume of blood is ejected.
(d) the maximum rate of ejection occurs.
(e) None of the above are correct.

ANSWER: b

34. The period lasting from closure of the AV valve to opening
     of the aortic valve is known as

(a) isovolumetric ventricular contraction.
(b) isovolumetric ventricular relaxation.
(c) the rapid ejection phase.
(d) the rapid filling phase.
(e) None of the above are correct.

ANSWER: a

35. The heart valves open and close due to

(a) attachment to the heart muscle.
(b) a pressure difference on the two sides of the valve.
(c) Na^+ and K^+ fluxes during ventricular depolarization.
(d) turbulent flow in the atria and ventricles.
(e) None of the above are correct.

ANSWER: b

36. The end-systolic volume

(a) is the volume of blood in the ventricle when ejection
     is complete.
(b) is the volume of blood in the ventricle when filling is
     complete.
(c) is always equal to the stroke volume.
(d) Both (a) and (c) above are correct.
(e) Both (b) and (c) above are correct.

ANSWER: a

37. The dicrotic notch on the aortic pressure curve

    (a) is due to a disturbance set up during closure of the aortic valve.
    (b) is due to a disturbance set up during closure of the left atrioventricular valve.
    (c) is due to elastic recoil of the arterial walls during ventricular diastole.
    (d) is due to turbulent flow through a stenotic valve.
    (e) is diagnostic of atherosclerosis.

ANSWER: a

38. An insufficient AV valve

    (a) fails to open completely.
    (b) fails to close completely.
    (c) produces a gurgling diastolic murmur.
    (d) Both (a) and (c) above are correct.
    (e) Both (b) and (c) above are correct.

ANSWER: b

39. A whistling murmur heard between the second and first heart sound would be indicative of

    (a) a stenotic AV valve.
    (b) an insufficient AV valve.
    (c) a stenotic aortic or pulmonary semilunar valve.
    (d) an insufficient aortic or pulmonary semilunar valve.
    (e) No conclusions can be reached based on the information provided.

ANSWER: a

40. Cardiac output

    (a) is the volume of blood pumped by each ventricle during each contraction or beat.
    (b) is the volume of blood pumped by each ventricle per minute.
    (c) equals heart rate x stroke volume.
    (d) Both (a) and (c) above are correct.
    (e) Both (b) and (c) above are correct.

ANSWER: e

41. If stroke volume is 80 ml and the heart rate is 70 beats
     per minute, the cardiac output is

     (a)   150 l/min
     (b)   560 ml/min
     (c)   5600 ml/min
     (d)   8700 ml/min
     (e)   None of the above are correct.

ANSWER: c

42. According to the Frank-Starling law of the heart,

     (a)   the shorter the initial length of the cardiac muscle
           fibers prior to contraction, the more forceful will be
           the subsequent contraction, because the fibers are
           already partially contracted.
     (b)   increasing the venous return increases the end-
           diastolic volume, which leads to an increased stroke
           volume, so the heart normally pumps out all of the blood
           returned to it.
     (c)   as cardiac output is reduced, blood pools in the
           blood vessels so that arterial blood pressure increases.
     (d)   the output of the left side of the heart must always
           exceed that of the right side of the heart, because the
           right side only pumps blood to the lungs, whereas the
           left side must pump blood to the rest of the body.
     (e)   the greater the stroke volume, the smaller will be the
           subsequent end-diastolic volume, because as more blood
           is squeezed out, the heart cannot fill as completely.

ANSWER: b

43. According to the Frank-Starling law of the heart,

     (a)   the heart completely empties with every beat.
     (b)   the heart empties more completely upon parasympathetic
           stimulation.
     (c)   the heart normally pumps out all the blood returned to
           it.
     (d)   when venous return decreases, stroke volume increases to
           compensate.
     (e)   the cardiac output cannot be varied, thereby maintaining
           circulatory stability.

ANSWER: c

44. During heart failure

(a) the Frank-Starling curve is shifted to the left.
(b) the heart pumps out a smaller stroke volume than normal for a given end-diastolic volume.
(c) a compensatory increase in sympathetic activity increases the contractility of the heart to normal in the early stages of the disease.
(d) Both (b) and (c) above are correct.
(e) All of the above are correct.

ANSWER: d

45. Parasympathetic innervation to the heart

(a) is the vagus nerve.
(b) decreases the rate at which spontaneous action potentials are initiated in the SA node.
(c) decreases the strength of ventricular contraction.
(d) Both (a) and (b) above are correct.
(e) All of the above are correct.

ANSWER: d

46. Sympathetic stimulation of the heart

(a) increases the heart rate.
(b) increases the contractile strength of the heart muscle.
(c) shifts the Frank-Starling curve to the left.
(d) Two of the above are correct.
(e) All of the above are correct.

ANSWER: e

47. The volume of blood pumped by the right ventricle in one minute is

(a) approximately one-fifth the total cardiac output.
(b) equal to coronary blood flow for one minute.
(c) equal to the volume pumped by the left ventricle in one minute.

ANSWER: c

48. The _____ nerves to the heart alter cardiac output by increasing heart rate and increasing contractility.

    (a) motor
    (b) sensory
    (c) sympathetic
    (d) parasympathetic
    (e) None of the above are correct.

ANSWER: c

49. Which of the following will **not** increase heart rate?

    (a) Increased parasympathetic nerve activity.
    (b) Increased sympathetic nerve activity.
    (c) Increased epinephrine secretion.

ANSWER: a

50. If the end-diastolic volume were held constant, increased stroke volume could be accomplished by

    (a) increased sympathetic nerve activity to the heart.
    (b) increased parasympathetic nerve activity to the heart.
    (c) decreased contractility.
    (d) sleep.
    (e) increased arterial blood pressure.

ANSWER: a

51. Which of the following will **not** increase stroke volume?

    (a) Increased end-diastolic volume.
    (b) Increased contractility of the heart.
    (c) Increased end-systolic volume.
    (d) Increased stretch of the cardiac muscle fibers during ventricular filling.
    (e) Increased venous return.

ANSWER: c

52. The cardiac muscle

   (a) extracts oxygen and nutrients from the blood within its
        chambers.
   (b) receives its blood supply primarily during ventricular
        systole when blood is forced into the vessels supplying
        the heart.
   (c) receives its blood supply as the blood returning to the
        heart from the lung passes through the cardiac
        circulation before being pumped to the systemic
        circulation.
   (d) receives most of its blood supply during ventricular
        diastole by means of the coronary circulation.
   (e) None of the above are correct.

ANSWER: d

53. Blood flow through the coronary circulation occurs

   (a) mainly during systole.
   (b) mainly during diastole.
   (c) almost equally during systole and diastole.
   (d) only during ventricular isovolumetric contraction.
   (e) None of the above are correct.

ANSWER: b

True/False

54. The pulmonary circulation carries oxygenated blood from the
     lungs to the body tissues.

ANSWER: False

55. The right ventricle pumps out blood low in oxygen content,
     whereas the left ventricle pumps out blood high in oxygen
     content.

ANSWER: True

56. The aortic valve prevents backflow of blood from the aorta
     into the left ventricle during ventricular diastole.

ANSWER: True

57. There are no valves guarding the veins entering the heart.

ANSWER: True

58.   The heart valves are innervated by the autonomic nervous system.

ANSWER: False

59.   The function of the chordae tendineae and papillary muscles is to hold the AV valves wide open during diastole to assure complete ventricular filling.

ANSWER: False

60.   The AV valve controls the amount of blood entering the atrium from the venous system.

ANSWER: False

61.   The SA node is the pacemaker of the heart.

ANSWER: True

62.   The only point of electrical contact between the atria and the ventricles is the AV valve.

ANSWER: False

63.   The action potential spreads through the atria by gap junctions, but there are no gap junctions present in the ventricles, so the impulse must be propagated throughout the ventricular myocardium by the bundle of His and Purkinje system.

ANSWER: False

64.   The bundle of His and Purkinje system facilitate the rapid spread of the action potential throughout the ventricles.

ANSWER: True

65.   The impulse is passing through the AV node between the P wave and QRS complex.

ANSWER: True

66.   The ECG is an actual recording of cardiac electrical activity.

ANSWER: False

67. The plateau phase of the action potential in a contractile cardiac muscle cell occurs as a result of activation of slow Ca^{2+} channels.

ANSWER: True

68. The ventricles <u>always</u> depolarize at the same rate as the SA node depolarizes.

ANSWER: False

69. Atrial repolarization does not occur.

ANSWER: False

70. Diastole refers to the period of cardiac relaxation.

ANSWER: True

71. The atria and the ventricles contract at the same time to assure efficient pumping action.

ANSWER: False

72. Atrial systole lasts throughout ventricular systole.

ANSWER: False

73. Ventricular filling occurs more rapidly early in diastole than it does later in diastole.

ANSWER: True

74. At rapid heart rates, the lengths of systole and diastole shorten equally.

ANSWER: False

75. Most ventricular filling is accomplished during atrial contraction.

ANSWER: False

76. The refractory period in cardiac muscle is much shorter than the refractory period in skeletal muscle to assure that the heart can quickly be restimulated to produce alternate periods of contraction and relaxation.

ANSWER: False

77. The long refractory period of cardiac muscle prevents tetanic contractions of the heart.

ANSWER: True

78. The heart undergoes tetanic contraction during sympathetic stimulation to squeeze out more blood.

ANSWER: False

79. All of the blood within the ventricles is ejected during ventricular systole.

ANSWER: False

80. Contraction of the spirally arranged cardiac muscle fibers produces a wringing effect for efficient pumping.

ANSWER: True

81. The AV and semilunar valves are never open at the same time.

ANSWER: True

82. The end-diastolic volume is the maximum amount of blood in the ventricle after ventricular filling is complete.

ANSWER: True

83. An insufficient valve is a valve that fails to open sufficiently.

ANSWER: False

84. The first heart sound signals the onset of ventricular systole.

ANSWER: True

85. The second heart sound is due to closure of the AV valves.

ANSWER: False

86. The stroke volume is the volume of blood ejected by each ventricle per minute.

ANSWER: False

87. Normally, the stroke volume of the right side of the heart is the same as the stroke volume of the left side of the heart.

ANSWER: True

88. When the heart rate is increased, the period of time devoted to diastole is reduced.

ANSWER: True

89. One important function of the intrinsic control of the heart (Frank-Starling law of the heart) is to maintain the left and right cardiac outputs in balance.

ANSWER: True

90. Parasympathetic stimulation slows the rate of depolarization of the SA node and thus decreases the heart rate.

ANSWER: True

91. Sympathetic stimulation increases the heart rate.

ANSWER: True

92. Parasympathetic stimulation of the AV node increases the speed of transmission of the impulse through the AV node.

ANSWER: False

93. Stroke volume can vary by alterations in both intrinsic and extrinsic control mechanisms.

ANSWER: True

94. The amount of blood pumped out of the heart during each beat is known as the cardiac output.

ANSWER: False

95. Cardiac output = stroke volume x heart rate.

ANSWER: True

96. According to the Frank-Starling law of the heart, the shorter the initial length of the cardiac muscle fibers prior to contraction, the more forceful will be the subsequent contraction, because the fibers are already partially contracted.

ANSWER: False

97. According to the Frank-Starling law of the heart, the greater the stroke volume the smaller will be the subsequent end-diastolic volume, because as more blood is squeezed out, the heart cannot fill as completely during the next diastole.

ANSWER: False

98. Left-sided congestive heart failure can lead to pulmonary edema.

ANSWER: True

99. Cardiac muscle receives its blood supply primarily during ventricular systole when blood is being pumped out into the aorta.

ANSWER: False

100. The heart muscle receives its oxygen and nutrients directly from the blood within its chambers during ventricular diastole.

ANSWER: False

101. Most blood flow through the coronary vessels occurs during ventricular systole when the heart is driving blood forward.

ANSWER: False

102. The heart utilizes glucose almost exclusively for energy production.

ANSWER: False

Fill-in-the-blanks

103. Ninety-nine percent of the cardiac fibers are specialized for _____, whereas the remainder are specialized for _____.

ANSWERS: contraction, initiating and conducting the action potential

104. The _____ is the normal pacemaker of the heart.

ANSWER: SA node

105. The _____ assures that atrial excitation and contraction are complete before ventricular excitation and contraction commence.

ANSWER: AV nodal delay

106. Tetanus of cardiac muscle is impossible because of _____.

ANSWER: the long refractory period

107. A swishy murmur heard between the second and first heart sounds is indicative of a(n) _____ (stenotic or insufficient) _____ (AV or semilunar) valve.

ANSWER: insufficient, semilunar

108. The _____ is the volume of blood pumped by each ventricle/beat.

ANSWER: stroke volume

109. The _____ is the volume of blood pumped by each ventricle/minute.

ANSWER: cardiac output

110. The _____ is the volume of blood in the ventricle when ejection is complete.

ANSWER: end-systolic volume

111. The _____ is the volume of blood in the ventricle when filling is complete.

ANSWER: end-diastolic volume

112. Insufficient circulation of oxygenated blood to the heart muscle to maintain aerobic metabolism is referred to as _____.

ANSWER: ischemia

113. Upon what two factors is the extent of myocardial infarction   dependent?   _____   and
    _____ .

ANSWERS: the size of the occluded vessel, the extent of
           collateral circulation

114. List the four possible outcomes of an acute myocardial
     infarction.

     _____   _____

     _____   _____

ANSWERS: immediate death, delayed death from complications,
           full functional recovery, recovery with impaired
           function

115. _____ carries cholesterol to cells whereas
     _____ transports it away from cells.

ANSWERS: LDL, HDL

116. The _____ extracts cholesterol from the blood
     and converts it into _____ , which are secreted into
     the bile.

ANSWERS: liver, bile salts

Sequencing

117. Indicate the proper sequence of blood flow through the
     heart by filling the appropriate letters in the blanks,
     using the following answer code.   Start with the right
     atrium, which is already filled in for you.

     (a) = left ventricle   (f) = bicuspid valve
     (b) = right ventricle   (g) = pulmonary valve
     (c) = left atrium   (h) = aortic valve
     (d) = right atrium   (i) = pulmonary circulation
     (e) = tricuspid valve   (j) = systemic circulation

     d - ___ - ___ - ___ - ___ - ___ - ___ - ___ -
     ___ - d

ANSWERS: d, e, b, g, i, c, f, a, h, j, d

118. Indicate the proper order of the events during the cardiac cycle by placing numbers in the blanks preceding the events in sequence. The first and last events are already so indicated as a guide.

   __1__ AV valve open; aortic valve closed; ventricular filling occurring
   _____ blood ejected from the ventricle
   _____ isovolumetric ventricular relaxation
   _____ atrial contraction
   __12_ AV valve opens; ventricular filling occurs again; one cardiac cycle is complete
   _____ aortic valve opens
   _____ SA node discharges
   _____ ventricular filling complete
   _____ ventricular relaxation begins
   _____ aortic valve closes
   _____ isovolumetric ventricular contraction
   _____ ventricular contraction begins; AV valve closes

ANSWERS: 1, 8, 11, 3, 12, 7, 2, 4, 9, 10, 6, 5

Matching

119. _____ encircles the heart and secretes a lubricating fluid
   _____ carries cholesterol to cells
   _____ prevents backflow of blood
   _____ area of low electrical resistance that allows an action potential to spread from one cardiac cell to surrounding cells
   _____ muscle mass that becomes excited and contracts as a unit
   _____ carries cholesterol away from cells

a. gap junction
b. HDL
c. functional syncytium
d. heart valve
e. pericardial sac
f. LDL

ANSWERS: e, f, d, a, c, b

120. _____ ventricular depolarization
_____ time during which ventricles
are contracting and emptying
_____ atrial depolarization
_____ time during which atria are
repolarizing
_____ time during which impulse
is traveling through the
AV node
_____ time during which ventricles
are filling

a. P wave
b. QRS complex
c. T wave
d. PR interval
e. TP interval
f. ST segment

ANSWERS: b, f, a, b, d, e

121. _____ consists of abnormal smooth
muscle cells, cholesterol
deposits, scar tissue, and
possible calcium deposits
_____ referred cardiac pain
_____ freely floating clot
_____ abnormal clot attached to
a vessel wall

a. angina pectoris
b. embolus
c. atherosclerotic
   plaque
d. thrombus

ANSWERS: c, a, b, d

122. Indicate the effects of sympathetic and parasympathetic
stimulation on the heart using the following answer code:

(a) = an effect caused by sympathetic stimulation
(b) = an effect caused by parasympathetic stimulation
(c) = not brought about by either sympathetic or parasympathetic stimulation

_____ increases the heart rate
_____ decreases the contractility of the atrial muscle
_____ increases the AV nodal delay
_____ decreases the rate of depolarization to threshold of
the SA node
_____ increases the contractility of the atrial and
ventricular muscle
_____ decreases the contractility of the ventricular muscle

ANSWERS: a, b, b, b, a, c

123. Use the following answer code to indicate which factor involved in the initiation and spread of cardiac excitation is being identified.

    (a) = SA node
    (b) = AV node
    (c) = Bundle of His and Purkinje system
    (d) = Gap junctions

    _____ has the fastest rate of pacemaker activity.
    _____ allows the impulse to spread from cell to cell.
    _____ delays conduction of the impulse.
    _____ only point of electrical contact between the atria and ventricles.
    _____ normal pacemaker of the heart.
    _____ rapidly conducts the impulse down the ventricular septum and throughout much of the ventricular musculature.

ANSWERS: a, d, b, b, a, c

124. Indicate which valve abnormality is being described using the answer code below.

    (a) = valvular stenosis
    (b) = valvular insufficiency

    _____ produces a "gurgling" murmur
    _____ produces a "whistling" murmur
    _____ valve does not close completely
    _____ valve does not open completely

ANSWERS: b, a, b, a

125. Using the following answer code, indicate which pressure relationship exists during the time in question.

    (a) = aortic pressure > ventricular pressure > atrial
          pressure
    (b) = ventricular pressure > aortic pressure > atrial
          pressure
    (c) = aortic pressure > atrial pressure > ventricular
          pressure
    (d) = ventricular pressure > atrial pressure > aortic
          pressure
    (e) = atrial pressure > ventricular pressure > aortic
          pressure

    _____ during ventricular diastole
    _____ when the atrioventricular valve closes
    _____ during isovolumetric ventricular contraction
    _____ when the aortic valve opens
    _____ when ventricular ejection is occurring
    _____ when the aortic valve closes
    _____ during isovolumetric ventricular relaxation
    _____ when the atrioventricular valve opens

ANSWERS: c, a, a, b, b, a, a, c

126. Use the answer code below to complete the following statements.

   (a) = stroke volume
   (b) = end-diastolic volume
   (c) = cardiac output
   (d) = heart rate
   (e) = end-systolic volume
   (f) = sympathetic activity

The volume of blood ejected by each ventricle each minute is known as the _____.

The two main determinants of cardiac output are _____ and _____.

The volume of blood ejected by each ventricle each beat is known as the _____.

The stroke volume may be calculated by _____ minus _____.

The maximum volume of blood that the ventricle contains after filling is complete is the _____.

The minimum volume of blood that the ventricle contains after emptying is complete is the _____.

Stroke volume can be increased by increasing _____ and _____.

The number of times the heart contracts each minute is the _____.

Heart rate can be increased by increasing _____.

ANSWERS: c, a-d, a, b-e, b, e, b-f, d, f

127. Use the following answer code to compare the magnitude of the items in question.

(a) = A is greater than B
(b) = B is greater than A
(c) = A and B are equal

_____ A. Resistance and pressure in the pulmonary circulation
       B. Resistance and pressure in the systemic circulation

_____ A. Volume of blood pumped out by the left side of the heart
       B. Volume of blood pumped out by the right side of the heart

_____ A. Spontaneous rate of depolarization in the SA node
       B. Spontaneous rate of depolarization in the ventricles

_____ A. Velocity of impulse conduction through the bundle of His and Purkinje system
       B. Velocity of impulse conduction through the AV node

_____ A. Rate of depolarization of the SA node on parasympathetic stimulation
       B. Rate of depolarization of the SA node on sympathetic stimulation

_____ A. Duration of systole at resting heart rate
       B. Duration of systole at rapid heart rate during exercise

_____ A. Duration of diastole at resting heart rate
       B. Duration of diastole at rapid heart rate during exercise

_____ A. Rate of ventricular filling in early diastole
       B. Rate of ventricular filling in late diastole

_____ A. Stroke volume when end-diastolic volume equals 130 ml
       B. Stroke volume when end-diastolic volume equals 160 ml

_____ A. Normal stroke volume
       B. Stroke volume on sympathetic stimulation

_____ A. Volume of blood in the ventricles at the onset of isovolumetric ventricular contraction
       B. Volume of blood in the ventricles at the end of isovolumetric ventricular contraction

_____ A. Volume of blood in the left ventricle when the aortic
            valve opens
         B. Volume of blood in the left ventricle when the aortic
            valve closes

_____ A. Volume of blood in the left ventricle when the left
            AV valve opens
         B. Volume of blood in the left ventricle when the left
            AV valve closes

_____ A. Duration of the refractory period in cardiac muscle
         B. Duration of contraction in cardiac muscle

_____ A. Duration of the refractory period in cardiac muscle
         B. Duration of the refractory period in skeletal muscle

_____ A. Coronary blood flow during systole
         B. Coronary blood flow during diastole

ANSWERS: b, c, a, a, b, c, a, a, b, b, c, a, b, c, a, b

Completion

128. Choose the response within the parentheses for each item
      that correctly completes this discussion of the sequence of
      events during the cardiac cycle.

    A.   During ventricular diastole, the atrial pressure
         is (greater than, less than, or equal to) the
         ventricular pressure, so the AV valve is (open, closed).

ANSWER: greater than, open

    B.   Thus blood entering the atria from the veins (remains
         in the atria, flows into the ventricle).

ANSWER: flows into the ventricle

    C.   Late in ventricular diastole, the P wave occurs. The
         P wave represents (ventricular depolarization,
         ventricular repolarization, atrial depolarization,
         atrial repolarization).

ANSWER: atrial depolarization

D. As a result of atrial contraction, ventricular filling
    is completed. The volume of blood in the ventricle at
    this time is known as the (stroke volume, end-diastolic
    volume, end-systolic volume, cardiac-output
    volume, maximal filling volume).

ANSWER: end-diastolic volume

E. The QRS wave follows the P wave on the ECG. What is
    initiated as a result of the QRS wave? (the AV nodal
    delay, SA node depolarization, ventricular contraction,
    ventricular relaxation)

ANSWER: ventricular contraction

F. At the beginning of ventricular systole, the AV valve
    (opens, closes) when the ventricular pressure (rises
    above, falls below) the atrial pressure.

ANSWER: closes, rises above

G. The period of isovolumetric ventricular contraction
    occurs after the AV valve has (opened, closed) and
    before the aortic valve has (opened, closed).

ANSWER: closed, opened

H. During the time of isovolumetric ventricular con-
    traction, the ventricular volume (is increasing, is
    decreasing, remains constant).

ANSWER: remains constant

I. Ventricular ejection takes place after the aortic valve
    (opens, closes), when ventricular pressure (rises above,
    falls below) the aortic pressure.

ANSWER: opens, rises above

J. During ventricular ejection, the ventricular volume (is
    increasing, is decreasing, remains constant).

ANSWER: is decreasing

K. The volume of blood left in the ventricle at the end of
    ejection is (the stroke volume, the end-diastolic
    volume, the end-systolic volume, zero ml).

ANSWER: the end-systolic volume

L.   The volume of blood ejected by the ventricle during a single contraction is known as (the stroke volume, the end-diastolic volume, the end-systolic volume, the cardiac output).

ANSWER: the stroke volume

M.   After the T wave occurs on the ECG, ventricular pressure (falls below, rises above) aortic pressure so the   aortic valve (opens, closes).

ANSWERS: falls below, closes

N.   During the period of isovolumetric ventricular relaxation, (both the aortic and AV valves are closed, the aortic valve is open and the AV valve is closed, the   aortic   valve   is closed and the AV valve is open, both the aortic and AV valve are open) because (the ventricular pressure is greater than the atrial pressure but less than the aortic pressure, the ventricular pressure is greater than both aortic and atrial pressures, the ventricular pressure is less than both aortic and atrial pressures, the ventricular pressure is less than atrial pressure but greater than aortic pressure).

ANSWERS: both the aortic and AV valves are closed, the ventricular pressure is greater than the atrial pressure but less than the aortic pressure

O.   Following isovolumetric ventricular relaxation, the AV valve (opens, closes).

ANSWER: opens

P.   Ventricular volume (increases, decreases, remains constant) as ventricular filling commences once again. One cardiac cycle is complete.

ANSWER: increases

129.   Complete the following discussion by circling the correct
       phrase within the parentheses.

If the venous return increases, at the end of diastole the ventricular volume will be (increased, decreased, the same as
before). Therefore, the length of the cardiac muscle cells will
be (increased, decreased, the same as before).   Consequently,
during the next contraction the tension developed by the heart
will be (greater than before, less than before, the same as
before). The amount of blood pumped out as a result of this
contraction will be (more than, less than, the same as) the amount
pumped out by the contraction prior to the increase in venous
return. Therefore, as venous return to the heart increases, the
stroke volume ejected by the heart (increases, decreases, remains
unchanged).

ANSWERS: increased, increased, greater than before, more
         than, increases.

130.   Indicate how the change listed in Column I affects the item
       listed in Column II by circling the appropriate letter.

Column I	increases	decreases	has no effect on	Column II
A. ↑ heart rate	a	b	c	cardiac output
B. ↑ stroke volume	a	b	c	cardiac output
C. exercise	a	b	c	cardiac output
D. ↑ cardiac sympathetic activity	a	b	c	rate of depolarization of the SA node
E. ↑ parasympathetic activity	a	b	c	rate of depolarization of the SA node

130. (cont.)

Column I	increases	decreases	has no effect on	Column II
F. ↑ parasympathetic activity	a	b	c	heart rate
G. ↑ venous return	a	b	c	end-diastolic volume
H. ↑ end-diastolic volume	a	b	c	stroke volume
I. ↑ length of cardiac muscle fiber prior to contraction	a	b	c	stroke volume
J. ↑ venous return	a	b	c	stroke volume
K. ↑ cardiac sympathetic activity	a	b	c	contractility of the ventricles
L. ↑ parasympathetic activity	a	b	c	stroke volume
M. ↑ parasympathetic activity	a	b	c	AV-nodal delay
N. ↑ cardiac sympathetic activity	a	b	c	stroke volume

130. (cont.)

Column I	increases	decreases	has no effect on	Column II
O. ↑ parasym-pathetic activity	a	b	c	atrial contractility
P. ↑ cardiac sympathetic activity	a	b	c	velocity of impulse conduction through the heart

ANSWERS: A.a, B.a, C.a, D.a, E.b., F.b, G.a, H.a, I.a, J.a, K.a, L.c, M.a, N.a, O.b, P.a

AUDIOVISUAL AIDS

Films

A list of films available from West Publishing Company is presented in Appendix A.   Following are other films that may be suitable.   The sources for these films, which are coded by abbreviation, are provided in Appendix B.

Action of Heart Valves, SU, 19 min.

Cardiac Arrest, USNAC, 36 min.

Cardiac Arrhythmias, SCI, 23 min.

Circulation, EI

Closed Chest Heart Massage, IF, 11 min.

Common Heart Disorders, MH, 17 min.

Coronary Counterattack, BYU, 21 min.

CPR: To Save a Life, EBF, 14 min.

CPR for Infants and Young Children, CF, 18 min.

Disorders of The Heart Beat, AHA, 30 min.

Dissection of the Heart, USNAC, 12 min.

Evaluation of Diagnostic Left Ventricular Function SNM, 30 min.

Heart, JBL, 6 min.

Heart and Circulation, EBE, 11 min.

Heart Attack, CF, 13 min.

Heart Disease, FHS, 19 min.

Heart Dissection and Anatomy, IM, 14 min.

Hearts and Circulatory Systems, COR, 14 min.

Heart Sounds and Murmurs - Origins and Characteristics, UW,   14 min.

Heart Formation in the Chick Embryo, HRW, 4 min.

Heart Valves: Repairing the Heart, FHS, 19 min.

Human Body: Circulatory System, COR, 13 min.

I am Joe's Heart, PYR, 25 min.

New Pulse of Life, PFP, 29 min.

Pacemakers: The Electrical Heartbeat, FHS, 19 min.

Partners for Life: The Human Heart and Lungs, EI

Sports for Life, BARR, 22 min.

The Heart, IM, 29 min.

The Heart Attack, MH, 20 min.

The Heart: Counterattack, MH, 30 min.

The Human Heart, MGHT, 26 min.

The Lymphatic System, IF, 15 min.

Transport Systems in Animals, IU, 17 min.

Two Hearts That Beat as One, FHS, 27 min.

Two Original Open-Heart Surgeries, UJ, 60 min.

Why Risk a Heart Attack, TLV, 14 min.

<u>Work of the Heart</u>, EBE, 19 min.

Software

<u>Cardiac Cycle of the Turtle</u>, SOV. A <u>VCR</u> program that covers the effect of temperature, refractory period, ECG, Starling's Law, and Vagal Stimulation.

<u>Cardiovascular Function</u>, EI. Covers principles of heart and vessel physiology.

<u>Cardiovascular System</u>, EI. Covers heart and blood vessels.

<u>Circulation</u>, EI. Covers blood, heart, arteries, capillaries, veins, and lungs.

<u>Experiments in Human Physiology</u>, SSS. Covers heart rate.

<u>Heart Abnormalities and EKG's: A Stimulation</u>, PLP. Stimulates heart disorders.

<u>Heartlab</u>, CDL. Covers the circulation of blood through the human heart.

<u>Human Electrocardiogram</u>, SOV. A <u>VCR</u> program covering the E C G , phonocardiogram, and arterial pulse wave.

<u>The Heart Stimulator</u>, CBS. Uses color graphics and animation to depict blood flowing through the heart as it beats.

<u>Transport</u>, CBS. Reviews the blood system, lymph system, blood cells, and blood types.

<u>Your Body: Series I</u>. Tests student's knowledge of blood and the circulatory system.

<u>Your Heart</u>, EI. Reviews the basic structures of the heart and the flow of blood through them.

Chapter 8
Blood Vessels and Blood Pressure

CONTENTS
(All page references are to the main text.)

-Extrinsic control of arteriolar radius is primarily important in the regulation of arterial blood pressure. p.250

Capillaries, p.251
-Capillaries are ideally suited to serve as sites of exchange. p.251
-Water-filled pores in the capillary wall permit passage of small, water-soluble substances that cannot cross the endothelial cells themselves. p.254
-Diffusion across the capillary wall is important in solute exchange. p.254
-Bulk flow across the capillary wall is important in extracellular-fluid distribution. p.256
-The lymphatic system is an accessory route by which interstitial fluid can be returned to the blood. p.257
-Edema occurs when too much interstitial fluid accumulates. p.260

Veins, p.261
-Veins serve as a blood reservoir as well as passageways back to the heart. p.261
-Venous return is enhanced by a number of extrinsic factors. p.262

Blood Pressure, p.265
-Regulation of mean arterial blood pressure is accomplished by controlling cardiac output, total peripheral resistance, and blood volume. p.265
-The baroreceptor reflex is the most important mechanism for short-term regulation of blood pressure. p.267
-Hypertension is a serious national public health problem, but its causes are largely unknown. p.268
-Inadequate sympathetic activity is responsible for dizziness or fainting accompanying transient orthostatic hypotension. p. 270

Beyond the Basics - The Ups and Downs of Hypertension and Exercise, p.270

-Circulatory shock can become irreversible. p.270

Chapter in Perspective: Focus on Homeostasis, p.272

Chapter Summary, p.273

LECTURE HINTS AND SUGGESTIONS

1. Use a chart, torso, or full-body manikin to demonstrate the locations of the various major blood vessels. These are available from Carolina Biological Supply Company, Burlington, NC.

2. Use 2 x 2 Carolina Biological Supply Company slides to illustrate cross sections of the various blood vessels.

3. Use a sphygmomanometer to demonstrate how to correctly measure blood pressure. See any general physiology lab manual for procedure.

4. Pathology slides of blood vessel problems are always interesting. These can be obtained from Carolina Biological Supply Company.

5. Have students draw a schematic road map tracing the flow of a drop of blood through various parts of the body, naming only those vessels that are used to transport the blood directly between two points.

6. The demonstration of circulation in the web of a frog foot is informative. See any general physiology lab manual for procedures.

7. Use Vinylite preparations of different organs to show blood vessel patterns.

8. Commercially prepared animals to show paths of general and visceral circulation are useful demonstrations. These can be obtained from many commercial sources.

CHAPTER TEST QUESTIONS

Multiple Choice

1.   Resistance

(a)   is a measure of the hindrance to blood flow through a vessel caused by friction between the moving fluid and stationary vascular walls.
(b)   is doubled when the radius of the vessel is reduced by one-half.
(c)   increases sixteen-fold when the radius of the vessel is reduced by one-half.
(d)   Both (a) and (b) above are correct.
(e)   Both (a) and (c) above are correct.

ANSWER: e

2.   Resistance increases when

(a)   radius decreases.
(b)   length decreases.
(c)   viscosity decreases.
(d)   hematocrit decreases.
(e)   None of the above are correct.

ANSWER: a

3.   Vasoconstriction

(a)   refers to a decrease in the radius of a vessel.
(b)   of an arteriole decreases blood flow through that vessel.
(c)   of a vein increases blood flow through that vessel.
(d)   Both (a) and (b) above are correct.
(e)   All of the above are correct.

ANSWER: e

4. Which of the following is the correct relationship between pressure, flow, and resistance?

    (a) flow = $\dfrac{\text{pressure gradient}}{\text{radius}^4}$

    (b) flow x pressure gradient = resistance

    (c) flow = $\dfrac{\text{pressure gradient}}{\text{resistance}}$

    (d) pressure gradient = $\dfrac{\text{flow}}{\text{resistance}}$

    (e) resistance = $\dfrac{\text{flow}}{\text{radius}^4}$

ANSWER: c

5. The major determinant influencing resistance to blood flow is

    (a) the viscosity of the blood.
    (b) the radius of the vessel through which the blood is flowing.
    (c) the pressure gradient in the vessel.
    (d) the hematocrit of the blood.
    (e) the amount of plasma protein.

ANSWER: b

6. Vasoconstriction

    (a) causes a decrease in resistance.
    (b) occurs when there is a decrease in the radius of a vessel.
    (c) occurs in response to a decrease in sympathetic activity.
    (d) Both (b) and (c) above are correct.
    (e) All of the above are correct.

ANSWER: b

7. Which of the following factors would produce the most profound change in blood flow?

   (a) Doubling the radius of the vessel.
   (b) Doubling the difference in the pressure gradient within the vessel.
   (c) Doubling the viscosity of the blood.
   (d) Doubling the length of the vessel.

ANSWER: a

8. Organs that recondition the blood

   (a) receive disproportionately large percentages of the cardiac output.
   (b) can withstand temporary reductions in blood flow much better than can organs that do not recondition the blood.
   (c) must receive a constant blood supply in order to maintain homeostasis.
   (d) Both (a) and (b) above are correct.
   (e) Both (a) and (c) above are correct.

ANSWER: d

9. The arteries

   (a) serve as rapid-transit passageways from the tissues to the heart because of their large radii.
   (b) act as a blood reservoir because they have the capacity to store large volumes of blood with little change in their internal pressure.
   (c) are the major resistive vessels of the vasculature.
   (d) are the site of exchange between the blood and surrounding tissues.
   (e) None of the above are correct.

ANSWER: e

10. What force continues to drive blood through the vasculature during ventricular diastole?

    (a) Ventricular contraction forces blood to the tissues during ventricular diastole.
    (b) The elastic recoil of the stretched arterial walls provides the force to continue blood flow in the remaining vascular system during ventricular diastole.
    (c) Sympathetic stimulation produces arterial vasoconstriction, which drives the blood forward into the arterioles during ventricular diastole.
    (d) Skeletal muscle contraction squeezes the blood forward from the arteries during ventricular diastole.
    (e) Respiratory movements produce pressure changes in the chest, which establishes a pressure gradient that drives blood forward from the arteries into the arterioles and capillaries.

ANSWER: b

11. Because the arteries have large radii, they serve as excellent rapid-transit passageways for blood. Their second function, related to their elasticity, is to act as a _____ for maintaining blood flow during diastole.

    (a) cardiac reserve
    (b) venous reserve
    (c) arterial capacitance
    (d) lymphatic reserve
    (e) pressure reservoir

ANSWER: e

12. The pressure measured in the arteries just before the next ventricular ejection of blood is

    (a) systolic pressure.
    (b) diastolic pressure.
    (c) pulse pressure.
    (d) mean pressure.
    (e) None of the above are correct.

ANSWER: b

13. The pulse pressure

    (a) is the difference between the systolic and diastolic pressure.
    (b) is the average pressure throughout the cardiac cycle.
    (c) is the maximum pressure exerted in the arteries.
    (d) is the minimum pressure exerted in the arteries.
    (e) is the change in pressure that can be felt in an artery due to the snapping shut of the aortic valve.

ANSWER: a

14. If the arterial blood pressure is recorded at 132/84, what is the mean arterial pressure?

    (a) 100 mm Hg
    (b) 93 mm Hg
    (c) 108 mm Hg
    (d) 48 mm Hg
    (e) None of the above are correct.

ANSWER: a

15. The major function of the arterioles is

    (a) to serve as a passageway to the tissues.
    (b) to distribute the cardiac output to the different organs.
    (c) to serve as a pressure reservoir.
    (d) to convert the intermittent flow from the heart to a steady outflow.
    (e) None of the above are correct.

ANSWER: b

16. The _____ are primarily responsible for determining the relative distribution of the cardiac output to different organs.

    (a) arteries
    (b) arterioles
    (c) capillaries
    (d) venules
    (e) veins

ANSWER: b

17. Which of the following factors is most important in matching the blood flow through a specific tissue with the metabolic needs of that tissue?

  (a) Sympathetically induced vasoconstriction of the arteries supplying a tissue forces more blood to flow into the tissue.
  (b) Parasympathetically induced vasodilation of the capillaries within a tissue allows more blood to flow into the tissue.
  (c) Local changes within a tissue resulting from increased metabolic activity can produce local arteriolar vasodilation to allow more blood to flow into the tissue.
  (d) Widespread venous vasoconstriction allows blood to dam up at the tissue level.
  (e) The amount of blood flowing through each tissue remains constant through reflex controls to assure that metabolic needs are continuously met.

ANSWER: c

18. Which of the following properties does **not** pertain to the arterioles?

  (a) Their radii cannot be changed.
  (b) Their walls contain a thick layer of smooth muscle.
  (c) They are responsible for the distribution of blood flow to the various organs.
  (d) They are the major vessels that contribute to total peripheral resistance.
  (e) They are richly innervated by sympathetic nerve fibers.

ANSWER: a

19. As metabolic activity of an organ or tissue increases, blood flow to that organ increases. This phenomenon is known as

  (a) tissue autoregulation.
  (b) tissue anoxia.
  (c) active hyperemia.
  (d) hypertension.
  (e) atherosclerosis.

ANSWER: c

20. Endothelial-derived relaxing factor (EDRF)

    (a) is a local chemical mediator released from the endothelial cells that induces relaxation of arteriolar smooth muscle in the vicinity.
    (b) is nitric oxide.
    (c) is produced in numerous other tissues besides endothelial cells.
    (d) Both (a) and (b) above are correct.
    (e) All of the above are correct.

ANSWER: e

21. Which of the following statements concerning nitric oxide (NO) is **incorrect?**

    (a) NO increases the total peripheral resistance by its action on arteriolar smooth muscle.
    (b) NO serves as endothelial-derived relaxing factor.
    (c) NO is the direct mediator of penile erection.
    (d) NO is released as "chemical warfare" by macrophages of the immune system.
    (e) NO serves as a novel type of neurotransmitter in the brain.

ANSWER: a

22. During exercise, there is **not** an increased blood flow to which of the following tissues?

    (a) Skeletal muscles.
    (b) Heart.
    (c) Skin.
    (d) Brain.
    (e) Blood flow is increased to all of these tissues during exercise.

ANSWER: d

23. During strenuous exercise, blood flow increases to the

    (a) heart because of local control factors.
    (b) brain because of reflex control factors.
    (c) skeletal muscles because of local control factors.
    (d) Both (a) and (c) above are correct.
    (e) All of the above are correct.

ANSWER: d

24. The major site of sympathetic blood flow control (resistance changes) is at the

    (a) arterioles.
    (b) capillaries.
    (c) atria.
    (d) arteries.
    (e) None of the above are correct.

ANSWER: a

25. Which of the following **does not** bring about arteriolar vasodilation?

    (a) Increased sympathetic stimulation.
    (b) Local decrease in O_2.
    (c) Histamine release.
    (d) Application of heat.

ANSWER: a

26. Extrinsic control of arteriolar radius

    (a) is accomplished primarily by the sympathetic nervous system.
    (b) is important in the regulation of arterial blood pressure.
    (c) can be overridden by local arteriolar adjustments.
    (d) Both (a) and (b) above are correct.
    (e) All of the above are correct.

ANSWER: e

27. Active hyperemia

    (a) refers to the arteriolar dilation that occurs within a tissue in response to local chemical changes that accompany increased metabolic activity of the tissue.
    (b) refers to local arteriolar mechanisms that are aimed at keeping tissue blood flow fairly constant in spite of rather wide deviations in mean arterial driving pressure.
    (c) is important in maintaining an adequate pressure head to drive blood forward into a tissue.
    (d) None of the above are correct.

ANSWER: a

28. The _____ are primarily responsible for nutrient
     exchange in different organs.

     (a) arteries
     (b) arterioles
     (c) capillaries
     (d) venules
     (e) veins

ANSWER: c

29. Which of the following is **not** a characteristic of
     capillaries?

     (a) Thin walls.
     (b) Short distance between adjacent vessels.
     (c) Distensible walls.
     (d) Slow blood velocity.
     (e) Large total surface area.

ANSWER: c

30. The largest total cross-sectional area is found in the

     (a) aorta.
     (b) arterioles.
     (c) capillaries.
     (d) venules.
     (e) veins.

ANSWER: c

31. Through which vessel is the velocity of blood flow the
     slowest?

     (a) Aorta.
     (b) Arterioles.
     (c) Capillaries.
     (d) Venules.
     (e) Veins.

ANSWER: c

32. As the total cross sectional area of the vascular tree
    _____, the velocity of blood flow _____.

    (a) increases; decreases.
    (b) increases; increases.
    (c) decreases; decreases.
    (d) increases; remains constant.
    (e) decreases; remains constant.

ANSWER: a

33. The site of exchange of nutrients and metabolic end
    products is

    (a) the arteries.
    (b) the arterioles.
    (c) the capillaries.
    (d) the veins.
    (e) the heart.

ANSWER: c

34. Glucose, a water-soluble, lipid-insoluble substance,
    crosses capillary walls

    (a) through water-filled pores.
    (b) directly through endothelial cells.
    (c) through water-filled pores and endothelial cells.
    (d) through gap junctions.
    (e) None of the above are correct.

ANSWER: a

35. What is the primary method by which materials such as O_2,
    CO_2 and nutrients are exchanged between the blood and
    surrounding tissues?

    (a) Passive diffusion of substances across the capillary
         wall down their concentration gradients.
    (b) Active transport of materials across the capillary
         wall.
    (c) Osmotic pressure drawing water and solutes out of the
         capillary, thereby bringing these dissolved nutrients
         into contact with the tissue cells.
    (d) The combined processes of ultrafiltration and
         reabsorption.
    (e) Bulk flow.

ANSWER: a

36.   The process of ultrafiltration

    (a)   refers to the movement of protein-free plasma from the capillaries into the interstitial-fluid.
    (b)   occurs when the outward forces (capillary blood pressure plus interstitial-fluid-colloid osmotic pressure) exceed the inward forces (plasma-colloid osmotic pressure plus interstitial-fluid hydrostatic pressure).
    (c)   occurs when the outward forces (capillary blood pressure plus plasma-colloid osmotic pressure exceed the inward forces (interstitial-fluid hydrostatic pressure plus interstitial-fluid-colloid osmotic pressure).
    (d)   Both (a) and (b) above are correct.
    (e)   Both (a) and (c) above are correct.

ANSWER: d

37.   Which two pressures act to move fluid into the capillary?

    (a)   Interstitial-fluid hydrostatic pressure and capillary blood pressure.
    (b)   Plasma-colloid osmotic pressure and interstitial-fluid-colloid osmotic pressure.
    (c)   Interstitial-fluid hydrostatic pressure and plasma-colloid osmotic pressure.
    (d)   Interstitial-fluid hydrostatic pressure and interstitial-fluid-colloid osmotic pressure.
    (e)   Capillary blood pressure and interstitial-fluid-colloid osmotic pressure.

ANSWER: c

38.   Fluid movement into and out of the capillary is dependent on _____ and _____ pressures working in _____ direction(s).

    (a)   hydrostatic, osmotic, opposite
    (b)   hydrostatic, osmotic, the same
    (c)   filtration, absorption, the same
    (d)   length, filling, the same
    (e)   protein content, blood pressure, the same

ANSWER: a

39. The principle force that causes movement of fluid from the tissues into the capillaries is

    (a) the hydrostatic pressure of the blood in the veins.
    (b) the hydrostatic pressure of the blood in the arteries.
    (c) the osmotic pressure created by the plasma proteins.
    (d) the pressure of the lymph.
    (e) None of the above are correct.

ANSWER: c

40. Plasma-colloid osmotic pressure

    (a) is due to the presence of the plasma proteins that cannot permeate the capillary wall.
    (b) tends to draw fluid into the capillary.
    (c) tends to force fluid out of the capillary.
    (d) Both (a) and (b) above are correct.
    (e) Both (a) and (c) above are correct.

ANSWER: d

41. The movements of fluid across the capillary wall depend on all the following **except**

    (a) capillary blood pressure.
    (b) interstitial-fluid hydrostatic pressure.
    (c) plasma protein concentration.
    (d) interstitial-fluid protein concentration.
    (e) concentration of glucose in the capillary.

ANSWER: e

42. Which change will **increase** fluid reabsorption by the capillaries?

    (a) Decreased interstitial-fluid hydrostatic pressure.
    (b) Increased capillary blood pressure.
    (c) Increased plasma-colloid osmotic pressure.
    (d) Increased interstitial-fluid-colloid osmotic pressure.
    (e) None of the above are correct.

ANSWER: c

43. Given the following forces acting at a given point across the capillary wall, what type of fluid movement will be taking place at that point?

    Capillary blood pressure = 32 mm Hg
    Plasma-colloid osmotic pressure = 23 mm Hg
    Interstitial-fluid hydrostatic pressure = 1 mm Hg
    Interstitial-fluid-colloid osmotic pressure = 0 mm Hg

    (a) Ultrafiltration will occur with a net outward pressure of 8 mm Hg.
    (b) Ultrafiltration will occur with a net outward pressure of 10 mm Hg.
    (c) Ultrafiltration will occur with a net outward pressure of 56 mm Hg.
    (d) Reabsorption will occur with a net inward pressure of 24 mm Hg.
    (e) Reabsorption will occur with a net inward pressure of 10 mm Hg.

ANSWER: a

44. Which of the following alterations could lead to edema?

    (a) A fall in capillary blood pressure.
    (b) A fall in the concentration of plasma proteins.
    (c) A rise in interstitial-fluid hydrostatic pressure.
    (d) Two of the above are correct.
    (e) All of the above are correct.

ANSWER: b

45. What is the primary reason that edema may occur with serious burns?

    (a) Increased venous pressure due to interference with circulation through scarring in the burned area.
    (b) Lowering of plasma-colloid osmotic pressure due to the loss of protein-rich fluid from the surface of the burn.
    (c) Blockage of lymphatic drainage from the burned area.
    (d) Loss of protein in the urine.
    (e) Increased tissue pressure.

ANSWER: b

46.   Edema could result from

1. blockage of lymph vessels.
2. increased capillary blood pressure.
3. decreased plasma-colloid osmotic pressure.

(a)   Answers (1), (2), and (3) above are correct.
(b)   Answers (1) and (2) above are correct.
(c)   Answers (2) and (3) above are correct.
(d)   Answers (1) and (3) above are correct.
(e)   None of the above are correct.

ANSWER: a

47.   Which of the following conditions might be associated with edema?

(a)   Extensive burns.
(b)   Congestive heart failure.
(c)   Kidney disease.
(d)   Two of the above are correct.
(e)   All of the above are correct.

ANSWER: e

48.   Which of the following is **not** a function of the lymphatic system?

(a)   Defense against disease.
(b)   Return of fluid to the circulatory system.
(c)   Transport of fat molecules absorbed in the intestine.
(d)   Transport of hormones.
(e)   Return of plasma proteins to the circulatory system.

ANSWER: d

49.   The veins

(a)   act as low-resistance passageways for blood flow from the tissues to the heart.
(b)   can serve as a blood reservoir by adjusting their total capacity to accommodate variations in blood volume.
(c)   contain one-way valves that prevent the backflow of blood.
(d)   Both (a) and (c) above are correct.
(e)   All of the above are correct.

ANSWER: e

50. Which vessels can act as a blood reservoir by adjusting their total capacity to accommodate variations in blood volume?

     (a)   Arteries.
     (b)   Arterioles.
     (c)   Capillaries.
     (d)   Veins.
     (e)   Lymph vessels.

ANSWER: d

51. The venous valves

     (a)   actively contract to force blood uphill against gravity.
     (b)   passively close to prevent the backflow of blood in the veins.
     (c)   are positioned at the entrances to the atria.
     (d)   Both (b) and (c) above are correct.
     (e)   All of the above are correct.

ANSWER: b

52. In addition to the heart, what other part of the circulatory system has valves?

     (a)   Arteries.
     (b)   Large veins.
     (c)   Blood capillaries.
     (d)   Lymphatic capillaries.
     (e)   Arterioles

ANSWER: b

53. Heart valves and venous valves serve a similar function. They prevent a _____ flow of blood.

     (a)   forward
     (b)   backward
     (c)   turbulent
     (d)   pulsatile
     (e)   laminar

ANSWER: b

54. The walls of the veins contain smooth muscle innervated by
     sympathetic nerve fibers. Sympathetic stimulation
     _____ venous pressure and drives _____ blood into
     the heart.

     (a) increases, more
     (b) increases, less
     (c) decreases, more
     (d) decreases, less
     (e) None of the above are correct.

ANSWER: a

55. Which of the following factors aids venous return to the
     heart?

     (a) Sympathetic stimulation increases venous pressure.
     (b) Skeletal muscle pump squeezes blood through the veins.
     (c) Respiratory pump provides a pressure gradient between
          the lower veins and the chest veins.
     (d) Venous valves prevent backflow of blood.
     (e) All of the above are correct.

ANSWER: e

56. Under resting conditions, over 60% of the total blood volume
     is found in which of the following?

     (a) Arteries.
     (b) Arterioles.
     (c) Capillaries.
     (d) Veins.
     (e) Heart chambers

ANSWER: d

57. The two determinants of mean arterial pressure are
     _____ and _____.

     (a) stroke volume, compliance of vessel walls
     (b) heart rate, stroke volume
     (c) heart rate, end-diastolic volume
     (d) cardiac output, total peripheral resistance
     (e) None of the above are correct.

ANSWER: d

58.   Mean arterial blood pressure

    (a)   equals stroke volume times heart rate.
    (b)   is 91 mm Hg when the blood pressure is recorded as 117/78.

    (c)   is 97.5 mm Hg when the blood pressure is recorded as 117/78.
    (d)   Both (a) and (b) above are correct.
    (e)   Both (a) and (c) above are correct.

ANSWER: b

59.   When the blood pressure becomes elevated above normal,

    (a)   the carotid-sinus and aortic-arch baroreceptors increase the rate of firing in the afferent nerves.
    (b)   the cardiovascular control center decreases sympathetic and increases parasympathetic activity to the heart and blood vessels.
    (c)   arteriolar vasodilation occurs as a compensatory response.
    (d)   Two of the above are correct.
    (e)   All of the above are correct.

ANSWER: e

60.   Which of the following does **not** occur to compensate for a fall in blood pressure below normal?

    (a)   Cardiac output is increased.
    (b)   Total peripheral resistance is decreased.
    (c)   Heart rate is increased.
    (d)   Venous vasoconstriction occurs.
    (e)   Stroke volume is increased.

ANSWER: b

61.   The cardiovascular center in the brain for regulation of systemic blood pressure is located in the

    (a)   carotid sinus.
    (b)   spinal cord.
    (c)   hypothalamus.
    (d)   medulla.
    (e)   sinoatrial node.

ANSWER: d

62. Regulation of arterial pressure is mediated by reflex mechanisms. One important pressure receptor, a _____, is located in the _____.

   (a) chemoreceptor, carotid sinus
   (b) exteroceptor, carotid sinus
   (c) baroreceptor, carotid sinus
   (d) chemoreceptor, skeletal muscles
   (e) baroreceptor, skeletal muscles

ANSWER: c

63. When the receptor potential of the baroreceptors decreases, the cardiovascular center responds by bringing about

   (a) an increase in stroke volume.
   (b) an increase in venous return.
   (c) an increase in total peripheral resistance.
   (d) Two of the above are correct.
   (e) All of the above are correct .

ANSWER: e

64. A sudden increase in pressure within the carotid sinus and aortic arch baroreceptors reflexly leads to

   (a) increased sympathetic nerve activity.
   (b) increased sympathetic nerve activity and decreased parasympathetic nerve activity.
   (c) decreased sympathetic nerve activity and increased parasympathetic nerve activity.
   (d) decreased sympathetic nerve activity.
   (e) None of the above are correct.

ANSWER: c

65. _____ refers to a chronic state of increased arterial pressure.

   (a) Shock
   (b) Congestive heart failure
   (c) Pulmonary edema
   (d) Angina pectoris
   (e) Hypertension

ANSWER: e

66. Which of the following does not occur as a compensation for hemorrhage?

   (a) A shift of fluid from the interstitial fluid into the plasma.
   (b) Reduced urinary output.
   (c) Increased capillary permeability.
   (d) Increased cardiac output.
   (e) Increased synthesis of plasma proteins.

ANSWER: c

67. Which of the following tissues have the most powerful local control mechanisms with which the override generalized sypathetic vasoconstriction?   (Indicate all answers that apply)

   (a) skin
   (b) heart
   (c) kidneys
   (d) digestive organs
   (e) skeletal muscle
   (f) brain

ANSWER: b, e

68. Which of the following characteristics apply to veins? (Indicate all answers that apply)

   (a) Low-resistance vessels
   (b) Slow velocity of blood flow
   (c) Highly distensible
   (d) Display elastic recoil
   (e) Innervated by sympathetic nerves
   (f) Serve as passageways from tissues to heart
   (g) Act as a pressure reservoir
   (h) Act as a blood reservoir
   (i) Contain one-way valves
   (j) Resistance increased upon vasoconstriction
   (k) Normally contain 60% of the total blood volume

ANSWER: a, c, e, f, h, i, k

True/False

69. Organs that recondition the blood normally receive considerably more of the cardiac output than is necessary to meet their metabolic needs.

ANSWER: True

70. Organs that do not adjust the blood are more vulnerable t
    reductions in blood flow than are the organs that perform
    homeostatic functions on the blood.

ANSWER: True

71. If driving pressure is constant, blood flow rate will double
    through a vessel when the radius of the vessel increases by
    two-fold.

ANSWER: False

72. Resistance to blood flow increases as the viscosity of the
    blood increases.

ANSWER: True

73. Vasoconstriction refers to a decrease in the radius of a
    vessel.

ANSWER: True

74. A major function of the arteries is to serve as a blood
    reservoir.

ANSWER: False

75. More blood is delivered to the tissues during ventricular
    systole than during ventricular diastole.

ANSWER: False

76. When the heart is not ejecting blood into the arterial
    system, the pressure in the arteries falls to zero as blood
    drains off into the rest of the vasculature.

ANSWER: False

77. There is a constant flow of blood through the capillaries
    even though the heart is forcing blood out into the arterial
    system only part of the time.

ANSWER: True

78. The sphygmomanometer and stethoscope can be used for a
    direct measurement of arterial blood pressure.

ANSWER: False

easurement of arterial pressure using a sphygmomanometer
.s possible because turbulent blood flow that occurs as
arterial pressure overcomes a partially occluded artery can
be heard by a stethoscope placed just over the artery.

ER: True

Arterial walls contain a thick layer of smooth muscle and
an abundance of collagen and elastin fibers.

JSWER: True

81.   The pulse pressure is the maximum pressure exerted in the
arteries.

ANSWER: False

82.   If the diastolic pressure and systolic pressure were both
increased by 10 mm Hg, then the pulse pressure would also
be increased by 10 mm Hg.

ANSWER: False

83.   Local control mechanisms can override sympathetic control
of arteriolar caliber.

ANSWER: True

84.   During exercise, blood flow to the digestive tract is
increased by dilation of the arterioles of the digestive
tract.

ANSWER: False

85.   Arteriolar resistance is regulated by both local controls
and extrinsic controls.

ANSWER: True

86.   Histamine released in injured areas produces local
arteriolar vasodilation.

ANSWER: True

87.   Differences in blood flow to an organ are related to the
resistance to flow offered by the arterioles that supply that
organ.

ANSWER: True

88. The regulation of blood flow in the arterioles of the brain is mainly under the control of the sympathetic nervou system.

ANSWER: False

89. Active hyperemia occurs in response to circulating epinephrine.

ANSWER: False

90. Increased sympathetic stimulation causes generalized vasoconstriction.

ANSWER: True

91. The greatest pressure drop in the vascular system occurs within the capillaries due to fluid leaving the capillaries by the process of ultrafiltration.

ANSWER: False

92. Normally the extra fluid filtered but not reabsorbed at the capillary level is picked up by the lymphatics.

ANSWER: True

93. The lymphatic system serves no useful function other than returning excess interstitial fluid to the blood.

ANSWER: False

94. The ultimate function of the circulatory system is accomplished by the heart.

ANSWER: False

95. All the fluid forced out of the capillaries is filtered through the lymphatics before being returned to the venous blood.

ANSWER: False

96. Velocity of blood flow is the slowest in the veins because the blood must move uphill against gravity in these vessels.

ANSWER: False

97. The velocity of blood flow through the capillaries is the slowest of all the blood vessels.

ANSWER: True

n   The primary means by which individual substances are
s   exchanged between the blood and surrounding tissues is by
     bulk flow.

ER: False

The main process by which exchange of solutes occurs
between the blood and interstitial fluid at the capillary
level is passive diffusion down concentration gradients.

ANSWER: True

100. Glucose is actively transported across the capillary walls.

ANSWER: False

101. Plasma proteins are responsible for the blood-colloid
     osmotic pressure.

ANSWER: True

102. The capillary vessel walls are more permeable than the
     lymphatic vessel walls.

ANSWER: False

103. Normally most of the blood at any one time is in the
     capillary beds, because this is where material exchange is
     taking place.

ANSWER: False

104. Bulk flow refers to the volume of blood ejected by each
     ventricle each minute.

ANSWER: False

105. The vessels with the greatest total cross-sectional area
     are the arteries.

ANSWER: False

106. Because the capillaries have the smallest radii of any
     vascular segment, they are the major resistive vessels.

ANSWER: False

107. An increase in blood-colloid osmotic pressure will
     decrease ultrafiltration and increase reabsorption at the
     capillary level.

ANSWER: True

108. Edema refers to excess interstitial fluid.

ANSWER: True

109. The skeletal-muscle pump helps counteract the effect of gravity on the venous system.

ANSWER: True

110. Cardiac contraction induces blood flow in the arterial system but it has no influence on blood flow in the veins.

ANSWER: False

111. Edema, venous pooling, and a reduction in cardiac output are consequences of standing still for a long time.

ANSWER: True

112. The effective circulating volume is reduced when blood collects in distended varicose veins.

ANSWER: False

113. It is important to try to hold a fainted person upright.

ANSWER: False

114. The flow rate of blood is the same in all segments of the vascular tree, but the velocity of blood flow is slower in the capillaries than in other segments of the vascular tree.

ANSWER: True

115. Primary hypertension refers to chronically elevated blood pressure of unknown origin.

ANSWER: True

116. The baroreceptors are usually no longer functional in the presence of hypertension.

ANSWER: False

117. Irreversible shock occurs when the cardiovascular system itself starts to deteriorate as a side effect from compensatory measures to the severe hypotension.

ANSWER: True

ι-the-blanks

ιist the two functions of arteries.
_____ and _____

ιR: passageway to tissues, pressure reservoir

Arteriolar smooth muscle normally displays a state of partial constriction known as _____.

ϽWER: tone

ι0. Relaxation of arteriolar smooth muscle causes the radius of the vessel to _____, a process known as _____, whereas contraction of arteriolar smooth muscle causes the radius of the vessel to _____, a process known as _____.

ANSWERS: increase, vasodilation, decrease, vasoconstriction

121. What category of controls (local or extrinsic) is primarily responsible for matching tissue blood flow with the metabolic needs of the specific tissue involved?
_____

ANSWER: local

122. What two hormones primarily involved in fluid balance are also potent vasoconstrictors? _____ and _____.

ANSWERS: vasopressin, angiotensin II

123. Movement of fluid out of the capillaries into the interstitial fluid is known as _____.

ANSWER: ultrafiltration

124. Movement of fluid from the interstitial fluid into the plasma is known as _____.

ANSWER: reabsorption

125. Accumulation of excess interstitial fluid is known as _____.

ANSWER: edema

126. The primary mechanism for exchange of individual solutes across the capillary wall is _____.

ANSWER: diffusion down individual concentration gradients

127. The process of _____ is responsible for determining the distribution of the extracellular flu volume between the plasma and interstitial fluid.

ANSWER: bulk flow

128. The presence of _____ in the blood is responsible for the plasma-colloid osmotic pressure.

ANSWER: plasma proteins

129. Mean arterial pressure = _____ x _____.

ANSWERS: cardiac output, total peripheral resistance

130. Cardiac output = _____ x _____.

ANSWERS: heart rate, stroke volume

131. Total peripheral resistance is primarily dependent on _____.

ANSWER: the degree of arteriolar vasoconstriction

132. The receptors for the baroreceptor reflex are located in the _____ and _____, whereas the integrating center is the _____ located in the _____. The efferent pathway for this reflex is the _____. The effector organs are the _____ and _____.

ANSWERS: carotid sinus, aortic arch; cardiovascular control center; medulla; autonomic nervous system; heart, blood vessels

133. Assume a person has a blood pressure recording of 125/77:

    (a) What is the systolic pressure?_____
    (b) What is the diastolic pressure?_____
    (c) What is the pulse pressure?_____
    (d) What is the mean arterial pressure?_____
    (e) Would any sound be heard when the pressure in an external cuff around the arm was 130 mm Hg - yes or no? _____
    (f) Would any sound be heard when cuff pressure was 118 mm Hg? _____
    (g) Would any sound be heard when cuff pressure was 75 mm Hg? _____

ANSWERS: a.125, b.77, c.48, d.93, e.no, f.yes, g.no

3

d

idicate which of the vessels performs the function listed
y writing the appropriate letter in the blank using the
nswer code below.

    (a) = arteries
    (b) = arterioles
    (c) = capillaries
    (d) = veins
    (e) = lymphatics

_____ Site of exchange of nutrients and waste products
between the blood and surrounding tissues.
_____ Serve as low-resistance passageways from the heart to
the tissues.
_____ Serve as a blood reservoir to accommodate variations in
blood volume.
_____ Major resistive vessels.
_____ Portion of the circulatory system through which the
velocity of blood flow is the slowest.
_____ Serve as low-resistance passageways from the tissues to
the heart.
_____ Act as a pressure reservoir to drive blood forward
throughout the vasculature during cardiac diastole.
_____ Changes in the radius of this vessel type regulate the
distribution of the cardiac output to various areas of
the body.
_____ Vessels that pick up fluid that is filtered but not
reabsorbed.

ANSWERS: c, a, d, b, c, d, a, b, e

135. Indicate what effect the changes in question would have on
blood flow, using the following answer code:

(a) = This change would increase blood flow
(b) = This change would decrease blood flow
(c) = This change would have no effect on blood flow

_____ Increasing the pressure gradient in a vessel.
_____ Increasing the resistance of a vessel.
_____ Increasing the radius of a vessel.
_____ Increasing the number of circulating red blood
cells.

ANSWERS: a, b, a, b

136. If the blood pressure is recorded as 118/76, indicate th[
correct value of the pressure in question by writing the
appropriate letter in the blank using the answer code belo[

(a) = 118 mm Hg
(b) = 42 mm Hg
(c) = 97 mm Hg
(d) = 76 mm Hg
(e) = 90 mm Hg

_____ What is the systolic pressure?
_____ What is the diastolic pressure?
_____ What is the pulse pressure?
_____ What is the mean pressure?

ANSWERS: a, d, b, e

137. Indicate what effect the change in question would have on
bulk flow using the answer code below:

(a) = the change would increase ultrafiltration and
        decrease reabsorption
(b) = the change would decrease ultrafiltration and
        increase reabsorption
(c) = the change would increase both ultrafiltration
        and reabsorption
(d) = the change would decrease both ultrafiltration
        and reabsorption
(e) = the change would not alter ultrafiltration and
        reabsorption

_____ loss of plasma protein in the urine due to kidney
        disease.
_____ rise in capillary blood pressure in connection with
        congestive heart failure.
_____ loss of plasma volume due to hemorrhage.
_____ escape of plasma proteins into the interstitial fluid
        due to capillary damage.
_____ reduced synthesis of plasma proteins due to liver
        disease.
_____ expanded plasma volume due to excessive fluid intake.

ANSWERS: a, a, b, a, a, a

e   dicate whether arteriolar vasoconstriction or
          sodilation would occur in the tissue in question by using
.   ie following answer code:

(a) = would produce arteriolar vasoconstriction
(b) = would produce arteriolar vasodilation
(c) = would not cause any change in arteriolar caliber

_____ decreased O_2 in skeletal muscle
_____ a hyperemic response in the heart
_____ histamine release in an injured tissue
_____ application of ice to a sprained ankle
_____ norepinephrine on cerebral arterioles
_____ sympathetic stimulation of kidney arterioles
_____ parasympathetic discharge on skeletal muscle
        arterioles

ANSWERS: b, b, b, a, c, a, c

Calculations

139. The calculations below are based on the following pressures:

Blood capillary pressure at arteriolar end of tissue capillaries: 35 mm Hg
Blood capillary pressure at venule end of tissue capillaries: 15 mm Hg
Plasma-colloid osmotic pressure: 20 mm Hg
Interstitial-fluid hydrostatic pressure: 1 mm Hg
Interstitial-fluid-colloid osmotic pressure: 0 mm Hg

_____ What would the ultrafiltration pressure be?
   (a)   14 mm Hg
   (b)   16 mm Hg
   (c)   9 mm Hg
   (d)   10 mm Hg
   (e)   35 mm Hg

_____ What would the reabsorption pressure be?
   (a)   21 mm Hg
   (b)   15 mm Hg
   (c)   6 mm Hg
   (d)   14 mm Hg
   (e)   20 mm Hg

_____ Would edema occur in this situation?
   (a)   yes
   (b)   no

ANSWERS: a, c, a

Identifying Relationships

140. Indicate the relative comparison of each of the paired items by writing the appropriate letter in the blank using the answer code below.

> (a) = A is greater than B
> (b) = B is greater than A
> (c) = A and B are equal

_____ A. Blood flow through an arteriole upon increased sympathetic activity.
        B. Blood flow through an arteriole upon decreased sympathetic activity.

_____ A. Blood flow through a vein upon increased sympathetic activity.
        B. Blood flow through a vein upon decreased sympathetic activity.

_____ A. Velocity of blood flow through the veins.
        B. Velocity of blood flow through the capillaries.

_____ A. Local arteriolar radius in the presence of local decreased O_2 concentration and increased CO_2 concentration.
        B. Local arteriolar radius with normal local concentration of O_2 and CO_2.

_____ A. Circulation through the skin during exercise.
        B. Circulation through the skin at rest.

_____ A. Circulation to the brain at rest.
        B. Circulation to the brain during an examination.

_____ A. Net ultrafiltration pressure at the arteriolar end of the capillary.
        B. Net reabsorption pressure at the venous end of the capillary.

ANSWERS: b, a, a, a, a, c, a

141. When blood pressure falls below normal, indicate what happens to each of the following factors to restore the blood pressure back toward normal.

I.   When the blood pressure falls below normal, the rate of firing in the afferent nerves originating from the carotid-sinus and aortic-arch baroreceptors _____.

   (a) increases
   (b) decreases
   (c) does not change

II. As a result of I., the medullary cardiovascular center responds by _____ the rate of firing in the sympathetic cardiac nerve.

   (a) increasing
   (b) decreasing
   (c) not changing

III. Also as a result of I., the cardiovascular center _____ the rate of firing in the parasympathetic nerve supply to the heart.

   (a) increases
   (b) decreases
   (c) does not alter

IV. Also as a result of I., the rate of firing in the sympathetic vasoconstrictor nerve _____ by the cardiovascular center.

   (a) is increased
   (b) is decreased
   (c) is not altered

V.   As a result of II. and III., the rate of firing of the SA node _____.

   (a) increases
   (b) decreases
   (c) remains unchanged

VI. As a result of V., the heart rate _____.

   (a) increases
   (b) decreases
   (c) remains unchanged

VII. As a result of IV., _____.

    (a) arteriolar vasoconstriction occurs
    (b) arteriolar vasodilation occurs
    (c) there is no change in arteriolar radius

VIII. As a result of VII., total peripheral resistance _____.

    (a) increases
    (b) decreases
    (c) remains unchanged

IX. Also as a result of IV., _____.

    (a) venous vasoconstriction occurs
    (b) venous vasodilation occurs
    (c) there is no change in venous radius

X. As a result of IX., venous return _____.

    (a) increases
    (b) decreases
    (c) remains unchanged

XI. As a result of X., end-diastolic volume _____.

    (a) increases
    (b) decreases
    (c) remains unchanged

XII. As a result of II. and XI., stroke volume _____.

    (a) increases
    (b) decreases
    (c) remains unchanged

XIII. As a result of VI. and XII., cardiac output _____.

    (a) increases
    (b) decreases
    (c) remains unchanged

XIV. As a result of VIII. and XIII., blood pressure _____.

    (a) increases to normal
    (b) decreases to normal
    (c) remains unchanged

ANSWERS: b, a, b, a, a, a, a, a, a, a, a, a, a, a

For questions 142 through 165, choose the appropriate letter
from the answer code below to make the statement true.

        (a) = stimulates or increases
        (b) = decreases or inhibits
        (c) = has no effect on

142. Increased blood pressure _____ the rate of firing in afferent nerves arising from the baroreceptors.

143. Decreased rate of firing in afferent nerves reaching the cardiovascular control center _____ the parasympathetic nerve activity to the cardiovascular system.

144. Decreased rate of firing in afferent nerves reaching the cardiovascular control center _____ the sympathetic nerve activity to the cardiovascular system.

145. Increased parasympathetic nerve activity _____ the strength of cardiac ventricular contraction.

146. Increased sympathetic nerve activity _____ the rate of depolarization of the SA node.

147. Increased sympathetic nerve activity _____ the strength of cardiac ventricular contraction.

148. Increased sympathetic nerve activity _____ the stroke volume.

149. Increased parasympathetic nerve activity _____ the heart rate.

150. Increased heart rate _____ cardiac output.

151. Decreased stroke volume _____ cardiac output.

152. Decreased stroke volume _____ heart rate.

153. Decreased sympathetic nerve activity _____ the arteriolar radius.

154. Increased arteriolar radius _____ the total peripheral resistance.

155. Increased total peripheral resistance _____ the mean systemic arterial blood pressure.

156. Decreased cardiac output _____ the mean systemic arterial blood pressure.

157. Increased skeletal muscle activity _____ venous return.

158. Decreased O_2 and increased CO_2, concentrations in a skeletal
      muscle _____ the radius of the arterioles supplying this
      skeletal muscle.

159. Increased sympathetic nerve activity _____ the venous
      radius.

160. Decreased venous radius _____ the venous return.

161. Increased venous return _____ the end-diastolic volume.

162. Decreased venous return _____ the stroke volume.

163. Decreased arteriolar radius _____ the blood flow through
      the arteriole.

164. Decreased venous radius _____ the blood flow through the
      vein.

165. Increased parasympathetic nerve activity _____ total
      peripheral resistance.

ANSWERS: 142-a, 143-b, 144-a, 145-c, 146-a, 147-a, 148-a,
           149-b, 150-a, 151-b, 152-c, 153-a, 154-b, 155-a,
           156-b, 157-a, 158-a, 159-b, 160-a, 161-a, 162-b,
           163-b, 164-a, 165-c

AUDIOVISUAL AIDS

Films

A list of films available from West Publishing Company is
presented in Appendix A.   Following are other films that may be
suitable. The sources for these films, which are coded by
abbreviation, are provided in Appendix B.

   Adrenergic Receptors, ICI, 20 min.

   Arterial and Venous Blood, IF, 3 min.

   Arterial and Venous Pressures, IF, 3 min.

   Arterial Blood Pressure Regulation, JW, 19 min.

   Atherosclerosis, MI, 33 min.

   Bleeding and Shock, USNAC, 51 min.

Blood Circulation   , EBF, 15 min.

Blood Pressure, Theory and Process, WAYNE

Circulation, UW, 16 min.

Circulation - Historical Perspective, MH, 29 min.

Disorders of the Cardiovascular System, TRA, 13 min.

Exercise Testing, TRA, 14 min.

Heart and Circulation, EBE, 11 min.

Hemo the Magnificent, WAV, 59 min.

High Blood Pressure, MF, 10 min.

Human Body: Circulatory System, COR, 13 min.

Hypertension, AMA, 20 min.

Hypoxia and the Role of the Peripheral Circulation, UI, 30 min.

Measuring Blood Pressure, WG, 10 min.

Risk Factors of Coronary Disease, MF, 12 min.

Shock, AMA, 19 min.

Shock Recognition and Management, AEF, 17 min.

Stroke, CF, 10 min.

Stroke Awareness and Prevention, MF, 10 min.

Software

Cardiovascular Fitness Lab, HRM. Provides a monitoring lab on aerobic exercise.

Cardiovascular System, PLP. Two part program that covers cardiovascular system.

Circulation, EI. Covers blood, heart, arteries, capillaries, veins, and lungs.

Dynamics of the Human Circulatory System, EI. Covers pulmonary, systemic, and lymphatic systems.

Flash: Blood Vessels, PLP. Studies aorta and more than 100 vessels.

Your Body (Series I), CBS. Tests student's knowledge of blood and the circulatory system.

Chapter 9
Blood and Body Defenses

CONTENTS
(All page references are to the main text.)

-Vascular spasm reduces blood flow through an injured
vessel. p.283
-Platelets aggregate to form a plug at a vessel defect.
 p.283
-A triggered chain reaction involving clotting factors in
the plasma results in blood coagulation. p.284
-Fibrinolytic plasmin dissolves clots and prevents inap-
propriate clot formation. p.286
-Inappropriate clotting is responsible for thromboembo-
lism. p.286
-Hemophilia is the primary condition responsible for
excessive bleeding. p.286

Leukocytes, p. 287
-Leukocytes function primarily outside of the blood. p.287
-Pathogenic bacteria and viruses are the major targets of
the immune defense system. p. 287
-There are five different types of leukocytes. p. 287
-Leukocytes are produced at varying rates, depending on
the changing defense needs of the body. p. 288

Nonspecific Immune Responses, p.290
-Immune responses may be either specific or nonspecific
-Nonspecific defenses include inflammation, interferon,
natural killer cells, and the complement system. p.290
-Inflammation is a nonspecific response to foreign invasion or tissue damage. p.290
-Salicylates and glucocorticoid drugs suppress the inflammatory response. p.293
-Interferon transiently inhibits multiplication of viruses
in most cells. p.293
-Natural killer cells destroy virus-infected cells and
tumor cells upon first exposure to them. p.293
-The complement system kills microorganisms directly on
its own and in conjunction with antibodies while augment-
ing the inflammatory response. p.294

Specific Immune Responses: General Concepts, p.295
-Specific immune responses include antibody-mediated
immunity accomplished by B lymphocyte derivatives and
cell-mediated immunity accomplished by T lymphocytes.
p.295
-An antigen induces an immune response against itself.
p.296

B Lymphocytes: Antibody-Mediated Immunity, p.296
-Antibodies amplify the inflammatory response to promote
destruction of the antigen that stimulated their produc
tion. p.296
-Each antigen stimulates a different clone of B lymphocytes to produce antibodies. p.299

-Natural immunity is actually a special case of actively acquired immunity. p.301

Beyond the Basics- Vaccination: A Victory Over Many Dreaded Diseases, p.302

   -Lymphocytes respond only to antigens that have been processed and presented to them by macrophages. p.303

T Lymphocytes: Cell-Mediated Immunity, p.303
   -The three types of T cells are specialized to kill virus-infected host cells and to help or suppress other immune cells. p.303
   -The immune system is normally tolerant of self-antigens. p.308
   -The major histocompatibility complex is the code for surface-membrane-bound human leukocyte-associated antigens unique for each individual. p.308
   -Immune surveillance against cancer cells involves an interplay among cytotoxic T cells, natural killer cells, macrophages, and interferon. p.309
   -A regulatory loop appears to link the immune system and the nervous and endocrine systems. p.310

Immune Diseases, p. 311
   -Immune deficiency diseases reduce resistance to foreign invaders. p.311
   -Inappropriate immune attacks against harmless environmental substances are responsible for allergies. p.311

External Defenses, p.313
   -The skin consists of an outer protective epidermis and an inner connective tissue dermis. p.313
   -Specialized cells in the epidermis produce keratin and melanin and participate in immune defense. p.406
   -Protective measures within body cavities that communicate with the external environment discourage pathogen invasion into the body. p.315

Chapter in Perspective: Focus on Homeostasis, p.316

Chapter Summary, p.317

LECTURE HINTS AND SUGGESTIONS

1.   Use colored slides to illustrate the various blood
     cells and their staining reactions. Also, use
     electron micrographs of various blood cells. These
     and the materials below can be obtained from Carolina
     Biological Supply Company, Burlington, NC.

2.   Demonstrate the technique for determining blood types
     and Rh factor. See any general physiology lab manual
     for procedures and supplies.

3.   Use models to illustrate the various components of
     blood.

4.   Display equipment used in determining the hematocrit,
     blood cell count, coagulation time, fibrin formation,
     etc. If available, demonstrate a Coulter counter.

5.   Put out demonstration microscope slides of
     histological preparations of normal and abnormal
     blood; e.g., sickle cell anemia and leukemia.

6.   Alert your students to the medical terminology
     associated with blood; for example, BUN, hematocrit,
     HDL, LDL, serum GOT.

7.   Use a bag of dated human blood to explain the
     information contained on the label. Labels can be
     obtained from local blood banks.

8.   Show blood and bone marrow slides from patients with
     anemia and leukemia.

9.   Use Carolina Biological Supply Company molecular
     models to demonstrate the various components of blood
     plasma.

10. Discuss a computer print-out of a typical blood
     profile from a physical examination. Examples to be
     covered include blood gases, BUN, cholesterol, LDL,
     creatinine, glucose, etc.

11. Discuss in further detail the pathogenesis and
     treatment of erythroblastosis fetalis. Do the same
     for sickle cell anemia.

12. Use a torso or full-body manikin to illustrate the locations of the various lymphoid tissues. This and other material suggested below is available from Carolina Biological Supply Company, Burlington NC, as well as other supply houses.

13. Demonstrate a lymph node model to illustrate its structure.

14. Direct students in the correct way to palpate their own lymph nodes; e.g., in the arm pits and neck. See a nursing textbook for examples.

15. Use Ouchterlony plates that demonstrate antigen-antibody reactions in vitro. These will need to be prepared ahead of time. See a general microbiology lab manual for procedure.

16. Use 2 x 2 slides to show the different defensive cells.

17. Good electron micrographs of phagocytosis are available.

18. Show some computer-generated models of antibody structure.

19. Show x-ray films of various cancers. These can be obtained from your local American Cancer Society chapter or from a local radiologist.

20. 2 x 2 slides of the various immune diseases are informative. Examples included could be blood transfusion reactions, hemolytic diseases of the newborn, allergies, AIDS, transplant rejection, etc.

21. Show slides of recombinant DNA technology.

22. Use a slide of bone marrow to demonstrate the genesis of leukocytes.

23. Obtain a 3-D model that illustrates the concept of antigen-antibody binding.

CHAPTER TEST QUESTIONS

   Multiple Choice

1. The normal constituents of blood plasma include all of the
    following **except**

      (a) water.
      (b) electrolytes.
      (c) proteins.
      (d) gases (O_2, CO_2, N_2).
      (e) red blood cells.

    ANSWER: e

2. Which of the following is **not** a function of plasma
    proteins?

      (a) Plasma proteins are responsible for the
           plasma colloid osmotic pressure.

      (b) Plasma proteins provide a source of readily available
           amino acids to be utilized by the tissue cells for
           the synthesis of new tissue proteins.
      (c) Antibodies are gamma globulins, a type of plasma
           protein that is important in the body's defense
           mechanism.
      (d) Plasma proteins play a role in buffering changes in pH
           in the body fluids.
      (e) The presence of plasma proteins in the blood is the
           primary factor responsible for preventing excessive
           loss of plasma from the capillaries into the inter-
           stitial fluid.

ANSWER: b

3. If the hematocrit is 42, what percentage of the whole blood
    is composed of plasma?

      (a) 42%
      (b) 55%
      (c) 58%
      (d) 45%
      (e) 50%

ANSWER: c

4. If the hematocrit is 40 then

    (a) the volume occupied by the red blood cells is 60%
         of the total blood volume.
    (b) the volume occupied by the white blood cells is
         40% of the total blood volume.
    (c) the volume occupied by the red blood cells is 40% of
         the total blood volume.
    (d) the volume occupied by the plasma and other cellular
         elements is 40% of the total blood volume.
    (e) More than one of the above are correct.

ANSWER: c

5. The hematocrit

    (a) refers to the percentage of plasma in the blood.
    (b) refers to the packed cell volume when a blood sample
         is centrifuged.
    (c) is increased in aplastic anemia.
    (d) Two of the above are correct.
    (e) None of the above are correct.

ANSWER: b

6. Antibodies

    (a) are gamma globulins.
    (b) are a type of plasma protein.
    (c) are produced by B lymphocytes.
    (d) Two of the above are correct.
    (e) All of the above are correct.

ANSWER: e

7. Which of the following statements concerning erythrocytes
    is **incorrect**?

    (a) Erythrocytes do not contain a nucleus,
         organelles, or ribosomes.
    (b) Erythrocytes are produced in the spleen.
    (c) Erythrocytes originate from the same undifferentiated
         pluripotential stem cells as leukocytes and platelets.
    (d) Erythrocytes are unable to utilize the O_2 they
         contain for their own ATP formation.
    (e) Erythrocytes only live about 120 days.

ANSWER: b

8. Erythrocytes

   (a) do not contain a nucleus.
   (b) survive an average of 120 days.
   (c) do not have the ability to use O_2 for energy production despite the fact that they transport O_2 to all the other tissues of the body.
   (d) Both (a) and (b) above are correct.
   (e) All of the above are correct.

ANSWER: e

9. Which is the most abundant type of cellular element in the blood?

   (a) Erythrocytes.
   (b) Neutrophils.
   (c) Leukocytes.
   (d) Lymphocytes.
   (e) Platelets.

ANSWER: a

10. Red blood cells

   (a) carry oxygen.
   (b) form the meshwork of a blood clot.
   (c) defend the body against foreign substances.
   (d) are capable of active movement.
   (e) possess all of the organelles found in other cell types.

ANSWER: a

11. Hemoglobin

   (a) consists of a protein made up of four highly folded polypeptide chains and four iron-containing, non protein, nitrogenous groups.
   (b) appears reddish when combined with O_2 and bluish when deoxygenated.
   (c) can combine only with O_2.
   (d) Both (a) and (b) above are correct.
   (e) All of the above are correct.

ANSWER: d

12. Hemoglobin

   (a)   is found in the nuclei of red blood cells.
   (b)   contains carbonic anhydrase.
   (c)   can combine with O_2, CO_2, H^+, and CO.
   (d)   Both (b) and (c) above are correct.
   (e)   All of the above are correct.

ANSWER: c

13. Iron

   (a)   can combine reversibly with O_2.
   (b)   deficiency can produce anemia.
   (c)   is converted into bilirubin and secreted into the
         bile when an old red blood cell ruptures and is
         degraded.
   (d)   Both (a) and (b) above are correct.
   (e)   All of the above are correct.

14. Which of the following statements concerning iron is
    incorrect?

   (a)   Iron is found in the heme portion of the
         hemoglobin molecule.
   (b)   Iron is converted into bilirubin upon
         erythrocyte degradation.
   (c)   Iron readily combines reversibly with O_2.
   (d)   Diets deficient in iron can lead to
         anemia.
   (e)   Iron is not adequately absorbed from the
         digestive tract in pernicious anemia.

ANSWER: b

15. Erythropoiesis

   (a)   is accomplished in the bone marrow upon stimulation
         by erythropoietin.
   (b)   is accomplished in the kidneys in response to reduced
         O_2 delivery to the kidneys.
   (c)   refers to an increase in the number of circulating
         red blood cells.
   (d)   refers to the destruction of erythrocytes by the
         macrophages.
   (e)   None of the above are correct.

ANSWER: a

16. Erythropoietin

    (a) is secreted by the bone marrow.
    (b) stimulates red blood cell production.
    (c) converts prothrombin to thrombin.
    (d) is deficient in pernicious anemia.
    (e) More than one of the above are correct.

ANSWER: b

17. Anemia results from a reduced O_2-carrying capacity of the blood, which can be caused by a decrease in the number of

    (a) leukocytes.
    (b) lymphocytes.
    (c) macrophages.
    (d) erythrocytes.
    (e) monocytes.

    ANSWER: d

18. Which of the following is **not** a possible cause of anemia?

    (a) Dietary deficiency of folic acid.
    (b) Deficiency of intrinsic factor.
    (c) Malaria.
    (d) Kidney disease
    (e) Living at high altitude.

ANSWER: e

19. In aplastic anemia

    (a) there is insufficient hemoglobin formation due to iron deficiency.
    (b) there is an acute loss of blood.
    (c) destruction of the bone marrow has occurred as a result of exposure to toxic chemicals or radiation.
    (d) the stomach secretes inadequate intrinsic factor, which is essential for intestinal absorption of vitamin B_{12}.
    (e) there is increased fragility of the erythrocyte cell membrane.

ANSWER: c

20. Which of the following statements concerning platelets is **incorrect**?

   (a) Platelets are produced in the bone marrow.
   (b) Platelets form the meshwork of a blood clot upon which the other cellular elements become entrapped.
   (c) Platelets form a plug when they adhere to the exposed collagen of a damaged vessel.
   (d) Aggregated platelets release ADP, which causes the surface of nearby circulating platelets to become sticky so that they also adhere to the enlarging platelet plug.
   (e) Platelets are small cell fragments that have budded off the outer edges of bone marrow - bound megakaryocytes.

ANSWER: b

21. Which of the following statements concerning platelets is **incorrect**?

   (a) Platelets do not adhere to normal vascular surfaces.
   (b) Aggregated platelets release ADP, which causes other platelets to become sticky and adhere to the platelet plug.
   (c) Platelets directly convert fibrinogen to fibrin.
   (d) A platelet plug releases chemicals that cause the injured vessel to constrict.
   (e) Platelets are produced in the bone marrow.

22. Platelets

   (a) are small cell fragments derived from large mega-karyocytes in the bone marrow.
   (b) lack nuclei.
   (c) contain high concentrations of actin and myosin, which enable them to contract.
   (d) Both (a) and (b) above are correct.
   (e) All of the above are correct.

ANSWER: e

23. Which of the following types of blood cellular elements
     lack nuclei?

     (a)   Platelets.
     (b)   Erythrocytes.
     (c)   Leukocytes.
     (d)   Both (a) and (b) above are correct.
     (e)   All of the above are correct.

ANSWER: d

24. Exposed collagen in a damaged vessel

     (a)   activates factor XII to initiate blood clotting.
     (b)   initiates platelet aggregation.
     (c)   secretes ADP, which causes platelets to become
           sticky.
     (d)   Both (a) and (b) above are correct.
     (e)   All of the above are correct.

ANSWER: d

25. Prostacyclin

     (a)   activates the clotting cascade.
     (b)   induces profound vasoconstriction of an injured
           vessel.
     (c)   profoundly inhibits platelet aggregation.
     (d)   is released by aggregated platelets.
     (e)   dissolves the clot.

ANSWER: c

26. What forms the meshwork of a clot?

     (a)   Red blood cells.
     (b)   Fibrin.
     (c)   Platelets.
     (d)   Thrombin.
     (e)   Hageman factor.

ANSWER: b

27. When small blood vessels are damaged, loss of blood is prevented by

    (a) platelet aggregation.
    (b) vasoconstriction of these vessels.
    (c) formation of a platelet plug.
    (d) All of the above are correct.
    (e) None of the above are correct.

ANSWER: d

28. Platelets

    (a) convert prothrombin to thrombin.
    (b) form the meshwork upon which the erythrocytes become trapped to produce a clot.
    (c) adhere and aggregate when they contact exposed collagen in the walls of a broken blood vessel.
    (d) release fibrinogen once a platelet plug is formed.
    (e) More than one of the above are correct.

ANSWER: c

29. Platelets

    (a) are important in hemostasis.
    (b) convert prothrombin to thrombin.
    (c) form the meshwork upon which the erythrocytes become trapped to produce a clot.
    (d) Two of the above are correct.
    (e) All of the above are correct.

ANSWER: a

30. The extrinsic clotting pathway

    (a) is set off by factor XII.
    (b) clots blood in an injured vessel.
    (c) has more steps than the intrinsic pathway.
    (d) More than one of the above are correct.
    (e) None of the above are correct.

ANSWER: e

31.   Tissue thromboplastin

       (a)   is released from traumatized tissue and triggers the
              extrinsic clotting pathway.
       (b)   converts fibrinogen to fibrin.
       (c)   forms the meshwork of the clot.
       (d)   activates factor XII (Hageman factor).
       (e)   More than one of the above are correct.

ANSWER: a

32.   Since fibrinogen is always present in the blood but the
       blood does not clot, _____ must normally be absent.

       (a)   prothrombin
       (b)   thrombin
       (c)   calcium
       (d)   red blood cells
       (e)   platelets

ANSWER: b

33.   Clots are slowly dissolved by

       (a)   tissue thromboplastin
       (b)   prostacyclin
       (c)   plasmin
       (d)   calcium
       (e)   exposed collagen

ANSWER: c

34.   Hemophilia results from

       (a)   a deficiency of platelets.
       (b)   inadequate hemoglobin production.
       (c)   vitamin B_{12} deficiency.
       (d)   a genetic inability to produce one of the factors in
              the clotting cascade.
       (e)   excess production of heparin.

ANSWER: d

35. White blood cells

  (a) are the most abundant type of blood cell.
  (b) do not have nuclei.
  (c) are actually only cell fragments.
  (d) defend the body against foreign invasion.
  (e) are found only in the blood.

ANSWER: d

36. Which of the following is **not** a function of white blood cells?

  (a) Activation of factor XII, which triggers the clotting cascade.
  (b) Production of antibodies.
  (c) Destruction of cancer cells.
  (d) Phagocytosis of foreign invaders.
  (e) Phagocytosis of cellular debris.

ANSWER: a

37. Polymorphonuclear granulocytes include

  (a) neutrophils.
  (b) eosinophils.
  (c) basophils.
  (d) Both (b) and (c) above are correct.
  (e) All of the above are correct.

ANSWER: e

38. Lymphocytes

  (a) are polymorphonuclear granulocytes.
  (b) are the most abundant type of leukocyte.
  (c) can be produced in lymphoid tissues as well as in the bone marrow.
  (d) Two of the above are correct.
  (e) All of the above are correct.

ANSWER: c

39.   Basophils

   (a)   contain granules that preferentially take up a basic
         blue dye.
   (b)   leave the blood to become macrophages.
   (c)   synthesize and store histamine and heparin.
   (d)   Two of the above are correct.
   (e)   All of the above are correct.

ANSWER: d

40.   An increase in the circulating number of _____ is
      associated with parasite infestations.

   (a)   neutrophils.
   (b)   eosinophils.
   (c)   basophils.
   (d)   lymphocytes.
   (e)   monocytes.

ANSWER: b

41.   _____ leave the blood after circulating for only a
      day or two and become the large tissue phagocytes known as
      macrophages.

   (a)   Neutrophils
   (b)   Eosinophils
   (c)   Basophils
   (d)   Lymphocytes
   (e)   Monocytes

ANSWER: e

42.   Which of the following can occur with leukemia?

   (a)   Inadequate defense capabilities against foreign
         invasion despite an excessive number of white blood
         cells.
   (b)   Anemia.
   (c)   Internal bleeding.
   (d)   Two of the above are correct.
   (e)   All of the above are correct.

ANSWER: e

43. Neutrophils

(a) are the most abundant type of white blood cell.
(b) attach to a parasitic worm and secrete substances
     that kill it.
(c) are stimulated to replicate and be released from the
     bone marrow in response to granulocyte colony-
     stimulating factor.
(d) are similar structurally to mast cells.
(e) Both (a) and (c) above are correct.

ANSWER: e

44. Viruses

(a) are single-celled microorganisms.
(b) consist only of nucleic acids enclosed by a
     protein coat.
(c) must invade a host cell in order to carry out metab-
     olism and reproduce.
(d) Both (a) and (c) above are correct.
(e) Both (b) and (c) above are correct.

ANSWER: e

45. Leukocytes

(a) are responsible for the body's various immune defense
     strategies.
(b) spend most of their time circulating in the blood.
(c) are all produced in the lymph nodes.
(d) Both (a) and (b) above are correct.
(e) All of the above are correct.

ANSWER: a

46. Which of the following are lymphoid tissues?

(a) Lymph nodes.
(b) Spleen.
(c) Bone marrow.
(d) Both (a) and (b) above are correct.
(e) All of the above are correct.

ANSWER: e

47. Which of the following is **not** attributable to the immune
     defense system?

     (a) Defends against pathogenic micro-
          organisms.
     (b) Converts foreign chemicals into compoundsthat
          can be more readily eliminated in the urine.
     (c) Removes worn-out cells and tissue debris.
     (d) Identifies and destroys abnormal or mutant cells.
     (e) Can inappropriately induce allergic responses and
          autoimmune disease.

ANSWER: b

48. Which of the following is **not** part of the inflammatory
     response?

     (a) localized vasodilation
     (b) migration of neutrophils and macrophages
          to the site of injury
     (c) phagocytosis of foreign invaders and cellular debris
     (d) interferon inhibition of viral replication
     (e) formation of interstitial-fluid clots that wall off
          bacterial invaders

ANSWER: d

49. Which of the following is **not** attributable to complement
     activity?

     (a) acting as opsonins
     (b) walling-off the inflamed area
     (c) serving as chemotaxins
     (d) bringing about direct lysis of invading bacteria
     (e) forming a membrane attack complex

ANSWER: b

50. Which of the following is (are) **not** accomplished by a
     chemical released from activated phagocytes?

     (a) triggering both the clotting and
          anticlotting systems
     (b) stimulating histamine release from mast
          cells
     (c) stimulating the synthesis of virus-blocking enzymes
     (d) inducing the development of fever
     (e) stimulating the synthesis and release of neutrophils
          and lymphocytes

ANSWER: c

51. Nonspecific immune responses

    (a) come into play whether or not there has been prior experience with the offending agent.
    (b) are triggered by invasion of infectious microorganisms, chemical injury, mechanical trauma, or burns.
    (c) are mediated by lymphocytes.
    (d) Both (a) and (b) above are correct.
    (e) All of the above are correct.

ANSWER: d

52. Which of the following is **not** a component of nonspecific immune responses?

    (a) Inflammation.
    (b) Antibody production.
    (c) Interferon.
    (d) Natural killer cells.
    (e) The complement system.

ANSWER: b

53. Which of the following are part of the inflammatory response?

    (a) Migration of neutrophils and macrophages to the involved area.
    (b) Localized vasodilation.
    (c) Formation of interstitial-fluid clots in the injured region.
    (d) Both (a) and (b) above are correct.
    (e) All of the above are correct.

ANSWER: e

54. Localized vasodilation in an inflamed area is brought about by the release of _____ from _____.

    (a) histamine, mast cells
    (b) opsonins, B lymphocytes
    (c) interleukin 1, mast cells
    (d) leukocyte endogenous mediator, phagocytes
    (e) prostaglandins, phagocytes

ANSWER: a

55. Which of the following properties does **not** apply to neutrophils?

    (a) Are produced only in lymph nodes.
    (b) Can perform phagocytosis.
    (c) Can leave the blood by wriggling through the capillary pores.
    (d) Can exhibit amoeboid movement.
    (e) Are attracted by chemotaxis.

ANSWER: a

56. Monocytes

    (a) are the first phagocytes to exit the blood and arrive at an injured or invaded area.
    (b) swell and mature into macrophages after exiting the blood.
    (c) act as opsonins.
    (d) Both (a) and (b) above are correct.
    (e) All of the above are correct.

ANSWER: b

57. Opsonins

    (a) enhance phagocytosis by linking the foreign cell to a phagocytic cell.
    (b) induce scar formation.
    (c) trigger the development of fever.
    (d) attract phagocytic cells to sites of damage or invasion.
    (e) cause localized vasodilation in an injured area.

ANSWER: e

58. Which of the following statements concerning endogenous pyrogen is **incorrect**? Endogenous pyrogen

    (a) is an acute-phase protein produced by the liver.
    (b) is secreted by phagocytes at a site of inflammation.
    (c) induces the development of fever.
    (d) is identical or closely related to interleukin 1.
    (e) causes the local release of prostaglandins within the hypothalamus.

ANSWER: a

59. The primary purpose of the blood vessel changes in an invaded or injured area is to

(a) produce swelling, redness, heat, and pain.
(b) bring to the affected area phagocytes and plasma proteins that defend against the offending agent.
(c) produce pus.
(d) exert an anti-inflammatory effect to protect against damage by potentially overreactive defense mechanisms.
(e) trigger specific immune responses.

ANSWER: b

60. Interferon

(a) is released from virus-infected cells.
(b) triggers the production of viral-blocking enzymes by cells that have not yet been invaded by viruses.
(c) directly breaks down viral messenger RNA and inhibits protein synthesis, both of which are essential for viral replication.
(d) Both (a) and (b) above are correct.
(e) All of the above are correct.

ANSWER: d

61. Which of the following is **not** accomplished by interferon? Interferon

(a) directly breaks down viral messenger RNA and inhibits protein synthesis, both of which are essential for viral replication.
(b) enhances macrophage phagocytic activity.
(c) stimulates antibody production.
(d) stimulates the activity of natural killer cells and cytotoxic T cells.
(e) slows cell division and suppresses tumor growth.

ANSWER: a

62. Virus-blocking enzymes

(a) are produced by cells that have been invaded by virus.
(b) are produced by cells in response to binding with interferon.
(c) are activated when a cell is invaded by virus.
(d) Both (b) and (c) above are correct.
(e) All of the above are correct.

ANSWER: d

63. Interferon

    (a) forms a membrane-attack complex.
    (b) causes lysis of invading microbes.
    (c) nonspecifically defends against viral invasion.
    (d) stimulates histamine release from mast cells.
    (e) is secreted by lymphoid tissues.

ANSWER: c

64. The complement system

    (a) consists of plasma proteins produced by the liver
        that circulate in the blood in inactive form.
    (b) is the primary mechanism activated by antibodies to
        kill foreign cells.
    (c) can be activated both nonspecifically and specifi-
        cally.
    (d) Both (a) and (b) above are correct.
    (e) All of the above are correct.

ANSWER: e

65. Which of the following is **not** attributable to activated
    components of the complement system?

    (a) Formation of a membrane-attack complex.
    (b) Walling-off of the inflamed area.
    (c) Serving as chemotaxins.
    (d) Acting as opsonins.
    (e) Enhancing local vascular changes.

ANSWER: b

66. T lymphocytes

    (a) produce thymosin.
    (b) secrete antibodies.
    (c) are converted into plasma cells.
    (d) mature and differentiate within the bone marrow.
    (e) None of the above are correct.

ANSWER: e

67. The thymus

    (a) is the site of maturational processing for T lymphocytes.
    (b) secretes a collection of hormones important in maintaining the T-cell lineage.
    (c) gradually atrophies and becomes less important as an individual matures.
    (d) Both (a) and (b) above are correct.
    (e) All of the above are correct.

ANSWER: e

68. Which type of leukocyte undergoes final maturation and differentiation in the thymus?

    (a) Neutrophils.
    (b) B lymphocytes.
    (c) T lymphocytes.
    (d) Macrophages.
    (e) Basophils.

ANSWER: c

69. B lymphocytes

    (a) are responsible for antibody-mediated immunity.
    (b) are activated by thymosin.
    (c) mature and differentiate into macrophages.
    (d) bind with foreign antigen in association with self-antigen.
    (e) are attacked by AIDS virus.

ANSWER: a

70. Plasma cells

    (a) are derived from B cells.
    (b) have an expanded rough endoplasmic reticulum.
    (c) do not secrete antibodies but remain dormant and expand the clone specific for the invading antigen.
    (d) Both (a) and (b) above are correct.
    (e) All of the above are correct.

ANSWER: d

71. A large, complex molecule that triggers a specific immune response against itself when it gains entry into the body is known as

    (a) interferon.
    (b) an antigen.
    (c) an antibody.
    (d) complement.
    (e) an opsonin.

ANSWER: b

72. Which of the following is **not** accomplished by antibodies?

    (a) neutralization of bacterial toxins
    (b) direct destruction of foreign cells
    (c) activation of the complement system
    (d) enhancement of phagocytosis
    (e) stimulation of killer (K) cells

ANSWER: b

73. The antigen-binding fragments (Fab) of antibodies

    (a) are located in the arm tips of the antibody molecule.
    (b) are located in the tail portion of the antibody molecule.
    (c) are unique for each different antibody so that each antibody can interact only with an antigen that specifically matches it.
    (d) Both (a) and (c) above are correct.
    (e) Both (b) and (c) above are correct.

ANSWER: d

74. The _____ of every antibody within each immunoglobulin subclass is identical.

    (a) antigen-binding fragments
    (b) tail portion
    (c) light chains
    (d) arm regions
    (e) Fab regions

ANSWER: b

75. Which of the following is **not** a way in which antibodies exert their protective influence?

   (a) Neutralization.
   (b) Agglutination
   (c) Direct destruction of foreign organisms.
   (d) Activation of the complement system.
   (e) Enhancement of phagocytosis.

ANSWER: c

76. A secondary response to an invading microorganism that has invaded a previous time

   (a) is launched by memory cells.
   (b) is slower and weaker than the primary response.
   (c) is more rapid, more potent, and longer-lasting than the primary response.
   (d) Both (a) and (b) above are correct.
   (e) Both (a) and (c) above are correct.

ANSWER: e

77. Type O blood

   (a) does not have any A or B red blood cell surface antigens.
   (b) contains both anti-A and anti-B antibodies.
   (c) can be transfused into individuals of any ABO blood type without a transfusion reaction involving this blood group system.
   (d) Both (a) and (b) above are correct.
   (e) All of the above are correct.

ANSWER: e

78. Lymphocytes respond only to antigens that have been processed and presented to them by

   (a) neutrophils.
   (b) eosinophils.
   (c) macrophages.
   (d) helper T cells.
   (e) interleukin 2.

ANSWER: c

79. Which of the following does **not** apply to
     macrophages?   Macrophages

     (a) participate in inflammation.
     (b) process and present antigen to lymphocytes.
     (c) secrete antibodies.
     (d) secrete interleukin 1.
     (e) participate in immune surveillance
          against cancer.

ANSWER: c

80. Which of the following is **not** secreted by
     helper T cells?

     (a) Interleukin 2.
     (b) Perforin.
     (c) Macrophage-migration inhibition factor.
     (d) B-cell growth factor.
     (e) T-cell growth factor.

ANSWER: b

81. _____ T cells destroy cells infected with virus.

     (a) Cytotoxic
     (b) Helper
     (c) Suppressor
     (d) Regulatory
     (e) Angry

ANSWER: a

82. What type of immune defense cell is selectively invaded by
     AIDS virus?

     (a) Cytotoxic T cells.
     (b) Helper T cells.
     (c) Suppressor T cells.
     (d) Macrophages.
     (e) Neutrophils.

ANSWER: b

83. Cytotoxic T cells

    (a) are the most numerous of the T cells.
    (b) secrete B-cell growth factor and T-cell growth factor.
    (c) confer greater phagocytic properties on macrophages, converting them into angry macrophages.
    (d) release perforin molecules, which join together to form a complex that punches a hole in the target cell's surface membrane, similar to the complement system's membrane-attack complex.
    (e) bind with class II MHC glycoproteins.

ANSWER: d

84. Chemicals other than antibodies secreted by lymphocytes are collectively known as

    (a) lymphokines.
    (b) antigens.
    (c) opsonins.
    (d) complement factors.
    (e) lymphogenous mediators.

ANSWER: a

85. HLA antigens

    (a) are plasma membrane-bound glycoproteins.
    (b) are coded for by the major histocompatibility complex.
    (c) are present only on the surface of leukocytes.
    (d) Both (a) and (b) above are correct.
    (e) All of the above are correct.

ANSWER: d

86. T cells

    (a) bind with free extracellular antigen.
    (b) bind with HLA self-antigens only when they are in association with a foreign antigen.
    (c) are responsible for cell-mediated immunity.
    (d) Both (a) and (c) above are correct.
    (e) Both (b) and (c) above are correct.

ANSWER: e

87. Which of the following statements regarding T cells is **incorrect**?

    (a) Cytotoxic T cells release chemicals that destroy targeted cells.
    (b) Helper T cells enhance the activity of other T cells and B cells.
    (c) Suppressor T cells are believed to play an important role in tolerance to self-antigens.
    (d) T cells produce antibodies.
    (e) The vast majority of T cells are helper T cells.

ANSWER: d

88. Which of the following does **not** play a direct role in immune surveillance against cancer?

    (a) B cells
    (b) natural killer cells
    (c) macrophages
    (d) cytotoxic T cells
    (e) interferon

ANSWER: a

89. Which of the following is **not** secreted by helper T cells?

    (a) B-cell growth factor
    (b) T-cell growth factor
    (c) interleukin 1
    (d) interleukin 2
    (e) macrophage migration inhibition factor

ANSWER: c

90. Which of the following statements concerning cancer cells is **incorrect**?

    (a) Cancer cells arise only when multiple independent mutations occur within the same cell.
    (b) Cancer cells lack the ability to perform the specialized functions of the normal cell-type from which they mutated.
    (c) The body has no means by which to defend against cancer cells.
    (d) Cancer cells usually do not adhere well to neighboring cells, so some of them may break away from the parent tumor.
    (e) All of the above are correct.

ANSWER: c

91. Which of the following does **not** help defend against cancer?

    (a) Interferon.
    (b) Macrophages.
    (c) Natural killer cells.
    (d) Cytotoxic T cells.
    (e) Antibodies.

ANSWER: e

92. With _____, the body fails to recognize and tolerate particular self-antigens.

    (a) delayed hypersensitivity
    (b) autoimmune disease
    (c) immune-complex disease
    (d) immediate hypersensitivity
    (e) inflammation

ANSWER: b

93. Which of the following does **not** characterize immediate hypersensitivity?

    (a) Is mediated by T cells.
    (b) Involves IgE antibodies.
    (c) Occurs within 20 minutes of exposure to the allergen.
    (d) Usually involves allergic responses to inhaled or ingested allergens.
    (e) Includes hayfever, asthma, and hives.

ANSWER: a

94. The epidermis

    (a) has an outermost keratinized layer that is tough, air-tight, and fairly waterproof.
    (b) contains melanocytes, keratinocytes, Langerhans cells, Granstein cells, and transient T lymphocytes.
    (c) has a richly vascularized inner layer.
    (d) Both (a) and (b) above are correct.
    (e) All of the above are correct.

ANSWER: d

95. Which of the following is **not** found in the epidermis?

(a) Blood vessels whose caliber can be adjusted as part of the temperature regulatory mechanisms.
(b) Keratinocytes.
(c) Melanocytes.
(d) Langerhans cells.
(e) Granstein cells.

ANSWER: a

96. Keratinocytes

(a) form the outer protective layer of the skin.
(b) secrete interleukin 1.
(c) present antigen to helper T cells.
(d) Both (a) and (b) above are correct.
(e) All of the above are correct.

ANSWER: d

97. Which cell type of the skin presents antigen to helper T cells?

(a) Keratinocytes.
(b) Melanocytes.
(c) Langerhans cells.
(d) Granstein cells.
(e) Sebaceous cells.

ANSWER: c

98. Which of the following does **not** contribute to defense of the respiratory system?

(a) Coughs and sneezes.
(b) Cilia-propelled mucus escalator.
(c) Alveolar macrophages.
(d) Normal microbial population of the lungs.

ANSWER: d

True/False

99. If the hematocrit is 47, this means that 47% of the whole blood consists of plasma.

ANSWER: False

100. If the hematocrit is 42%, this means that 58% of the whole blood is comprised of plasma.

ANSWER: True

101. Antibodies are gamma globulins produced by B lymphocytes.

ANSWER: True

102. All of the constituents present in the plasma are freely diffusible across the capillary walls.

ANSWER: False

103. The bone marrow is the major site for the formation of most blood cells.

ANSWER: True

104. Red blood cells are produced by the yellow bone marrow.

ANSWER: False

105. Hemoglobin is found within the nuclei of erythrocytes.

ANSWER: False

106. Erythropoietin stimulates erythropoiesis by the kidneys.

ANSWER: False

107. Anemia is a condition in which the oxygen-carrying capacity of the blood is increased.

ANSWER: False

108. Polycythemia often occurs in those who live at high altitudes.

ANSWER: True

109. Aplastic anemia is due to intrinsic factor deficiency.

ANSWER: False

110. Pernicious anemia occurs when the bone marrow is destroyed by drugs or radiation.

ANSWER: False

111. Polycythemia can occur in association with chronic lung disease.

ANSWER: True

112. Polycythemia increases the viscosity of the blood, thus increasing the total peripheral resistance.

ANSWER: True

113. All types of white blood cells can be produced in the bone marrow as well as in lymphoid tissues, such as the lymph nodes and tonsils.

ANSWER: False

114. Antibodies are produced by both B and T lymphocytes.

ANSWER: False

115. Lymphocytes are polymorphonuclear granulocytes.

ANSWER: False

116. Platelets are important in the process of hemostasis.

ANSWER: True

117. Specific hormones direct the differentiation and proliferation of the various types of white blood cells.

ANSWER: True

118. Granulocyte colony-stimulating factor stimulates the replication and release of neutrophils from the bone marrow.

ANSWER: True

119. The first step in hemostasis is the formation of a blood clot.

ANSWER: False

120. Thrombin forms the meshwork of the clot.

ANSWER: False

121. Platelets adhere to exposed collagen, forming a plug at the site of a vessel defect.

ANSWER: True

122. Serum is identical in composition to plasma; that is, both of them contain all of the components of blood except for the blood cells.

ANSWER: False

123. Being a cell fragment, a platelet lacks a nucleus and organelles and does not have any synthetic ability.

ANSWER: False

124. Hemostatic mechanisms are effective for completely arresting bleeding from small vessels, but rupture of medium to large vessels requires external intervention to stop bleeding.

ANSWER: True

125. Serum is identical to plasma.

ANSWER: False

126. The intrinsic clotting pathway stops blood in an injured vessel, whereas the extrinsic pathway clots blood that has escaped into the tissues.

ANSWER: True

127. Clot formation is a temporary measure to halt blood loss from an injured vessel until the more powerful platelet plug can be formed.

ANSWER: False

128. Pathogenic bacteria induce tissue damage and produce disease by invading host cells and taking over the cellular biochemical facilities for their own purposes.

ANSWER: False

129. Immune surveillance refers to the body's ability to resist or eliminate potentially harmful foreign invaders.

ANSWER: False

130. The spleen clears the lymph that passes through it of bacteria and other foreign matter.

ANSWER: False

131. Specific immune responses are selectively targeted against particular foreign material to which the body has previously been exposed.

ANSWER: True

132. Neutrophils are the first phagocytes to leave the blood and arrive at a site of bacterial invasion or tissue damage.

ANSWER: True

133. Neutrophils swell and mature into macrophages after they enter the tissues.

ANSWER: False

134. Chemotaxis refers to the ability of leukocytes to squeeze through small capillary pores.

ANSWER: False

135. The early stage of inflammation is predominated by neutrophils.

ANSWER: True

136. Phagocytes can destroy foreign microbes only after they have engulfed these invaders.

ANSWER: False

137. Endogenous pyrogen (EP), and interleukin 1 (IL-1) are believed to be identical or closely related chemical mediators.

ANSWER: True

138. The only means by which macrophages can defend against microbial invaders is phagocytosis.

ANSWER: False

139. Virus-blocking enzymes induced by interferon are activated only upon viral invasion of the cell.

ANSWER: True

140. Interferon is released only from phagocytic cells that have been invaded by viruses.

ANSWER: False

141. Interferon, natural killer cells, and cytotoxic T cells all exert antiviral and anticancer effects.

ANSWER: True

142. The membrane-attack complex is formed by the five final activated components of the complement system.

ANSWER: True

143. Interferon is secreted by lymphoid tissues.

ANSWER: False

144. Antibodies are not able to directly destroy invading organisms.

ANSWER: True

145. The arm regions of an antibody determine with what antigen the antibody can bind, whereas the tail portion determines the destiny of the antibody once it is bound.

ANSWER: True

146. When an antigen gains entry to the body, it stimulates all of the B cells to produce antibodies specific against it.

ANSWER: False

147. The primary response to microbial invasion is mediated by memory cells.

ANSWER: False

148. The formation of memory cells against a particular disease-causing microorganism can only occur as a result of the person actually having the disease.

ANSWER: False

149. Type AB blood has both A and B antigens and no anti-A or anti-B antibodies.

ANSWER: True

150. Type AB blood can be donated to anyone because it lacks both anti-A and anti-B antibodies.

ANSWER: False

151. Persons with type A blood produce anti-B antibodies without ever being exposed to type B blood, but Rh-negative individuals produce anti-Rh antibodies only if they are exposed to Rh-positive blood.

ANSWER: True

152. One of the most lethal consequences of mismatched blood transfusions is acute kidney failure caused by blockage of urine-forming structures by hemoglobin precipitation.

ANSWER: True

153. HLA antigens are found only on the surface of leukocytes.

ANSWER: False

154. T cells typically bind with HLA self-antigens only when they are in association with foreign antigen.

ANSWER: True

155. B cells bind with HLA self-antigens.

ANSWER: False

156. Histamine is primarily responsible for causing the bronchial constriction associated with asthma.

ANSWER: False

157. Eosinophils are attracted to sites involved with delayed allergic reactions.

ANSWER: False

158. B lymphocytes are involved with immediate hypersensitivity reactions, whereas T lymphocytes are involved with delayed hypersensitivity reactions.

ANSWER: True

159. A single mutation induced by a carcinogen is usually sufficient to convert a normal cell into a cancer cell.

ANSWER: False

160. The immune system functions entirely independently of the body's two major control systems, the nervous and endocrine systems.

ANSWER: False

161. Immediate hypersensitivity reactions are mediated by IgE antibodies secreted by B cells, whereas delayed hypersensitivity is mediated by T cells.

ANSWER: True

162. Antihistamines are effective in combating the allergic symptoms induced by slow-reactive substance of anaphylaxis.

ANSWER: False

163. Hair and nails are both special keratinized products.

ANSWER: True

164. Most fat cells in the body are located in the dermis.

ANSWER: False

165. Severe burns of the skin can result in life-threatening circulatory disturbances.

ANSWER: True

166. Adipose tissue is located within the hypodermis.

ANSWER: True

167. Saliva is destructive to bacteria because it is highly acidic.

ANSWER: False

168. The large intestine's normal microbial population helps defend against infection within the lower intestine.

ANSWER: True

169. Debris trapped on the sticky mucus lining the respiratory airways is primarily cleared away by the aveolar macrophages.

ANSWER: False

170. A sneeze expels irritant material from the trachea.

ANSWER: False

Fill-in-the-blanks

171. The percentage of whole blood occupied by erythrocytes, known as the _____, is normally (greater than, less than) the plasma volume.

ANSWER: hematocrit, less than

172. The three types of cellular elements in the blood are _____, _____ and _____.

ANSWERS: erythrocytes (red blood cells), leukocytes (white blood cells), platelets (thrombocytes)

173. By far the most abundant of the cellular elements in the blood are the _____.

ANSWER: erythrocytes (red blood cells)

174. Most of the old erythrocytes are removed from the circulation as they rupture passing through the narrow capillaries of the _____.

ANSWER: spleen

175. Red blood cell production by the _____ is stimulated by the hormone _____, which is secreted from the kidney into the blood in response to _____.

ANSWER: bone marrow, erythropoietin, reduced O_2 delivery

176. Undifferentiated _____ reside in the bone marrow, where they continuously divide and differentiate to give rise to each of the types of blood cells.

ANSWER: pluripotential stem cells

177. Which of the types of leukocytes are categorized as polymorphonuclear granulocytes? _____ _____.

ANSWER: neutrophils, eosinophils, basophils

178. In what two different ways do leukocytes defend against foreign invasion by infectious agents? _____ and _____.

ANSWER: by phagocytosis; by immune responses, such as the production of antibodies that mark invaders for destruction in more subtle ways

179. List the three major steps in hemostasis:

_____   _____

_____

ANSWERS: vascular spasm, formation of a platelet plug, blood coagulation

180. _____ refers to the body's ability to resist or eliminate potentially harmful foreign materials or abnormal cells.

ANSWER: Immunity

181. _____ refer collectively to the tissues that store, produce, or process lymphocytes.

ANSWER: Lymphoid tissues

182. _____ in an infected wound is a collection of phagocytic cells, dead tissue liquified by enzymes released from the phagocytic cells, and bacteria.

ANSWER: Pus

183. _____ refers to the chemical attraction of leukocytes to the site of invasion.

ANSWER: Chemotaxis

184. _____ is released from virally-invaded cells and, transiently, nonselectively inhibits multiplication of viruses in other cells.

ANSWER: Interferon

185. The _____ of the complement system imbeds itself in the microbial membrane surface, thereby bringing about lysis of the victim cell.

ANSWER: membrane-attack complex

186. _____ are lymphocytelike cells that nonspecifically destroy virus-infected cells and tumor cells.

ANSWER: Natural killer cells

187. The T lymphocyte lineage undergoes maturational processing and differentiation in the _____.

ANSWER: thymus

188. According to the _____ theory, when an antigen enters the body, it activates the particular clone of B cells that bear receptors on their surface uniquely specific for that antigen.

ANSWER: clonal selection

189. Most of the progeny of an activated B-cell clone differentiate into _____, which produce antibodies, and _____, which remain dormant and expand the specific clone.

ANSWERS: plasma cells, memory cells

190. A(n) _____ is a large complex molecule that triggers an immune response against itself.

ANSWER: antigen

191. A(n) _____ is a low molecular weight molecules that becomes antigenic by attaching to body proteins.

ANSWER: hapten

192. _____ cells derived from activated B lymphocytes are specialized for antibody production.

ANSWER: Plasma

193. Clumping of foreign cells brought about by the formation of antigen-antibody complexes is known as _____.

ANSWER: agglutination

194. The _____ theory proposes that a diversity of lymphocytes are produced during development, each preprogrammed to synthesize antibody against only one of an almost limitless variety of antigens.

ANSWER: clonal selection

195. Lymphocytes can only recognize and be activated by antigens that have been processed and presented to them by _____.

ANSWER: macrophages

196. The type of immune cells selectively invaded by AIDS virus is the _____.

ANSWER: helper T cell

197. _____ refers to the phenomenon of the immune system not attacking a person's own tissues.

ANSWER: Tolerance

198. _____ are plasma membrane-bound glycoproteins that serve as self-antigens.

ANSWER: Human leukocyte-associated antigens (HLA antigens)

199. The group of genes that codes for self-antigens is known as the _____.

ANSWER: major histocompatibility complex (MHC)

200. _____ against cancer cells involves an interplay among cytotoxic T cells, NK cells, macrophages, and interferon.

ANSWER: Immune surveillance

201. A mass of transformed cells that is slow-growing, stays put, and does not infiltrate surrounding tissue is known as a _____ tumor, whereas rapidly-growing, invasive masses are called _____ tumors or _____. The spreading of mutant cells that have broken away from the parent tumor to other body sites is called _____.

ANSWER: benign, malignant, cancer, metastasis

202. _____ disease occurs when destructive inflammatory processes "spill over" into normal tissue in the presence of excessive numbers of antigen-antibody complexes.

ANSWER: Immune-complex

203. The type of antibodies responsible for inducing allergic manifestations are _____.

ANSWER: IgE

204. _____ refers to the life-threatening
allergic phenomenon characterized by severe hypotension
and profound bronchial constriction due to the presence of
large amounts of chemical mediators in the blood released
from mast cells and basophils in response to a particular
allergen.

ANSWER: Anaphylactic shock

205. The _____ refers to the cilia-propelled upward
movement of the respiratory airways' mucus layer to which
inspired particulates are stuck.

ANSWER: mucus escalator

206. Name two categories of drugs that exert anti-inflammatory
effects.

    (1)_____
    (2)_____

ANSWER: salicylates, glucocorticoids

207. Distinguish between the two pathways by which the
complement system can be activated.

    (1)_____
    (2)_____

ANSWERS: classical pathway: antibodies activate complement
          system; alternate pathway: particular carbohydrate
          chains on microbial surfaces activate complement
          system

208.   List two functions of dermal blood vessels.

    (1)_____
    (2)_____

ANSWERS: supply blood to both the dermis and epidermis; play
          a major role in temperature regulation

209. Indicate the secretory product and function of the
following three specialized skin structures.

Name	Secretory Product	Function
(1) sweat glands	_____	_____
(2) sebaceous glands	_____	_____
(3) hair follicles	_____	_____

ANSWERS: (1) sweat; important in temperature regulation by
cooling the skin; (2) sebum; oils hairs and outer
layers of skin, thereby waterproofing and
softening them; (3) hairs; increase the skin's
sensitivity in touch and important in lower
species in heat conservation

Matching

210. _____ Lack of red blood cell
production due to poisoning
of the bone marrow.
_____ Lack of intrinsic factor.
_____ Premature rupture of
erythrocytes.
_____ Vitamin B_{12} is not
absorbed.
_____ Associated with prolonged
exposure to low oxygen, such
as at high altitude or with
chronic lung disease.
_____ Associated with sickle cell anemia.
_____ Associated with malaria.
_____ Associated with acute loss of blood.
_____ Uncontrolled production of white
blood cells.

a. aplastic anemia
b. pernicious anemia
c. hemolytic anemia
d. hemorrhagic
   anemia
e. polycythemia
f. leukemia

ANSWERS: a, b, c, b, e, c, c, d, f

211. _____ most abundant type of
     granulocyte
     _____ become tissue macrophages
     _____ produce antibodies
     _____ first phagocytes to
     arrive at site of
     bacterial invasion
     _____ release histamine and
     heparin
     _____ destroy parasitic worms
     _____ participate in cell-
     mediated immune responses
     _____ most abundant type of
     agranulocyte
     _____ similar to mast cells

a. neutrophils
b. eosinophils
c. basophils
d. monocytes
e. lymphocytes

ANSWERS: a, d, e, a, c, b, e, e, d

212. _____ formation of a
     platelet plug
     _____ thromboplastin
     _____ thrombin
     _____ prothrombin
     _____ fibrin
     _____ blood coagulation
     _____ collagen
     _____ adenosine
     diphosphate
     _____ plasminogen
     _____ vascular spasm

a. Converts fibrinogen to fibrin.
b. When platelets come into contact with this substance in an
   injured vessel wall, it causes
   them to adhere and aggregate.
c. When activated, this substance
   digests the fibrin threads,
   causing dissolution of the
   clot.
d. Substance released by the
   platelet plug which causes
   more platelets to aggregate.
e. First step in hemostasis.
f. Forms the meshwork of the
   clot.
g. A plasma protein activated by
   factor X.
h. Second step in hemostasis.
i. Released from injured tissues;
   activates extrinsic clotting
   pathway.
j. Third step in hemostasis.

ANSWERS: h, i, a, g, f, j, b, d, c, e

213. Indicate the characteristics that apply to bacteria and viruses by using the following code:

> (a) = pertains to bacteria
> (b) = pertains to viruses

_____ consists of nucleic acids enclosed by a protein coat
_____ self-sustaining, single-celled organisms
_____ can secrete enzymes or toxins that are injurious to host cells
_____ can invade a host cell and take over the cellular biochemical facilities for their own purposes

ANSWERS: b, a, a, b

214. Indicate whether the following characteristics apply to the Fab or Fc region of an antibody by using the answer code below:

> (a) = applies to the Fab region
> (b) = applies to the Fc region

_____ located in the "arm" regions of an antibody
_____ located in the "tail" region of an antibody
_____ highly variable between different antibodies of the same class
_____ constant between different antibodies of the same class

ANSWERS: a, b, a, b

215. Indicate the immune disease being described by using the following answer code:

> (a) = immediate hypersensitivity
> (b) = acquired immune deficiency syndrome
> (c) = delayed hypersensitivity
> (d) = immune-complex disease
> (e) = autoimmune disease
> (f) = severe combined immunodeficiency

_____ Allergic response mediated by IgE antibodies.
_____ Damage of normal cells brought about by excessive formation of antigen-antibody complexes.
_____ Helper T cells are destroyed by viral invasion.
_____ The immune system fails to recognize and tolerate particular self-antigens.
_____ Hereditary condition in which both B and T cells are lacking.
_____ Allergic response mediated by T cells.

ANSWERS: a, d, b, e, f, c

216. ____ enhance(s) phagocytosis by   (a) Lactoferrin
         linking the foreign cell to   (b) Glucocorticoids
         a phagocytic cell.   (c) Histamine
     ____ form(s) a membrane-attack   (d) Endogenous
         complex.   pyrogen
     ____ released from mast cells and   (e) Opsonins
         causes localized vasodilation   (f) Complement
         in a region of tissue damage.   system
     ____ stimulates production of   (g) Antibodies
         virus-blocking enzymes.   (h) Interferon
     ____ produced by plasma cells.
     ____ induce(s) the development of fever.
     ____ potent anti-inflammatory drug(s).

ANSWERS: d, e, b, g, f, c, a

217. Indicate which type of T cell is being described by
     writing the appropriate letter in the blank using the
     answer code below.

         (a) = applies to cytotoxic T cell
         (b) = applies to helper T cells
         (c) = applies to suppressor T cells
         (d) = applies to both helper T cells and suppressor
               T cells
         (e) = applies to all three types of T cells

     _____ destroy host cells bearing foreign antigen
     _____ suppress both B-cell and T-cell activity
     _____ secrete B-cell growth factor
     _____ called regulatory T cells
     _____ secrete interleukin 2
     _____ release perforin
     _____ secrete macrophage-migration inhibition factor
     _____ attacked by AIDS virus
     _____ most numerous of the T cells
     _____ serve to limit immune reactions in a check and
            balance relationship with the other lymphocytes
     _____ believed to play a role in tolerance

ANSWERS: a, c, b, d, b, a, b, b, b, c, c

151. _____ secrete a pigment
responsible for
varying shades of
brown color in the
skin
_____ secrete interleukin 1
_____ produce the tough
protective surface of
the skin
_____ secrete a substance that
absorbs harmful
ultraviolet rays
_____ present antigen to
helper T cells
_____ present antigen to
suppressor T cells
_____ the most abundant cell
type in the skin
_____ produce hair and nails

a. keratinocytes
b. melanocytes
c. Langerhans cells
d. Granstein cells

ANSWERS: b, a, a, b, c, d, a, a

AUDIOVISUAL AIDS

Films

A list of films available from West Publishing Company is
presented in Appendix A.   Following are other films that may
be suitable. The sources for these films, which are coded by
abbreviation, are provided in Appendix B.

Accident, FM, 26 min.

Aids and Other Epidemics, FHS, 26 min.

AIDS: On the Trail of a Killer, FHS, 58 min.

Aids: What Everyone Needs to Know, CF, 20 min.

Anaphylaxis in Guinea Pigs, UC, 8 min.

A New View of Corticosteroid Action in Inflammatory Dermatoses,
SYN, 14 min.

Antibody Diversity and Immunoregulation, ISC, 24 min.

Arterial and Venous Blood, IF, 3 min.

Autoimmunity and Disease, UC, 33 min.

B Cells and Antibodies, ISC, 24 min.

Blood, EBE, 16 min.

Blood Components and Their Use, AF, 45 min.

Blood Composition and Function, CFV, 15 min.

Blood Grouping, ICIA, 21 min.

Blood: The Microscopic Miracle, EBE, 22 min.

Blood: River of Life, Mirror of Health, EI

Blueprints in the Bloodstream, TL, 57 min.

Body Defenses Against Disease, EBE, 11 min.

Cancer: Common and Curable, BNA, 25 min.

Circulation, IM, 29 min.

Circulatory System, CFV, 16 min.

Death of a Disease, TLV, 58 min.

Fundamental Principles of Immunization, WFL, 40 min.

Hemoglobin, UI, 25 min.

How Blood Clots, BFA, 13 min.

Hunt for a Cancer Killer, MH, 26 min.

Immune System Disorders, FHS, 28 min.

Immunity, IM, 29 min.

Immunization, EBE, 11 min.

Immunodeficiency: A Disease of Life, IM, 19 min.

Immunology: An Overview, ISC, 22 min.

Infectious Diseases and Man-Made Defenses, COR, 10 min.

Infectious Diseases and Natural Body Defenses, COR, 11 min.

Life and Structure of Hemoglobin, ISC, 29 min.

Normal Homeostasis, TRA, 19 min.

Phagocytes: The Body's Defenders, ASF, 10 min.

Rh: The Disease and its Conquest, MF, 18 min.

Secret of the White Blood Cell, NET, 24 min.

Sickle Cell Fundamentals, NIH, 30 min.

T Cells, ISC, 24 min.

The Blood, EBE, 16 min.

The Blood, FHS, 9 min.

The Common Cold, FHS, 28 min.

The Genetics of Transplantation, MF, 19 min.

The Human Body: Circulatory System, KSU, 16 min.

The Human Immune System: The Fighting Edge, FHS, 52 min.

The Immune Response, COR, 20 min.

The Immune Response, IM, 22 min.

The Inflammatory Process, SYN, 31 min.

The Inflammatory Reaction, LL, 25 min.

The Lymphatic System, ISC, 15 min.

The Microbiology of Aids, FHS, 10 min.

The Nature and Transmission of Aids, FHS, 20 min.

The Structure and Function of Hemoglobin, UM, 25 min.

The Sickle Cell Story, PF, 16 min.

The Transplant Experience, TLV, 50 min.

To Make Man Immune from Disease, UI, 20 min.

Transport Systems in Animals, IU, 17 min.

Vaccines and Preventive Medicine, FHS, 26 min.

Viruses: The Mysterious Energy, IM, 38 min.

White Blood Cells, MH, 12 min.

Work of the Blood, EBF, 13 min.

<u>Wound Healing</u>, AMA, 24 min.

Software

<u>Aids: The Investigation</u>, PLP. How does an unsuspecting victim contract Aids.

<u>Aids: The New Epidemic</u>, PLP. Covers symptoms, treatment, transmission, and prevention.

<u>Antigen-Antibody Reactions</u>, MAC. The specificity of antigen-antibody reactions is the focus of this lesson.

<u>Biochemistry of the Immune System</u>, EI. Covers all aspects of immune system

<u>Biochemistry of Viruses: Viruses and Cancer</u>, EI. Basic principles of viruses and their life cycles.

<u>Circulation</u>, EI. Covers blood, heart, arteries, capillaries, veins, and lungs.

<u>Dysfunctional Immunity</u>, MAC. Examines a number of different types of dysfunctional conditions of the immune system.

<u>Host Non-specific Defense System Against Infectious Diseases</u>, MAC. Examines the variety of non-specific defense systems that protect the human body.

<u>Identification and Alleviation of Allergies</u>, MAC. Examines the allergic response.

<u>Immunoglobulins</u>, MAC. The properties of immunoglobulins are covered.

<u>Microbe</u>, CBS. Covers virus attacks and natural defense mechanisms.

<u>The Immune Defense System</u>, MAC. Covers the immune response. Transport, CBS. Reviews the blood system, lymph system, blood cells, and blood types.

<u>Vaccines and Immunoglobulins</u>, MAC. The use of vaccines for preventing disease and the use of antibodies for treating specific disease conditions are reviewed.

Chapter 10
Respiratory System

CONTENTS
(All page references are to the main text.)

-Elastic behavior of the lungs is due to elastic connective-tissue fibers and alveolar surface tension. p.333
-Pulmonary surfactant decreases surface tension and contributes to lung stability. p.335
-A deficiency of pulmonary surfactant is responsible for newborn respiratory distress syndrome. p.335
-Normally, the lungs contain about 2 to 2.5 liters of air during the respiratory cycle but can be filled to over 5.5 liters or emptied to about 1 liter. p.336
-Alveolar ventilation is less than pulmonary ventilation because of the presence of dead space. p.338

Gas Exchange, p.339
-Gases move down partial pressure gradients. p.339
-Oxygen enters and CO_2 leaves the blood in the lungs passively down partial pressure gradients. p.341

Beyond the Basics: How to Find Out How Much Work You're Capable of Doing, p.343

-Factors other than the partial pressure gradient influence the rate of gas transfer. p.344
-Gas exchange across the systemic capillaries also occurs down partial pressure gradients. p.344

Gas Transport, p.345
-Most O_2 in the blood is transported bound to hemoglobin. p.345
-The P_{O2} is the primary factor determining the percent hemoglobin saturation. p.346
-By acting as a storage depot, hemoglobin promotes the net transfer of O_2 from the alveoli to the blood. p.347
-Increased CO_2, acidity, temperature, and 2,3-diphosphoglycerate shift the O_2-Hb dissociation curve to the right. p.348
-Oxygen-binding sites on hemoglobin have a much higher affinity for carbon monoxide than for O_2. p.349
-The majority of CO_2 is transported in the blood as bicarbonate. p.450
-Various respiratory states are characterized by abnormal blood-gas levels. p.351

Beyond the Basics - Effects of Heights and Depths on the Body, p.352

Control of Respiration, p.353
-Respiratory centers in the brain stem establish a rhythmic breathing pattern. p.353   -Carbon-dioxide-generated hydrogen-ion concentration in the brain extracellular fluid is normally the primary regulator of the magnitude of ventilation. p.354

-During apnea, a person subconsciously "forgets to breathe," whereas during dyspnea, a person consciously feels that ventilation is inadequate. p.356

Chapter in Perspective: Focus on Homeostasis, p.357

Chapter Summary, p.357

LECTURE HINTS AND SUGGESTIONS

1. Use a torso or whole-body manikin to demonstrate the anatomical location of the respiratory organs. This and other materials required below can be obtained from Carolina Biological Supply Company, Burlington, NC, as well as from other supply houses.

2. A skull is very useful to review the bones associated with the nasal sinuses.

3. Use a balloon and bell jar model of the respiratory system to illustrate the mechanics of breathing. Several mechanical variations are available that illustrate the movement of gases.

4. Demonstrate the Colins or other commercial respirometer to illustrate how volumes and capacities can be measured.

5. Have students palpate their own larynx and trachea.

6. Demonstrate the Heimlich maneuver. Charts are available from local Red Cross chapters.

7. Bubble air through blood in order to demonstrate the color changes associated with O_2 and hemoglobin. Do the same with carbon dioxide. See any general physiology lab manual for examples.

8. Demonstrate preserved specimens of whole normal and diseased lungs; e.g., black lung, emphysema, tuberculosis.

9. Use microscope slides of histological preparations of normal and diseased lung tissue.

10. Set up a diffusion demonstration showing diffusion of a solid in a liquid to illustrate how slow the process is. See any general physiology lab manual for examples.

11. Cardiopulmonary resuscitation demonstration with a Resusci-Annie or similar manikin is useful and informative. Fire rescue personnel, local heart associations or local hospitals have these for public use.

12. Obtain and demonstrate biomounts of animal respiratory structures.

13. Have students use their imaginations to construct a mechanical model to demonstrate the mechanics of breathing.

14. Have students hold their breath, then ask them to describe the physiological events resulting from this action. Follow this with a discussion of regulatory mechanisms.

CHAPTER TEST QUESTIONS

Multiple Choice

1. The entire sequence of events involved in the exchange of O_2 and CO_2 between the cells of the body and the external environment is known as

    (a) internal respiration.
    (b) external respiration.
    (c) ventilation.
    (d) breathing.
    (e) Both (c) and (d) above are correct.

ANSWER: b

2. Which of the following is **not** a function of the respiratory system?

    (a) Transports O_2 to the tissues.
    (b) Contributes to maintenance of normal acid-base balance.
    (c) Provides a route for heat and water elimination.
    (d) Enables speech, singing, and other vocalization.
    (e) Removes, modifies, activates, or inactivates various materials passing through the pulmonary circulation.

ANSWER: a

3. Which of the following is a function of the respiratory system?

    (a) Contributes to maintenance of normal acid-base balance.
    (b) Route for heat and water elimination.
    (c) Enhances venous return.
    (d) Two of the above are correct.
    (e) All of the above are correct.

ANSWER: e

4. Which of the following structures serves as a common passageway for both the respiratory and digestive systems?

    (a) Nose.
    (b) Pharynx.
    (c) Trachea.
    (d) Bronchi.
    (e) Esophagus.

ANSWER: b

5. Type I alveolar cells

    (a) form the wall of the alveoli.
    (b) secrete pulmonary surfactant.
    (c) contract during expiration to force air out of the alveoli.
    (d) Both (a) and (b) above are correct.
    (e) All of the above are correct.

ANSWER: a

6. Which of the following statements concerning alveoli is (are) correct?

    (a) Alveoli are the site of gas exchange in the lungs.
    (b) Alveolar Type II cells secrete pulmonary surfactant.
    (c) The walls of the alveoli are very thin and are surrounded by a network of capillaries so that air and blood are separated by only a very thin barrier.
    (d) Both (a) and (c) above are correct.
    (e) All of the above are correct.

ANSWER: b

7. The intra-alveolar pressure

    (a) is the pressure within the air sacs of the lung.
    (b) always equilibrates with atmospheric pressure.
    (c) is always less than intrapleural pressure.
    (d) Both (a) and (b) above are correct.
    (e) All of the above are correct.

ANSWER: d

8. The transmural pressure gradient

   (a) stretches the lungs to fill the thoracic cavity, which is larger than the lungs.
   (b) does not exist in pneumothorax.
   (c) does not exist at rest.
   (d) Both (a) and (b) above are correct.
   (e) All of the above are correct.

ANSWER: d

9. A transmural pressure gradient exists across the lung wall because the _____ pressure is less than the _____ pressure.

   (a) intrapleural, intra-alveolar
   (b) intra-alveolar, intrapleural
   (c) intrapleural, atmospheric
   (d) atmospheric, intra-alveolar
   (e) None of the above are correct.

ANSWER: a

10. The inspiratory muscles include the

    (a) diaphragm and internal intercostal muscles.
    (b) diaphragm and external intercostal muscles.
    (c) diaphragm and abdominal muscles.
    (d) internal and external intercostal muscles.
    (e) None of the above are correct.

ANSWER: b

11. When intra-alveolar pressure becomes greater than atmospheric pressure,

    (a) air will flow out of the lungs.
    (b) air will flow into the lungs.
    (c) there will be no air flow.

ANSWER: a

12. During which of the following cases would the intra-alveolar pressure be greater than atmospheric pressure?

    (a) During inspiration.
    (b) During passive expiration.
    (c) During active expiration.
    (d) During pneumothorax.
    (e) Both (b) and (c) above are correct.

ANSWER: c

13. At the end of a normal expiration when outward air flow
     has ceased,

     (a) intra-alveolar pressure is less than atmospheric
          pressure.
     (b) intra-alveolar pressure is greater than atmospheric
          pressure.
     (c) intra-alveolar pressure is equal to atmospheric
          pressure.
     (d) intrapleural pressure is greater than atmospheric
          pressure.
     (e) intrapleural pressure is greater than intra-alveolar
          pressure.

ANSWER: c

14. Which of the following does **not** occur during expiration
     when a person is breathing quietly?

     (a) The size of the thoracic cavity is reduced.
     (b) The intra-alveolar pressure becomes greater than
          atmospheric pressure.
     (c) Air flows out of the lungs.
     (d) The expiratory muscles contract.
     (e) Intrapleural pressure is less than intra-alveolar
          pressure.

ANSWER: d

15. During inspiration,

     (a) intra-alveolar pressure falls below atmospheric
          pressure.
     (b) the diaphragm contracts.
     (c) the internal intercostal muscles contract.
     (d) Both (a) and (b) above are correct.
     (e) All of the above are correct.

ANSWER: d

16. When the diaphragm contracts,

     (a) the size of the thoracic cavity increases.
     (b) lung volume increases as the lungs are forced
          to expand.
     (c) the intra-alveolar pressure increases.
     (d) Both (a) and (b) above are correct.
     (e) All of the above are correct.

ANSWER: d

17. Airway resistance

   (a) is normally the primary factor that determines the amount of air flow into and out of the lungs.
   (b) is increased when the radius of the airways becomes reduced.
   (c) when elevated requires that the person must increase the pressure gradient between the lungs and atmosphere through vigorous respiratory efforts to move even normal volumes of air into and out of the lungs.
   (d) Both (b) and (c) above are correct.
   (e) All of the above are correct.

ANSWER: d

18. Which of the following does **not** bring about increased airway resistance?

   (a) Histamine-induced edema of the walls of the small airways.
   (b) Epinephrine's action on the smooth muscle of the airways.
   (c) Allergy-induced spasm of the smooth muscle in the walls of the small airways.
   (d) Collapse of the smaller airways as a result of emphysema.
   (e) Excess mucus production in the airways.

ANSWER: b

19. Which of the following promotes elastic recoil of the lungs?

   (a) Elastic fibers in the lung.
   (b) Surface tension of the fluid lining the alveoli.
   (c) Pulmonary surfactant.
   (d) Both (a) and (b) above are correct.
   (e) All of the above are correct.

ANSWER: d

20. Which of the following statements concerning pulmonary surfactant is __incorrect__?

  (a) Pulmonary surfactant is secreted by Type II alveolar cells.
  (b) Pulmonary surfactant is deficient in newborn respiratory distress syndrome.
  (c) Pulmonary surfactant promotes elastic recoil of the lungs.
  (d) The cohesive force between a water molecule and an adjacent pulmonary surfactant molecule is much lower than the cohesive force between two adjacent water molecules.
  (e) Pulmonary surfactant reduces surface tension.

ANSWER: c

21. Pulmonary surfactant

  (a) is secreted by Type I alveolar cells.
  (b) decreases surface tension of the fluid lining the alveoli.
  (c) is one of the factors responsible for causing elastic recoil of the lungs.
  (d) Two of the above are correct.
  (e) All of the above are correct.

ANSWER: b

22. The minimum volume of air that remains in the lungs after a maximal expiration is termed the

  (a) tidal volume.
  (b) functional residual capacity.
  (c) residual volume.
  (d) vital capacity.
  (e) No air remains in the lungs after maximal expiration.

ANSWER: c

23. The vital capacity

  (a) is the volume of air normally entering or leaving the lungs during a single breath.
  (b) is the maximum volume of air that can be moved in or out during a single breath.
  (c) is the maximum volume of air that the lungs can hold.
  (d) is the minimum volume of air that the lungs can hold.
  (e) None of the above are correct.

ANSWER: b

24. Which type of chronic obstructive pulmonary disease is characterized by a breakdown of alveolar walls and collapse of the smaller airways?

    (a) Asthma.
    (b) Chronic bronchitis.
    (c) Emphysema.
    (d) Two of the above are correct.
    (e) All of the above are correct.

ANSWER: c

25. Which of the following spirometry results would **not** be expected of a patient suffering from obstructive lung disease?

    (a) Normal total lung capacity.
    (b) Increased functional residual capacity.
    (c) Decreased residual volume.
    (d) Decreased FEV_1.

ANSWER: c

26. Which of the following forces does **not** contribute to keeping the alveoli open?

    (a) Alveolar surface tension.
    (b) Transmural pressure gradient.
    (c) Pulmonary surfactant.

ANSWER: a

27. A person who has a tidal volume of 400 ml/breath, a respiratory rate of 14 breaths/minute, and an anatomic dead space volume of 120 ml will have a pulmonary ventilation rate of

    (a) 3,000 ml/minute.
    (b) 3,920 ml/minute.
    (c) 4,260 ml/minute.
    (d) 5,600 ml/minute.
    (e) 6,240 ml/minute.

ANSWER: d

28. A person who has a tidal volume of 400 ml/breath, a respiratory rate of 14 breaths/minute and an anatomic dead space volume of 120 ml will have an alveolar ventilation rate of

    (a) 3,000 ml/minute.
    (b) 3,920 ml/minute.
    (c) 4,260 ml/minute.
    (d) 5,600 ml/minute.
    (e) 6,240 ml/minute.

ANSWER: b

29. If 20% of the air is composed of O_2, the partial pressure of oxygen at sea level where atmospheric pressure is 760 mm Hg would be

    (a) 20 mm Hg.
    (b) 760 mm Hg.
    (c) 70 mm Hg.
    (d) 350 mm Hg.
    (e) 152 mm Hg.

ANSWER: e

30. If 20% of the air is composed of O_2, the partial pressure of oxygen at an altitude of 20,000 feet where atmospheric pressure is 350 mm Hg would be

    (a) 20 mm Hg.
    (b) 760 mm Hg.
    (c) 74 mm Hg.
    (d) 350 mm Hg.
    (e) 160 mm Hg.

ANSWER: c

31. Po_2 in the blood

    (a) refers to the pressure exerted by the amount of oxygen dissolved in the blood.
    (b) is the most important factor determining the per cent saturation of hemoglobin.
    (c) is normal in carbon monoxide poisoning.
    (d) Both (a) and (b) above are correct.
    (e) All of the above are correct.

ANSWER: e

32. Po$_2$

    (a) of atmospheric air averages 20% of total atmospheric pressure.
    (b) of blood is the most important factor that determines the extent to which O$_2$ will combine with hemoglobin.
    (c) of arterial blood is decreased when hemoglobin preferentially combines with CO rather than O$_2$.
    (d) Both (a) and (b) above are correct.
    (e) All of the above are correct.

ANSWER: d

33. If the alveolar Po$_2$ is 100 mm Hg, the blood leaving the pulmonary capillaries in a normal person will have a Po$_2$ of

    (a) 40 mm Hg.
    (b) 46 mm Hg.
    (c) 100 mm Hg.
    (d) 760 mm Hg.
    (e) None of the above are correct.

ANSWER: c

34. Which of the following would decrease diffusion of a gas across the alveolar/pulmonary capillary membrane?

    (a) An increase in thickness of the membrane.
    (b) An increase in surface area of the membrane.
    (c) An increase in the partial pressure gradient.
    (d) Two of the above are correct.
    (e) All of the above are correct.

ANSWER: a

35. Systemic venous Po$_2$ is _____ alveolar Po$_2$ and systemic venous Pco$_2$ is _____ alveolar Pco$_2$.

    (a) greater than, greater than
    (b) greater than, less than
    (c) less than, greater than
    (d) less than, less than
    (e) equal to, equal to

ANSWER: c

36. Systemic arterial P_{O_2} is _____ tissue P_{O_2} and systemic
      arterial P_{CO_2} is _____ tissue P_{CO_2}.

    (a) greater than, greater than
    (b) greater than, less than
    (c) less than, greater than
    (d) less than, less than
    (e) equal to, equal to

ANSWER: b

37. Hemoglobin

    (a) plays a critical role in determining the total amount
         of O_2 that is exchanged because it acts as a storage
         depot, removing dissolved O_2 and thus keeping the P_{O_2}
         low so that net diffusion is allowed to continue.
    (b) combines only with O_2.
    (c) is found only in erythrocytes.
    (d) Both (a) and (c) above are correct.
    (e) All of the above are correct.

ANSWER: d

38. The percent hemoglobin saturation

    (a) decreases as P_{O_2} increases.
    (b) decreases as P_{CO_2} increases.
    (c) decreases as H^+ decreases.
    (d) decreases as body temperature decreases.
    (e) More than one of the above are correct.

ANSWER: b

39. Which of the following will **not** cause the oxygen-hemo-
      globin dissociation curve to shift to the right?

    (a) An increase in P_{O_2}.
    (b) An increase in temperature.
    (c) An increase in P_{CO_2}.
    (d) An increase in acidity.
    (e) An increase in DPG.

ANSWER: a

40. Oxygen-binding sites on hemoglobin have the highest affinity for

    (a) carbon dioxide.
    (b) oxygen.
    (c) carbon monoxide.
    (d) nitrogen.

ANSWER: c

41. Which of the following factors does **not** shift the Hb-O_2 curve to the right?

    (a) increased CO_2
    (b) increased CO
    (c) increased H^+
    (d) increased temperature
    (e) increased DPG

ANSWER: b

42. Approximately what percent of oxygen is transported in the blood physically dissolved?

    (a) 10%.
    (b) 30%.
    (c) 1.5%.
    (d) 98.5%.
    (e) 60%.

ANSWER: c

43. The primary factor determining the percent hemoglobin saturation is

    (a) blood P_{O_2}.
    (b) blood P_{CO_2}.
    (c) diphosphoglycerate concentration.
    (d) the temperature of the blood.
    (e) the acidity of the blood.

ANSWER: a

44. The plateau portion of the O_2-Hb curve

    (a)   is in the blood-Po_2 range that exists at the pulmonary capillaries.
    (b)   means that hemoglobin becomes almost nearly saturated in the lungs unless the pulmonary capillary Po_2 falls below 60 mm Hg.
    (c)   is in the blood-Po_2 range that exists at the systemic capillaries.
    (d)   Both (a) and (b) above are correct.
    (e)   Both (b) and (c) above are correct.

ANSWER: d

45. Because of the steep portion of the O_2-Hb curve,

    (a)   there is a good margin of safety in O_2-carrying capacity of the blood.
    (b)   a small drop in systemic capillary Po_2 in a metabolically active tissue automatically makes large amounts of O_2 available, because O_2 is released from hemoglobin as a result of a big drop in percent hemoglobin saturation.
    (c) O_2 loading is still almost normal even when alveolar Po_2 falls up to 40%.
    (d)   more O_2 is physically dissolved in the systemic capillaries than in the pulmonary capillaries.
    (e)   the affinity of hemoglobin for O_2 is increased as the blood Po_2 decreases.

ANSWER: b

46. Which of the following statements concerning hemoglobin is (are) correct?

    (a)   The presence of hemoglobin keeps the blood Po_2 low and favors O_2 movement into the blood despite a very large transfer of O_2 until hemoglobin is completely saturated.
    (b)   Hemoglobin can combine with O_2, CO_2, H^+, and CO.
    (c)   Hemoglobin unloads more O_2 in the presence of increased tissue acidity.
    (d)   Both (a) and (b) above are correct.
    (e)   All of the above are correct.

ANSWER: e

47. Hemoglobin

    (a) combines preferentially with O_2 over any other sub-
         stance.
    (b) when combined with carbon dioxide is known as
         carboxyhemoglobin.
    (c) plays a critical role in determining the amount of O_2
         that is exchanged between alveoli and blood, because
         it acts as a storage depot, removing dissolved O_2 from
         the blood, thereby keeping Po_2 low and allowing net
         diffusion of O_2 to continue until the hemoglobin is
         completely saturated.
    (d) Both (b) and (c) above are correct.
    (e) All of the above are correct.

ANSWER: c

48. The amount of oxygen unloaded from hemoglobin at the
    tissue level increases when

    (a) Pco_2 in the tissue increases.
    (b) the concentration of DPG in the red blood cells
         increases.
    (c) the concentration of DPG in the red blood cells
         decreases.
    (d) Both (a) and (b) above are correct.
    (e) Both (a) and (c) above are correct.

ANSWER: d

49. Compare the changes in percent hemoglobin saturation that
    would occur in the two following situations:

    I. If the blood Po_2 dropped from 100 mm Hg to 80 mm Hg.
    II. If the blood Po_2 dropped from 40 mm Hg to 20 mm Hg.

    (a) In both situations, the percent hemoglobin saturation
         would decrease by 20%.
    (b) There would be very little reduction in percent
         hemoglobin saturation in I but a large reduction in
         II.
    (c) There would be a large reduction in percent hemo-
         globin saturation in I but very little reduction in
         II.

ANSWER: b

50. The normal percent saturation of hemoglobin in venous
     blood is

     (a)   97%.
     (b)   75%.
     (c)   50%.
     (d)   40%.
     (e)   10%.

ANSWER: b

51. Approximately what percent of carbon dioxide is trans-
     ported in the blood physically dissolved?

     (a)   5%.
     (b)   10%.
     (c)   20%.
     (d)   30%.
     (e)   None of the above are correct.

ANSWER: b

52. What is the primary method by which CO_2 is transported in
     the blood?

     (a)   Physically dissolved.
     (b)   Bound to hemoglobin.
     (c)   Bound to plasma protein.
     (d)   As bicarbonate.
     (e)   As carbonic anhydrase.

ANSWER: d

53. Carbonic anhydrase

     (a)   is found in the red blood cells.
     (b)   catalyzes the formation of carbonic acid from
           carbonic dioxide and water.
     (c)   catalyzes the formation of oxyhemoglobin from oxygen
           and reduced hemoglobin.
     (d)   Both (a) and (b) above are correct.
     (e)   Both (a) and (c) above are correct.

ANSWER: d

54. 2,3-diphosphoglycerate

    (a) is produced within red blood cells.
    (b) production is inhibited by HbO_2.
    (c) concentration gradually increases whenever Hb in the arterial blood is chronically undersaturated.
    (d) Both (a) and (b) above are correct.
    (e) All of the above are correct.

ANSWER: e

55. Which of the following conditions exists at high altitudes?

    (a) Histotoxic hypoxia.
    (b) Hypoxic hypoxia.
    (c) Anemic hypoxia.
    (d) Hypocapnia.
    (e) None of the above are correct.

ANSWER: b

56. Hypercapnia

    (a) refers to excess CO_2 in the arterial blood.
    (b) occurs when CO_2 is blown off to the atmosphere at a rate faster than it is being produced by the tissues.
    (c) is caused by hyperventilation.
    (d) Both (a) and (c) above are correct.
    (e) All of the above are correct.

ANSWER: a

57. The primary respiratory center that provides output to the respiratory muscles is located in the

    (a) pons.
    (b) medulla.
    (c) cerebral cortex.
    (d) cerebellum.
    (e) hypothalamus.

ANSWER: b

58. Which of the following statements concerning the dorsal
     respiratory group (DRG) is correct?

     (a) The DRG consists of both inspiratory neurons and
          expiratory neurons.
     (b) The neurons of the DRG remain inactive during normal
          quiet breathing.
     (c) The DRG is called into play by the VRG as an
          "overdrive" mechanism during periods when demands for
          ventilation are increased.
     (d) All of the above are correct.
     (e) None of the above are correct.

ANSWER: e

59. Pacemaker activity that establishes the rhythmicity of
     breathing resides in

     (a) the lung tissue.
     (b) the respiratory muscles.
     (c) the respiratory control centers in the brain.
     (d) the phrenic nerve.
     (e) the relationship between the inspiratory and
          expiratory neurons of the ventral respiratory group.

ANSWER: c

60. The inspiratory neurons

     (a) rhythmically send impulses down the spinal cord to
          activate the phrenic nerve, bringing about contrac-
          tion of the diaphragm.
     (b) are stimulated by the pulmonary stretch receptors.
     (c) are located in the pneumotaxic respiratory center in
          the pons.
     (d) Both (a) and (b) above are correct.
     (e) All of the above are correct.

ANSWER: d

61. The apneustic center

     (a) is located in the medulla.
     (b) stimulates the inspiratory neurons.
     (c) inhibits inspiratory activity.
     (d) Both (a) and (b) above are correct.
     (e) Both (a) and (c) above are correct.

ANSWER: b

62. Expiratory neurons

    (a)   are found in both the DRG and VRG.
    (b)   send impulses to the expiratory muscles during normal
          quiet breathing.
    (c)   are stimulated by the pneumotaxic center.
    (d)   Both (a) and (b) above are correct.
    (e)   None of the above are correct.

ANSWER: d

63. The primary regulator of the magnitude of ventilation in
    normal circumstances is

    (a)   the H^+ concentration of the brain extracellular
          fluid monitored by central chemoreceptors.
    (b)   the Po_2 of the arterial blood monitored by central
          chemoreceptors.
    (c)   the Po_2 of the arterial blood monitored by peripheral
          chemoreceptors.
    (d)   the Pco_2 of arterial blood monitored by central
          chemoreceptors.
    (e)   the Pco_2 of arterial blood monitored by peripheral
          chemoreceptors.

ANSWER: a

64. Which of the following statements concerning the periph-
    eral chemoreceptors is **incorrect**?   The peripheral chemo-
    receptors

    (a)   are stimulated whenever the arterial Po_2 falls below
          normal.
    (b)   are weakly stimulated by a rise in arterial Pco_2.
    (c)   are stimulated by an increase in arterial H^+, which
          plays an important role in acid-base balance.
    (d)   are located at the bifurcation of the common carotid
          arteries and in the aortic arch.
    (e)   when stimulated, reflexly increase ventilation.

ANSWER: a

65. The receptors that are stimulated by a large drop in the
    blood Po_2 level are located

    (a)   in the respiratory center of the brain.
    (b)   in the carotid and aortic bodies.
    (c)   in the tissue capillaries.
    (d)   Two of the above are correct.
    (e)   All of the above are correct.

ANSWER: b

66. Ventilation is increased the most by

    (a) a small increase in arterial Pco_2.
    (b) a small decrease in arterial Pco_2.
    (c) a small increase in arterial Po_2.
    (d) a small decrease in arterial Po_2.

ANSWER: a

67. At high altitudes

    (a) the alveolar Po_2 is higher than normal.
    (b) the alveolar Po_2 is lower than normal.
    (c) the alveolar Pco_2 is higher than normal.
    (d) Both (a) and (c) above are correct.
    (e) Both (b) and (c) above are correct.

ANSWER: b

True/False

68. The respiratory system is the only system involved with the exchange of gas between the cells of an organism and the external environment.

ANSWER: False

69. Respiration is accomplished entirely by the respiratory system.

ANSWER: False

70. Both the respiratory system and the circulatory system are involved in the process of respiration.

ANSWER: True

71. All steps of external respiration are accomplished by the respiratory system.

ANSWER: False

72. The respiratory system provides a route for water and heat elimination.

ANSWER: True

73. The respiratory airways filter, warm, and humidify incoming air.

ANSWER: True

74. The sole purpose of the vocal cords is related to their role in initiating the sounds of speech.

ANSWER: False

75. Air flow through the smaller bronchioles can be adjusted by varying the contractile activity of the smooth muscle within their walls.

ANSWER: True

76. The site of gas exchange in the lungs is the alveoli.

ANSWER: True

77. The pleural cavity normally is not in direct communication with the lungs or atmosphere.

ANSWER: True

78. At the end of inspiration and at the end of expiration, intra-alveolar pressure is always equal to atmospheric pressure.

ANSWER: True

79. At the end of inspiration and at the end of expiration, intrapleural pressure is always equal to atmospheric pressure.

ANSWER: False

80. Intrapleural pressure is usually less than atmospheric pressure.

ANSWER: True

81. Intrapleural pressure always equilibrates with intra-alveolar pressure.

ANSWER: False

82. The abdominal muscles are expiratory muscles.

ANSWER: True

83. The internal intercostal muscles are inspiratory muscles because they lift the ribs upward and outward to enlarge the thoracic cavity.

ANSWER: False

84. At a constant temperature, the pressure that a gas exerts depends on the volume that it occupies.

ANSWER: True

85. The quantity of air that will flow into and out of the lungs depends solely on the radius of the respiratory airways.

ANSWER: False

86. Inspiration is **always** an active process.

ANSWER: True

87. Expiration is **always** a passive process.

ANSWER: False

88. Stimulation of the sympathetic nervous system and epinephrine release lead to an increase in airway resistance.

ANSWER: False

89. Elastic recoil refers to how readily the lungs rebound after having been stretched.

ANSWER: False

90. Pulmonary surfactant decreases alveolar surface tension and makes the lung easier to expand.

ANSWER: True

91. Pulmonary surfactant is secreted by Type II alveolar cells.

ANSWER: True

92. Pulmonary surfactant reduces the work of breathing and increases lung stability by increasing alveolar surface tension.

ANSWER: False

93. Newborn respiratory distress syndrome is caused by an excess of pulmonary surfactant.

ANSWER: False

94. If there is a deficient supply of pulmonary surfactant, the lungs become more compliant.

ANSWER: False

95. A highly compliant lung is easier to stretch than a less compliant one.

ANSWER: True

96. Atelectasis refers to air in the pleural cavity.

ANSWER: False

97. Emphysema most commonly is brought about by excessive release of destructive enzymes from alveolar macrophages in response to chronic exposure to inhaled irritants.

ANSWER: True

98. Patients suffering from chronic obstructive pulmonary disease generally have more trouble exhaling than inhaling.

ANSWER: True

99. To produce a normal tidal volume, the expiratory muscles must be stimulated.

ANSWER: False

100. The residual volume is the amount of air remaining in the lungs at the end of a normal expiration.

ANSWER: False

101. If a person is breathing rapidly, it is safe to assume that s/he is getting adequate ventilation.

ANSWER: False

102. The 500 ml of air that is inspired is the same 500 ml of air that enters the alveoli during a single breath.

ANSWER: False

103. If the tidal volume is 500 ml and the anatomical dead space volume is 150 ml, only 350 ml of air enters the alveoli during inspiration.

ANSWER: False

104. Slow, deep breathing is more effective for increasing alveolar ventilation than is rapid, shallow breathing.

ANSWER: True

105. O_2 moves from the alveoli to the blood by active transport.

ANSWER: False

106. The partial pressure of oxygen in blood is a measure of the total content of oxygen in the blood.

ANSWER: False

107. The partial pressure of a gas in blood depends on the amount that is physically dissolved and not on the total content of the gas present in the blood.

ANSWER: True

108. Alveolar partial pressures do not fluctuate to any extent between inspiration and expiration.

ANSWER: True

109. The quantity of O_2 that will diffuse between the alveolar air and pulmonary blood depends solely on the partial pressure gradients that exist between the alveoli and blood.

ANSWER: False

110. Alveolar P_{O_2} is greater than systemic venous P_{O_2}.

ANSWER: True

111. Alveolar P_{CO_2} is greater than systemic venous P_{CO_2}.

ANSWER: False

112. Systemic arterial P_{O_2} is greater than tissue P_{O_2}.

ANSWER: True

113. Systemic arterial P_{CO_2} is greater than tissue P_{CO_2}.

ANSWER: False

114. A molecule of nitrogen exerts more pressure than a molecule of oxygen because nitrogen is a larger molecule.

ANSWER: False

115. Alveolar Po_2 is higher following inspiration than following expiration.

ANSWER: False

116. The most important factor that determines the extent to which hemoglobin is saturated with oxygen is the blood Po_2.

ANSWER: True

117. O_2 is much more soluble in blood than CO_2 is.

ANSWER: False

118. At the systemic capillaries, the Po_2 is in the range of the steep portion of the O_2-Hb curve.

ANSWER: True

119. Carbonic anhydrase is found only in the plasma.

ANSWER: False

120. During hyperventilation, arterial Pco_2 levels decrease because CO_2 is blown off more rapidly than it is being produced in the tissues.

ANSWER: True

121. In the plateau region of the Hb-O_2 curve, a large decrease in Po_2 results in a small decrease in Hb saturation, whereas in the steep portion of the curve a small decrease in Po_2 results in a large decrease in % Hb saturation.

ANSWER: True

122. Hemoglobin, by acting as a storage depot, plays an important role in permitting the transfer of large quantities of O_2 between the blood and surrounding tissues down Po_2 gradients because the O_2 bound to Hb does not directly contribute to the blood Po_2.

ANSWER: True.

123. The combination of Hb and CO_2 is known as carboxyhemo-globin.

ANSWER: False

124. The peripheral chemoreceptors are not activated during carbon monoxide poisoning despite the fact that the total O_2 content in the blood can become lethally low.

ANSWER: True

125. Respiration is reflexly inhibited by a fall in arterial H^+ concentration.

ANSWER: True

126. The most important factor controlling respiration is the Po_2 of arterial blood.

ANSWER: False

127. O_2 levels are much more closely regulated than CO_2 levels in the arterial blood.

ANSWER: False

128. A slight decrease in arterial Po_2 below normal is a more potent stimulus toward increasing respiration than is a slight increase in Pco_2 above normal.

ANSWER: False

129. The aortic and carotid body chemoreceptors are primarily sensitive to changes in arterial Pco_2 levels.

ANSWER: False

130. The pulmonary stretch receptors inhibit the inspiratory neurons.

ANSWER: True

131. When the inspiratory neurons stop firing, expiration occurs.

ANSWER: False

132. The inspiratory and expiratory neurons both display pacemaker activity.

ANSWER: False

133. The pneumotaxic and apneustic centers are located in the pons.

ANSWER: True

134. Receptors in the CNS that detect changes in arterial Pco_2 are actually sensitive to the H^+ concentration of the brain extracellular fluid.

ANSWER: True

Fill-in-the-blanks

135. The _____ serve as the conducting portion of the respiratory system and the _____ are the gas-exchanging portion.

ANSWER: respiratory airways, alveoli

136. The exchange of O_2 and CO_2 between the external environment and tissue cells is known as _____.

ANSWER: external respiration

137. The _____ serves as a common passageway for both the respiratory and digestive systems.

ANSWER: pharynx

138. The alveolar wall is (how many) _____ cell layer(s) thick. The wall of the pulmonary capillaries surrounding an alveolus is (how many) cell _____ layer(s) thick.

ANSWER: one, one

139. The most profound changes in thoracic volume can be accomplished by contraction of the _____.

ANSWER: diaphragm

140. According to _____ law, at any constant temperature, the pressure of a gas varies inversely with the volume of the gas.

ANSWER: Boyle's

141. _____ refers to air in the pleural cavity.

ANSWER: Pneumothorax

142. _____ refers to a collapsed lung.

ANSWER: Atelectasis

143. The _____ nerve supplies the diaphragm.

ANSWER: phrenic

144. The site of gas exchange in the lungs is the _____.

ANSWER: alveoli

145. The _____ is a double-walled, closed sac that separates each lung from the thoracic wall and other surrounding structures.

ANSWER: pleural sac

146. _____ is a respiratory disease characterized by collapse of the smaller airways and a breakdown of alveolar walls.

ANSWER: Emphysema

147. The maximum volume of air that can be moved in and out of the lungs in a single breath is known as the _____.

ANSWER: vital capacity

148. The volume occupied by the conducting airways is known as the _____.

ANSWER: anatomical dead space

149. The primary factor that determines the % Hb saturation is the _____.

ANSWER: P_{O_2}

150. The _____ effect refers to the reduced affinity of Hb for O_2 in the presence of increased CO_2 and H^+.

ANSWER: Bohr

151. The _____ effect refers to the increased affinity of Hb for CO_2 and H^+ after O_2 unloading.

ANSWER: Haldane

152. _____ refers to a ventilation rate that exceeds the metabolic needs of the body.

ANSWER: hyperventilation

153. The primary respiratory control center that provides output to the respiratory muscles is located in the _____.

ANSWER: medulla of the brain stem

154. The apneustic and pneumotaxic centers are located in the _____.

ANSWER: pons of the brain stem

155. The DRG consists mostly of _____ neurons.

ANSWER: inspiratory

156. The expiratory neurons are located in the _____.

ANSWER: VRG

157. _____ is normally the most important input in regulating the magnitude of ventilation under resting conditions.

ANSWER: Arterial P_{CO_2} (by means of brain ECF H^+)

158. The peripheral chemoreceptors include the _____ and _____ bodies.

ANSWER: carotid, aortic

159. _____ is the transient cessation of breathing.

ANSWER: Apnea

160. The subjective sensation of not getting enough air is known as _____.

ANSWER: dyspnea

161. List the substances that can combine with Hb. _____, _____, _____, _____

ANSWER: O_2, CO_2, H^+, CO

162.   If a person ascended a mountain where the atmospheric pressure was only 500 mmHg, what would the P_{O_2} of the air be, assuming that the air consisted of 21% O_2?

_____

ANSWER: 105 mmHg

(Go to next page.)

Matching

163.   Indicate which lung volume or capacity is being described in the column below by filling in the appropriate letter in the blank. <u>There is only one correct answer for each question and each answer may be used more than once.</u>

(a) = vital capacity
(b) = respiratory rate
(c) = FEV_1
(d) = tidal volume
(e) = residual volume
(f) = total lung capacity
(g) = functional residual capacity

(h) = alveolar ventilation
(i) = pulmonary ventilation
(j) = inspiratory reserve volume
(k) = expiratory reserve volume
(l) = inspiratory capacity
(m) = anatomical dead space volume

_____ respiratory rate x (tidal volume - dead space volume)
_____ maximum volume of air that the lungs can hold
_____ the volume of air entering or leaving the lungs in a single breath during quiet breathing
_____ the minimum volume of air remaining in the lungs after maximal expiration
_____ the extra volume of air that can be maximally inspired over and above the tidal volume
_____ amount of air breathed in and out in one minute
_____ maximum volume of air that can be moved in and out during a single breath
_____ volume of air that can be expired during the first second of expiration in a vital-capacity determination
_____ the maximum volume of air that can be inspired at the end of a normal expiration
_____ inspiratory reserve volume + tidal volume + expiratory reserve volume
_____ vital capacity + residual volume
_____ volume of air in the respiratory airways
_____ the extra volume of air that can be actively expired by contraction of expiratory muscles beyond that normally expired
_____ respiratory rate x tidal volume
_____ volume of air in the lungs at the end of a normal passive expiration
_____ amount of air that is available for exchange of gases with the blood per minute
_____ breaths/minute

ANSWERS: h, f, d, e, j, i, a, c, l, a, f, m, k, i, g, h, b

164. _____ newborn respiratory distress syndrome
     _____ dyspnea
     _____ chronic obstructive pulmonary disease
     _____ apnea
     _____ hyperventilation
     _____ hyperpnea

a. transient cessation of breathing
b. rate of ventilation is in excess of the body's metabolic needs
c. deficiency of pulmonary surfactant
d. increased ventilation that matches an increase metabolic demand.
e. subjective sensation of not getting enough breath
f. increased airway resistance

ANSWERS: c, e, f, a, b, d

165. Indicate which type of hypoxia would be present in each of the circumstances listed below by writing the appropriate letter in the blank using the following answer code.

> (a) = anemic hypoxia
> (b) = circulatory hypoxia
> (c) = histotoxic hypoxia
> (d) = hypoxic hypoxia

_____ cyanide poisoning
_____ high altitude
_____ carbon monoxide poisoning
_____ emphysema
_____ hemoglobin deficiency
_____ congestive heart failure

ANSWERS: c, d, a, d, a, b

166. Indicate the effect the following changes would have on
      the rate of gas transfer using the answer code below:

      (a) = this change would increase the rate of gas
            transfer
      (b) = this change would decrease the rate of gas
            transfer
      (c) = this change would have no effect on the rate
            of gas transfer

      _____ the effect of pulmonary fibrosis on O_2 and CO_2
             exchange within the lungs
      _____ the effect of emphysema on O_2 and CO_2 exchange within
             the lungs
      _____ the effect of a fall in atmospheric Po_2 on O_2 exchange
             within the lungs
      _____ the effect on O_2 exchange in the lungs of replacing
             part of the nitrogen with helium so that the inspired
             air consists of 60% N, 19% He, and 21% O_2
      _____ the effect of increased metabolism of a cell on O_2 and
             CO_2 exchange between the cell and blood
      _____ the effect of tissue edema on O_2 and CO_2 exchange
             between the surrounding cells and blood
      _____ the effect of reduced systemic venous Po_2 on O_2
             exchange within the lungs

ANSWER: b, b, b, c, a, b, a

167. Indicate which chemical factor is responsible for the
      effect described by writing the appropriate letter in the
      blank using the following answer code:

      (a) = arterial Po_2 between 60 to 100 mm Hg
      (b) = arterial Po_2 less than 60 mm Hg
      (c) = arterial Pco_2 increased above normal
      (d) = brain ECF H^+ increased above normal
      (e) = arterial H^+ increased above normal

      _____ stimulates the peripheral chemoreceptors and is
             important in the regulation of acid-base balance
      _____ directly depresses the central chemoreceptors
      _____ weakly stimulates the peripheral chemoreceptors
      _____ stimulates peripheral chemoreceptors as an emergency
             mechanism
      _____ directly stimulates the central chemoreceptors and
             represents the dominant control of ventilation
      _____ blood-borne factor that has no effect on the
             peripheral chemoreceptors

ANSWERS: e, b, c, b, d, a

Completion

168. Circle the correct answers to complete the following statements concerning changes during a normal respiratory cycle.

As the diaphragm contracts, the size of the thoracic cavity is (increased, decreased). As a result, the lungs (expand, collapse), which causes the intra-alveolar pressure to (increase, decrease). The intra-alveolar pressure is now (greater than, less than) the atmospheric pressure. Since air flows from an area of (higher to lower, lower to higher) pressure, air (enters, leaves) the lungs. This process is known as an (inspiration, expiration).

During (inspiration, expiration) the size of the thoracic cage is decreased. As a result, the lungs (increase, decrease) in volume, which causes an (increase, decrease) in intra-alveolar pressure. The intra-alveolar pressure is now (greater than, less than) atmospheric pressure, so air (enters, leaves) the lungs.

ANSWERS: increased, expand, decrease, less than, higher to lower, enters, inspiration, expiration, decrease, increase, greater than, leaves

169. Indicate the relationship that exists between the two items in question by circling:

> (greater than),   < (less than),   or = (equal to)

   (a)   The size of the thoracic cavity when the diaphragm is contracting is (>, <, =) the size of the thoracic cavity when the diaphragm is relaxed.

   (b)   Lung volume before the diaphragm contracts is (>, <, =) lung volume after the diaphragm contracts.

   (c)   Intra-alveolar pressure during inspiration when air is flowing into the lungs is (>, <, =) intra-alveolar pressure before the onset of inspiration when no air is flowing.

   (d)   Intra-alveolar pressure at the end of inspiration is (>, <, =) atmospheric pressure.

(continued on page 338)

(e)   The number of molecules of air in the lungs at the onset of inspiration is (>, <, =) the number of molecules of air in the lungs at the end of inspiration.

(f)   Intra-alveolar pressure during expiration when air is flowing out of the lungs is (>, <, =) intra-alveolar pressure before the onset of expiration when no air is flowing.

(g)   Intra-alveolar pressure at the end of expiration, prior to the onset of inspiration, is (>, <, =) atmospheric pressure.

(h)   Intrapleural pressure at any point during the respiratory cycle is (>, <, =) intra-alveolar pressure.

(i)   The number of molecules of air in the lungs at the onset of expiration is (>, <, =) the number of molecules of air in the lungs at the end of expiration.

(j)   Intra-alveolar pressure upon relaxation of the diaphragm is (>, <, =) intra-alveolar pressure upon relaxation of the diaphragm plus contraction of the abdominal muscles.

(k)   The size of the thoracic cavity during contraction of the internal intercostal muscles is (>, <, =) the size of the thoracic cavity during contraction of the external intercostal muscles.

(l)   During quiet breathing, energy expenditure during inspiration is (>, <, =) energy expenditure during expiration.

(m)   Air flow during passive expiration is (>, <, =) air flow during active expiration.

(n)   Intrapleural pressure in the presence of pneumothorax is (>, <, =) atmospheric pressure.

(o)   The pressure gradient needed to move a normal tidal volume in a healthy individual is (>, <, =) the pressure gradient needed to move a normal tidal volume in a person with obstructive lung disease.

(p)   The total lung capacity of a person with restrictive lung disease is (>, <, =) the total lung capacity of a person with obstructive lung disease.

(q)   The residual volume of a person with restrictive lung disease is (>, <, =) the residual volume of a person with obstructive lung disease.

(r)   The FEV_1/VC % of a person with restrictive lung disease is (>, <, =) the FEV_1/VC % of a person with obstructive lung disease.

(s)   Alveolar surface tension of normal lungs is (>, <, =) alveolar surface tension of an infant with newborn respiratory distress syndrome.

ANSWERS: (a) >, (b) <, (c) <, (d) =, (e) <, (f) >, (g) =,
           (h) <, (i) >, (j) <, (k) <, (l) >, (m) <, (n) =,
           (o) <, (p) <, (q) <, (r) >, (s) <

AUDIOVISUAL AIDS

Films

A list of films available from West Publishing Company is presented in Appendix A.   Following are other films that may be suitable. The sources for these films, which are coded by abbreviation, are provided in Appendix B.

Asthma, FHS, 19 min.

Blood Gases, USNAC, 27 min.

Breath of Life, PSP, 10 min.

Breath of Life, FM, 26 min.

Breathing and Respiration, PHC, 19 min.

Carbon Monoxide Poisoning, IF, 3 min.

Carbon Monoxide Poisoning - Hyperhemoglobinemia Hypoxia, IOWA, 3 min.

Cell Respiration, MH, 28 min.

Chemical Balance Through Respiration, NFM, 29 min.

Choking to Save a Life, EBE, 12 min.

CPR Trainer, TLV, 21 min.

Cystic Fibrosis, FHS, 26 min.

Effects of Altitude, IF, 3 min.

Gas Exchange in the Respiratory System, HR, 4 min.

How to Save a Choking Victim: The Heimlich Maneuver, PAR, 11 min.

Human Body: Respiratory System, COR, 19 min.

Hypoxia, USNAC, 29 min.

Lungs and Pressure Volume Relationships, NFM, 20 min.

Mechanisms of Breathing, EBE, 11 min.

New Breath of Life, PF, 20 min.

Partners for Life: The Human Heart and Lungs, EI

Principles of Artificial Respiration, NFM, 29 min.

Principles of Respiratory Mechanics, AMA, 22 min.

Pulmonary Physiology: Ventilation, Diffusion, and Perfusion (VCR), OER, 60 min.

Respiration, MH, 28 min.

Respiration, PMR, 20 min.

Respiration in Man, EBE, 26 min.

Respiratory System, CFV, 13 min.

Smoking - Emphysema, MH, 19 min.

Smoking, Emphysema: A Fight for Breath, MH, 12 min.

Spirometry: Early Detection of Chronic Pulmonary Disease, WX, 25 min.

The Nose, EBE, 11 min.

The Tobacco Problem, EBE, 17 min.

Transport Systems in Animals, IU, 17 min.

Software

Dynamics of the Respiratory System, EI. An interactive animation allows students to simulate changes in activity and note its effect on respiratory system.

<u>Gas Laws</u>, CBS. Presents relationships between volume, pressure, and temperature.

<u>Respiration</u>, SSS. Reviews the main concepts.

<u>Respiratory Diseases and Disorders</u>, PLP. Covers bronchitis, cystic fibrosis, emphysema, tuberculosis, pneumonia, and asthma.

<u>Respiratory System</u>, PLP. Covers the human respiratory system including CNS centers.

Chapter 11
Urinary System

CONTENTS
(All page references are to the main text.)

-Tubular reabsorption involves transepithelial transport. p.372
-An energy-dependent Na^+-K^+ ATPase transport mechanism in the basolateral membrane is essential for Na^+ reabsorption. p.373
-Aldosterone stimulates Na^+ reabsorption in the distal and collecting tubules; atrial natriuretic peptide inhibits it.   p.374
-Glucose and amino acids are reabsorbed by Na^+-dependent secondary active transport.   p.376
-With the exception of Na^+, actively reabsorbed substances exhibit a transport maximum.   p.376
-Active Na^+ reabsorption is responsible for the passive reabsorption of Cl^-, H_2O, and urea.   p.378
-In general, unwanted waste products are not reabsorbed. p.378

Tubular Secretion
-The most important secretory processes are those for H^+, K^+, and organic ions.   p.378

Urine Excretion and Plasma Clearance, p.380
-On the average, one ml of urine is excreted per minute. p.380
-Plasma clearance refers to the volume of plasma cleared of a particular substance per minute.   p.381
-The ability to excrete urine of varying concentrations depends on the medullary countercurrent system and vaso pressin.   p.382
-Urine is temporarily stored in the bladder, from which it is emptied by the process of micturition.   p.389
-Renal failure has wide-ranging consequences.   p.388

Beyond the Basics - When Protein in the Urine Does Not Mean Kidney Disease, p.390

Beyond the Basics - Dialysis: Cellophane Tubing or Abdominal Lining as an Artificial Kidney, p.391

Chapter in Perspective: Focus on Homeostasis, p.392

Chapter Summary, p.393

LECTURE HINTS AND SUGGESTIONS

1. Use a torso model or whole body manikin to illustrate the locations of the organs of the urinary system. This and other materials required below can be obtained from Carolina Biological Supply Company, Burlington, NC, as well as from other supply houses.

2. Use a sectioned beef, sheep, or cow kidney to illustrate gross anatomy. Injected latex kidneys are very informative since they show the large amount of vasculature present in the kidney.

3. Kidney and nephron models are useful.

4. Show how to perform a urinalysis and explain what is being tested for during each step. Also use commercially prepared reagent strips. See any general physiology lab manual for examples.

5. Discuss the situations that require the use of commercial hemodialysis. Obtain used hemodialysis systems from a local hospital to illustrate their construction and function.

6. Set up demonstration slides of the urinary system histology.

7. Use vinylite molds of renal blood vessels and renal pelvis for demonstration.

8. Obtain and demonstrate three-dimensional models of the human urinary system.

CHAPTER TEST QUESTIONS

Multiple Choice

1. Which of the following is **not** a function of the kidneys?

    (a) Excrete the end products of bodily metabolism
    (b) Maintain proper plasma volume.
    (c) Secrete aldosterone to regulate sodium balance in the body.
    (d) Maintain proper osmolarity of body fluids.
    (e) Assist in maintaining the proper acid-base balance of the body.

ANSWER: c

2. Which of the following is **not** accomplished by the kidneys? The kidneys:

    (a) contribute significantly to long-term regulation of arterial blood pressure by maintaining the proper plasma volume.
    (b) act directly on the interstitial fluid, the fluid that bathes the cells, to maintain constancy in its composition.
    (c) excrete the metabolic waste products.
    (d) assist in maintaining the proper acid-base balance of the body.
    (e) secrete several hormones.

ANSWER: b

3. The kidneys

    (a) produce a minimum volume of about 500 ml of urine per day, even if a person is stranded without water.
    (b) can compensate more efficiently for excesses than for deficits of plasma constituents that they regulate.
    (c) produce urine of fixed composition in order to maintain homeostasis.
    (d) Both (a) and (b) above are correct.
    (e) All of the above are correct.

ANSWER: d

4. The functional unit of the kidneys is

    (a) the renal medulla.
    (b) the nephron.
    (c) the countercurrent system.
    (d) the loop of Henle.
    (e) the glomerulus.

ANSWER: b

5. Which of the following is **not** part of the nephron?

    (a) The glomerulus.
    (b) The proximal tubule.
    (c) The renal pelvis.
    (d) The collecting duct.
    (e) Bowman's capsule.

ANSWER: c

6. The peritubular capillaries

   (a)   supply nutrients and O_2 to the tubular cells.
   (b)   take up the substances that are reabsorbed by the tubules.
   (c)   supply substances that are secreted by the tubules.
   (d)   All of the above are correct.
   (e)   None of the above are correct.

ANSWER: d

7. The blood that flows through the kidneys

   (a)   is normally about 20 to 25% of the total cardiac output.
   (b)   is all filtered through the glomeruli.
   (c)   is all used to supply the renal tissue with O_2 and nutrients.
   (d)   Both (a) and (b) above are correct.
   (e)   All of the above are correct.

ANSWER: a

8. The glomerular filtration rate

   (a)   averages 125 ml/minute.
   (b)   averages 180 l/day.
   (c)   represents about 20 to 25% of the total cardiac output.
   (d)   Both (a) and (b) above are correct.
   (e)   All of the above are correct.

ANSWER: d

9. The glomerular filtrate as it enters Bowman's capsule

   (a)   is a protein-free plasma.
   (b)   is identical in composition to urine.
   (c)   contains only substances that are not needed by the body.
   (d)   is formed as a result of active forces.
   (e)   is formed at a constant rate under all circumstances.

ANSWER: a

10. The glomerular filtrate as it enters Bowman's capsule

    (a) is a protein-free plasma.
    (b) is formed as a result of an imbalance of passive
         forces acting across the glomerular membrane.
    (c) does not contain foreign compounds because these
         substances are secreted by special transport mecha-
         nisms in the proximal tubule instead.
    (d) Both (a) and (b) above are correct.
    (e) All of the above are correct.

ANSWER: d

11. Which of the following does **not** normally appear in the
    glomerular filtrate?

    (a) Plasma proteins.
    (b) Glucose.
    (c) Sodium.
    (d) Urea.
    (e) Calcium.

ANSWER: a

12. Filtered substances do **not** pass through which of the
    following as they move across the glomerular membrane?

    (a) Glomerular capillary pores.
    (b) Basement membrane.
    (c) Podocytes.
    (d) Filtration slits.

ANSWER: c

13. Which of the following forces oppose glomerular filtra-
    tion?

    (a) Plasma-colloid osmotic pressure.
    (b) Bowman's capsule hydrostatic pressure.
    (c) Glomerular-capillary blood pressure.
    (d) Both (a) and (b) above are correct.
    (e) Both (b) and (c) above are correct.

ANSWER: d

14. Bowman's capsule

    (a) filters water and solute from the blood.
    (b) exerts a hydrostatic pressure that opposes filtration.
    (c) exerts a hydrostatic pressure that favors filtration.
    (d) Both (a) and (b) above are correct.
    (e) Both (a) and (c) above are correct.

ANSWER: b

15. Which of the following statements concerning the process of glomerular filtration is correct?

    (a) Bowman's capsule hydrostatic pressure opposes filtration.
    (b) The glomerular filtration rate is limited by a T_m.
    (c) All of the plasma that enters the glomerulus is filtered.
    (d) Two of the above are correct.
    (e) All of the above are correct.

ANSWER: a

16. Glomerular filtration

    (a) occurs in the loop of Henle.
    (b) is the process by which plasma water, electrolytes, and small molecules, which enter Bowman's capsule, are separated from blood cells and protein, which remain in the glomerular capillaries.
    (c) is the process by which a substance is transported from the tubular fluid to the peritubular capillaries.
    (d) Both (a) and (b) above are correct.
    (e) None of the above are correct.

ANSWER: b

17. Which of the following factors would **decrease** the GFR?

    (a) A fall in plasma protein concentration.
    (b) An obstruction such as a kidney stone in the tubular system, which increases Bowman's capsule hydrostatic pressure.
    (c) Vasodilation of the afferent arterioles.
    (d) Two of the above are correct.
    (e) All of the above would increase the GFR.

ANSWER: b

350   Chapter 11

18. Afferent arteriolar vasoconstriction _____ blood flow
     into the glomerulus, which causes the glomerular-capillary
     blood pressure to _____, leading to a(n) _____
     in the net filtration pressure and a resultant _____
     in the GFR.

     (a) increases, increase, increase, increase
     (b) decreases, decrease, decrease, decrease
     (c) increases, increase, decrease, decrease
     (d) decreases, decrease, increase, increase
     (e) None of the above are correct.

ANSWER: b

19. Extrinsic control of the GFR

     (a) is mediated by sympathetic nervous system input to
          the afferent arterioles.
     (b) is aimed at the regulation of arterial blood pres-
          sure.
     (c) does not require a special mechanism but occurs as
          part of the baroreceptor reflex.
     (d) Both (a) and (b) above are correct.
     (e) All of the above are correct.

ANSWER: e

20. Tubular reabsorption

     (a) refers to the movement of a substance from the
          peritubular capillary blood into the tubular fluid.
     (b) occurs by either active or passive transport.
     (c) involves the process of transepithelial transport.
     (d) Both (b) and (c) above are correct.
     (e) All of the above are correct.

ANSWER: d

21. Which of the following statements regarding tubular
     reabsorption is **incorrect**? Tubular reabsorption

     (a) refers to the movement of a substance from the
          tubular fluid to the peritubular capillary blood.
     (b) is important for the conservation of substances
          important to the body such as Na^+, Cl^-, glucose, and
          amino acids.
     (c) can occur by active or passive transport mechanisms.
     (d) involves the process of transepithelial transport.
     (e) takes place only in the proximal tubule.

ANSWER: e

22. Tubular reabsorption

    (a) involves the movement of substances from the peri-
        tubular capillaries into the tubular fluid.
    (b) involves the movement of substances from the tubular
        fluid into the peritubular capillaries.
    (c) is considered to be active if any one of the five
        steps of transepithelial transport is active.
    (d) Both (a) and (c) above are correct.
    (e) Both (b) and (c) above are correct.

ANSWER: e

23. The vessels that substances enter during tubular reab-
    sorption are the

    (a) afferent arterioles.
    (b) efferent arterioles.
    (c) peritubular capillaries.
    (d) glomerular capillaries.
    (e) collecting tubules.

ANSWER: c

24. Which of the following is **not** a step in transepithelial
    transport?

    (a) Movement of the substance through the cytosol of the
        tubular cell.
    (b) Movement of the substance across the glomerular
        capillary wall.
    (c) Movement of the substance across the luminal membrane
        of the tubular cell.
    (d) Movement of the substance through the interstitial
        fluid.
    (e) Movement of the substance across the basolateral
        membrane of the tubular cell.

ANSWER: b

25. The Na^+ -K^+ ATPase transport system that plays a pivotal
    role in much of tubular reabsorption is located in the

    (a) luminal membrane of tubular cells.
    (b) basolateral membrane of tubular cells.
    (c) podocytes.
    (d) glomerular capillary membrane.
    (e) basement membrane.

ANSWER: b

26. The proximal tubule

    (a) reabsorbs about 65% of the filtered water.
    (b) is the site of action of aldosterone.
    (c) is the location where glucose is reabsorbed.
    (d) Both (a) and (c) above are correct.
    (e) All of the above are correct.

ANSWER: d

27. The T_m

    (a) represents the maximum amount of a particular
         substance that can be.excreted in the urine per unit
         of time.
    (b) represents the plasma concentration at which a
         substance first appears in the urine.
    (c) for phosphate is equal to the normal plasma concen-
         tration of phosphate.
    (d) More than one of the above are correct.
    (e) None of the above are correct.

ANSWER: e

28. Tubular maximum (T_m)

    (a) is the maximum amount of a substance that the tubular
         cells can actively transport within a given time
         period.
    (b) is the maximum rate at which a substance is filtered
         at the glomerulus.
    (c) occurs when the membrane carrier becomes saturated.
    (d) Both (a) and (c) above are correct.
    (e) Both (b) and (c) above are correct.

ANSWER: d

29. T_m is

    (a) the maximum rate of glomerular filtration.
    (b) the maximum rate a substance can be reabsorbed
         because of saturation of the carrier molecule.
    (c) the maximum rate of urine excretion.
    (d) the maximum rate a substance can be cleared from the
         blood.
    (e) the maximum % of renal blood flow that can be
         converted to filtrate.

ANSWER: b

30. The renal threshold is

    (a) the maximum amount of a particular substance that can
         be excreted in the urine per unit of time.
    (b) the maximum amount of a particular substance that the
         tubular cells are capable of actively reabsorbing per
         unit of time.
    (c) the plasma concentration of a particular substance at
         which its T_m is reached and the substance first
         appears in the urine.
    (d) the maximum amount of waste products that can be
         concentrated in the urine per unit of time.
    (e) the maximum amount of water that can be osmotically
         absorbed across the tubules per unit of time.

ANSWER: c

31. Which of the following plasma constituents is **not** regu-
    lated by the kidneys?

    (a) Glucose
    (b) Na^+
    (c) H^+
    (d) Phosphate
    (e) Water

ANSWER: a

32. The plasma concentration of which of the following
    substances is regulated by the kidneys?

    (a) Plasma proteins
    (b) Urea
    (c) Glucose
    (d) PO_4^{3-}
    (e) Amino acids

ANSWER: d

33. Which of the following substances exhibits a T_m?

    (a) Na^+
    (b) Cl^-
    (c) Amino acids
    (d) Urea
    (e) H_2O

ANSWER: c

34. Given the following data for substance X (GFR = 125 ml/minute, T_m = 125 mg/minute, at a plasma concentration of 200 mg/100 ml), how much of substance X is filtered, reabsorbed, and excreted?

    (a) 200 mg/minute filtered, 125 mg/minute reabsorbed, 75 mg/minute excreted.
    (b) 250 mg/minute filtered, 125 mg/minute reabsorbed, 125 mg/minute excreted.
    (c) 125 mg/minute filtered, 125 mg/minute reabsorbed, 0 mg/minute excreted.
    (d) 250 mg/minute filtered, 200 mg/minute reabsorbed, 50 mg/minute excreted.
    (e) None of the above are correct.

ANSWER: b

35. The juxtaglomerular apparatus

    (a) secretes renin in response to sodium depletion or plasma volume reduction.
    (b) consists of specialized tubular and vascular cells at a point where the ascending limb passes through the fork formed by the afferent and efferent arterioles of the same nephron.
    (c) is the site of Na^+ reabsorption in the kidneys.
    (d) Both (a) and (b) above are correct.
    (e) All of the above are correct.

ANSWER: d

36. Aldosterone

    (a) stimulates Na^+ reabsorption in the distal and collecting tubules.
    (b) is secreted by the juxtaglomerular apparatus.
    (c) stimulates K^+ secretion in the distal tubule.
    (d) Both (a) and (b) above are correct.
    (e) Both (a) and (c) above are correct.

ANSWER: e

37. Aldosterone secretion

    (a) occurs in the kidney.
    (b) is stimulated by angiotensin II.
    (c) is controlled by the plasma concentration of Cl^-.
    (d) All of the above are correct.
    (e) None of the above are correct.

ANSWER: b

38. Na⁺ reabsorption

     (a) uses 80% of the energy requirement of the kidney.
     (b) is under control of the hormone aldosterone in the distal portions of the nephron.
     (c) is linked to the reabsorption of water, Cl⁻, glucose, amino acids, and urea.
     (d) Both (a) and (b) above are correct.
     (e) All of the above are correct.

ANSWER: e

39. The greatest percentage of Na⁺ reabsorption takes place in the

     (a) proximal tubule.
     (b) loop of Henle.
     (c) distal tubule.
     (d) collecting tubule.
     (e) renal pelvis.

ANSWER: a

40. Which of the following substances is reabsorbed by secondary active transport?

     (a) Water.
     (b) Chloride.
     (c) Glucose.
     (d) Phosphate.
     (e) Urea.

ANSWER: c

41. Angiotensin I

     (a) is formed as a result of activation of angiotensinogen by renin.
     (b) is transformed into angiotensin II as a result of converting enzyme action in the lungs.
     (c) acts on the adrenal cortex to stimulate aldosterone secretion.
     (d) Both (a) and (b) above are correct.
     (e) All of the above are correct.

ANSWER: d

42. Sodium reabsorption in the distal portions of the nephron is stimulated by

    (a) atrial natriuretic peptide.
    (b) vasopressin.
    (c) angiotensin II.
    (d) aldosterone.
    (e) renin.

ANSWER: d

43. Which of the following is (are) attributable to atrial natriuretic peptide (ANP)?

    (a) ANP is released from the cardiac atria when the ECF volume is reduced.
    (b) ANP inhibits Na^+ reabsorption in the distal parts of the nephron.
    (c) ANP inhibits sympathetic nervous activity to the heart and blood vessels.
    (d) Both (b) and (c) above are correct.
    (e) All of the above are correct.

ANSWER: d

44. The energy requirement for glucose reabsorption is used to

    (a) run the Na^+ -K^+ ATPase pump.
    (b) run the Na^+-glucose cotransport carrier.
    (c) synthesize renin, which controls glucose reabsorption.
    (d) maintain the T_m for glucose.
    (e) insert additional glucose carriers in the tubular membranes, thus increasing the permeability of the tubules to glucose.

ANSWER: a

45. Which of the following does **not** play a role in Na^+ reabsorption?

    (a) Renin.
    (b) Vasopressin.
    (c) Angiotensinogen.
    (d) Aldosterone.
    (e) Atrial natriuretic peptide.

ANSWER: b

46. The distal and collecting tubules

(a) are the site of the cotransport carriers for
glucose and amino acid reabsorption.
(b) are the site of the organic ion secretory systems.
(c) are the site of aldosterone and vasopressin action.
(d) Both (a) and (c) above are correct.
(e) Both (b) and (c) above are correct.

ANSWER: c

47. Water reabsorption is under the control of vasopressin

(a) along the entire length of the nephron.
(b) only in the loop of Henle.
(c) only in the distal and collecting tubules.
(d) only in the proximal tubule.

ANSWER: c

48. Water reabsorption

(a) occurs passively by osmosis in the proximal tubule.
(b) is under the control of vasopressin in the distal and
collecting tubules.
(c) occurs by active transport in the distal and collecting tubules.
(d) Both (a) and (b) above are correct.
(e) All of the above are correct.

ANSWER: d

49. Which of the following statements concerning water
reabsorption is correct?

(a) Water reabsorption is under control of vasopressin
throughout the length of the nephron.
(b) The ascending limb of the loop of Henle is always
impermeable to water.
(c) Vasopressin makes the distal and collecting tubules
impermeable to water.
(d) 15% of the filtered water osmotically follows the
absorption of Na^+ and other solutes in the proximal
tubule.
(e) Water reabsorption is passive in the early portions
of the nephron but is active in the distal portions
of the nephron under vasopressin control.

ANSWER: b

50.   Water reabsorption

   (a)   cannot occur from any portion of the nephron in the
         absence of vasopressin.
   (b)   occurs to the greatest extent in the proximal
         convoluted tubule.
   (c)   is under vasopressin control in the proximal tubule.
   (d)   is under vasopressin control in the distal and
         collecting tubules.
   (e)   Both (b) and (d) above are correct.

ANSWER: e

51.   Urea

   (a)   is the waste product with the smallest molecular size
         in the glomerular filtrate.
   (b)   is in greater concentration at the end of the
         proximal tubule than in other body fluids.
   (c)   clearance rate is less than the GFR.
   (d)   Both (a) and (b) above are correct.
   (e)   All of the above are correct.

ANSWER: e

52.   Urea

   (a)   reabsorption occurs by active transport.
   (b)   is only 50% reabsorbed in the proximal tubule because
         the carrier has a low T_m.
   (c)   is a waste product of protein metabolism.
   (d)   Both (b) and (c) above are correct.
   (e)   All of the above are correct.

ANSWER: c

53.   Tubular secretion

   (a)   refers to the movement of a substance from the
         peritubular capillary blood into the tubular lumen.
   (b)   can occur by active or passive transport mechanisms.
   (c)   of K^+ occurs in the distal and collecting tubules and
         is stimulated by aldosterone.
   (d)   of organic anions and cations occurs in the proximal
         tubule by two distinct types of carriers.
   (e)   All of the above are correct.

ANSWER: e

54.   Tubular secretion

(a)   is important in the renal regulation of H⁺ concen-
      tration.
(b)   refers to the movement of substances from the tubular
      lumen to the peritubular capillaries.
(c)   is important in the renal regulation of Na⁺ balance.
(d)   Two of the above are correct.
(e)   All of the above are correct.

ANSWER: a

55.   Tubular secretion

(a)   involves transepithelial transport.
(b)   is the movement of a substance from the peritubular
      capillary blood into the tubular fluid.
(c)   always occurs by active transport.
(d)   Both (a) and (b) above are correct.
(e)   Both (b) and (c) above are correct.

ANSWER: d

56.   Tubular secretion

(a)   refers to the movement of a substance from the
      peritubular capillary blood into the tubular fluid.
(b)   involves transepithelial transport.
(c)   is important for removing foreign compounds from the
      body.
(d)   Both (a) and (b) above are correct.
(e)   All of the above are correct.

ANSWER: e

57.   Tubular secretion

(a)   is important in the renal regulation of hydrogen ion
      concentration.
(b)   is important for the elimination of metabolic waste
      products from the body.
(c)   is important in the renal regulation of sodium
      balance.
(d)   Both (a) and (b) above are correct.
(e)   All of the above are correct.

ANSWER: a

58. Secretion of foreign substances such as drugs generally occurs in the

    (a) distal tubule.
    (b) loop of Henle.
    (c) proximal tubule.
    (d) collecting duct.
    (e) glomerulus.

ANSWER: c

59. Potassium

    (a) is actively reabsorbed in the proximal tubule.
    (b) is actively secreted in the distal and collecting tubules.
    (c) secretion is controlled by aldosterone.
    (d) Both (b) and (c) above are correct.
    (e) All of the above are correct.

ANSWER: e

60. Which of the following stimulates aldosterone secretion?

    (a) An increase in plasma K^+.
    (b) A decrease in plasma K^+.
    (c) Activation of the renin-angiotensin pathway.
    (d) Both (a) and (c) above are correct.
    (e) Both (b) and (c) above are correct.

ANSWER: d

61. Plasma clearance

    (a) is the volume of plasma that is completely cleared of a substance by the kidneys in one minute of time.
    (b) is the amount of a substance appearing in the urine in one minute of time.
    (c) is the amount of a substance that is filtered in one minute of time.
    (d) is the amount of a substance secreted in one minute of time.

ANSWER: a

62. The plasma clearance of a substance can be used to calculate the glomerular filtration rate (GFR) if that substance is

    (a) freely filtered at the glomerulus and secreted and reabsorbed by the tubules.
    (b) freely filtered at the glomerulus and neither reabsorbed nor secreted by the tubules.
    (c) freely filtered at the glomerulus and secreted by the tubules.
    (d) freely filtered at the glomerulus and reabsorbed by the tubules.

ANSWER: b

63. When the GFR is 125 ml/minute, given the clearance rates for the following substances, which of these substances is being reabsorbed?

    (a) Substance A (clearance rate = 500 ml/minute).
    (b) Substance B (clearance rate = 125 ml/minute).
    (c) Substance C (clearance rate = 0 ml/minute).
    (d) Substance D (clearance rate = 75 ml/minute).
    (e) Substances C and D are both being reabsorbed.

ANSWER: e

64. The plasma clearance of what substance can be used to determine the GFR?

    (a) Urea.
    (b) Inulin.
    (c) Glucose.
    (d) Phosphate.
    (e) Para-aminohippuric acid.

ANSWER: b

65. When the body fluids are hypotonic

    (a) they are too dilute at an osmolarity less than 300 mosm/l.
    (b) a H_2O deficit exists.
    (c) vasopressin secretion is stimulated.
    (d) Two of the above are correct.
    (e) All of the above are correct.

ANSWER: a

66. Which of the following statements concerning the medullary vertical osmotic gradient is **incorrect**?

(a) The loops of Henle of long-looped nephrons establish a medullary vertical osmotic gradient by means of countercurrent multiplication.
(b) The countercurrent system establishes and maintains a medullary vertical osmotic gradient ranging from 300 to 1200 mosm/l.
(c) The collecting tubules of the long-looped nephrons but not the short-looped nephrons descend through the medullary vertical osmotic gradient before emptying into the renal pelvis.
(d) The medullary vertical osmotic gradient permits excretion of urine of differing concentrations by means of vasopressin-controlled, variable H_2O reabsorption from the final tubular segments.

ANSWER: c

67. The ascending limb of the loop of Henle of a long-looped nephron

(a) actively transports NaCl out of the lumen into the interstitial fluid.
(b) is highly impermeable to H_2O.
(c) is always impermeable to H_2O.
(d) Both (a) and (b) above are correct.
(e) Both (a) and (c) above are correct.

ANSWER: e

68. The tubular fluid is _____ as it enters Bowman's capsule, _____ at the beginning of the loop of Henle, _____ at the tip of the loop, and _____ as it leaves the loop to enter the distal tubule.

(a) isotonic, hypertonic, hypertonic, isotonic
(b) isotonic, isotonic, hypotonic, hypotonic
(c) isotonic, isotonic, hypertonic, hypotonic
(d) hypertonic, hypotonic, hypertonic, isotonic
(e) None of the above are correct.

ANSWER: c

69. The vertical osmotic gradient in the kidney

(a) is established and maintained by the countercurrent system.
(b) makes it possible to put out urine of variable concentration depending on the needs of the body by varying the degree of water permeability of the distal portions of the nephron.
(c) is found in the renal cortex.
(d) Both (a) and (b) above are correct.
(e) All of the above are correct.

ANSWER: d

70. The ascending limb of the loop of Henle of long-looped nephrons.

(a) is where NaCl passively leaves the tubular fluid down its concentration gradient.
(b) is where NaCl is actively transported into the interstitial fluid, leaving water behind because the tubular cells are not permeable to water.
(c) is where K^+ is secreted.
(d) is where aldosterone stimulates Na^+ reabsorption.
(e) None of the above are correct.

ANSWER: b

71. The ascending limb of the loop of Henle of long-looped nephrons.

(a) actively transports NaCl into the surrounding interstitial fluid.
(b) is impermeable to water.
(c) is found in the renal cortex.
(d) drains into the proximal convoluted tubule.
(e) Both (a) and (b) above are correct.

ANSWER: e

72. Which of the following statements concerning the countercurrent system is **incorrect**?

    (a) The loops of Henle of long-looped nephrons are responsible for establishing a vertical osmotic gradient in the interstitial fluid of the renal medulla by countercurrent multiplication.
    (b) The active NaCl pump of the ascending limb of Henle's loop can establish a 1200 mosm/l concentration difference between the ascending and descending limbs at any given horizontal level.
    (c) The collecting tubules of all nephrons utilize the driving force of the vertical osmotic gradient to accomplish variable H_2O reabsorption under the control of vasopressin, which governs their permeability.

ANSWER: b

73. Which of the following statements concerning the loop of Henle of long-looped nephrons is (are) correct?

    (a) The ascending limb of the loop of Henle is freely permeable to H_2O and NaCl.
    (b) The filtrate is isotonic as it enters the loop of Henle, hypertonic at the tip of the loop of Henle, and hypotonic as it leaves the loop of Henle.
    (c) The descending limb of the loop of Henle actively transports NaCl out of the tubule into the interstitial fluid.
    (d) More than one of the above are correct.
    (e) None of the above are correct.

ANSWER: b

74. Which part of the long-looped nephron is responsible for establishing the vertical osmotic gradient in the medulla of the kidney?

    (a) Collecting duct.
    (b) Afferent arteriole.
    (c) Loop of Henle.
    (d) Juxtaglomerular apparatus.
    (e) Distal tubule.

ANSWER: c

75. Identify the proper sequence of structures through which filtered plasma that does not get reabsorbed travels.

   (a) Glomerular capillaries, proximal tubule, distal tubule, loop of Henle, collecting duct.
   (b) Glomerular capillaries, proximal tubule, loop of Henle, distal tubule, collecting duct.
   (c) Glomerular capillaries, loop of Henle, proximal tubule, collecting duct, distal tubule.
   (d) Glomerular capillaries, proximal tubule, loop of Henle, collecting duct, distal tubule.
   (e) None of the above are correct.

ANSWER: b

76. Vasopressin

   (a) secretion is stimulated by a water deficit.
   (b) increases the permeability of the distal and collecting tubules to water.
   (c) increases the permeability of the late portion of the collecting tubule to urea.
   (d) Both (a) and (b) above are correct.
   (e) All of the above are correct.

ANSWER: e

77. Vasopressin

   (a) is produced in the hypothalamus.
   (b) increases the permeability of the distal and collecting tubules to water.
   (c) secretion is stimulated by a water deficit in the body.
   (d) Both (b) and (c) above are correct.
   (e) All of the above are correct.

ANSWER: e

78. Vasopressin

    (a) can completely halt urine production during periods
         of water deprivation to conserve water for the body.
    (b) activates the cyclic AMP second-messenger system
         within the tubular cells.
    (c) renders the distal and collecting tubules impermeable
         to water.
    (d) increases Na^+ reabsorption by the distal portions of
         the nephron.
    (e) stimulates the active salt pump of the ascending limb
         of the long loops of Henle to establish the medullary
         vertical osmotic gradient.

ANSWER: b

79. Vasopressin secretion

    (a) induces the kidneys to produce a small volume of
         concentrated urine.
    (b) is stimulated when the body fluids are hypertonic.
    (c) is inhibited when the arterial blood pressure is
         dangerously low.
    (d) Both (a) and (b) above are correct.
    (e) All of the above are correct.

ANSWER: d

80. The _____ and _____ enable the kidneys to
    produce urine of varying concentrations and volumes
    depending on the body's needs.

    (a) Na^+ -K^+ ATPase pump, co-transport carriers
    (b) juxtaglomerular apparatus, podocytes
    (c) podocytes, peritubular capillaries
    (d) medullary vertical osmotic gradient, vasopressin
    (e) renin-angiotensin-aldosterone system, renal pyramids

    ANSWER: d

81. Substances that appear in the urine have been

    (a) filtered and reabsorbed.
    (b) filtered and/or secreted but not reabsorbed.
    (c) reabsorbed but not secreted.
    (d) secreted and reabsorbed but not filtered.
    (e) None of the above are correct.

ANSWER: b

82. The segment of the nephron that is not permeable to H_2O even in the presence of vasopressin is the

    (a) proximal tubule.
    (b) ascending limb of a long loop of Henle.
    (c) descending limb of a long loop of Henle.
    (d) distal tubule.
    (e) collecting tubule.

ANSWER: b

83. Which of the following is a potential consequence of kidney disease?

    (a) Cardiac disturbances.
    (b) Skeletal abnormalities.
    (c) Anemia.
    (d) Acidosis.
    (e) All of the above are correct.

ANSWER: e

84. Excretion

    (a) is the removal from the body in the urine of substances that were filtered at the glomerulus or secreted but not reabsorbed.
    (b) is the process by which a substance moves from the peritubular capillary blood to the tubular fluid.
    (c) conserves substances that are important to the body.
    (d) occurs by active transport of substances into the urinary bladder.

ANSWER: a

85. Urine moves from the kidneys to the urinary bladder through the ureters

    (a) by active transport.
    (b) passively by the force of gravity.
    (c) by peristaltic contraction of the smooth muscle of the ureters.
    (d) when the bladder empties and creates a negative pressure that pulls the urine to the bladder.

ANSWER: c

86. The urinary bladder

   (a) is a temporary storage site for urine.
   (b) wall is stretched by 200 to 400 ml of urine, which
        stimulates stretch receptors that initiate the
        micturition reflex.
   (c) contracts when parasympathetic nerves stimulate it.
   (d) All of the above are correct.
   (e) None of the above are correct.

ANSWER: d

87. When the bladder wall is distended as a result of urine
     accumulation, the stretch receptors are stimulated and
     send afferent impulses to the spinal cord that

   (a) stimulate parasympathetic nerves, which return to the
        bladder and cause it to contract.
   (b) inhibit the motor neurons that normally keep the
        external urethral sphincter closed.
   (c) stimulate nerves that go to the kidney and
        prevent glomerular filtration until the bladder
        is empty.
   (d) Both (a) and (b) above are correct.
   (e) All of the above are correct.

ANSWER: d

88. When the bladder of an infant is filled with urine,

   (a) the stretch receptors in the bladder wall are
        inhibited.
   (b) the parasympathetic nerve supplying the bladder is
        inhibited, allowing the bladder to relax.
   (c) the motor neuron supplying the external urethral
        sphincter is stimulated, causing the sphincter to
        open.
   (d) the motor neuron supplying the external urethral
        sphincter is inhibited, allowing the sphincter to
        open.
   (e) the parasympathetic nerve supplying the internal
        urethral sphincter is stimulated, causing the
        sphincter to close.

ANSWER: d

89. The process of preventing micturition in spite of initiation of the micturition reflex involves

   (a) the cerebral cortex.
   (b) voluntary stimulation of the motor neuron supplying the external urethral sphincter.
   (c) voluntary stimulation of the internal urethral sphincter via its parasympathetic nerve supply.
   (d) Both (a) and (b) above are correct.
   (e) All of the above are correct.

ANSWER: d

90. Which of the following does **not** occur during the micturition reflex in a baby?

   (a) The motor neuron supplying the external sphincter is stimulated.
   (b) The parasympathetic nerve supply to the bladder is stimulated.
   (c) The internal urethral sphincter mechanically opens due to changes in the shape of the bladder.
   (d) The external urethral sphincter is relaxed.
   (e) The bladder contracts.

ANSWER: a

True/False

91. The kidneys are the organs that are primarily responsible for maintaining constancy of the volume and electrolyte composition of the internal fluid environment.

ANSWER: True

92. The kidneys keep the urine volume and composition essentially constant.

ANSWER: False

93. The functional unit of the kidneys is the glomerulus.

ANSWER: False

94. The afferent arteriole is the blood vessel that carries blood to the glomerular capillaries.

ANSWER: True

95.   Only long-looped nephrons contain a juxtaglomerular apparatus.

ANSWER: False

96.   The group of specialized tubular and vascular cells located where the ascending limb passes through the fork formed by the afferent and efferent arterioles of the same nephron is known as the juxtaglomerular apparatus.

ANSWER: True

97.   In the kidney, blood is filtered in the cortex, drains through the renal pelvis into the renal medulla, and from there travels in the ureter to the urinary bladder.

ANSWER: False

98.   The renal pelvis stores urine until it can be voided.

ANSWER: False

99.   Glomerular filtration occurs primarily by active transport.

ANSWER: False

100. Twenty-five percent of the cardiac output goes to the kidneys because of their tremendous nutrient requirement for the active transport of Na^+.

ANSWER: False

101. All of the plasma that enters the glomerulus is normally filtered into Bowman's capsule except for the plasma proteins.

ANSWER: False

102. The glomerular filtrate is almost identical in composition to the plasma.

ANSWER: True

103. The vast majority of the filtered fluid is reabsorbed.

ANSWER: True

104. In general, the substances in the filtrate that need to be conserved are selectively reabsorbed whereas the unwanted substances that need to be eliminated fail to be reabsorbed.

ANSWER: True

105. Glomerular filtration occurs by active transport of Na^+, which then creates an osmotic gradient for the filtration of water.

ANSWER: False

106. The glomerular filtrate contains only substances that are not needed by the body.

ANSWER: False

107. The average GFR is 125 ml/minute.

ANSWER: True

108. Bowman's capsule hydrostatic pressure opposes filtration.

ANSWER: True

109. Blood pressure in the glomerular capillaries is the same as in capillaries elsewhere in the body.

ANSWER: False

110. The glomerular capillary blood pressure is higher than capillary pressure elsewhere in the body primarily because the afferent arteriole has a larger diameter than the efferent arteriole.

ANSWER: True

111. If a kidney stone blocked the renal pelvis and consequently caused a build-up of fluid pressure in the tubules and Bowman's capsule, the net filtration pressure across the glomerular capillary membrane would increase.

ANSWER: False

112. The glomerular capillary wall contains filtration slits formed by the clefts between the foot processes of adjacent podocytes.

ANSWER: False

113. The kidneys receive a disproportionately large share of the cardiac output for the purpose of adjusting and purifying the plasma.

ANSWER: True

114. Sympathetic vasoconstriction of the afferent arterioles and a resultant fall in the GFR occur as part of the baroreceptor reflex response when the blood pressure is too low.

ANSWER: True

115. When a substance is reabsorbed, it moves from the tubular fluid back into the blood.

ANSWER: True

116. In active reabsorption, all of the steps involved in transepithelial transport are active.

ANSWER: False

117. Transepithelial transport occurs only for substances that are actively reabsorbed.

ANSWER: False

118. The amount of a substance that is filtered = its plasma concentration x GFR.

ANSWER: True

119. The T_m represents the maximum amount of a particular substance that can be excreted in the urine per unit of time.

ANSWER: False

120. The amount of glucose filtered is directly proportional to the plasma glucose concentration at all plasma glucose concentrations.

ANSWER: True

121. The amount of glucose reabsorbed is directly proportional to the plasma glucose concentration at all plasma glucose concentrations.

ANSWER: False

122. The renal threshold represents the maximum amount of a particular substance that the tubular cells are capable of actively reabsorbing per unit of time.

ANSWER: False

123. For a substance to be actively reabsorbed, all of the steps of transepithelial transport require energy expenditure.

ANSWER: False

124. The tubular cells display a T_m for urea.

ANSWER: False

125. The renal threshold for glucose is well above the normal plasma glucose concentration, but the renal threshold for PO_4^{3-} is equal to the normal plasma PO_4^{3-} concentration.

ANSWER: True

126. During acidosis, H^+ secretion increases.

ANSWER: True

127. A rise in ECF K^+ concentration leads to increased excitability of heart muscle, possibly producing fatal cardiac arrhythmias.

ANSWER: True

128. The Na^+ cotransport system in the proximal tubule facilitates elimination of foreign organic compounds from the body.

ANSWER: False

129. ACE inhibitor drugs promote diuresis by blocking the conversion of angiotensin I into angiotensin II.

ANSWER: True

130. Water reabsorption cannot occur from any portion of the nephron in the absence of vasopressin.

ANSWER: False

131. Vasopressin increases H_2O reabsorption in the proximal tubule.

ANSWER: False

132. Urea is passively reabsorbed down the osmotic gradient created by active Na^+ reabsorption.

ANSWER: False

133. Tubular secretion involves the movement of substances from the peritubular capillary blood into the tubular fluid.

ANSWER: True

134. Potassium is both actively reabsorbed and actively secreted.

ANSWER: True

135. The organic ion secretory systems only secrete foreign compounds.

ANSWER: False

136. Tubular reabsorption and tubular secretion are highly selective processes, whereas glomerular filtration is not.

ANSWER: True

137. The clearance rate for a substance that is filtered and secreted but not reabsorbed is greater than the GFR.

ANSWER: True

138. The clearance rate for inulin is equal to the GFR.

ANSWER: True

139. Inulin clearance is used to determine the renal plasma flow.

ANSWER: False

140. Urea clearance rate is less than the GFR.

ANSWER: True

141. A plasma clearance of 135 ml/min for a substance when the GFR is 125 ml/min indicates that net secretion of the substance occurs.

ANSWER: True

142. The osmolarity of the medullary interstitial fluid always equilibrates with the descending limb of the loop of Henle.

ANSWER: True

143. The driving force for H_2O reabsorption across all permeable segments of the kidney tubule is an osmotic gradient.

ANSWER: True

144. The receptor sites for vasopressin binding are located on the basolateral border, yet the end result is an increase in H_2O permeability of the luminal border of the tubular cells.

ANSWER: True

145. In the tubular segments permeable to H_2O, solute reabsorption is always accompanied by comparable H_2O reabsorption.

ANSWER: True

146. The permeability and transport properties of the loops of Henle of long-looped nephrons are important in establishing the vertical osmotic gradient in the renal medulla.

ANSWER: True

147. NaCl is actively transported from the descending limb of the loop of Henle to establish the medullary osmotic gradient.

ANSWER: False

148. When tubular fluid enters the distal tubule, it is hypotonic.

ANSWER: True

149. The presence of vasopressin acts to prevent the reabsorption of water from the distal and collecting tubules.

ANSWER: False

150. The functional unit of the kidney is the countercurrent system.

ANSWER: False

151. Because of countercurrent multiplication, the long loop of Henle is able to establish a vertical osmotic gradient in the renal medulla ranging from 300 to 1,200 mosm/l, despite the fact that the active salt pump of the ascending limb is only able to produce a 200 mosm/l osmotic gradient at each horizontal level.

ANSWER: True

152. Acute renal failure may be reversible, whereas chronic renal failure is not reversible.

ANSWER: True

153. Urine moves from the kidneys to the urinary bladder through the ureters passively by the force of gravity.

ANSWER: False

154. Urine is prevented from refluxing from the bladder back into the ureters by the internal ureteral sphincter.

ANSWER: False

155. The micturition reflex controls bladder emptying in adults.

ANSWER: False

156. During the micturition reflex, the motor neuron supplying the external urethral sphincter is stimulated.

ANSWER: False

157. The average rate of urine formation is 1 ml/minute.

ANSWER: True

158. One can deliberately prevent urination in spite of the micturition reflex by voluntarily inhibiting the parasympathetic supply to the bladder to halt bladder contraction.

ANSWER: False

Fill-in-the-blanks

159. The functional unit of the kidneys is the _____.

ANSWER: nephron

160. The two regions of the kidney are an outer _____ and an inner _____.

ANSWERS: cortex, medulla

161. _____% of the plasma that enters the glomerulus is filtered.

ANSWER: 20

162. The average GFR is _____ ml/min.

ANSWER: 125

163. The specialized cells of the _____ secret the hormone _____ into the blood when they detect a fall in NaCl/ECFvolume/blood pressure. This hormone in turn activates a pathway that ultimately leads to secretion of the hormone _____, which increases _____ reabsorption by the distal and collecting tubules.

ANSWERS: juxtaglomerular apparatus, renin, aldosterone, sodium

164. The energy-dependent step in Na^+ reabsorption involves the _____ located at the _____ membrane of the tubular cell.

ANSWERS: Na^+-K^+ pump, basolateral

165. If the plasma concentration of substance X is 200 mg/100 ml and the GFR is 125 ml/min, the filtered load of this substance is _____.

ANSWER: 250 mg/min

166. If the T_m for substance X is 200 mg/min, how much of the substance will be reabsorbed at a plasma concentration of 200 mg/100 ml and a GFR of 125 ml/min? _____ How much of substance X will be excreted? _____

ANSWERS: 200 mg/min, 50 mg/min

167. The plasma concentration of a particular substance at which its T_m is reached and the substance first starts appearing in the urine is known as the _____.

ANSWER: renal threshold

168. On the average, of the 125 ml/min of plasma filtered, _____ ml/min is reabsorbed and _____ ml/min is excreted as urine.

ANSWERS: 124, 1

169. The plasma clearance of the harmless foreign compound _____ is equal to the GFR.

ANSWER: inulin

170. The plasma clearance of the organic anion _____ is equal to the renal plasma flow.

ANSWER: para-aminohippuric acid

171. _____% of the filtered H_2O is variably reabsorbed under the control of the hormone _____ in the distal and collecting tubules.

ANSWER: Twenty, vasopressin

172. Vasopressin is also known as _____, indicative of its effect on the kidneys.

ANSWER: antidiuretic hormone

173. _____ renal failure has a rapid onset but may be reversible; _____ renal failure is slow, progressive, and irreversible.

ANSWER: Acute, chronic

174. _____% of the renal tissue can adequately perform all excretory and regulatory functions of the kidney.

ANSWER: Twenty-five

175. _____ is the inability to prevent the discharge of urine.

ANSWER: Urinary incontinence

176. Two means by which substances can enter the renal tubules are _____ and _____. Two means by which substances can leave the kidney tubules are _____ and _____.

ANSWERS: glomerular filtration, tubular secretion, tubular reabsorption, urine excretion

Matching

177. _____ glomerular filtration
     _____ tubular reabsorption
     _____ tubular secretion
     _____ urine excretion

a. movement of substances from the peritubular capillary blood into the tubular lumen
b. movement of substances from the glomerular capillary blood into the tubular lumen
c. everything filtered or secreted that is not subsequently reabsorbed
d. movement of substances from the tubular lumen into the peritubular capillary blood

ANSWERS: b, d, a, c

178. _____Plays a pivotal role in the reabsorption of glucose, amino acids, H_2O, Cl_-, and urea.
     _____Subject to hormonal control
     _____Plays a critical role in the kidneys' ability to produce urine of varying concentrations and volumes.
     _____Is important in the regulation of ECF volume

a. sodium reabsorption in the distal and collecting tubules
b. sodium reabsorption in the proximal tubule
c. sodium reabsorption coupled with chloride reabsorption in the long loop of Henle

ANSWERS: b, a, c, a

279.

_____ Afferent arteriole
_____ Renal pelvis
_____ Tubular reabsoprtion
_____ Tubular secretion
_____ Glomerular filtration
_____ Distal and collecting tubules
_____ Bowman's capsule
_____ Peritubular capillary
_____ Ureter
_____ Proximal tubule
_____ Loop of Henle
_____ Urethra
_____ Efferent arteriole
_____ Urinary bladder
_____ Glomerulus
_____ Nephron

a. Collecting tubules empty into this structure.
b. Stores the urine.
c. Passage of substances from the peritubular capillaries into the tubular lumen.
d. Carries blood to the glomerulus.
e. Tuft of capillaries that forms the filtrate.
f. Passage of protein-free plasma into Bowman's capsule.
g. Urine is forced through this structure by peristalsis.
h. Collects the glomerular filtrate.
i. Passage of substances from the tubular lumen into the peritubular capillaries.
j. Functional unit of the kidney.
k. Supplies the renal tissue with O_2 and nutrients.
l. Carries blood from one capillary network to another capillary net work.
m. Tube through which urine leaves the body.
n. Variable water and sodium reabsorption occur here under hormon-al control.
o. Responsible for the ver-tical osmotic gradient in the medulla of the kidney.
p. Glucose and amino acid reabsorption occur here.

ANSWERS: d, a, i, c, f, n, h, k, g, p, o, m, l, b, e, j

180. Indicate whether the first item in the statement increases, decreases, or has no effect on the second item by
filling in the appropriate letter using the following
answer code.

(a) = increases
(b) = decreases
(c) = has no effect on

Water deficit in the body _____ vasopressin
secretion.
Decreased vasopressin secretion _____ H$_2$O reabsorption.
Decreased Na$^+$ in body fluids (Na$^+$ depletion) _____
renin secretion.
Increased renin secretion _____ angiotensin I activa-
tion.
Increased vasopressin secretion _____ urinary output.
Increased angiotensin II activation _____ aldosterone
secretion.
Increased aldosterone secretion _____ Na$^+$ reabsorption.
Increased vasopressin secretion _____ Na$^+$ reabsorption.

ANSWERS: a, b, a, a, b, a, a, c

181. Indicate which substance in the right column undergoes the
process in the left column by writing the appropriate
letter in the blank.

_____ Filtered and actively reabsorbed,   a. K$^+$
but not secreted.   b. glucose
_____ Filtered and passively reabsorbed.   c. inulin
_____ Filtered and secreted, but not   d. plasma
reabsorbed.   protein
_____ Filtered and both actively re-   e. urea
absorbed and actively secreted.   f. H$^+$
_____ Filtered but not reabsorbed or
secreted.
_____ Not filtered.

ANSWERS: b, e, f, a, c, d

182. Indicate whether the factor in question would ultimately lead to (a) an increase, or (b) a decrease in Na⁺ reabsorption by means of the renin-angiotensin-aldosterone mechanism.

$$(a) = \text{an increase in Na}^+ \text{ reabsorption}$$
$$(b) = \text{a decrease in Na}^+ \text{ reabsorption}$$

_____ a precipitous fall in arterial blood pressure as during hemorrhage

_____ a reduction in total Na⁺ load in the body

_____ a reduction in ECF volume

ANSWERS: a, a, a

183. _____ directly stimulates Na⁺ reabsorption by the distal and collecting tubules

_____ acted upon by renin

_____ secreted by the adrenal cortex

_____ produced by the liver

_____ acted upon by converting enzyme in the lung

_____ its secretion is directly stimulated by angiotensin II

_____ stimulates K⁺ secretion by the distal and collecting tubules

_____ secreted by the juxtaglomerular apparatus

_____ inhibits Na⁺ reabsorption by the renal tubules

_____ its secretion is directly stimulated by a low plasma K⁺ concentration

_____ a potent constrictor of arterioles

a. renin
b. angiotensinogen
c. angiotensin I
d. angiotensin II
e. aldosterone
f. atrial natriuretic peptide

ANSWERS: e, b, e, b, c, e, e, a, f, e, d

184. Indicate whether the portion of the tubule in question is permeable or impermeable to the substance in question using the following answer code:

> (a) = permeable
> (b) = impermeable

The ascending limb of Henle's loop is _____ to H_2O.
The descending limb of Henle's loop is _____ to H_2O.
The vasa recta is _____ to salt and _____ to H_2O.
The distal and collecting tubules in the absence of vasopressin are _____ to H_2O.
The distal and collecting tubules in the presence of vasopressin are _____ to H_2O.

ANSWERS: b; a; a, a; b; a

Completion

185. Circle the answer that correctly completes the statement.

If a person ingests excess H_2O, the body fluids become (hypertonic, hypotonic). In response, vasopressin secretion is (stimulated, inhibited). As a result, a (small, large) volume of (hypertonic, hypotonic) urine is excreted to help ameliorate the fluid imbalance.

ANSWERS: hypotonic, inhibited, large, hypotonic

AUDIOVISUAL AIDS

Films

A list of films available from West Publishing Company is presented in Appendix A.   Following are other films that may be suitable.   The sources for these films, which are coded by abbreviation, are provided in Appendix B.

Dialysis Procedures, LER, 20 min.

Diuresis, AMA, 48 min.

Elimination, UW, 11 min.

Excretion, IM, 29 min.

Excretion, MH, 28 min.

Excretory System, CFV, 14 min.

Functional Anatomy of the Human Kidney, AMA, 25 min.

Human Body: Excretory System, COR, 12 min.

Kidney Disease, FHS, 26 min.

Kidneys, FI, 11 min.

Kidney Function in Health, EL, 38 min.

Kidney Function in Disease, LER, 46 min.

Kidneys, Ureters, and Bladders, IU, 11 min.

Physiology: The Work of the Kidney, IU, 20 min.

Renal Hypertension/Bilateral Nephrectomy Kidney Transplantation, UP, 23 min.

Renal Structure and Function, SNM, 90 min.

The Dynamic Kidney, EL, 29 min.

The Mammalian Kidney, EI, 20 min.

The Physiology of the Kidney, PH, 6 min.

The Urinary Tract (VCR), FM, 26 min.

Vascular and Tubular Organization of the Kidney, AHP, 20 min.

The Vertebrate Kidney, PS, 24 min.

Water, FHS, 26 min.

The Work of the Kidneys, EBE, 20 min.

Software

Dynamics of the Human Urinary System, EI. Follows the formation of wastes from the cells to their final expulsion from the body.

Excretion, CBS. Reviews the nature of metabolic wastes and waste removal in simple organisms and kidney functions in humans.

The Kidney, PLP. Studies the relation between renal structure and function.

<u>The Kidney: Structure and Function</u>, EI. Covers anatomy and physiology of renal systems.

<u>Urinary System and Reproductive Systems</u>, PLP.   Covers both systems in both sexes.

Chapter 12
Fluid Balance and Acid-Base Balance

CONTENTS
(All page references are to the main text.)

387

LECTURE HINTS AND SUGGESTIONS

1. Fill dialysis bags with normal tap water and place in beakers containing solutions that are isotonic, hypertonic, and hypotonic. Weigh the bags before placing in beaker and after 15 minutes. See any general physiology lab manual for procedure.

2. Measure the pH of some body fluids; e.g., urine, sweat, saliva.

3. Demonstrate the buffering capability of blood by adding small amounts of HCl and NaOH and checking the pH of each solution.

4. Demonstrate the use of a pH meter for measuring the pH of various body fluids, such as blood or urine. Demonstrate the buffering activity of blood by adding various acids or bases and checking the pH after each addition.

5. The slide-tape series "Acid-Base Physiology and Buffer Chemistry: Physiological Applications," Program 501 of the American Physiological Society, is excellent.

CHAPTER TEST QUESTIONS

Multiple Choice

1. Variation in percent body water among individuals is primarily due to differences in

    (a) amount of adipose tissue.
    (b) total muscle mass.
    (c) vasopressin secretion.
    (d) drinking habits.
    (e) glomerular filtration rate.

ANSWER: a

2. The tissue in the body containing the lowest percentage of water is the

    (a) skin.
    (b) skeleton.
    (c) muscle.
    (d) internal organs.
    (e) adipose (fat).

ANSWER: e

3.   The component that constitutes the largest percentage of body weight is

(a)   protein.
(b) H_2O.
(c) Na^+.
(d)   carbohydrate.
(e)   phospholipid.

ANSWER: b

4.   A _____ exists when total body input of a particular substance equals its total body output.

(a)   positive balance
(b)   negative balance
(c)   stable balance
(d)   state of equilibrium
(e)   steady state

ANSWER: c

5.   Extracellular fluid

(a)   includes plasma.
(b)   includes interstitial fluid.
(c)   constitutes a greater percentage of total body water than does intracellular fluid.
(d)   Both (a) and (b) above are correct.
(e)   All of the above are correct.

ANSWER: d

6.   Extracellular fluid

(a)   constitutes a greater percentage of total body water than does intracellular fluid.
(b)   osmolarity must be regulated to prevent an acid-base imbalance, because the hydrogen ions might become too concentrated or too dilute in the body fluids.
(c)   volume must be regulated to prevent the cells from swelling or shrinking.
(d)   More than one of the above are correct.
(e)   None of the above are correct.

ANSWER: e

7. Interstitial fluid

   (a) is the largest component of the extracellular fluid.
   (b) is the true internal environment of the body.
   (c) represents a larger percentage of total body weight than does intracellular fluid.
   (d) Both (a) and (b) above are correct.
   (e) All of the above are correct.

ANSWER: d

8. Transcellular fluid

   (a) is the sum of fluid within all of the cells.
   (b) consists of a number of small specialized fluid volumes, all of which are secreted by specific cells into a particular body cavity to perform a specialized function.
   (c) plays a crucial role in fluid balance.
   (d) includes the lymph.
   (e) lies in the spaces between the cells.

ANSWER: b

9. The barrier between the plasma and interstitial fluid

   (a) is the blood vessel walls.
   (b) is the plasma membrane.
   (c) transports materials between these two fluid com-partments by both passive and active means.
   (d) Both (a) and (c) above are correct.
   (e) Both (b) and (c) above are correct.

ANSWER: a

10. Interstitial fluid

   (a) constitutes the true internal environment.
   (b) is very similar in composition to the plasma.
   (c) is very similar in composition to the intracellular fluid.
   (d) Both (a) and (b) above are correct.
   (e) Both (a) and (c) above are correct.

ANSWER: d

11. The primary ECF cation is _____ and the primary ICF cation is _____.

    (a) K^+, Na^+
    (b) K^+, Ca^{2+}
    (c) Ca^{2+}, Na^+
    (d) Na^+, K^+
    (e) Na^+, Ca^{2+}

ANSWER: d

12. The main reason that extracellular fluid volume must be closely regulated is

    (a)   to prevent changes in ICF osmolarity.
    (b)   to maintain adequate urine formation.
    (c)   to maintain proper blood pressure.
    (d)   to prevent cells from swelling or shrinking.
    (e)   to allow changes in ICF volume.

ANSWER: c

13. Which of the following are compensatory measures for a fall in arterial blood pressure?

    (a)   Increased cardiac output and increased total peripheral resistance as a result of the baroreceptor reflex.
    (b)   A shift of fluid out of the interstitial compartment into the vasculature.
    (c)   A reduction in the urinary excretion of salt and accompanying fluid.
    (d)   Both (a) and (b) above are correct.
    (e)   All of the above are correct.

ANSWER: e

14. The most important factor in the long-term regulation of ECF volume is

    (a)   maintenance of salt balance.
    (b)   maintenance of water balance.
    (c)   thirst.
    (d)   the baroreceptor reflex.
    (e)   fluid shifts between the interstitial fluid and plasma.

ANSWER: a

15. The vast majority of the extracellular fluid's osmotic activity is contributed by

    (a) plasma proteins.
    (b) Na$^+$ and its attendant anions.
    (c) K$^+$ and its attendant anions.
    (d) Ca^{2+} and its attendant anions.
    (e) red blood cells.

ANSWER: b

16. Osmotic activity

    (a) across the capillary wall is due to the unequal distribution of plasma proteins in the plasma and interstitial fluid.
    (b) across the cellular plasma membranes is related to any differences in ionic concentration between the ECF and ICF.
    (c) across the cellular plasma membranes is related to differences in protein composition between the ECF and ICF.
    (d) Both (a) and (b) above are correct.
    (e) Both (a) and (c) above are correct.

ANSWER: d

17. The importance of regulating ECF osmolarity is

    (a) to help maintain blood pressure.
    (b) to prevent the urine from becoming too concentrated.
    (c) to prevent fluid shifts between the cells and the extracellular fluid, which could produce profound symptoms as the cells swell or shrink.
    (d) to prevent spontaneous depolarization of nerve and muscle cell membranes because of shifts in Na$^+$ balance.
    (e) to prevent an acid-base imbalance if the hydrogen ions were to become too concentrated or too dilute in the body fluids.

ANSWER: c

18. Which of the following is **not** a potential cause of hypertonicity in the body?

 (a)   Water deprivation.
 (b)   Heavy sweating.
 (c)   Excess vasopressin secretion.
 (d)   Diabetes insipidus.
 (e)   Severe diarrhea.

ANSWER: c

19. Diabetes insipidus

 (a)   is due to excess vasopressin secretion.
 (b)   is due to vasopressin deficiency.
 (c)   gives rise to hypertonicity of the body fluids.
 (d)   Both (a) and (c) above are correct.
 (e)   Both (b) and (c) above are correct.

ANSWER: e

20. In compensating for dehydration,

 (a)   vasopressin secretion increases.
 (b)   urinary output increases.
 (c)   thirst increases.
 (d)   Two of the above are correct.
 (e)   All of the above are correct.

ANSWER: d

21. Which of the following statements concerning hypotonicity of the body fluids is **incorrect**?

 (a)   Hypotonicity can occur as a result of diabetes insipidus.
 (b)   Hypotonicity occurs when excess free H_2O is present.
 (c)   Drowsiness, headache, confusion, lethargy, weakness, and edema are symptoms associated with hypotonicity.
 (d)   Drinking excess fluid is a cause of hypotonicity.
 (e)   The cells become swollen.

ANSWER: a

22. Which of the following statements concerning hypotonicity is correct?

    (a) During hypotonicity, water enters the cells by osmosis.
    (b) The only cause of hypotonicity is drinking excess fluid.
    (c) Hypotonicity is a major consequence of diabetes mellitus, which is a deficiency of vasopressin.
    (d) Hypotonicity is usually associated with a negative water balance.
    (e) Common symptoms of hypotonicity include dry skin and sunken eyeballs.

ANSWER: a

23. If an individual is overhydrated,

    (a) H_2O will move by osmosis into the cells.
    (b) both the ECF and ICF compartments will be hypotonic after the fluid shift has occurred.
    (c) symptoms might include confusion, headache, lethargy, weakness, and edema.
    (d) Two of the above are correct.
    (e) All of the above are correct.

ANSWER: e

24. When the ECF becomes hypotonic, fluid will

    (a) shift from the ICF into the ECF.
    (b) not shift between the ECF and the ICF.
    (c) shift from the ECF into the ICF.
    (d) None of the above are correct.

ANSWER: c

25. When isotonic fluid is added to the ECF, fluid will

    (a) shift from the ICF into the ECF.
    (b) not shift between the ECF and ICF.
    (c) shift from the ECF into the ICF.
    (d) None of the above are correct.

ANSWER: b

26.   Salt balance in humans

    (a)   depends primarily upon control of Na$^+$ intake through salt hunger.
    (b)   depends primarily upon control of Na$^+$ output by the kidneys.
    (c)   is poorly regulated.
    (d)   depends upon Na$^+$ secretion by the kidneys.
    (e)   is not affected by aldosterone secretion.

ANSWER: b

27.   The main control for salt balance is

    (a)   control of salt intake.
    (b)   control of salt output in the sweat.
    (c)   control of salt output in the feces.
    (d)   control of salt output in the urine.
    (e)   regulation through salt hunger.

ANSWER: d

28.   When there is excess Na$^+$ in the body,

    (a)   the plasma volume is expanded and arterial blood pressure is increased.
    (b)   as a compensatory measure, the GFR is reflexly increased to increase the amount of Na$^+$ filtered.
    (c)   as a compensatory measure, aldosterone secretion is increased to increase the amount of Na$^+$ reabsorbed.
    (d)   Both (a) and (b) above are correct.
    (e)   All of the above are correct.

ANSWER: d

29.   The amount of Na$^+$ excreted in the urine equals the amount of Na$^+$ _____ minus the amount of Na$^+$ _____.

    (a)   filtered, reabsorbed
    (b)   ingested, filtered
    (c)   ingested, metabolically consumed
    (d)   ingested, placed in storage
    (e)   secreted, reabsorbed

ANSWER: a

30. Which of the following is a source of water input?

    (a) Fluid intake.
    (b) Ingested food.
    (c) Chemical reactions within the cells that convert food and O_2 into energy.
    (d) Both (a) and (b) above are correct.
    (e) All of the above are correct.

ANSWER: e

31. Insensible water loss includes

    (a) loss during cellular metabolism.
    (b) loss from the lungs.
    (c) loss from sweat.
    (d) loss in the feces.
    (e) More than one of the above are correct.

ANSWER: b

32. What is the primary regulatory mechanism to maintain water balance in the body?

    (a) Control of intake through thirst.
    (b) Control of sweating.
    (c) Control of output through regulation of urine production by the kidney.
    (d) Oral metering.
    (e) Control of insensible water loss.

ANSWER: c

33. Which of the following statements concerning acids is **incorrect**?

    (a) Acids can dissociate in solution to yield free hydrogen ions and anions.
    (b) All substances that contain hydrogen are considered to be acids.
    (c) A strong acid has a greater tendency to dissociate than does a weak acid.
    (d) The extent of dissociation for a given acid is a constant, K.
    (e) Only free hydrogen ions contribute to the acidity of a solution.

ANSWER: b

34. pH

    (a)   is equal to log $1/[H^+]$.
    (b)   is low when acidosis is present.
    (c)   is higher in arterial blood than venous blood.
    (d)   Both (a) and (b) above are correct.
    (e)   All of the above are correct.

ANSWER: e

35. Which of the following is **not** influenced by a change in the pH of body fluids?

    (a)   Phosphate excretion.
    (b)   Enzyme activity.
    (c)   Potassium excretion.
    (d)   Protein shape and activity.
    (e)   Nerve and muscle excitability.

ANSWER: a

36. Which of the following symptoms is associated with acidosis?

    (a)   Extreme nervousness.
    (b)   Disoriented and comatose.
    (c)   Tingling, "pins and needles" sensations.
    (d)   Muscle twitches and muscle spasms.
    (e)   Convulsions.

ANSWER: b

37. Which of the following symptoms is **not** associated with alkalosis?

    (a)   Disoriented and comatose.
    (b)   Tingling, "pins and needles" sensations.
    (c)   Muscle twitches and muscle spasms.
    (d)   Extreme nervousness.
    (e)   Convulsions.

ANSWER: a

38. Which of the following is normally the major source of hydrogen ions in the body?

    (a) Phosphoric and sulfuric acids formed during the metabolism of dietary proteins.
    (b) Lactic acid production by the muscles during exercise.
    (c) Carbonic acid generated from metabolically produced CO_2.
    (d) Natural acids found in foods, such as citric acid.
    (e) Fatty acids produced during fat metabolism.

ANSWER: c

39. H^+ generated from CO_2 at the tissue level

    (a) is the major source of hydrogen ion in the body.
    (b) is normally buffered in transit between the tissues and the lungs by hemoglobin.
    (c) is responsible for the fact that the pH of the venous blood is higher than the pH of the arterial blood.
    (d) Both (a) and (b) above are correct.
    (e) All of the above are correct.

ANSWER: d

40. Which of the following statements concerning chemical buffer systems is **incorrect**?

    (a) A chemical buffer system consists of a pair of substances involved in a reversible reaction, one that can yield free H^+ and one that can bind with free H^+.
    (b) A chemical buffer system minimizes changes in the pH of a solution when an acid or base is added to or removed from the solution.
    (c) Buffers respond to changes in pH in 1 to 3 minutes.
    (d) A buffer system cannot actually eliminate hydrogen ions from the body.
    (e) Buffer systems act according to the law of mass action.

ANSWER: c

41. Chemical buffer systems

    (a) respond in 1 to 3 minutes to changes in hydrogen ion concentration.
    (b) stimulate the respiratory center when acidosis is present.
    (c) promote H^+ excretion by the kidneys when acidosis is present.
    (d) are the most powerful mechanism available for regulating changes in $[H^+]$ within the body.
    (e) None of the above are correct.

ANSWER: e

42. Chemical buffer systems

    (a) can act within a fraction of a second to buffer changes in $[H^+]$.
    (b) are the only mechanism available for regulating changes in $[H^+]$ within the body.
    (c) actually eliminate acid from the body.
    (d) Both (a) and (c) above are correct.
    (e) All of the above are correct.

ANSWER: a

43. H^+ generated at the tissue level from CO_2 is buffered in transit between the tissues and the lungs primarily by

    (a) reduced hemoglobin.
    (b) phosphate buffer system.
    (c) H_2CO_3: HCO_3^- buffer system.
    (d) plasma proteins.
    (e) respiratory regulation.

ANSWER: a

44. Which of the following reactions would occur to compensate for excess lactic acid accumulation in the ECF during heavy exercise?

    (a) $CO_2 + H_2O \rightarrow H_2CO_3 \rightarrow H^+ + HCO_3^-$
    (b) $H^+ + HCO_3^- \rightarrow H_2CO_3 \rightarrow CO_2 + H_2$
    (c) $H^+ + Hb \rightarrow HHb$
    (d) $HHb \rightarrow H^+ + Hb$
    (e) $NH_4^+ \rightarrow NH_3 + H^+$

ANSWER: b

45. Which of the following is an important urinary buffer?

    (a) H_2CO_3 : HCO_3^- buffer system.
    (b) Hemoglobin buffer system.
    (c) Phosphate buffer system.
    (d) Protein buffer system.
    (e) Calcium buffer system.

ANSWER: c

46. Which of the following statements concerning the respiratory mechanism of pH control is **incorrect**?

    (a) Respiratory rate and depth increase as a compensatory measure to combat metabolic acidosis.
    (b) The respiratory system can compensate completely for metabolic acidosis.
    (c) The respiratory responses to acid-base imbalances represent the second line of defense against changes in pH of the body fluids.
    (d) Metabolic alkalosis inhibits (depresses) respiration.
    (e) The respiratory system responds to changes in $[H^+]$ within 1 to 3 minutes.

ANSWER: b

47. Which of the following statements concerning the respiratory mechanism of pH control is correct?

    (a) Respiratory rate and depth decrease as a compensatory measure to combat metabolic acidosis.
    (b) The respiratory system can compensate completely for uremic acidosis.
    (c) Metabolic alkalosis inhibits (depresses) the respiratory center.
    (d) The respiratory responses to acid-base imbalances represent the first line of defense against changes in pH of the body fluids.
    (e) The respiratory system responds to changes in $[H^+]$ only if the kidneys are unable to cope with the change.

ANSWER: c

48. If the tubular filtrate becomes too acidic, which of the following substances is secreted by the tubular epithelial cells to buffer the secreted H^+?

   (a) HCO_3^-
   (b) OH^-
   (c) NH_3
   (d) NH_4^+
   (e) Basic phosphate

ANSWER: c

49. The kidney tubular cells secrete NH_3

   (a) when the urinary pH becomes too high.
   (b) when the body is in a state of alkalosis.
   (c) to buffer the acid phosphate excreted in the urine.
   (d) when there is excess NH_3 in the body fluids.
   (e) to enable further renal secretion of H^+ to occur.

ANSWER: e

50. Which of the following statements concerning the kidneys' response to increased $[H^+]$ in the body fluids is **<u>incorrect</u>**?

   (a) When $[H^+]$ increases, the kidneys conserve HCO_3^- by reabsorbing more HCO_3^- and reducing its excretion in the urine.
   (b) When $[H^+]$ increases, the kidneys secrete more H^+ to be eliminated in the urine.
   (c) When $[H^+]$ increases, the kidneys secrete more basic phosphate to buffer the H^+ in the tubular filtrate.
   (d) When $[H^+]$ decreases, the kidneys excrete more HCO_3^- into the urine.
   (e) When severe acidosis is present, the kidney tubules secrete NH_3.

ANSWER: c

51. Which of the following conditions would be a cause of metabolic acidosis?

   (a) Severe diarrhea.
   (b) Severe vomiting.
   (c) Aspirin poisoning.
   (d) Emphysema.
   (e) None of the above are correct.

ANSWER: a

52. Vomiting of gastric contents

    (a)   can lead to dehydration.
    (b)   can cause metabolic acidosis.
    (c)   can cause metabolic alkalosis.
    (d)   Both (a) and (b) above are correct.
    (e)   Both (a) and (c) above are correct.

ANSWER: e

53. During respiratory compensation for metabolic alkalosis

    (a)   breathing becomes faster and deeper.
    (b)   breathing becomes slower and shallower.
    (c) CO_2 levels in the body decrease.
    (d)   Both (a) and (c) above are correct.
    (e)   Both (b) and (c) above are correct.

ANSWER: b

54. Which of the following do **not** occur in response to the acidosis accompanying diabetes mellitus?

    (a)   the $H^+ + HCO_3^- \leftrightarrow H_2CO_3 \leftrightarrow CO_2 + H_2O$ reaction shifts to the right to compensate for the rise in $[H^+]$.
    (b)   ventilation is increased to reduce the concentration of H^+-generating CO_2 in the body fluids.
    (c)   the kidneys secrete more H^+.
    (d)   the kidneys conserve HCO_3^-.
    (e)   an alkaline urine is produced to compensate for the acidosis.

ANSWER: e

True/False

55. Water is the most abundant component of the body, making up over 95% of the body weight.

ANSWER: False

56. The tissue with the lowest percentage of water is the skeleton.

ANSWER: False

57. There is more fluid outside of the cells than inside all of the cells collectively in the body.

ANSWER: False

58. The greatest percentage of body water is found in the intracellular fluid compartment.

ANSWER: True

59. The extracellular fluid is all the body fluid not contained within cells.

ANSWER: True

60. Interstitial fluid is the true internal environment, because it bathes all the cells of the body.

ANSWER: True

61. Intracellular fluid is divided into two compartments, the plasma fluid and the interstitial fluid.

ANSWER: False

62. Extracellular fluid volume depends primarily on the sodium load in the body.

ANSWER: True

63. The main reason that extracellular fluid volume must be closely regulated is to prevent fluid shifts from occurring between the ICF and ECF.

ANSWER: False

64. The main reason ECF volume must be regulated is to maintain proper cell volume.

ANSWER: False

65. The ECF volume and osmolarity are regulated primarily by the kidneys.

ANSWER: True

66. Osmolarity is a measure of the concentration of the individual solute particles dissolved in a fluid.

ANSWER: True

67. Each intracellular protein exerts more osmotic effect than each intracellular phosphate ion because the proteins are larger.

ANSWER: False

68. Diabetes insipidus often leads to hypertonicity of the body fluids.

ANSWER: True

69. A hypertonic solution has a higher concentration of solutes and a lower concentration of H_2O than an isotonic solution.

ANSWER: True

70. When the body becomes dehydrated (H_2O deficit), both urinary output and thirst increase as compensatory measures.

ANSWER: False

71. Diabetes insipidus is a potential cause of hypertonicity in the body.

ANSWER: True

72. The only cause of hypotonicity is drinking excess fluid.

ANSWER: False

73. Common symptoms of hypotonicity include dry skin, parched tongue, and sunken eyeballs.

ANSWER: False

74. Control of salt balance in humans is accomplished primarily by control of salt intake via a well-developed salt hunger.

ANSWER: False

75. Salt concentration in the body varies markedly between individuals depending on how much salt they consume.

ANSWER: False

76. Renal regulation of salt is the primary means of achieving salt balance.

ANSWER: True

77. In a normal, healthy person, H_2O intake equals H_2O output.

ANSWER: True

78.   Insensible water loss includes water lost from the lungs during expiration and water lost from the skin during sweating.

ANSWER: False

79.   Insensible H_2O loss includes water lost as a result of metabolic reactions within the cells.

ANSWER: False

80.   The primary factor responsible for regulating H_2O balance in the body is control of fluid intake via the thirst mechanism.

ANSWER: False

81.   The thirst center is closely related to or perhaps identical with the cells that secrete vasopressin.

ANSWER: True

82.   The hypothalamus controls both thirst and vasopressin secretion.

ANSWER: True

83.   If the pH of body fluids is 7.30, then alkalosis is present because neutral pH equals 7.0.

ANSWER: False

84.   If the pH of body fluids is 7.30, acidosis is said to exist even though a solution with a pH of 7.30 is chemically considered to be basic.

ANSWER: True

85.   A high pH is associated with acidosis.

ANSWER: False

86.   The pH of arterial blood is higher than the pH of venous blood.

ANSWER: True

87.   A pH of less than 6.8 or greater than 8.0 is not compatible with life.

ANSWER: True

88. Alkalosis eventually leads to unconsciousness and coma.

ANSWER: False

89. Regulation of hydrogen ion concentration is important in the maintenance of proper enzyme function.

ANSWER: True

90. As H^+ secretion increases, K^+ secretion also increases because of the intimate relationship between H^+ secretion and K^+ secretion by the kidneys.

ANSWER: False

91. When H^+ secretion increases, K^+ retention occurs because less K^+ can be secreted.

ANSWER: True

92. Normally the major source of H^+ in the body is from the formation of sulfuric and phosphoric acid produced during metabolism of dietary proteins that contain sulfate and phosphate groups.

ANSWER: False

93. The major source of H^+ in the body fluids is the carbonic acid generated from metabolic production of CO_2.

ANSWER: True

94. A chemical buffer system consists of a pair of substances involved in a reversible reaction, one that can yield free H^+ and one that can bind with free H^+.

ANSWER: True

95. Buffer systems act according to the law of mass action.

ANSWER: True

96. A chemical buffer system enables a solution to resist a marked change in pH upon addition or loss of acid or base.

ANSWER: True

97. Chemical buffer systems are the most powerful mechanism available for defending against changes in [H^+] because they respond the fastest.

ANSWER: False

98.   The most powerful mechanism for regulating [H⁺] in the body is the H_2CO_3 : HCO_3^- buffer system.

ANSWER: False

99.   The phosphate buffer system serves as an important urinary buffer.

ANSWER: True

100.   During respiratory compensation for metabolic alkalosis, breathing becomes slower and shallower.

ANSWER: True

101.   The kidneys are the first line of defense against changes in acid-base balance because they are the most powerful mechanism for maintaining pH.

ANSWER: False

102.   Basic phosphate is secreted by the kidney tubular cells to buffer hydrogen ion when the tubular fluid becomes too acidic.

ANSWER: False

103.   When [H⁺] decreases, the kidneys excrete more HCO_3^- into the urine.

ANSWER: True

104.   The kidneys secrete additional H^+ and conserve HCO_3^- to compensate for increased H^+ concentration in the body fluids.

ANSWER: True

105.   Metabolic acidosis can result from vomiting of gastric contents.

ANSWER: False

106.   Respiratory alkalosis occurs as a consequence of hyper-ventilation, because CO_2 is blown off more quickly than it is produced, decreasing the amount of carbonic acid in the body fluids.

ANSWER: True

107. The respiratory system can compensate completely for metabolic acidosis.

ANSWER: False

108. Carbon dioxide is unintentionally increased as a cause of respiratory acidosis but is deliberately increased as a compensation for metabolic alkalosis.

ANSWER: True

109. Respiratory adjustments can fully compensate for uremic acidosis.

ANSWER: False

Fill-in-the-blanks

110. On the average _____% of the body weight consists of H_2O.

ANSWER: 60

111. The quantity of any particular substance in the ECF is considered to be a readily available internal _____.

ANSWER: pool

112. When total body input of a particular substance equals its total body output, a _____ balance exists.

ANSWER: stable

113. The two components of the ECF compartment are _____ and _____.

ANSWER: plasma, interstitial fluid

114. The true internal environment is the _____.

ANSWER: interstitial fluid

115. The force responsible for movement of H_2O between the ECF and ICF is _____.

ANSWER: osmotic pressure differences

116. The principal ECF cation is _____, which is
      accompanied primarily by the anion _____ and
      to a lesser extent _____.

ANSWER: sodium, chloride, bicarbonate

117. The barrier between the plasma and interstitial fluid is
      the _____.

ANSWER: blood vessel walls

118. An imbalance in the physical forces, _____ and
      _____, is primarily responsible for
      producing movement of fluid between the plasma and
      interstitial fluid.

ANSWERS: capillary blood pressure, plasma colloid osmotic
          pressure

119. The barrier between the ECF and ICF is the _____
      _____.

ANSWER: plasma membrane of cells

120. The major intracellular cation is _____
      whereas the major intracellular anions are
      _____ and _____.

ANSWERS: potassium, phosphate, negatively charged intracellu-
          lar proteins

121. The amount of Na^+ excreted depends on _____
      minus _____.

ANSWERS: the amount of Na^+ filtered, the amount of Na^+
          reabsorbed

122. The amount of Na^+ filtered is controlled by regulating the
      _____.

ANSWER: GFR

123. The amount of Na^+ reabsorbed is regulated primarily by the
      _____ system.

ANSWER: renin-angiotensin-aldosterone

124. The amount of free H_2O reabsorbed is regulated primarily
      by the hormone _____.

ANSWER: vasopressin.

125.   _____ are a special group of hydrogen-containing substances that dissociate in solution to liberate free H^+ and anions.

ANSWER: Acids

126.   A _____ is a substance that can combine with a free H^+, thus removing it from solution.

ANSWER: base

127.   A pH of _____ is considered to be chemically neutral. The normal pH of plasma is _____. The pH range compatible with life is _____ to _____.

ANSWERS: 7.0, 7.4, 6.8, 8.0

128.   A _____ is a pair of chemical compounds involved in a reversible reaction, one that can yield free H^+ and one that can bind free H^+, which together minimize changes in pH when either an acid or a base in added to or removed from the solution.

ANSWER: chemical buffer system

Matching

129.   Indicate which fluid imbalance is being described by writing the appropriate letter in the blank using the answer code below.

           (a) = overhydration
           (b) = dehydration
           (c) = both overhydration and dehydration
           (d) = neither overhydration or dehydration

_____ Symptoms include dry skin, parched tongue, and sunken eyeballs.
_____ Water enters the cells by osmosis.
_____ The body fluids have a lower concentration of solutes than normal.
_____ ECF and ICF become hypertonic.
_____ Cells become swollen.
_____ No fluid shift occurs between the ECF and ICF.
_____ Occurs as a consequence of water deprivation.
_____ Cells shrink.
_____ ECF and ICF become hypotonic.
_____ Convulsions and coma may occur.
_____ Occurs as a consequence of diabetes insipidus.
_____ Occurs as a consequence of heavy vomiting.
_____ Osmolarity of the body fluids is decreased.
_____ Occurs as a consequence of excessive fluid intake.
_____ Occurs as a consequence of excessive vasopressin secretion.
_____ Vasopressin secretion is stimulated as a compensatory mechanism.
_____ Increased urinary output occurs as a compensatory mechanism.

ANSWERS: b, a, a, b, a, d, b, b, a, c, b, b, a, a, a, b, a

130. When a person has diarrhea, s/he loses excessive
      salt and water from the body. This fluid loss results in
      Na^+ depletion, dehydration, a decreased extracellular
      fluid volume, a reduction in plasma volume, and a
      decreased systemic arterial blood pressure.

      The following refer to the sequence of events that occur
      to compensate for this fluid loss. Indicate whether each
      factor listed

              (a) = exhibits no change,
              (b) = is increased,
        or (c) = is decreased, to compensate for fluid loss.

      _____ Sympathetic activity to the afferent
              arterioles of the nephrons.
      _____ Caliber of the afferent arterioles.
      _____ Glomerular capillary blood pressure.
      _____ Net filtration pressure.
      _____ GFR.
      _____ Amount of Na^+ and H_2O filtered.
      _____ Renin secretion.
      _____ Angiotensin I and II production.
      _____ Aldosterone secretion.
      _____ Amount of Na^+ reabsorbed.
      _____ Amount of Na^+ excreted.
      _____ Vasopressin secretion.
      _____ Permeability of distal and collecting
              tubules to H_2O.
      _____ Amount of H_2O reabsorbed.
      _____ Amount of H_2O excreted.
      _____ Urinary volume.
      _____ Thirst.

ANSWERS: b, c, c, c, c, c, b, b, b, b, c, b, b, b, c, c, b

131.   Indicate whether the item in question is referring to regulation of ECF volume or regulation of ECF osmolarity by using the answer code below:

(a) = refers to regulation of ECF volume
(b) = refers to regulation of ECF osmolarity

_____ primarily important to prevent fluid shifts between the ECF and ICF
_____ primarily important in the long-term regulation of arterial blood pressure
_____ depends primarily on Na^+ balance
_____ depends primarily on H_2O balance
_____ monitored primarily by hypothalamic osmoreceptors
_____ monitored primarily by arterial baroreceptors

ANSWERS: b, a, a, b, b, a

132.   _____ buffers H^+ generated from carbonic acid   a. hemoglobin buffer system
        _____ primary ECF buffer for non-carbonic acids   b. phosphate buffer system
        _____ primary intracellular buffer   c. protein buffer system
        _____ important urinary buffer   d. $H_2CO_3 : HCO_3^-$ buffer system

ANSWERS: a, d, c, b

133. Indicate which type of acid-base imbalance might occur in each of the following situations by writing the appropriate letter in the blank.

_____ Fever	(a) respiratory acidosis
_____ Excessive ingestion	(b) respiratory alkalosis
of alkaline drugs	(c) metabolic acidosis
such as NaHCO$_3$	(d) metabolic alkalosis
_____ Aspirin poisoning	
_____ Anxiety	
_____ Severe exercise	
_____ Uremia	
_____ Damage to the	
respiratory center	
_____ Severe diarrhea	
_____ Pneumonia	
_____ Excessive vomiting of	
gastric contents	
_____ Diabetes mellitus	

ANSWERS: b, d, b, b, c, c, a, c, a, d, c

Completion

134. Indicate the changes in ECF and ICF volume and osmolarity that exist after equilibrium has been established during overhydration (e.g., drinking excess H$_2$O) and indicate the compensations that occur by circling the appropriate item in parentheses.

During overhydration, ECF volume is (normal, increased above normal, decreased below normal) and ECF osmolarity is (isotonic, hypotonic, hypertonic). After the resultant fluid shift has occurred, ICF volume is (normal, increased above normal, decreased below normal) and ICF osmolarity is (isotonic, hypotonic, or hypertonic). As compensatory measures, vasopressin secretion is (increased, decreased, unchanged), resulting in (increased, decreased, no change in) urinary output, and thirst is (increased, decreased, unchanged).

ANSWERS: increased above normal, hypotonic, increased above normal, hypotonic, decreased, increased, decreased

135. The following refer to the acid-base abnormality that
      would result from extensive pneumonia in which gas
      exchange is impaired. Indicate the correct answers by
      selecting the appropriate letter for each item.

_____ If a patient has extensive pneumonia, before
        compensation occurs his/her P_{CO_2} would be
        (a) decreased.
        (b) increased.
        (c) normal.

_____ As a consequence of this change in P_{CO_2},
        his/her [H$^+$] would be
        (a) decreased.
        (b) increased.
        (c) normal.

_____ Therefore, the pH of his/her body fluids
        would be
        (a) below normal.
        (b) above normal.
        (c) normal.

_____ Which of the following acid-base
        abnormalities would be present?
        (a) Respiratory alkalosis.
        (b) Respiratory acidosis.
        (c) Metabolic alkalosis.
        (d) Metabolic acidosis.

_____ For which of the following reasons must this
        change in pH be restored to normal?
        (a) If the acid-base abnormality is not
             corrected, the patient will experience
             muscle twitches, muscle spasms, "pins
             and needles" sensations, and may exhibit
             extreme nervousness and even
             convulsions.
        (b) If the acid-base abnormality is not
             corrected, the patient may become
             disoriented and later comatose.
        (c) K^+ retention and cardiac arrhythmias can
             occur.
        (d) Both (a) and (c) above are correct.
        (e) Both (b) and (c) above are correct.

_____ The first line of defense against this change in [H⁺] is the chemical buffer systems. What will be the primary buffer system that will respond to this change?

(a) Phosphate buffer system.
(b) NH_4^+: NH_3 buffer system.
(c) Protein buffer system.
(d) Hemoglobin buffer system.
(e) Carbonic acid: bicarbonate buffer system.

_____ The second line of defense will be the respiratory mechanism of pH control. Which of the following statements concerning respiratory response in this situation is correct?
(a) The respiratory mechanism of pH control cannot occur in this situation.
(b) Faster, deeper respirations will occur to compensate for the change in [H⁺].
(c) Slower, shallower respirations will occur to compensate for the change in [H⁺].

_____ The third line of defense will be the renal mechanism of pH control. Which of the following renal compensations will occur in response to this condition?
(a) HCO_3^- excretion will increase.
(b) H⁺ excretion will increase.
(c) NH_3 secretion is likely to occur.
(d) Both (b) and (c) above are correct.
(e) All of the above are correct.

ANSWERS: b, b, a, b, e, d, a, d

AUDIOVISUAL AIDS

Films

A list of films available from West Publishing Company is presented in Appendix A. Following are other films that may be suitable. The sources for these films, which are coded by abbreviation, are provided in Appendix B.

Acid-Base Balance, WAYNE, 31 min.

Acid-Base Physiology and Buffer Chemistry, APS.

Acids, Bases, and Salts, COR, 21 min.

Buffers, EI

Chemical Balance Through Respiration, ASF, 23 min.

<u>Diuresis</u>, AMA, 48 min.

<u>Dynamics of Fluid Exchange</u>, ACC, 30 min.

<u>Simple and Mixed Acid-Base Disorders</u>, EUT, 56 min.

<u>The Patient Who Cannot Drink</u>, MF, 18 min.

<u>Water</u>, FM, 26 min.

Software

<u>Acid-Base Chemistry</u>, SSS. Covers pH, buffers, molarity, and much more.

<u>Acids and Bases</u>, PLP. Tutorial with calculations of pH.

Chapter 13
Digestive System

CONTENTS
(All page references are to the main text.)

Chapter in Perspective: Focus on Homeostasis, p.458

Chaper Summary, p.458

LECTURE HINTS AND SUGGESTIONS

1. Use a skull model to show teeth and dentition. This and other supplies suggested below can be obtained from Carolina Biological Supply Company or other supply houses.

2. Use microscope slides of the esophagus, stomach, small intestine, and large intestine to show the similarity of histological structure.

3. Use a torso or whole-body manikin to illustrate the location and structure of the organs of the digestive system.

4. Have students observe the neck area for the different swallowing movements.

5. A villus model is informative and can be used effectively in lecture.

6. Use molecular models to illustrate the digestive process.

7. If available from schools that are medically affiliated and work with cadavers, preserved human viscera make excellent demonstration material.

8. A small animal (frog, mouse or rat) can be dissected to illustrate, in situ, the various organs of this system. Of special interest are the length of the intestine, the stomach's rugae, and the hepatic portal system.

9. X-ray films showing ulcers or cancer of the colon are of interest. These can be obtained from local hospitals or radiologists.

10. Have students examine different teeth to see how they are adapted to function in different ways. Teeth models are available at general supply houses.

11. Mix soap or detergents, oil and water together to illustrate emulsification. See any general physiology lab manual for procedures.

12. Consider having a nutrition specialist talk to the class.

CHAPTER QUESTIONS

Multiple Choice

1. Mixing movements

    (a) promote digestion by mixing food with digestive juices.
    (b) facilitate absorption by exposing luminal contents to absorptive surfaces.
    (c) take place only in the stomach.
    (d) Both (a) and (b) above are correct.
    (e) All of the above are correct.

ANSWER: d

2. Which of the following is **not** an accessory digestive organ?

    (a) Salivary glands.
    (b) Exocrine pancreas.
    (c) Stomach.
    (d) Gall bladder.
    (e) Liver.

ANSWER: c

3. Which of the following statements concerning the intrinsic plexuses is **incorrect**?

    (a) The myenteric plexus is located in the submucosa.
    (b) The plexuses innervate smooth muscle cells and exocrine and endocrine gland cells.
    (c) The plexuses are influenced by extrinsic nerves.
    (d) The plexuses coordinate local digestive tract activity.
    (e) There are two major networks of nerve fibers forming the plexuses of the gut.

ANSWER: a

4. The intrinsic nerve plexuses

    (a) produce spontaneous depolarization of the smooth muscle cells in the wall of the digestive tract.
    (b) are located in the mucosa.
    (c) coordinate local activity in the digestive tract.
    (d) Both (a) and (c) above are correct.
    (e) All of the above are correct.

ANSWER: c

5. Which of the following statements concerning parasympa-
    thetic innervation to the digestive tract is **incorrect**?

    (a) In general, parasympathetic stimulation is
         excitatory to the digestive system.
    (b) Parasympathetic innervation to the digestive tract
         come primarily through the vagus nerve.
    (c) Parasympathetic innervation is part of the
         extrinsic nerve supply to the digestive tract.
    (d) Parasympathetic stimulation of the salivary glands
         produces a saliva rich in mucus.
    (e) Parasympathetic stimulation increases salivary,
         gastric, pancreatic, and biliary secretion.

ANSWER: d

6. The BER

    (a) refers to the <u>b</u>asic <u>e</u>ating <u>r</u>eflex, which assures that
         food is moved along the digestive tract at an
         appropriate rate.
    (b) refers to the <u>b</u>asic <u>e</u>lectrical <u>r</u>hythm consisting of
         spontaneous, rhythmic, wavelike fluctuations in
         membrane potential.
    (c) refers to the <u>b</u>asic <u>e</u>mptying <u>r</u>eflex, which governs the
         rate of gastric emptying.
    (d) refers to the <u>b</u>owel <u>e</u>vacuation <u>r</u>eflex, or defecation
         reflex.
    (e) None of the above are correct.

ANSWER: b

7. 9,500 ml of fluid is absorbed from the digestive tract
    daily. The ultimate source of most of this fluid is

    (a) food and fluid ingested during meals.
    (b) stored within secretory cells of the
         digestive tract.
    (c) the plasma.
    (d) the accessory digestive organs.
    (e) metabolic water.

ANSWER: c

8. Chewing reflexly increases which of the following secretions?

    (a) Salivary secretion.
    (b) Gastric secretion.
    (c) Pancreatic secretion.
    (d) Both (a) and (b) above are correct.
    (e) All of the above are correct.

ANSWER: e

9. Which of the following is (are) accomplished by chewing?

    (a) grinding and breaking up food
    (b) mixing food with saliva to facilitate swallowing
    (c) reflexly increasing salivary, gastric, pancreatic, and bile secretion
    (d) Two of the above are correct
    (e) All of the above are correct

ANSWER: e

10. Salivary secretion is

    (a) entirely under neural control (i.e., there is no hormonal control of salivary secretion).
    (b) a passive secretion.
    (c) stimulated by the parasympathetic nervous system and inhibited by the sympathetic nervous system.
    (d) Two of the above are correct.
    (e) All of the above are correct.

ANSWER: a

11. Which of the following is **not** a function of saliva? Saliva

    (a) facilitates swallowing.
    (b) serves as a solvent for molecules that stimulate taste buds.
    (c) dissolves glucose to facilitate its absorption by the oral mucosa.
    (d) has antibacterial action.
    (e) aids speech.

ANSWER: c

12. Which of the following statements concerning the process of salivation is **incorrect**?

    (a) Salivation is entirely under neural control.
    (b) Parasympathetic stimulation and sympathetic stimulation both increase salivary secretion.
    (c) The acquired salivary reflex occurs upon stimulation of chemoreceptors and/or pressure receptors in the mouth.
    (d) Parasympathetic stimulation produces a watery saliva rich in enzymes.
    (e) The salivary center is located in the medulla.

ANSWER: c

13. Which of the following is entirely under nervous control and has no hormonal regulatory component?

    (a) Salivary secretion.
    (b) Gastric secretion.
    (c) Pancreatic secretion.
    (d) Liver secretion.
    (e) All of the above have a hormonal regulatory component.

ANSWER: a

14. Swallowing

    (a) includes the movement of the bolus from the mouth to the stomach.
    (b) includes only the movement of the bolus from the mouth to the esophagus.
    (c) is a sequentially programmed, multiple response, all-or-none reflex.
    (d) Both (a) and (c) above are correct.
    (e) Both (b) and (c) above are correct.

ANSWER: d

15. The swallowing center is located in the

    (a) cerebral cortex.
    (b) medulla.
    (c) hypothalamus.
    (d) throat.
    (e) spinal cord.

ANSWER: b

16. During the oropharyngeal phase of swallowing,

(a) food is prevented from reentering the mouth by elevation of the uvula, which lodges against the back of the throat.
(b) food is prevented from entering the nasal passages by closure of the nasopharyngeal sphincter.
(c) food is prevented from entering the trachea primarily by the epiglottis blocking the opening between the vocal cords.
(d) More than one of the above are correct.
(e) None of the above are correct.

ANSWER: e

17. The pharyngoesophageal sphincter is normally closed

(a) to prevent air from entering the esophagus during breathing.
(b) to prevent gastric contents from refluxing back into the esophagus.
(c) to prevent vomiting.
(d) to prevent esophageal secretions from leaking into the stomach.
(e) to prevent food from entering the pharynx.

ANSWER: a

18. What prevents food from entering the nasal passages during swallowing?

(a) Elevation of the uvula.
(b) Contraction of the pharyngeal muscles.
(c) Positioning of the tongue.
(d) Tight apposition of the vocal cords over the glottis.
(e) Elevation of the epiglottis over the nasopharynx.

ANSWER: a

19. What prevents food from entering the trachea during swallowing?

(a) Elevation of the uvula.
(b) Contraction of the pharyngeal muscles.
(c) Positioning of the tongue.
(d) Tight apposition of the vocal cords over the glottis.
(e) Elevation of the epiglottis over the pharyngoesophageal sphincter.

ANSWER: d

20. Secondary peristaltic waves in the esophagus

    (a) occur when a large or sticky bolus becomes stuck in the esophagus.
    (b) are coordinated by the swallowing center.
    (c) are coordinated by the intrinsic nerve plexus within the esophageal wall.
    (d) Both (a) and (b) above are correct.
    (e) Both (a) and (c) above are correct.

ANSWER: e

21. Assume that the primary peristaltic wave in the esophagus is insufficient to carry an especially large bolus of food through the esophagus to the stomach. What happens to dislodge this trapped food?

    (a) A secondary peristaltic wave is initiated by the swallowing center.
    (b) A secondary peristaltic wave is initiated by distention of the esophagus, mediated by the intrinsic nerve plexuses.
    (c) The food remains in the esophagus until the swallowing mechanism is voluntarily initiated once again.
    (d) Increased esophageal mucus secretion occurs to lubricate the stuck bolus so that it can slide to the stomach.
    (e) Food never becomes stuck in the esophagus because it is very distensible.

ANSWER: b

22. The gastroesophageal sphincter is normally closed

    (a) to prevent air from entering the esophagus during breathing.
    (b) to prevent gastric contents from refluxing back into the esophagus.
    (c) to prevent vomiting.
    (d) to prevent esophageal secretions from leaking into the stomach.
    (e) to prevent food from entering the pharynx.

ANSWER: b

23. The most important function of the stomach is

(a) digestion of starch.
(b) digestion of protein.
(c) digestion of fat.
(d) absorption of monosaccharides.
(e) storage of food.

ANSWER: e

24. Receptive relaxation refers to

(a) relaxation of the pharyngoesophageal sphincter during swallowing.
(b) relaxation of the pyloric sphincter when the duodenum is prepared to receive the chyme.
(c) relaxation of the external anal sphincter when the individual is receptive to the defecation reflex.
(d) relaxation of the stomach as it starts to fill, thereby allowing an increase in volume with very little increase in pressure.
(e) None of the above are correct.

ANSWER: d

25. In which part of the stomach does gastric mixing occur?

(a) Body.
(b) Fundus.
(c) Pylorus.
(d) Antrum
(e) Food is only stored in the stomach, not mixed.

ANSWER: d

26. Gastric mixing

(a) occurs primarily in the body of the stomach.
(b) occurs as a result of the stomach's contents being tumbled back and forth in the antrum because of vigorous peristaltic contractions.
(c) mixes the food with gastric secretions to convert it to a finely divided liquid form known as chyme.
(d) Both (b) and (c) above are correct.
(e) All of the above are correct.

ANSWER: d

27. Which of the following factors is the most potent stimulus for inhibition of gastric motility?

    (a) Fat in the duodenum.
    (b) Acid in the duodenum.
    (c) Acid in the stomach.
    (d) Distention of the stomach.
    (e) Hypertonicity of the duodenal contents.

ANSWER: a

28. Which of the following factors will **not** influence the rate at which a meal will empty from the stomach?

    (a) Fat in the duodenum.
    (b) Acid in the duodenum.
    (c) Caffeine in the duodenum.
    (d) Hypertonicity of the duodenal contents.
    (e) Distention of the duodenum.

ANSWER: c

29. Gastric emptying is decreased by

    (a) distention of the stomach.
    (b) gastrin.
    (c) carbohydrate in the stomach.
    (d) fat in the duodenum.
    (e) fat in the stomach.

ANSWER: d

30. Peristaltic antral contractions

    (a) occur at a rate of 3/minute.
    (b) are responsible for emptying of food into the duodenum.
    (c) are responsible for mixing of food and gastric enzymes within the antrum.
    (d) Both (a) and (b) above are correct.
    (e) All of the above are correct.

ANSWER: e

31. Which of the following breakfasts would remain in the stomach the longest?

(a) Toast, orange juice, and coffee.
(b) Black coffee.
(c) Fried eggs, bacon, and hash browns.
(d) A bowl of cereal with skim milk.
(e) Boiled egg, toast, and juice.

ANSWER: c

32. The enterogastrones include

1. secretin.
2. cholecystokinin.
3. gastrin.

(a) Both (1) and (2) above are correct.
(b) Both (1) and (3) above are correct.
(c) Both (2) and (3) above are correct.
(d) All of the above are correct.
   (e) None of the above are correct.

ANSWER: a

33. Which of the following is **not** secreted by the stomach in response to parasympathetic (acetylcholine) stimulation?

(a) Pepsinogen.
(b) HCl.
(c) Gastrin.
(d) Histamine.
(e) Both (c) and (d) above are not secreted in response to parasympathetic stimulation.

ANSWER: d

34. During the cephalic phase of gastric secretion,

(a) thinking about, seeing, smelling, and chewing food reflexly increases gastric secretion.
(b) vagal stimulation of the gastric glands occurs.
(c) gastrin is released.
(d) Both (a) and (b) above are correct.
(e) All of the above are correct.

ANSWER: e

35. The parietal cells of the gastric mucosa secrete

    (a) HCl.
    (b) pepsinogen.
    (c) intrinsic factor.
    (d) Both HCl and pepsinogen.
    (e) Both HCl and intrinsic factor.

ANSWER: e

36. Which of the following statements concerning HCl secretion by the stomach is correct?

    (a) HCl inactivates salivary amylase and the pancreatic enzymes.
    (b) HCl activates pepsinogen.
    (c) H^+ is actively secreted with Cl- following passively down the electrical gradient.
    (d) Both (a) and (b) above are correct.
    (e) All of the above are correct.

ANSWER: d

37. Intrinsic factor

    (a) is secreted by the parietal cells in the stomach.
    (b) is necessary for absorption of vitamin B_{12}.
    (c) is deficient in pernicious anemia.
    (d) Two of the above are correct.
    (e) All of the above are correct.

ANSWER: e

38. Pernicious anemia

    (a) can occur when the stomach has been removed.
    (b) can occur when the terminal ileum has been removed.
    (c) can occur when there is a deficiency of intrinsic factor.
    (d) Both (a) and (c) above are correct.
    (e) All of the above are correct.

ANSWER: e

39. Which of the following is secreted by the chief cells of the gastric mucosa?

    (a) Pepsinogen.
    (b) HCl.
    (c) Intrinsic factor.
    (d) Gastrin.
    (e) Mucus.

ANSWER: a

40. After pepsinogen is activated,

    (a) it autocatalytically activates more pepsinogen.
    (b) it activates the pancreatic proteolytic enzymes in the duodenal lumen after gastric emptying has occurred.
    (c) it inhibits the pyloric gland area in a negative-feedback fashion.
    (d) Both (a) and (b) above are correct.
    (e) All of the above are correct.

ANSWER: a

41. Inhibition of gastric secretion following a meal is accomplished by

    (a) the enterogastric reflex.
    (b) inhibition of the pyloric gland area by vagal stimulation.
    (c) a high concentration of H^+, which directly inhibits the release of gastrin from the pyloric gland area.
    (d) Both (a) and (c) above are correct.
    (e) All of the above are correct.

ANSWER: d

42. As food leaves the stomach, gastric secretion is reduced. Which of the following factors does **not** contribute to this reduction?

    (a) Fat in the duodenum.
    (b) Low gastric pH.
    (c) Distention of the duodenum.
    (d) High concentration of acid in the stomach or duodenum.
    (e) Pepsinogen in the duodenum.

ANSWER: e

43.   The pyloric gland area of the stomach antrum

  (a)   secretes gastrin.
  (b)   is inhibited when the gastric pH falls too low.
  (c)   is stimulated by the presence of protein, alcohol, caffeine, and distention in the stomach.
  (d)   Both (a) and (b) above are correct.
  (e)   All of the above are correct.

ANSWER: e

44.   The pyloric gland area of the stomach antrum secretes

  (a)   histamine.
  (b)   gastrin.
  (c)   intrinsic factor.
  (d)   Both (a) and (b) above are correct.
  (e)   Both (a) and (c) above are correct.

ANSWER: b

45.   Alcohol

  (a)   stimulates gastric secretion.
  (b)   can be absorbed more rapidly from the small intestine than from the stomach.
  (c)   inhibits gastric emptying through the enterogastric reflex.
  (d)   Both (a) and (b) above are correct.
  (e)   All of the above are correct.

ANSWER: d

46.   Which of the following digestive processes occurs in the stomach?

  (a)   Carbohydrate digestion occurs in the antrum of the stomach.
  (b)   Protein digestion occurs in the antrum of the stomach.
  (c)   Fat digestion occurs in the body of the stomach.
  (d)   Protein digestion occurs in the body of the stomach.
  (e)   Two of the above are correct.

ANSWER: b

47. Which of the following substances is absorbed by the stomach?

    (a) Glucose.
    (b) Caffeine.
    (c) Aspirin.
    (d) Amino acids.
    (e) Fatty acids.

ANSWER: c

48. Which of the following does **not** occur during vomiting?

    (a) The diaphragm contracts.
    (b) The abdominal muscles contract.
    (c) The stomach contracts.
    (d) Respiration is inhibited.
    (e) The glottis is closed.

ANSWER: c

49. Which of the following does **not** occur during vomiting?

    (a) The diaphragm contracts.
    (b) Reverse peristalsis occurs in the esophagus.
    (c) The stomach relaxes.
    (d) The abdominal muscles contract.
    (e) Respiration is inhibited and the airways are closed off.

ANSWER: b

50. During vomiting,

    (a) the diaphragm contracts.
    (b) the abdominal muscles contract.
    (c) the stomach contracts.
    (d) Both (a) and (b) above are correct.
    (e) All of the above are correct.

ANSWER: d

51. Cholecystokinin

    (a) is secreted by the endocrine portion of the pancreas.
    (b) stimulates pancreatic enzyme secretion.
    (c) causes contraction of the gall bladder.
    (d) Both (b) and (c) above are correct.
    (e) All of the above are correct.

ANSWER: d

52. Which of the following accurately describes chymotrypsinogen?

    (a) Chymotrypsinogen is activated by enterokinase.
    (b) Once activated, chymotrypsinogen is involved in protein digestion.
    (c) Chymotrypsinogen is secreted by the endocrine pancreas.
    (d) All of the above are correct.
    (e) None of the above are correct.

ANSWER: b

53. The intestinal hormone secretin is released by endocrine cells in the duodenal mucosa in response to

    (a) distention of the stomach.
    (b) carbohydrate in the duodenum.
    (c) acid in the duodenum.
    (d) gastrin secreted by the pyloric gland area of the stomach.
    (e) None of the above are correct.

ANSWER: c

54. Which of the following statements about pancreatic enzymes is **<u>incorrect</u>**?

    (a) Trypsinogen is secreted in an inactive form.
    (b) Pancreatic amylase digests carbohydrate.
    (c) Pancreatic lipase is responsible for triglyceride digestion.
    (d) Except for trypsinogen, other proteolytic enzymes are secreted in active form.
    (e) Trypsinogen is activated by enterokinase.

ANSWER: d

55. Which of the following are functions of aqueous $NaHCO_3$ secreted by the pancreas into the duodenum?

    (a) Neutralization of acidic gastric contents emptied into the duodenum.
    (b) Prevention of irritation of the duodenal mucosa.
    (c) Actively digests fat molecules into fatty acids.
    (d) Both (a) and (b) above are correct.
    (e) All of the above are correct.

ANSWER: d

56. Which of the following statements concerning secretin is correct?

   (a) The most potent stimulus for secretin secretion is the presence of fat in the duodenum.
   (b) Secretin stimulates pancreatic enzyme secretion.
   (c) Secretin stimulates the parietal and chief cells.
   (d) Secretin stimulates the pancreatic acinar cells.
   (e) None of the above are correct.

ANSWER: e

57. The most potent choloretic is

   (a) vagal stimulation.
   (b) bile salts.
   (c) CCK.
   (d) secretin.
   (e) cholera toxin.

ANSWER: b

58. Which of the following is **not** true of bile?

   (a) Bile contains an excretory product, bilirubin.
   (b) Bile salts aid in protein digestion by transporting amino acids to the intestinal mucosa cells for absorption.
   (c) Bile salts emulsify fat in the lumen of the small intestine.
   (d) Bile salts exert a detergent action.
   (e) Bile contains bile salts which, along with other constituents of bile, form water-soluble micelles that aid fat absorption.

ANSWER: b

59. Bile is secreted by the

   (a) gallbladder.
   (b) pancreas.
   (c) duodenum.
   (d) liver.
   (e) jejunum.

ANSWER: d

60. Bile salts

    (a) aid fat digestion through their detergent action.
    (b) aid fat absorption through micelle formation.
    (c) are lost in the feces once secreted into the bile.
    (d) Both (a) and (b) above are correct.
    (e) All of the above are correct.

ANSWER: d

61. Which of the following stimulates gallbladder contraction?

    (a) CCK
    (b) secretin
    (c) sympathetic stimulation
    (d) Both (a) and (c) above are correct
    (e) Both (b) and (c) above are correct

ANSWER: a

62. Which of the following is **not** a function of the liver?

    (a) metabolic processing of carbohydrates, proteins, and fats
    (b) secretion of proteolytic digestive enzymes
    (c) detoxification and/or degradation of body wastes, hormones, drugs, and foreign compounds
    (d) synthesis of plasma proteins essential to the clotting process
    (e) storage of glycogen, fats, iron, copper, and many vitamins

ANSWER: b

63. Cholecystokinin exerts which of the following actions?

    (a) Stimulates contraction of the gallbladder.
    (b) Stimulates HCl secretion by parietal cells.
    (c) Increases motility of the stomach.
    (d) Stimulates motility of the small intestine.
    (e) Inhibits pancreatic secretion of digestive enzymes.

ANSWER: a

64. Which of the following is the most important stimulus for contraction of the gallbladder?

    (a) CCK causes contraction of the gallbladder.
    (b) Mechanical contraction of the small intestine causes bile to be forced out of the gallbladder.
    (c) Sympathetic stimulation causes contraction of the gallbladder.
    (d) An increase in bile secretion by the liver causes contraction of the gallbladder.
    (e) Bile salts cause contraction of the gallbladder.

ANSWER: a

65. What is responsible for the brown color of the feces?

    (a) Bile salts.
    (b) Undigested cellulose.
    (c) Aqueous $NaHCO_3$ secretion.
    (d) Bilirubin.
    (e) Disintegrated epithelial cells.

ANSWER: d

66. The formation of a lipid emulsion

    (a) facilitates digestion of fat by lipase.
    (b) is accomplished by bile salts.
    (c) takes place in the stomach.
    (d) Both (a) and (b) above are correct.
    (e) All of the above are correct.

ANSWER: d

67. Which of the following enter the duodenum?

    (a) Pancreatic secretions.
    (b) Bile.
    (c) Gastric contents.
    (d) Both (a) and (b) above are correct.
    (e) All of the above are correct.

ANSWER: e

68.   The small intestinal digestive enzymes

 (a)   are secreted into the lumen where they perform their
       function.
 (b)   act intracellularly within the brush borders.
 (c)   complete the digestion of carbohydrates and protein.
 (d)   Both (a) and (c) above are correct.
 (e)   Both (b) and (c) above are correct.

ANSWER: e

69.   Which of the following does **not** enter the duodenal lumen?

 (a)   Trypsinogen.
 (b)   Bile salts.
 (c)   Disaccharidases.
 (d)   Gastric contents.
 (e)   Amylase.

ANSWER: c

70.   The primary factor responsible for moving the chyme
      forward in the small intestine is

 (a)   mass movements.
 (b)   migrating motility complex.
 (c)   a gradient in the frequency of segmentation along the
       length of the small intestine.
 (d)   sequential ringlike contractions that move progres-
       sively forward along the length of the small intestine
       in a stripping motion, pushing the chyme ahead of the
       contraction.
 (e)   stimulation of the intestinal smooth muscle by
       enterokinase.

ANSWER: c

71.   Segmentation

 (a)   is the primary motility in the small intestine during
       digestion of a meal.
 (b)   is both mixing and propulsive.
 (c)   refers to sequential ringlike contractions that sweep
       downward, creating a stripping motion that pushes the
       chyme forward.
 (d)   Both (a) and (b) above are correct.
 (e)   All of the above are correct.

ANSWER: d

72. The primary motility in the small intestine during digestion of a meal is

(a) peristalsis.
(b) segmentation.
(c) haustral contractions.
(d) deglutition.
(e) mastication.

ANSWER: b

73. Epithelial cells are continually being shed from the villi because

(a) the intracellular enzymes digest important cellular constituents, causing the cells to disintegrate and slough.
(b) the body needs a continual new source of protein derived from the digestion of these cells.
(c) new cells are continually being produced in the crypts at the base of the villi and migrate upward, pushing off the old cells at the tip in the process.
(d) acid entering the small intestine from the stomach constantly destroys the small intestinal lining, causing the cells to slough.
(e) None of the above are correct.

ANSWER: c

74. Which of the following enzymes is **not** secreted into the duodenal lumen?

(a) Aminopeptidase.
(b) Lipase.
(c) Trypsinogen.
(d) Procarboxypeptidase.
(e) Amylase.

ANSWER: a

75. In the small intestine, how long does it take for an epithelial cell to migrate from the base of the villi to the tip?

(a) 3 hours.
(b) 3 days.
(c) 1 day.
(d) 3 months.
(e) Several weeks.

ANSWER: b

76. The brush border of the small intestine epithelial cells is responsible for digestion and absorption of food substances by which of the following mechanisms?

    (a) By exerting a stroking action that sweeps the end products of digestion to the absorptive surfaces.
    (b) By supplying digestive enzymes and specific carriers for membrane transport.
    (c) By propelling chyme down the digestive tract.
    (d) By breaking food particles into smaller sizes by "brushing" action.

ANSWER: b

77. Where is digestion completed?

    (a) Stomach.
    (b) Small intestine lumen.
    (c) Intracellularly in the brush borders of the small-intestine epithelial cells.
    (d) Colon.
    (e) Rectum.

ANSWER: c

78. Which of the following absorptive processes occurs?

    (a) Carbohydrate is absorbed by active transport in the small intestine and enters the blood.
    (b) Fat is absorbed by active transport in the small intestine and enters the lymph.
    (c) Protein is absorbed primarily by pinocytosis.
    (d) The water soluble vitamins are carried in the micelles, which are water soluble.
    (e) Chylomicrons dissolve in the lipid portion of the plasma membrane to enable fat to enter the intestinal cell from the lumen.

ANSWER: a

79. Which of the following substances is absorbed by special active transport mechanisms found only in the terminal ileum?

   (a) Fatty acids and monoglycerides.
   (b) Bile salts.
   (c) Vitamin B_{12}.
   (d) Both (b) and (c) above are correct.
   (e) All of the above are correct.

ANSWER: d

80. Absorption of which of the following substances is linked to active sodium absorption at the basolateral border of the epithelial cell?   (Indicate all correct answers.)

   (a) water
   (b) glucose
   (c) galactose
   (d) fructose
   (e) amino acids
   (f) small peptides
   (g) monoglycerides and free fatty acids

ANSWERS: a,b,c,e

81. Which of the following does **not** directly enter the blood upon being absorbed from the digestive tract?

   (a) Glucose.
   (b) Monoglycerides and free fatty acids.
   (c) Amino acids.
   (d) Alcohol.
   (e) Vitamin B_{12}.

ANSWER: b

82. The primary site of absorption in the digestive system is the

   (a) stomach.
   (b) small intestine.
   (c) colon.
   (d) esophagus.
   (e) mouth.

ANSWER: b

83. Which of the following correctly describes carbohydrate absorption by intestinal cells?

    (a) The absorbable units of carbohydrate are monosaccharides.
    (b) Fructose is absorbed by facilitated diffusion.
    (c) Glucose is absorbed by secondary active transport.
    (d) Carbohydrates are absorbed into the blood.
    (e) All of the above are correct.

ANSWER: e

84. Which of the following substances is **not** absorbed from the duodenum?

    (a) Amino acids.
    (b) Glucose.
    (c) Monoglycerides.
    (d) Bile salts.
    (e) Fatty acids.

ANSWER: d

85. Chylomicrons

    (a) are aggregations of triglycerides formed within intestinal epithelial cells and covered with a layer of lipoprotein, which renders them water soluble.
    (b) are aggregations of bile salts, monoglycerides, and free fatty acids.
    (c) are small fat globules held apart by the action of bile salts.
    (d) are secreted in the succus entericus.
    (e) are digested by bacteria in the colon.

ANSWER: a

86. Of the fluid entering the small intestine, _____ % is reabsorbed.

    (a) 100%
    (b) 95%
    (c) 85%
    (d) 50%

ANSWER: b

87. Which of the following statements concerning the colon is **incorrect**?

   (a) Absorption of salt and water converts the colonic contents into fecal material.
   (b) Colonic bacteria digest cellulose for their own growth and reproduction.
   (c) When mass movements of the colon propel feces into the rectum, stimulation of the stretch receptors in the rectal wall reflexly causes contraction of the internal and external anal sphincters to prevent defecation from occurring until an opportune time.
   (d) No digestive enzymes are secreted by the colon.
   (e) Haustral contractions in the colon are a type of mixing motility.

ANSWER: c

88. Which of the following statements concerning the colon is correct?

   (a) The colon has as much absorptive capacity as the small intestine.
   (b) The final stages of carbohydrate and protein digestion occur in the colon.
   (c) Colonic movements are slower than those in small intestine.
   (d) Two of the above are correct.
   (e) All of the above are correct.

ANSWER: c

89. The defecation reflex

   (a) is initiated when mass movements force fecal material into the rectum, stimulating stretch receptors in the rectal wall.
   (b) involves relaxation of the internal anal sphincter and contraction of the sigmoid colon and rectum.
   (c) can be overridden by voluntary contraction of the external anal sphincter.
   (d) Both (a) and (b) above are correct.
   (e) All of the above are correct.

ANSWER: e

90. Which of the following structures secrete mucus?

    (a) Salivary glands.
    (b) Esophagus.
    (c) Stomach.
    (d) Colon.
    (e) All of the above are correct.

ANSWER: e

91. Which of the following is **not** a side effect of constipation?

    (a) Headache.
    (b) Nausea.
    (c) Gradual build-up of toxins.
    (d) Lack of appetite.
    (e) All of the above are correct.

ANSWER: c

92. The symptoms of constipation (e.g., abdominal discomfort, headache, and nausea) are due to which of the following?

    (a) Inhibition of gastric emptying.
    (b) Absorption of toxins of bacterial origin from the colon.
    (c) Prolonged distention of the large intestine by the fecal mass.
    (d) Exhaustion due to frequent straining movements in an effort to initiate the defecation reflex.
    (e) The accumulation of large amounts of fluid in the colon.

ANSWER: c

True/False

93. The majority of metabolic waste products are excreted via the digestive system.

ANSWER: False

94. The only waste product eliminated in the feces is bilirubin.

ANSWER: True

95. The outer muscle layer of the digestive tract consists of circular smooth muscle.

ANSWER: False

96. The ultimate source of the fluids secreted into the digestive tract is the plasma.

ANSWER: True

97. Secretion of some digestive juices occurs passively.

ANSWER: False

98. The function of mixing movements is to promote digestion and facilitate absorption.

ANSWER: True

99. The contents of the digestive tract are technically outside of the body.

ANSWER: True

100. The main sympathetic nerve supply to the digestive tract is the vagus.

ANSWER: False

101. In general, sympathetic stimulation is excitatory to digestive activity.

ANSWER: False

102. The myenteric plexus is a nerve network located in the submucosa.

ANSWER: False

103. The intrinsic nerve plexuses innervate smooth muscle and exocrine gland cells but do not influence endocrine gland cells within the digestive system.

ANSWER: False

104. The BER refers to the basic eating reflex whereby digestive juices are secreted upon seeing, thinking about, or smelling food in anticipation of the arrival of food.

ANSWER: False

105. Slow-wave potentials are always accompanied by contractile activity.

ANSWER: False

106. The only function of chewing is to break food up into smaller pieces and soften it by mixing it with saliva to facilitate swallowing.

ANSWER: False

107. Deglutition refers to the process of chewing.

ANSWER: False

108. After the food has been chewed and mixed with salivary secretion, it is referred to as chyme.

ANSWER: False

109. Protein digestion is initiated by salivary amylase.

ANSWER: False

110. Salivary secretion is a passive process.

ANSWER: False

111. Sympathetic stimulation inhibits salivary secretion.

ANSWER: False

112. There is continuous salivary secretion due to constant low-level stimulation by the parasympathetic nerve endings within the salivary glands.

ANSWER: True

113. Parasympathetic and sympathetic stimulation both increase salivary secretion, contrary to the usual antagonistic activity of these two components of the autonomic nervous system.

ANSWER: True

114. Parasympathetic stimulation of the salivary glands produces a large volume of watery saliva high in enzyme concentration.

ANSWER: True

115. Salivary secretion is entirely under neural control and does not have any hormonal regulation.

ANSWER: True

116. Lysozyme activates salivary amylase.

ANSWER: False

117. Movement of a bolus of food from the mouth into the esophagus takes an average of five to nine seconds.

ANSWER: False

118. Swallowing propels a bolus of food from the mouth through the pharynx and esophagus into the stomach via a complex, sequential, multiple-response reflex.

ANSWER: True

119. The swallowing center initiates and coordinates secondary peristaltic waves.

ANSWER: False

120. The swallowing center is located in the medulla.

ANSWER: True

121. The pharyngoesophageal sphincter is normally closed to prevent esophageal secretions from entering the pharynx during breathing.

ANSWER: False

122. Respiration is inhibited throughout the entire time swallowing is taking place.

ANSWER: False

123. Salivary amylase and the pancreatic enzymes are inactivated by acid.

ANSWER: True

124.   The stomach mucosa is thrown into folds known as villi.

ANSWER: False

125.   The body of the stomach exhibits vigorous peristaltic contractions at a frequency of about 3/minute.

ANSWER: False

126.   The most important function of the stomach is to begin protein digestion.

ANSWER: False

127.   Segmentation contractions in the stomach at a rate of three contractions/minute, keeping pace with the BER.

ANSWER: False

128.   Gastric secretion does not begin until the arrival of food in the stomach.

ANSWER: False

129.   Absorption of foodstuffs begins in the stomach.

ANSWER: False

130.   Gastric mixing takes place primarily in the antrum of the stomach.

ANSWER: True

131.   The rate of gastric emptying depends entirely on the volume and fluidity of gastric contents.

ANSWER: False

132.   The enterogastric reflex promotes gastric emptying.

ANSWER: False

133.   The rate of gastric emptying is influenced both by factors in the stomach and in the duodenum.

ANSWER: True

134. The primary factor governing the rate of gastric emptying is the volume of the gastric contents.

ANSWER: False

135. The presence of protein in the stomach stimulates the release of histamine, which in turn promotes HCl and pepsinogen secretion.

ANSWER: False

136. Gastric secretion occurs only when food is present in the stomach.

ANSWER: False

137. Gastrin is not secreted during the cephalic phase of gastric secretion.

ANSWER: False

138. HCl activates pepsinogen.

ANSWER: True

139. The parietal cells secrete both pepsinogen and intrinsic factor.

ANSWER: False

140. Intrinsic factor is necessary for the absorption of vitamin B_{12}.

ANSWER: True

141. H^+ ions are actively secreted against a large concentration gradient into the stomach; Cl^- secretion follows passively.

ANSWER: False

142. As the gastric pH falls very low, the pyloric gland area is inhibited.

ANSWER: True

143. Pepsinogen inhibits the pyloric gland area in negative-feedback fashion.

ANSWER: False

144. The process of digestion starts as food enters the stomach.

ANSWER: False

145. Most nutrients are absorbed in the stomach.

ANSWER: False

146. A glass of milk drunk shortly before several beers will slow the absorption of alcohol, delaying its effects on the body by decreasing the rate of gastric emptying.

ANSWER: True

147. Alcohol can be absorbed by the stomach mucosa more quickly than by the small intestine mucosa.

ANSWER: False

148. Vomiting is accomplished by strong peristaltic contractions in the stomach.

ANSWER: False

149. The enterogastric reflex and enterogastrones inhibit gastric motility but stimulate gastric secretion.

ANSWER: False

150. The pancreatic enzymes function best in an acid medium.

ANSWER: False

151. The pancreatic digestive enzyme secretions are referred to collectively as succus entericus.

ANSWER: False

152. All the pancreatic enzymes are secreted in inactive form.

ANSWER: False

153. The pancreas secretes enzymes involved in the digestion of all three categories of foodstuff.

ANSWER: True

154. Chymotrypsinogen is activated by enterokinase.

ANSWER: False

155. Trypsin inhibitor blocks the action of trypsin within the duodenal lumen once protein digestion has been completed.

ANSWER: False

156. The principal clinical manifestation of pancreatic exocrine insufficiency is incomplete protein digestion resulting from the deficiency of the powerful pancreatic proteolytic enzymes.

ANSWER: False

157. The liver receives venous blood coming directly from the digestive tract and arterial blood coming from the aorta.

ANSWER: True

158. Bile is secreted continuously by the gallbladder.

ANSWER: False

159. Bile is secreted by the liver and stored and concentrated in the gallbladder.

ANSWER: True

160. Bile salts are important in fat digestion and absorption.

ANSWER: True

161. Bilirubin aids fat digestion and absorption.

ANSWER: False

162. Bile salts are responsible for the brown color of feces.

ANSWER: False

163. Enterohepatic circulation is important in the secretion of bile salts.

ANSWER: True

164. CCK causes relaxation of the sphincter of Oddi.

ANSWER: True

165. The most potent choloretic is CCK.

ANSWER: False

166.   The primary factor responsible for forward propulsion of chyme through the small intestine is mass movements.

ANSWER: False

167.   The ileocecal juncture serves as a barrier to prevent bacteria-laden contents of the large intestine from contaminating the small intestine.

ANSWER: True

168.   Excessive small intestinal motility can lead to diarrhea because there is less time for absorption to take place.

ANSWER: True

169.   The main motility seen in the small intestine during digestion of a meal is the migrating motility complex.

ANSWER: False

170.   The main function of the ileocecal valve/sphincter is to prevent small intestinal contents from entering the large intestine before digestion of food is completed.

ANSWER: False

171.   The small intestinal epithelium actively secretes digestive enzymes into the intestinal lumen.

ANSWER: False

172.   Digestive enzymes produced by the small intestine are not secreted into the lumen but act intracellularly.

ANSWER: True

173.   Migration of a new intestinal epithelial cell from the crypt at the base of the villus to the tip of the villus requires about three weeks.

ANSWER: False

174. Protein digestion begins in the stomach under the influence of pepsin, continues in the duodenal lumen under the influence of pancreatic proteolytic enzymes, and is completed intracellularly in the small intestinal brush border.

ANSWER: True

175. The primary site of absorption of foodstuffs is the small intestine.

ANSWER: True

176. Most of the fluid presented to the small intestine for absorption has been ingested.

ANSWER: False

177. Amino acids and glucose are both absorbed by secondary active transport by the small intestinal epithelial cells.

ANSWER: True

178. Fat is absorbed into the lymph in the form of micelles.

ANSWER: False

179. The central lacteal picks up chylomicrons.

ANSWER: True

180. Chylomicrons are aggregates of bile salts, monoglycerides, and free fatty acids.

ANSWER: False

181. Most vitamin absorption occurs passively in the small intestine.

ANSWER: True

182. Haustrations propel the feces 1/3 to 3/4 the length of the colon in a few seconds.

ANSWER: False

183. Succus entericus refers to the mucus alkaline secretion of the colon.

ANSWER: False

184. Colonic secretion contains no digestive enzymes.

ANSWER: True

185. Humans are not capable of digesting cellulose but some of the colonic bacteria have this capability.

ANSWER: True

186. Most of the digestive secretions remain in the fecal material.

ANSWER: False

187. The primary absorption of nutrients, water, and electrolytes takes place in the large intestine, converting chyme to fecal material.

ANSWER: False

188. Toxin accumulation in the blood is the biggest hazard of constipation.

ANSWER: False

189. Receptive relaxation refers to the voluntary relaxation of the external anal sphincter when the individual is receptive to the defecation reflex.

ANSWER: False

190. Upon arrival of a new meal in the stomach, the gastro-colic reflex pushes the colonic contents into the rectum, triggering the defecation reflex to eliminate the remains of a preceding meal.

ANSWER: True

191. Symptoms associated with constipation are attributable to toxins absorbed from the retained fecal material.

ANSWER: False

192. The external anal sphincter is voluntarily relaxed to permit flatus to escape.

ANSWER: False

Fill-in-the-blanks

193.   The four basic digestive processes are _____,
       _____, _____ and
       _____.

ANSWERS: motility, secretion, digestion, absorption

194.   In general, the parasympathetic nervous system is
       (excitatory or inhibitory) _____ to the
       digestive tract, whereas the sympathetic nervous system
is _____.

ANSWERS: excitatory, inhibitory

195.   The _____ is a common passageway for both
       the digestive and respiratory systems.

ANSWER: pharynx

196.   The primary wave of peristalsis in the esophagus is
       initiated by the _____. If this primary
       wave fails to push the bolus to the stomach, a secondary
       peristaltic wave is initiated by the
       _____.

ANSWERS: swallowing center, intrinsic nerve plexus

197.   Gastric storage takes place in the _____ (what
       part?) of the stomach whereas gastric mixing takes place
       in the _____.

ANSWERS: body, antrum

198.   The most potent stimulus for inhibiting gastric motility
       and emptying is _____.

ANSWER: fat in the duodenal lumen

199.   The three gastrointestinal hormones that function as
       enterogastrones are _____, _____,
       and _____.

ANSWERS: secretin, cholecystokinin, gastric inhibitory
           peptide

200.   The most potent stimulus for gastrin release is
        _____. Gastrin, in turn, is a powerful
        stimulus for _____. The PGA is directly
        inhibited from releasing gastrin by _____.

ANSWERS: protein in the stomach, hydrochloric acid and
           pepsinogen secretion, high hydrogen-ion concentra
           tion

201.   Carbohydrate digestion takes place in the (what part)
        _____ of the stomach under the influence of
        _____ (what enzyme), while protein
        digestion takes place in the _____ under the
        influence of _____.

ANSWERS: body, salivary amylase, antrum, pepsin

202.   The pancreatic _____ secretion
        neutralizes acidic gastric contents in the duodenal
        lumen.

ANSWER: aqueous alkaline

203.   Secretin stimulates the pancreatic _____
        cells to secrete _____, whereas CCK
        stimulates the pancreatic _____ cells to
        secrete _____.

ANSWERS: duct, aqueous alkaline fluid, acinar, digestive
           enzymes

204.   When worn-out red blood cells are destroyed, the
        hemoglobin is degraded to a yellow pigment known as
        _____, which is excreted into the bile.

ANSWER: bilirubin

205.   Excessive accumulation of bilirubin in the body produces
        the condition of _____.

ANSWER: jaundice

206.   The primary mixing and propulsive motility of the small
        intestine is _____.

ANSWER: segmentation

207. The three modifications of the small intestine mucosa that greatly increase the surface area available for absorption are _____, _____, and _____.

ANSWERS: circular folds, villi, microvilli

208. _____ contractions are responsible for mixing the colonic contents, while _____ periodically propel the contents long distances.

ANSWERS: Haustral, mass movements

209. Colonic secretion consists of _____.

ANSWER: an alkaline mucus solution

210. List the three categories of foodstuffs and their absorbable units.

Category of foodstuff   Absorbable unit

(a) _____   (b) _____
(c) _____   (d) _____
(e) _____   (f) _____

ANSWERS: (a) carbohydrates (polysaccharides, disaccharides); (b) monosaccharides (especially glucose); (c) proteins; (d) amino acids; (e) fats (triglycerides); (f) monoglycerides, free fatty acids

Matching

211. _____ pathway by which factors outside of the digestive system can influence digestion

_____ travels via the blood to alter digestive motility and secretion

_____ responsible for coordinating local activity within the digestive tract

_____ responsible for establishing the rate of rhythmic contractility

_____ coordinates activity between different regions of the digestive tract

a. autonomous smooth muscle function
b. extrinsic (autonomic) nerves
c. hormones
d. intrinsic nerve plexuses

ANSWERS: b, c, d, a, b

460   Chapter 13

212. _____ secretes digestive juices   a. serosa
     _____ suspends digestive organs   b. inner circular
           from the inner wall of the   smooth muscle
           abdominal cavity   layer
     _____ secretes a watery   c. mucous membrane
           lubricating fluid   d. lamina propria
     _____ absorbs luminal contents   e. mesentery
     _____ provides distensibility   f. muscularis
           and elasticity   mucosa
     _____ constricts the lumen   g. submucosa
     _____ shortens the digestive   h. outer
           tract   longitudinal
     _____ houses gut-associated   smooth muscle
           lymphoid tissue   layer
     _____ secretes gastrointestinal
           hormones
     _____ can alter pattern of surface
           folding

ANSWERS: c, e, a, c, g, b, h, d, c, f

213. _____ secrete HCl   a. chief cells
     _____ secrete gastrin   b. parietal cells
     _____ serve as parent cells of   c. mucous cells
           all new cells of the   d. endocrine cells of
           gastric mucosa   PGA
     _____ secrete pepsinogen
     _____ secrete intrinsic factor

ANSWERS: b, d, c, a, b

214. Indicate which hormone(s) is (are) being described by writing the appropriate letter in the blank using the following answer code.

> (a) = Both secretin and CCK
> (b) = Secretin
> (c) = CCK
> (d) = Gastrin

_____ Secreted by the pyloric gland area.
_____ Stimulated primarily by the presence of fat (fatty acids).
_____ Stimulated primarily by the presence of protein.
_____ Secretion is inhibited by a low pH.
_____ Inhibit(s) gastric secretion.
_____ Stimulate(s) gastric secretion.
_____ Inhibits gastric motility.
_____ Stimulate(s) pancreatic digestive enzyme secretion.
_____ Stimulate(s) pancreatic aqueous $NaHCO_3$ secretion.
_____ Stimulate(s) gallbladder contraction.
_____ Known as an enterogastrone.
_____ Secreted by the small intestine mucosa.
_____ Stimulate(s) the pancreatic acinar cells.
_____ Stimulate(s) the pancreatic duct cells.
_____ Stimulated primarily by the presence of acid.

ANSWERS: d, c, d, d, a, d, a, c, b, c, a, a, c, b, b

215. Identify which part of the digestive system is associated
      with each item in question by writing the appropriate
      letter in the blank using the following answer code.

                    (a) = Small intestine
                    (b) = Large intestine
                    (c) = Mouth
                    (d) = Esophagus
                    (e) = Stomach

      _____ Absorbs weak acids such as aspirin.
      _____ Primary motility is haustrations.
      _____ Receptive relaxation occurs.
      _____ Secondary peristaltic waves occur.
      _____ Primary motility is segmentation.
      _____ BER occurs at a rate of 3 contractions/minute.
      _____ Absorbs nitroglycerin.
      _____ Involved with second stage of deglutition.
      _____ Involved with mastication.
      _____ Food is converted into chyme.
      _____ Chyme is converted into feces.
      _____ Main site of digestion and absorption.
      _____ Secretion is entirely mucus.
      _____ Protein digestion begins.
      _____ Carbohydrate digestion begins.
      _____ Fat digestion begins.

ANSWERS: e, b, e, d, a, e, c, d, c, e, b, a, d, e, c, a

216. Indicate the site at which digestion of each of the three
      main categories of foodstuff begins and is completed by
      writing the appropriate letter in the blank using the
      following answer code.

                    (a) = Mouth
                    (b) = Stomach
                    (c) = Small intestine lumen
                    (d) = Intracellularly in the small intestine
                          brush border
                    (e) = Colon

      _____ Carbohydrate digestion begins.
      _____ Protein digestion begins.
      _____ Fat digestion begins.
      _____ Carbohydrate digestion is completed.
      _____ Protein digestion is completed.
      _____ Fat digestion is completed.

ANSWERS: a, b, c, d, d, c

217. Indicate which digestive secretion is being described in each question by writing the appropriate letter in the blank using the following answer code.

        (a) = Bile salts
        (b) = Pepsin(ogen)
        (c) = Amylase
        (d) = Lipase
        (e) = Trypsin(ogen)

    _____ Pancreatic enzyme that digests protein.
    _____ Gastric enzyme that digests protein.
    _____ Enzyme that digests fat.
    _____ Secreted by the salivary glands.
    _____ Recycled many times through enterohepatic circulation.
    _____ Exerts detergent action.
    _____ Pancreatic enzyme that digests carbohydrate.
    _____ Forms micelles to aid fat absorption.
    _____ Activated by enterokinase.
    _____ Activated by HCl.
    _____ Potent choloretic.

ANSWERS: e, b, d, c, a, a, c, a, e, b, a

218. Indicate the stimulus for the item in question stion by writing the appropriate letter in the blank using the following answer code.

        (a) = Fat in the duodenum
        (b) = Acid in the duodenum
        (c) = Acid in the stomach
        (d) = Protein in the stomach

    _____ Stimulates secretion of CCK.
    _____ Stimulates secretion of secretin.
    _____ Most potent stimulus for inhibition of gastric motility.
    _____ Stimulates secretion of gastrin.
    _____ Directly inhibits secretion of gastrin.

ANSWERS: a, b, a, d, c

219. Indicate which item in the right column best describes the item in the left column by writing the appropriate letter in the blank. <u>There is only one correct answer per question and each answer may be used only once.</u>

_____ Salivary amylase	a. secretes $NaHCO_3$.
_____ HCl	b. enzyme for protein digestion secreted by pancreas.
_____ Cholecystokinin	
_____ Trypsin(ogen)	
_____ Lipase	c. activates pepsinogen.
_____ Gastrin	d. enzyme for fat digestion.
_____ Pepsin(ogen)	
_____ Pyloric gland area	e. functions inside brush border.
_____ Secretion	f. secretes gastrin
_____ Pancreatic acinar cell	g. stimulates parietal and chief cells
_____ Aminopeptidase	h. enzyme for carbohydrate digestion that functions primarily in the body of the stomach.
_____ Pancreatic duct cell	

i. secreted by chief cells.
j. secretes pancreatic enzymes.
k. secreted by duodenal cells in response to the presence of acid.
l. stimulates pancreatic acinar cells.

ANSWERS: h, c, l, b, d, g, i, f, k, j, e, a

220.
_____ activation initiated by enterokinase	a. amylase
_____ only enzyme for fat digestion	b. trypsin
_____ similar to digestive enzyme found in saliva	c. chymotrypsin
_____ activation initiated by trypsin	d. lipase

ANSWERS: b, d, a, c

AUDIOVISUAL AIDS

Films

A list of films available from West Publishing Company is presented in Appendix A. Following are other films that may be suitable. The sources for these films, which are coded by abbreviation, are provided in Appendix A.

Alimentary Tract, EBE, 11 min.

Breakdown, FM, 26 min.

Colorectal Cancer, FHS, 49 min.

Diet: The Cancer Connection, FHS, 26 min.

Digestion, IM, 29 min.

Digestion and the Food We Eat, BFA, 9 min.

Digestion: Breakdown (VCR), FM, 26 min.

Digestion: Eating to Live (VCR), FM, 26 min.

Digestion: Mechanics, UW, 18 min.

Digestive System, CFV, 16 min.

Digestive System, FI, 12 min.

Eat, Drink and be Wary, CH, 21 min.

Eating to Live, FM, 26 min.

Good Sense About Your Stomach, TLV, 14 min.

Human Body: Chemistry of Digestion, COR, 14 min.

Human Body: Nutrition and Metabolism, COR, 13 min.

Human Gastric Function, ASF, 18 min

I Am Joe's Stomach, PYR, 26 min.

Let's Eat Food, MGHT, 35 min.

Look Before You Eat, CH, 22 min.

Metabolic Diversity, MH, 26 min.

<u>Nova: Fat Chance in a Thin World</u>, CBS, 60 min.

<u>Nutrition: The Inner Environment</u>, AEF, 15 min.

<u>Regulation of Pancreatic Secretion</u>, USNAC, 28 min.

<u>Stomatal Opening and Closing</u>, EF, 3 min.

<u>The Digestive System</u>, EBE, 15 min.

<u>The Human Body: Digestive System</u>, COR, 16 min.

<u>The Liver</u>, IU, 15 min.

<u>The Mechanisms of Swallowing</u>, WARDS, 3 min.

<u>You Are What You Eat</u>, CH, 10 min.

<u>William Beaumont</u>, UC, 30 min.

Software

<u>Digestion</u>, CBS. Deals with nutrients, digestion in simple organisms, and digestion in humans.

<u>Digestion</u>, SSS. Reviews the main concepts.

<u>Digestive System</u>, PLP. Two part program covering all physiological aspects.

<u>Dynamics of Human Teeth</u>, EI. Teeth as they relate to ingestion of nutrients.

<u>Dynamics of the Human Digestive System</u>, EI. Follows the food through the digestive process.

<u>Nutrition - A Balanced Diet</u>, CBS. This program allows students to evaluate the nutritional quality of their daily diets.

<u>The Digestion Simulation</u>, PLP. The dynamics of digestion with unique animated graphics.

Chapter 14
Energy Balance and Temperature Regulation

CONTENTS
(All page references are to the main text.)

-Shivering is the primary involuntary means of increasing heat production.   p.472
-The magnitude of heat loss can be adjusted by varying the flow of blood through the skin.   p.472
-The hypothalamus simultaneously coordinates heat-production mechanisms and heat-loss and heat-conservation mechanisms to regulate core temperature homeostatically.   p.473
-During a fever, the hypothalamic thermostat is "reset" at an elevated temperature.   p.473

Beyond the Basics - The Extremes of Heat and Cold Can Be Fatal, p.474

Chapter in Perspective: Focus on Homeostasis, p.475

Chapter Summary, p.475

LECTURE HINTS AND SUGGESTIONS

1.   Show how a metabolator can be used to determine one's BMR.

2.   The game <u>Metabolism</u> is available from Carolina Biological Supply Company. This game helps students become familiar with cellular respiration.

3.   Display a bomb calorimeter and explain how it works. See any general physiology laboratory manual.

CHAPTER TEST QUESTIONS

Multiple Choice

1.   Which of the following is a potential source of energy to support energy expenditure needs?

   (a)   Food intake.
   (b)   Fat stores.
   (c)   Shivering.
   (d)   Both (a) and (b) above are correct.
   (e)   All of the above are correct.

ANSWER: d

2. Which of the following is **not** internal work?

    (a) Energy required for active transport.
    (b) Energy required to pump blood.
    (c) Energy required to move the body in
         relation to the environment.
    (d) Energy used during synthetic reactions.
    (e) Energy used to maintain body posture.

ANSWER: c

3. Internal work

    (a) includes all of the energy-expending activities that
         must go on all of the time to sustain life.
    (b) .refers to all energy expenditure by tissues other than
         skeletal muscles.
    (c) includes the energy expenditure required to move
         external objects.
    (d) Both (a) and (b) above are correct.
    (e) All of the above are correct.

ANSWER: a

4. The energy equivalent of oxygen

    (a) is the number of calories contained in every liter of
         oxygen consumed.
    (b) is the value that equates how much energy is liberated
         from food for every liter of oxygen consumed.
    (c) is the oxygen consumption required for the processing
         and storage of ingested foodstuff.
    (d) is the energy required to raise 1 gram of H_2O 1°C.
    (e) None of the above are correct.

ANSWER: b

5. The energy equivalent of O_2 is

    (a) 4.8 kilocalories of energy liberated per liter of O_2
         consumed.
    (b) used to indirectly measure the metabolic rate.
    (c) the energy required to raise 1 gm of H_2O 1°C.
    (d) Both (a) and (b) above are correct.
    (e) All of the above are correct.

ANSWER: d

6. The lowest metabolic rate occurs

   (a) during sleep.
   (b) during a basal metabolic rate determination.
   (c) during exercise.
   (d) after a meal.
   (e) in males compared to females.

ANSWER: a

7. The factor that increases the metabolic rate to the greatest extent is

   (a) increased skeletal-muscle activity.
   (b) increased mental effort.
   (c) increased dietary fiber intake.
   (d) increased epinephrine secretion.
   (e) increased brown fat deposition.

ANSWER: a

8. When a negative energy balance exists,

   (a) the individual gains weight because s/he is using less than normal energy or "negative" energy.
   (b) the caloric content of the food ingested is less than the energy output.
   (c) the caloric content of the food ingested exceeds the energy lost due to heat or work.
   (d) energy has been destroyed by catabolic processes within the body.
   (e) external work exceeds internal work so more energy is expended via external work than is produced via internal work.

ANSWER: b

9. If more energy is contained in the food eaten than is expended,

   (a) a positive energy balance will exist.
   (b) the excess energy will be destroyed.
   (c) the excess energy will be stored, primarily as adipose tissue.
   (d) Both (a) and (b) above are correct.
   (e) Both (a) and (c) above are correct.

ANSWER: e

10. Which of the following is **not** a theory of satiety?

   (a) Hydrostatic theory.
   (b) Glucostatic theory.
   (c) Lipostatic theory.
   (d) Ischymetric theory.

ANSWER: a

11. Which of the following statements concerning control of food intake is **incorrect**?

   (a) There are a pair of feeding centers and a pair of satiety centers in the hypothalamus that play a major role in controlling food intake.
   (b) Stimulation of the feeding centers drives the individual to eat.
   (c) Stimulation of the satiety centers brings about the feeling of having had enough to eat.
   (d) Distention of the digestive tract constitutes the major input for regulating food intake.
   (e) Destruction of the satiety centers in an experimental animal leads to profound overeating and obesity.

ANSWER: d

12. The leading theory believed responsible for maintenance of body weight as a result of long-term matching of food intake to energy expenditure relates to

   (a) the amount of triglyceride fat stored in adipose tissue.
   (b) the extent of glucose utilization.
   (c) the magnitude of cellular ATP production.
   (d) the extent of gastrointestinal distention.
   (e) the extent of behavioral modification associated with eating habits.

ANSWER: a

13. Core temperature is

   (a) normally maintained relatively constant around 100°F.
   (b) the temperature of the abdominal and thoracic organs, the central nervous system, and the skeletal muscles.
   (c) the temperature of the skin and subcutaneous fat.
   (d) Both (a) and (b) above are correct.
   (e) Both (a) and (c) above are correct.

ANSWER: d

14. "Normal" body temperature may vary slightly as a result of

    (a) exercise.
    (b) recent food intake.
    (c) the time of day.
    (d) exposure to extremes in environmental temperature.
    (e) All of the above are correct.

ANSWER: e

15. Radiation

    (a) refers to heat emission from a warm object in the
         form of electromagnetic waves.
    (b) is only a source of heat loss for the body (i.e., the
         body can lose but not gain heat by radiation).
    (c) refers to the transfer of heat by direct contact
         between a warmer and cooler object.
    (d) involves the continued cycling of cool air over the
         body.
    (e) refers to the transformation of water from a gaseous
         to a liquid state.

ANSWER: a

16. Radiation and conduction are two types of heat exchange
    between the body and environment. The magnitude of heat
    loss via these two processes is determined by the

    (a) amount of sweating.
    (b) temperature difference between body surface and its
         surroundings.
    (c) absolute core temperature.
    (d) the extent of evaporation from the body surface.

ANSWER: b

17. When the surrounding temperature is low, heat is lost from
    the body by means of

    (a) radiation.
    (b) conduction/convection.
    (c) nonshivering thermogenesis.
    (d) Both (a) and (b) above are correct.
    (e) All of the above are correct.

ANSWER: d

18. A person can lose heat to an environment warmer than the body by means of

    (a) radiation.
    (b) evaporation.
    (c) conduction.
    (d) Both (a) and (b) above are correct.
    (e) All of the above are correct.

ANSWER: b

19. The type of heat loss that occurs by sitting on a cold car seat is

    (a) radiation.
    (b) convection.
    (c) conduction.
    (d) evaporation.

ANSWER: c

20. On the average, about half of the body heat that is lost is due to loss by

    (a) radiation.
    (b) convection.
    (c) conduction.
    (d) evaporation.

ANSWER: a

21. Sweating

    (a) is an active evaporative heat-loss process under sympathetic nervous control.
    (b) is the only means of losing heat when the environmental temperature is warmer than body temperature.
    (c) is the only means by which evaporative heat loss can take place in the body.
    (d) Both (a) and (b) above are correct.
    (e) All of the above are correct.

ANSWER: d

22. Where are the temperature control centers located?

    (a) Hypothalamus.
    (b) Cerebellum.
    (c) Skin.
    (d) Cerebral cortex.
    (e) Medulla.

ANSWER: a

23. The temperature control center within the anterior region of the hypothalamus is activated by _____ and initiates reflexes that mediate _____.

    (a) cold, heat production and heat conservation
    (b) cold, heat loss
    (c) warmth, heat loss
    (d) warmth, heat production and heat conservation

ANSWER: c

24. Receptors that relay temperature information to the hypothalamic temperature control centers include

    (a) peripheral warmth and cold thermoreceptors in the skin.
    (b) central thermoreceptors in the hypothalamus.
    (c) central thermoreceptors in internal organs.
    (d) Both (a) and (b) above are correct.
    (e) All of the above are correct.

ANSWER: e

25. Which of the following is **not** a means of increasing heat production?

    (a) Shivering.
    (b) Skin vasoconstriction.
    (c) Nonshivering thermogenesis.
    (d) Increased muscle tone.
    (e) Increased exercise.

ANSWER: b

26.   The major means of increasing heat production in response
      to a cold environmental temperature is

      (a)   skin vasoconstriction.
      (b)   wearing warm clothing.
      (c)   increased skeletal muscle activity, such as through
            shivering and increased voluntary exercise.
      (d)   formation of "goose bumps."
      (e)   increased food intake to elevate the metabolic rate.

ANSWER: c

27.   The major means of decreasing heat loss in response to a
      cold environmental temperature is

      (a)   skin vasoconstriction.
      (b)   skin vasodilation.
      (c)   increasing the temperature gradient between the skin
            and environment.
      (d)   formation of "goose bumps."
      (e)   shivering.

ANSWER: a

28.   Nonshivering thermogenesis

      (a)   is stimulated by epinephrine and thyroid hormone.
      (b)   refers to the general increase in muscle tone in
            response to abrupt exposure to cold.
      (c)   enhances the insulative capacity of the skin by
            promoting increased deposition of brown fat under the
            skin.
      (d)   refers to the elevation of body temperature in
            response to pyrogen release.
      (e)   None of the above are correct.

ANSWER: a

29.   Sweating

   (a)   causes vasodilation of the skin vessels.
   (b)   increases the insulative capacity of the skin so that
         less heat can be gained from the environment.
   (c)   is the only heat-loss mechanism available to the body
         when the environmental temperature is so high that a
         normal temperature gradient between the skin and the
         environment cannot be established.
   (d)   Both (a) and (c) above are correct.
   (e)   All of the above are correct.

ANSWER: c

30.   On a hot summer day with a temperature of 101°F, body heat
      is lost by

   (a)   radiation.
   (b)   conduction/convection.
   (c)   evaporation.
   (d)   Both (b) and (c) above are correct.
   (e)   All of the above are correct.

ANSWER: c

31.   When vasodilation of the blood vessels in the skin occurs,

   (a)   the skin temperature becomes warmer than the core
         temperature.
   (b)   the insulative capacity of the skin is increased.
   (c)   heat will be lost from the body if the air tempera-
         ture is cooler than the skin temperature.
   (d)   Both (b) and (c) above are correct.
   (e)   All of the above are correct.

ANSWER: c

32.   Which of the following mechanisms help to maintain body
      temperature on hot days?

   (a)   Decreased muscle tone.
   (b)   Skin vasodilation.
   (c)   Sweating.
   (d)   Two of the above are correct.
   (e)   All of the above are correct.

ANSWER: e

33. Which of the following statements about thermoregulation is correct?

    (a) In a cold environment, the body will be losing heat by conduction, convection, radiation, and evaporation.
    (b) In a hot environment when the temperature of the environment exceeds that of the skin surface, evaporation is the only means for the body to lose heat.
    (c) The temperature control centers in the hypothalamus receive afferent input from peripheral thermoreceptors in the skin and central thermoreceptors in the hypothalamus and internal organs.
    (d) Both (b) and (c) above are correct.
    (e) All of the above are correct.

    ANSWER: e

34. In fever production

    (a) endogenous pyrogen released from white blood cells in response to an infection elevates the hypothalamic "set point."
    (b) cold response mechanisms are initiated by the hypothalamus to raise the body temperature to the new set point.
    (c) heat loss mechanisms are triggered to eliminate the excess heat from the body.
    (d) Both (a) and (b) above are correct.
    (e) Both (a) and (c) above are correct.

ANSWER: d

35. Which of the following does **not** characterize heat exhaustion?

    (a) Reduced plasma volume.
    (b) Extensive sweating.
    (c) Rapidly rising body temperature.
    (d) Fainting.
    (e) Reduced blood pressure.

ANSWER: c

True/False

36. Energy cannot be created or destroyed, but it can be transformed from one form of energy into another.

ANSWER: True

37. Internal energy expenditure is the energy utilized by the skeletal muscles when external objects are moved.

ANSWER: False

38. All energy liberated from ingested food that is not directly used for movement of external objects or stored in the body eventually becomes thermal energy.

ANSWER: True

39. Metabolic rate equals energy expenditure/unit of time.

ANSWER: True

40. Metabolic rate can be measured indirectly by measuring the rate of oxygen consumption.

ANSWER: True

41. The basal metabolic rate is the body's lowest metabolic rate.

ANSWER: False

42. The most dominant factor influencing the BMR is the level of active circulation thyroid hormone.

ANSWER: True

43. As the level of active circulating thyroid hormone increases, the BMR increases correspondingly.

ANSWER: True

44. Weight loss occurs when the energy derived from the food consumed is less than the energy expended by the body.

ANSWER: True

45. The appetite centers stimulate feeding behavior, whereas the satiety centers inhibit feeding behavior.

ANSWER: True

46. The feeding and satiety centers are located in the hypothalamus.

ANSWER: True

47. An animal can be driven to overeat either by selective stimulation of the appetite centers or destruction of the satiety centers.

ANSWER: True

48. Fat people tend to eat more on a daily basis than thin persons.

ANSWER: False

49. The core temperature is maintained at a fairly constant level, but skin temperature is quite variable.

ANSWER: True

50. Oral temperature is lower than the core temperature.

ANSWER: True

51. Oral temperature is the same as core temperature.

ANSWER: False

52. The normal core temperature is 98.6°F (37°C).

ANSWER: False

53. The skin thermoreceptors are capable of regulating core temperature in the absence of the hypothalamic temperature control centers.

ANSWER: False

54. The temperature control center in the posterior region of the hypothalamus is activated in response to cold exposure.

ANSWER: True

55.   Sweat that drips off the skin instead of being evaporated does not produce a cooling effect.

ANSWER: True

56.   Skin vasoconstriction increases the skin's insulative capacity.

ANSWER: True

57.   Upon exposure to heat, skin vasodilation occurs, which increases the temperature gradient between the skin and environment, thus promoting heat loss.

ANSWER: True

58.   Heat loss from the body by evaporation occurs even in very cold weather.

ANSWER: True

59.   The nude body absorbs more radiant heat energy than the body covered in light colored clothing.

ANSWER: True

60.   Skin vasoconstriction reduces the temperature of the skin.

ANSWER: True

61.   The body temperature is normally maintained at an elevated level during sustained exercise.

ANSWER: True

62.   An elevated body temperature is always indicative of an infection.

ANSWER: False

63.   Heat exhaustion is accompanied by extensive sweating, whereas heat stroke is characterized by an absence of sweating.

ANSWER: True

64.   Profuse sweating occurs during heat stroke as body temperature climbs rapidly upward.

ANSWER: False

Fill-in-the-blanks

65. _____ work refers to the energy expended by contracting skeletal muscles to accomplish movement of objects or the body within the external environment.

ANSWER: External

66. _____ work constitutes all forms of biological energy expenditure that do not accomplish mechanical work outside of the body.

ANSWER: Internal

67. The _____ is the energy expenditure (i.e., rate of heat production) per unit of time.

ANSWER: metabolic rate

68. The unit of heat energy used in energy balance is the _____.

ANSWER: kilocalorie

69. The minimal waking rate of energy expenditure determined under standardized conditions is known as the _____.

ANSWER: basal metabolic rate (BMR)

70. Regulation of _____ is the most important factor in the long-term maintenance of energy balance and body weight.

ANSWER: food intake

71. The region of the brain primarily responsible for controlling food intake is the _____.

ANSWER: hypothalamus

72. The disorder characterized by a pathological fear of gaining weight and a distorted body image is _____.

ANSWER: anorexia nervosa

73. _____ may serve as a satiety signal to stop eating before ingested food is actually digested, absorbed, and made available to meet the body's energy needs.

ANSWER: Cholecystokinin (CCK)

74. The most important factor determining the extent of evaporation of sweat is the _____ of the air.

ANSWER: humidity

75. The _____ serves as the body's thermostat.

ANSWER: hypothalamus

76. The temperature-sensitive receptors that monitor skin and core temperature are termed _____.

ANSWER: thermoreceptors

77. The amount of heat lost to the environment by radiation and conduction-convection is largely determined by the _____ between the skin and the external environment.

ANSWER: temperature gradient

78. The only means of heat loss when the environmental temperature exceeds core temperature is _____.

ANSWER: sweating

79. _____ refers to a state of collapse resulting from reduced blood pressure brought about as a consequence of overtaxing the heat loss mechanisms.

ANSWER: Heat stroke

80. Freezing of exposed tissues produces the condition of _____.

ANSWER: frostbite

81. An elevation in body temperature due to reasons other than an infection is known as _____.

ANSWER: hyperthermia

Matching

82. Match the item in the right column with its description in the left column by writing the appropriate letter in the blank.

_____ Energy expended by contracting skeletal muscles to move external objects or to move the body.

_____ All forms of biological energy that do not accomplish work outside the body.

_____ Amount of heat required to raise the temperature of 1 gram of H_2O 1°C.

_____ Quantity of heat produced per liter of O_2 consumed.

_____ Minimal waking rate of internal energy expenditure.

a. energy equivalent of oxygen
b. external work
c. calorie expenditure
d. basal metabolic rate
e. internal work

ANSWERS: b, e, c, a, d

83. Match the method of heat exchange in the right column with its description in the left column by writing the appropriate letter in the blank.

_____ Emission of heat energy from the surface of a warm body in the form of electromagnetic waves.

_____ Heat loss by means of conversion of water from a liquid to a gaseous state.

_____ Transfer of heat between objects of differing temperatures that are in direct contact with each other.

_____ Transfer of heat by air or water currents.

a. convection
b. evaporation
c. radiation
d. conduction

ANSWERS: c, b, d, a

84.   _____ Excessive fat content in
adipose tissues stores.
_____ Morbid fear of becoming
overweight.
_____ State of collapse resulting
from reduced blood pressure
brought about as a consequence
of overtaxing the heat loss
mechanisms.
_____ Heat loss mechanisms are absent
despite the fact that the body
temperature is rapidly rising.
_____ Freezing of tissues as a result
of cold exposure.
_____ Elevation in body temperature due
to reasons other than an infection.
_____ Slowing of all body processes as a
result of generalized cooling.

a. hypothermia
b. obesity
c. frostbite
d. hyperthermia
e. anorexia
   nervosa
f. heat stroke
g. heat
   exhaustion

ANSWERS: b, e, g, f, c, d, a

85.   Indicate by circling the appropriate letter which of the
following physiological and behavioral responses occur to
restore core temperature to normal when (a) it starts to
fall upon cold exposure or (b) it starts to rise upon
heat exposure. Furthermore, indicate whether each of
these responses represents a means of (c) altering heat
gain or (d) altering heat loss by circling the appropriate letter.

A. shivering	a	b	c	d
skin vasoconstriction	a	b	c	d
B. skin vadodilation	a	b	c	d
C. decreased muscle tone	a	b	c	d
D. reduced voluntary activity	a	b	c	d
E. sweating	a	b	c	d
F. increasing the insulative capacity of the skin	a	b	c	d
G. hunching over	a	b	c	d
H. panting in dogs	a	b	c	d
I. putting on light colored clothing	a	b	c	d
J. bouncing up and down; hand clapping	a	b	c	d
K. erection of hair shafts in furred animals	a	b	c	d

ANSWERS: A. a,c; B. a,d; C. b,d; D. b, c; D. b,c; F.
b,d; G. a,d; H. a,d; I. b,d; J. b,c; K. a,c;
L. a,d

AUDIOVISUAL AIDS

Films

A list of films available from West Publishing Company is presented in Appendix A. Following are other films that may be suitable. The sources for these films, which are coded by abbreviation, are provided in Appendix B.

A Chemical Feast, BNF, 11 min.

A Declaration: "The Right to Eat," SRS, 20 min.

Cholesterol - Eat Your Heart Out, SEF, 14 min.

Diets for all Reasons, CH, 20 min.

Eat, Drink, and be Wary, CH, 19 min.

Energetics of Life, JW, 23 min.

Energy, MH, 27 min.

Energy - A Conversation, MH, 17 min.

Energy and Living Things, MH, 17 min.

Energy Cycles in the Cell, MH, 16 min.

Energy Released from Food, UJ, 26 min.

Food, Energy and You, PE, 20 min.

For Tomorrow We Shall Diet, CH, 24 min.

Hot and Cold, FM, 26 min.

How the Body Uses Energy, MH, 15 min.

Human Body: Nutrition and Metabolism, COR, 13 min.

Metabolic Diversity, MH, 28 min.

Metabolism: The Fire of Life, PLP, 30 min.

Nutrition and Metabolism, COR, 14 min.

Nutrition - Energy, Carbohydrates, Fats, and Proteins, BFA, 54 min.

Nutrition - Fueling the Human Machine, BFA, 18 min.

Nutrition Is ...., WG, 26 min.

Nutrition: The Inner Environment, AEF, 15 min.

Oxidation-Reduction, MH, 9 min.

Patterns of Energy Transfer, MH, 20 min.

Regulating Body Temperature, EBE, 22 min.

The Curious Case of Vitamin E, UC, 29 min.

Vitamins from Foods, IU, 26 min.

You're Too Fat, NBC, 49 min.

Software

Advanced Cell Respiration, EI. An integrated lesson on the chemical pathways.

Energy, SSS. Emphasis is on the physical principles of energy changes.

Experiments in Metabolism, EI. Utilizes graphics and animation to guide students to calculate BMR.

Matter and Energy, SSS. Covers elements, compounds, mixtures, physical and chemical changes, potential and kinetic energy, and energy changes.

Metabolism and the Production of ATP, EI. How organisms metabolize carbohydrates, fats, and proteins. All on one disk!

Nutrition - A Balanced Diet, CBS. Allows students to evaluate the nutritional value of their diets, taking into account such factors as age, sex, etc.

Chapter 15
Endocrine System

CONTENTS
(All page references are to the main text.)

-Abnormalities of thyroid function include both hypothyroidism and hyperthyroidism. p.503
-A goiter may or may not accompany either hypothyroidism or
hyperthyroidism. p.504

Adrenal Glands, p.505

-Each adrenal gland consists of an outer, steroid-secreting
adrenal cortex and an inner, catecholamine-secreting
medulla. p.505
-The adrenal cortex secretes mineralocorticoids, glucocorticoids, and sex hormones. p.505
-Mineralocorticoids' major effects are on electrolyte balance and blood-pressure homeostasis. p.505
-Glucocorticoids exert metabolic effects and have an important role in adaptation to stress. p.506
-Cortisol secretion is directly regulated by ACTH. p.507
-The adrenal cortex secretes both male and female sex
hormones in both sexes. p.508
-The adrenal gland may secrete too much or too little of any
one of its hormones. p.508
-The catecholamine-secreting adrenal medulla is a modified
sympathetic postganglionic neuron. p.509
-Epinephrine reinforces the sympathetic nervous system and
exerts additional metabolic effects as well. p.509
-Adrenomedullary dysfunction is very rare. p.510
-The stress response is a generalized, nonspecific pattern
of neural and hormonal reactions to any situation that
threatens homeostasis. p.510
-The multifaceted stress response is coordinated by the
hypothalamus. p.511
-Activation of the stress response by chronic psychosocial
stressors may be harmful. p.511

Endocrine Control of Fuel Metabolism, p.512

-All three classes of nutrient molecules can be used to
provide cellular energy and, to a large extent, can be
interconverted. p.512
-The brain must be continuously supplied with glucose, even
between meals when no new nutrients are being taken up from
the digestive tract. p.514
-Metabolic fuels are stored during the absorptive state and
are mobilized during the postabsorptive state. p.515
-The pancreatic hormones, insulin and glucagon, are most
important in regulating fuel metabolism. p.515
-Insulin lowers blood glucose, amino acid, and fatty acid
levels and promotes anabolism of these small nutrient
molecules. p.515
-The primary stimulus for increased insulin secretion is an
increase in blood glucose concentration. p.516
-There are two types of diabetes mellitus, depending on the
insulin-secreting capacity of the cells. p.517

-The symptoms of diabetes mellitus are characteristic of an exaggerated postabsorptive state. p.518
-Insulin excess causes brain-starving hypoglycemia. p.518
-Glucagon in general opposes the actions of insulin. p.520
-Glucagon secretion is increased during the postabsorptive state. p.520
-Glucagon excess can aggravate the hyperglycemia of diabetes mellitus. p.521
-Epinephrine, cortisol, growth hormone, and thyroid hormone also exert direct metabolic effects. p.521

Endocrine Control of Calcium Metabolism, p.522
-Plasma calcium must be closely regulated to prevent changes in neuromuscular excitability. p.522
-Parathyroid hormone raises free plasma calcium levels by its effects on bone, kidneys, and intestine. p.522
-The primary regulator of PTH secretion is the plasma concentration of free calcium. p.523
-Calcitonin lowers the plasma calcium concentration but is not important in the normal control of calcium metabolism. p.524
-Vitamin D is actually a hormone that increases calcium absorption in the intestine. p.524
-Disorders in calcium metabolism may arise from abnormal levels of parathyroid hormone or vitamin D. p.524

Beyond the Basics - Osteoporosis: The Bane of Brittle Bones, p.526

Chapter in Perspective: Focus on Homeostasis, p.526

Chapter Summary, p.527

LECTURE HINTS AND SUGGESTIONS

1. Use a dissectible torso or whole-body manikin to illustrate the location of the various endocrine glands. Charts are also very useful in illustrating this concept. This and other materials suggested below are available from Carolina Biological Supply Company, Burlington, NC, and other supply houses.

2. Use molecular models to illustrate the major types of hormones.

3. Show a brain model to illustrate the relationships of the hypothalamus to the pituitary gland.

4. Use of a sheep brain (obtained from a local slaughter house) is an excellent way to show the hypothalamus-pituitary relationship.

5. Use a human skull to show the sella turcica (a "small house") and its relationship to the pituitary.

6. Stress the integration of neural and endocrine tissues in regulatory body functions.

7. Use familiar examples of endocrine functions to initiate classroom dialogue. For example, changes in urine volume can be used as a basis for a discussion of endocrine regulatory mechanisms.

8. Provoke a hormonal response in students, then ask what happened (e.g., startle them to induce epinephrine release).

9. Sheep endocrine glands are excellent demonstration material of endocrine gland anatomy. These are available from local slaughter houses.

10. Demonstration slides as well as 2 x 2 slides of various endocrine glands are useful.

11. Have students locate the thyroid gland by gently exploring the anterior surface of the trachea while swallowing.

12. Biochemical flow charts are very useful for this chapter.

CHAPTER TEST QUESTIONS

Multiple Choice

1. The specificity of hormones is due to

    (a) specialized hormone secretion.
    (b) molecular rearrangement at the site of action.
    (c) specific binding of hormones to plasma proteins.
    (d) specialization of target-cell receptors.
    (e) discrete inactivation of hormones by the liver or kidneys.

ANSWER: d

2.   Hormones

   (a)   are all of similar chemical composition.
   (b)   combine with specific receptors on the target cell's
         surface or inside the target cell.
   (c)   are secreted at a constant rate.
   (d)   all act by activating adenylate cyclase, which
         transforms ATP into cyclic AMP.
   (e)   All of the above are correct.

ANSWER: b

3.   All hormones

   (a)   are cholesterol derivatives.
   (b)   initiate synthesis of new proteins.
   (c)   are secreted by endocrine glands through ducts into
         the blood.
   (d)   must combine with specific receptors on the target
         cells in order to exert their effects.
   (e)   Both (b) and (d) above are correct.

ANSWER: d

4.   Which of the following is true about hormones?   Hormones

   (a)   are released from exocrine glands.
   (b)   interact with receptors at target-cell sites.
   (c)   are synthesized in the lymph nodes.
   (d)   interact with receptors in the blood.
   (e)   are all similar chemically.

ANSWER: b

5.   Hormones

   (a)   are long-distance chemical mediators synthesized by
         endocrine glands.
   (b)   are secreted into the blood.
   (c)   always exert tropic effects.
   (d)   Both (a) and (b) above are correct.
   (e)   All of the above are correct.

ANSWER: d

6. Hormones

    (a)   are secreted through ducts into the blood.
    (b)   are all peptides.
    (c)   are all secreted at a constant rate to maintain homeostasis.
    (d)   exert their effects by altering intracellular protein activity within their target cells.
    (e)   Both (c) and (d) above are correct.

ANSWER: d

7. Which of the following is **not** accomplished by the endocrine system?

    (a)   Coordination of rapid, precise interactions with the external environment.
    (b)   Regulation of organic metabolism and H_2O and electrolyte balance.
    (c)   Promoting growth and development.
    (d)   Controlling reproduction.
    (e)   Helping body cope with stressful situations.

ANSWER: a

8. Which of the following is **not** controlled at least in partly by hormones?

    (a)   homeostasis
    (b)   organic metabolism
    (c)   rapid interactions with the external environment
    (d) H_2O and electrolyte balance
    (e)   adaptation to stress
    (f)   growth and development
    (g)   red blood cell production
    (h)   circulation
    (i)   digestion and absorption of food
    (j)   reproduction

ANSWER: c

9. Tropic hormones

    (a)   are produced by the posterior pituitary.
    (b)   are secreted only by the hypothalamus.
    (c)   primarily regulate hormone secretion by certain other endocrine glands.
    (d)   all have nontropic functions, too.
    (e)   are the hormones that stimulate athletes to win trophies.

ANSWER: c

10. Hormones may be divided into the following three classes:

    (a) amines, peptides, and steroids.
    (b) free fatty acids, peptides, and steroids.
    (c) amines, phospholipids, and steroids.
    (d) amines, free fatty acids, and peptides.
    (e) amines, steroids, and phospholipids.

ANSWER: a

11. Amines

    (a) consist of a chain of specific amino acids of varying length.
    (b) are derived from the amino acid tyrosine.
    (c) include the hormones secreted by the thyroid gland and adrenal medulla.
    (d) Both (a) and (c) above are correct.
    (e) Both (b) and (c) above are correct.

ANSWER: e

12. Which of the classes of hormones are polar and, accordingly, hydrophilic and lipophobic?

    (a) Peptides.
    (b) Catecholamines.
    (c) Steroids.
    (d) Both (a) and (b) above are correct.
    (e) All of the above are correct.

ANSWER: d

13. Which of the classes of hormones are synthesized by the endoplasmic reticulum/Golgi complex mechanism?

    (a) Peptides.
    (b) Catecholamines.
    (c) Steroids.
    (d) Thyroid hormone.
    (e) Both (a) and (b) above are correct.

ANSWER: a

14. Which of the classes of hormones are **not** stored within the endocrine cell after being synthesized?

    (a) Peptides.
    (b) Catecholamines.
    (c) Steroids.
    (d) Thyroid hormone.
    (e) Both (c) and (d) above are correct.

ANSWER: c

15. Which of the classes of hormones are released by exocytosis upon appropriate stimulation?

    (a) Peptides.
    (b) Catecholamines.
    (c) Steroids.
    (d) Thyroid hormone.
    (e) Both (a) and (b) above are correct.

ANSWER: e

16. Which of the following statements concerning peptide hormones is **incorrect**?

    (a) Peptides are synthesized by the endoplasmic reticulum-Golgi complex system.
    (b) Peptides circulate largely bound to plasma proteins.
    (c) Peptides bind to surface receptors of their target cells.
    (d) Peptides exert their effect largely by means of second-messenger systems.
    (e) Peptides are released by exocytosis upon appropriate stimulation.

ANSWER: b

17. Steroids

    (a) are lipophilic.
    (b) are derived from cholesterol.
    (c) initiate the synthesis of specific new proteins within their target cells.
    (d) Both (a) and (b) above are correct.
    (e) All of the above are correct.

ANSWER: e

18. Lipophilic hormones

    (a) include steroids and thyroid hormone.
    (b) bind with receptors located inside their target cells.
    (c) activate second-messenger systems within their target cells.
    (d) Both (a) and (b) above are correct.
    (e) All of the above are correct.

ANSWER: d

19. Which of the classes of hormones acts by means of the second-messenger system?

    (a) Peptides.
    (b) Catecholamines.
    (c) Steroids.
    (d) Thyroid hormone.
    (e) Both (a) and (b) above are correct.

ANSWER: e

20. Which of the classes of hormones triggers the synthesis of new intracellular proteins within the target cell?

    (a) Peptides.
    (b) Catecholamines.
    (c) Steroids.
    (d) Thyroid hormone.
    (e) Both (c) and (d) above are correct.

ANSWER: e

21. The most common second messenger used by hydrophilic hormones is

    (a) calcium.
    (b) cyclic AMP.
    (c) chromatin.
    (d) messenger RNA.
    (e) plasma proteins.

ANSWER: b

22.   In the second-messenger system of hormonal action,

(a)   the presence of a small amount of one hormone (the second messenger) is essential to permit another hormone (the first messenger) to exert its full effect.

(b)   a tropic hormone (the first messenger) stimulates secretion of another hormone (the second messenger).

(c)   the hormone first binds to a specific surface receptor (the first messenger), whereupon the hormone-receptor complex moves into the cell to combine with a specific intracellular receptor (the second messenger).

(d)   releasing hormones (the first messenger) from the hypothalamus regulate the release of many anterior pituitary hormones (the second messenger).

(e)   the combination of a hormone (the first messenger) with membrane surface receptors activates adenylate cylase, which catalyzes the transformation of cellular ATP to cyclic AMP, which in turn acts as a "second messenger" to produce alteration of cell function associated with that hormone.

ANSWER: e

23.   Which of the classes of hormones gain entry inside their target organ cells?

(a)   Peptides.
(b)   Catecholamines.
(c)   Steroids.
(d)   Thyroid hormone.
(e)   Both (c) and (d) above are correct.

ANSWER: e

24.   Which of the following situations represents negative feedback?

(a)   When hormone A stimulates hormone B, hormone B inhibits hormone C.

(b)   when hormone A inhibits hormone B, hormone B inhibits hormone A.

(c)   When hormone A stimulates hormone B, hormone B inhibits hormone A.

(d)   When hormone A inhibits hormone B, hormone B inhibits hormone C.

(e)   When hormone A stimulates hormone B, hormone B stimulates hormone A.

ANSWER: c

25. In the process of negative feedback,

   (a) TSH inhibits thyroid hormone secretion by the thyroid gland.
   (b) thyroid hormone inhibits TSH secretion by the anterior pituitary.
   (c) thyroid hormone directly inhibits further thyroid hormone secretion by the thyroid gland.
   (d) TRH inhibits TSH secretion by the anterior pituitary.

ANSWER: b

26. Which of the following statements concerning control of hormone secretion is **not** correct?

   (a) Normally the effective plasma concentration of a hormone is regulated by appropriate adjustments in the rate of its secretion.
   (b) In order to maintain homeostasis, the rate of hormone secretion remains constant.
   (c) Negative-feedback control is important in maintaining the plasma concentration of a hormone at a relatively constant set-point.
   (d) Neuroendocrine reflexes produce a sudden increase in hormone secretion in response to a specific, usually external, stimulus.
   (e) Hormonal secretion fluctuates with time as a result of endogenous oscillators that are entrained to external cues.

ANSWER: b

27. Diurnal rhythms

   (a) are inherent cyclical peaks and ebbs of hormone secretion that are a function of time and are entrained to the twenty-four hour light-dark cycle.
   (b) are important in maintaining hormone levels at a relatively constant set point no matter the time of day.
   (c) occur only with cortisol secretion.
   (d) Both (a) and (c) above are correct.
   (e) None of the above are correct.

ANSWER: a

28. Permissiveness of hormones refers to the fact that

(a) hormones permit cellular processes to occur.
(b) hormones permit their target organs to function at the optimal rate.
(c) in some instances an adequate amount of one hormone must be present for the full exertion of another hormone's effect, even though the first hormone itself does not directly elicit the response.
(d) the nervous system through numerous neuroendocrine relationships permits the endocrine system to function.
(e) the tropic hormones permit other endocrine glands to secrete their hormones.

ANSWER: c

29. Synergism occurs when

(a) one hormone induces the loss of another hormone's receptors.
(b) the actions of several hormones are complementary and their combined effect is greater than the sum of their separate effects.
(c) one hormone must be present in adequate amounts for the full exertion of another hormone's effect, even though the first hormone does not directly elicit the response.
(d) one hormone increases the number of target-tissue receptors for another hormone.
(e) the number of target tissue receptors for a hormone is reduced as a direct consequence of the hormone's effect on its own receptors.

ANSWER: b

30. Too little activity of a particular hormone can arise from

(a) an abnormality within the endocrine gland that produces this hormone.
(b) a deficiency of this hormone's tropic hormone.
(c) an inborn lack of target-cell receptors for this hormone.
(d) Both (a) and (b) above are correct.
(e) All of the above are correct.

ANSWER: e

31.   The posterior pituitary

 (a)   secretes vasopressin and oxytocin in response to hypothalamic hypophysiotropic hormones.
 (b)   stores anterior pituitary hormones.
 (c)   stores vasopressin and oxytocin, which are secreted by the hypothalamus and travel to the posterior pituitary along nerve axons.
 (d)   secretes vasopressin and oxytocin into the hypothalamic-hypophyseal portal system.
 (e)   None of the above are correct.

ANSWER: c

32.   The posterior pituitary

 (a)   is composed of nervous tissue.
 (b)   stores anterior pituitary hormones, which are released into the blood upon hypothalamic stimulation.
 (c)   synthesizes and secretes vasopressin and oxytocin.
 (d)   Both (a) and (c) above are correct.
 (e)   All of the above are correct.

ANSWER: a

33.   Which of the following has a direct anatomical connection to the hypothalamus?

 (a)   Adrenal gland.
 (b)   Posterior lobe of the pituitary.
 (c)   Thyroid gland.
 (d)   Parathyroid gland.
 (e)   None of the above are correct.

ANSWER: b

34.   Which of the following is a neurohormone?

 (a)   Vasopressin.
 (b)   Thyroid hormone.
 (c)   Growth hormone.
 (d)   Cortisol.
 (e)   Luteinizing hormone.

ANSWER: a

35. Which of the following does **not** produce hormones?

    (a) Posterior pituitary.
    (b) Liver.
    (c) Pancreas.
    (d) Stomach.
    (e) Adrenal medulla.

ANSWER: a

36. Melanocyte-stimulating hormone

    (a) are responsible for the deposition of melanin in the skin during the process of tanning.
    (b) are not present in humans.
    (c) are present in varying amounts in races of different skin color.
    (d) are important for color adaptations associated with camouflage in certain lower vertebrates.
    (e) More than one of the above are correct.

ANSWER: d

37. Melanocyte-stimulating hormone

    (a) are secreted by the intermediate lobe of the pituitary in some lower vertebrates.
    (b) are known to cause skin darkening in certain lower vertebrates.
    (c) are believed to be responsible for the tanning phenomenon in humans.
    (d) Both (a) and (b) above are correct.
    (e) All of the above are correct.

ANSWER: d

38. Which of the following hormones is **not** secreted by the anterior pituitary?

    (a) CRH.
    (b) TSH.
    (c) FSH.
    (d) LH.
    (e) GH.

ANSWER: a

39. The anterior pituitary

    (a)   is also known as the adenohypophysis.
    (b)   is composed primarily of nervous tissue.
    (c)   primarily secretes tropic hormones.
    (d)   Both (a) and (c) above are correct.
    (e)   All of the above are correct.

ANSWER: d

40. The anterior pituitary

    (a)   is also known as the adenohypophysis.
    (b)   is composed of glandular tissue.
    (c)   does not contain prolactin-secreting cells in males.
    (d)   Both (a) and (b) above are correct.
    (e)   All of the above are correct.

ANSWER: d

41. Which of the following hormones secreted by the anterior
pituitary is purely nontropic?

    (a)   TSH.
    (b)   Prolactin.
    (c)   LH.
    (d)   ACTH.
    (e)   FSH.

ANSWER: b

42. Hormone secretion from the anterior pituitary gland is
controlled

    (a)   by hypophysiotropic hormones from the hypothalamus.
    (b)   directly by neural innervation of anterior pituitary
          cells.
    (c)   by negative-feedback action of target-tissue hor-
          mones.
    (d)   Both (a) and (c) above are correct.
    (e)   All of the above are correct.

ANSWER: d

43. Which of the following hormones is regulated by the anterior pituitary?

    (a) Parathyroid hormone.
    (b) Cortisol.
    (c) Aldosterone.
    (d) Insulin.
    (e) TRH.

ANSWER: b

44. Hypophysiotropic hormones from the hypothalamus

    (a) control the release of oxytocin and vasopressin from the posterior pituitary.
    (b) travel via neuron axons from the hypothalamus to the anterior pituitary.
    (c) are carried in the hypothalamic-hypophyseal portal system.
    (d) are released upon positive-feedback stimulation via the anterior pituitary tropic hormones.
    (e) always act to stimulate the release of anterior pituitary hormones.

ANSWER: c

45. Which of the following statements concerning hypophysio-tropic hormones is correct?

    (a) Each hypophysiotropic hormone influences only one anterior pituitary hormone.
    (b) All hypophysiotropic hormones stimulate the release of anterior pituitary hormones.
    (c) Hypophysiotropic hormones are also produced outside of the hypothalamus, where they serve different functions.
    (d) Hypophysiotropic hormones are secreted into the general circulation.

ANSWER: c

46. Which of the following hormones is **not** secreted by the hypothalamus?

    (a) vasopressin
    (b) ACTH
    (c) TRH
    (d) somatostatin
    (e) prolactin-inhibiting hormone

ANSWER: d

47.   The hypothalamic-hypophyseal portal system

   (a)   carries anterior pituitary hormones from the anterior
         pituitary gland to the hypothalamus to regulate the
         release of hypophysiotropic hormones.
   (b)   diverts blood directly to the pituitary, completely
         bypassing the hypothalamus.
   (c)   carries hypophysiotropic hormones from the hypotha-
         lamus to the anterior pituitary to regulate anterior
         pituitary hormone secretion.
   (d)   carries the anterior pituitary hormones into the
         general systemic circulation.
   (e)   connects the hypothalamus and posterior pituitary.

ANSWER: c

48.   The hypothalamic-hypophyseal portal system

   (a)   carries vasopressin and oxytocin from the hypotha-
         lamus to the posterior pituitary for storage.
   (b)   carries hypophysiotropic hormones from the hypotha-
         lamus to the posterior pituitary to control the
         release of posterior pituitary hormones.
   (c)   carries hypophysiotropic hormones from the hypotha-
         lamus to the anterior pituitary to control the
         release of anterior pituitary hormones.
   (d)   carries vasopressin and oxytocin from the hypotha-
         lamus to the anterior pituitary to control the
         release of anterior pituitary hormones.
   (e)   Both (b) and (c) above are correct.

ANSWER: c

49.   Which of the following represent long-loop negative
      feedback in the CRH-ACTH-cortisol system?

   (a)   Cortisol inhibits CRH secretion.
   (b)   CRH inhibits ACTH secretion.
   (c)   ACTH inhibits CRH secretion.
   (d)   ACTH inhibits cortisol secretion.
   (e)   CRH inhibits cortisol secretion.

ANSWER: a

50. Which of the following is **not** an effect of growth hormone?

    (a) Increased fat breakdown.
    (b) Increased bone growth.
    (c) Decreased glucose entry into muscle cells.
    (d) Decreased protein synthesis.
    (e) Increased rate of cell division.

ANSWER: d

51. Growth hormone

    (a) levels in the blood are directly correlated with the rate of growth throughout life.
    (b) stimulates the secretion of somatomedins.
    (c) stimulates osteoblast activity.
    (d) Both (b) and (c) above are correct.
    (e) All of the above are correct.

ANSWER: d

52. Hypertrophy

    (a) refers to an increase in the size of cells.
    (b) refers to an increase in the number of cells.
    (c) is promoted by growth hormone.
    (d) Both (a) and (c) above are correct.
    (e) Both (b) and (c) above are correct.

ANSWER: d

53. Growth hormone

    (a) increases the uptake of amino acids by cells.
    (b) promotes triglyceride breakdown.
    (c) conserves glucose for glucose-dependent tissues such as the brain.
    (d) Both (a) and (b) above are correct.
    (e) All of the above are correct.

ANSWER: e

54. Which of the following is **not** a function of growth
     hormone?

     (a) Increases uptake of amino acids by cells.
     (b) Stimulates the synthesis of somatomedins.
     (c) Enhances glucose uptake by muscle cells.
     (d) Stimulates cell division.
     (e) Promotes bone growth until the epiphyseal plate is
          closed.

ANSWER: c

55. Growth hormone

     (a) closes the epiphyseal plate of long bones.
     (b) promotes hypertrophy and hyperplasia.
     (c) secretion is stimulated by an increased blood glucose
          level.
     (d) is the only factor responsible for governing the
          growth of an individual.
     (e) All of the above are correct.

ANSWER: b

56. Growth hormone

     (a) directly stimulates bone growth.
     (b) exerts its effects on bones via somatomedin release.
     (c) promotes closure of the epiphyseal plate.
     (d) Both (a) and (c) above are correct.
     (e) Both (b) and (c) above are correct.

ANSWER: b

57. Excessive growth hormone secretion in an adult leads to

     (a) gigantism.
     (b) disproportionate growth resulting in thickened bones
          and coarse features.
     (c) no symptoms because growth is already complete.
     (d) acromegaly.
     (e) Both (b) and (d) above are correct.

ANSWER: e

58.   Somatomedins are released from the liver in response to

       (a)   increased plasma growth hormone levels.
       (b)   increased plasma somatostatin levels.
       (c)   decreased plasma growth hormone levels.
       (d)   decreased plasma somatostatin levels.

ANSWER: a

59.   Dwarfism may be the result of a deficiency of

       (a)   growth-hormone releasing hormone.
       (b)   GH.
       (c)   Somatomedins.
       (d)   Both (b) and (c) above are correct.
       (e)   All of the above are correct.

ANSWER: e

60.   Osteoblasts

       (a)   secrete the organic matrix components of bone.
       (b)   become osteocytes once they become entrapped in the
              bone that they form.
       (c)   dissolve bone.
       (d)   form cartilage.
       (e)   Both (a) and (b) above are correct.

ANSWER: e

61.   Which of the following factors does **not** increase growth
       hormone secretion?

       (a)   Deep sleep.
       (b)   Exercise.
       (c)   Low blood amino acid level.
       (d)   Stress.
       (e)   Low blood glucose level.

ANSWER: c

62.   Which of the following hormones does **not** promote growth
       either directly or indirectly?

       (a)   growth hormone
       (b)   androgens
       (c)   thyroid hormone
       (d)   cortisol
       (e)   insulin

ANSWER: d

63. Iodine is necessary for the formation of

   (a)   thyroid hormone.
   (b)   ACTH.
   (c)   insulin.
   (d)   calcitonin.
   (e)   cortisol.

ANSWER: a

64. Thyroid hormones are

   (a)   stored attached to thyroglobulin in the colloid.
   (b)   released from the thyroid gland immediately after
         synthesis.
   (c)   not bound by plasma proteins.
   (d)   Both (a) and (c) above are correct.
   (e)   None of the above are correct.

ANSWER: a

65. The "iodine pump" refers to

   (a)   the mechanism whereby target-cells extract iodine-
         containing thyroid hormone from the blood.
   (b)   the active transport mechanism that concentrates
         iodine in the thyroid.
   (c)   the mechanism whereby T_3 and T_4 are released from
         thyroglobulin and pumped into the circulation.
   (d)   the protein binding process whereby T_3 and T_4 are
         pumped throughout the body bound to plasma proteins.
   (e)   the mechanism whereby ingested iodine is absorbed by
         the small intestine.

ANSWER: b

66. Which of the following statements concerning the synthesis
     and storage of thyroid hormones is **incorrect**?

   (a)   The "iodine pump" of the follicular cells
         is important for thyroid hormone
         production.
   (b)   Thyroid hormones are formed within a much
         larger molecule called thyroglobulin.
   (c)   Thyroid-hormone synthesis is greatly stimulated by
         the presence of TSH.
   (d)   A one- to two-hour supply of thyroid hormone is
         stored within the colloid in the lumen of the folli-
         cle.
   (e)   The coupling of two DIT molecules yields thyroxine.

ANSWER: d

67.   Thyroxine (T_4)

    (a)   is formed by coupling one MIT and one DIT within the colloid.
    (b)   is produced by the C cells of the thyroid gland.
    (c)   exerts a calorigenic effect.
    (d)   inhibits thyroid-stimulating immunoglobulin in negative-feedback fashion.
    (e)   is more potent than triiodothyronine.

ANSWER: c

68.   Which of the following biochemical events does **not** take place within the thyroid gland during hormone synthesis?

    (a)   Four iodine molecules combine with one tyrosine molecule to form one tetraiodothyronine molecule.
    (b)   Two iodine molecules combine with one tyrosine molecule to form one diiodotyrosine molecule.
    (c)   Two diiodotyrosine molecules combine to form one molecule of thyroxine.
    (d)   One monoiodotyrosine molecule combines with one diiodotyrosine molecule to form one triiodothyronine molecule.

69.   During thyroid hormone secretion,

    (a)   the follicular cells phagocytize a piece of colloid.
    (b) T_4 and T_3 are split off of thyroglobulin by lysosomal enzymes within the follicular cell and subsequently diffuse out of the cell into the blood.
    (c) T_4 and T_3 are secreted by exocytosis of the colloid that has been internalized by the follicular cells.
    (d)   Both (a) and (b) above are correct.
    (e)   Both (a) and (c) above are correct.

ANSWER: d

70.   The most abundant product secreted from the thyroid gland is _____ and the most potent thyroid secretory product is _____.

    (a) T_4, T_4
    (b) T_3, T_4
    (c) T_4, T_3
    (d) T_4, MIT
    (e)   DIT, T_3

ANSWER: c

71. What happens to most of the secreted T_4?

  (a) It is phagocytized by target tissues.
  (b) It is converted into T_3 by being peripherally stripped of one of its I atoms.
  (c) It is the major biologically active form of thyroid hormone at the cellular level.
  (d) It is split to form two DIT molecules, which are excreted in the urine.
  (e) It is permitted to exert its full biological effect as a result of epinephrine's permissive actions.

ANSWER: b

72. Which of the following hormones is very important during early development of the nervous system?

  (a) Growth hormone.
  (b) Thyroid hormone.
  (c) Cortisol.
  (d) Parathyroid hormone.
  (e) None of the above are correct.

ANSWER: b

73. Thyroid hormone

  (a) increases the metabolic rate.
  (b) secretion is increased in response to TSH.
  (c) inhibits TSH secretion.
  (d) Both (a) and (b) above are correct.
  (e) All of the above are correct.

ANSWER: e

74. Which of the following hormones secreted by the thyroid gland are categorized as thyroid hormone?

  (a) Thyroxine.
  (b) Triiodothyronine.
  (c) Calcitonin.
  (d) Both (a) and (b) above are correct.
  (e) All of the above are correct.

ANSWER: d

75. Which of the following is **not** an effect of thyroid hormone?

   (a) Increased metabolic rate.
   (b) Increased tissue responsiveness to catecholamines.
   (c) Increased absorption of iodine from the digestive tract into the blood.
   (d) Essential for normal growth.
   (e) Essential for normal development of the nervous system.

ANSWER: c

76. TSH

   (a) is stimulated by thyrotropin-releasing hormone (TRH).
   (b) is inhibited by T_3 and T_4.
   (c) increases the rate of thyroid hormone secretion.
   (d) promotes hypertrophy and hyperplasia of thyroid cells.
   (e) All of the above are correct.

ANSWER: e

77. Which of the following hormones is **not** part of the hypothalamus-pituitary-thyroid axis?

   (a) TSH.
   (b) Thyroxine.
   (c) Calcitonin.
   (d) Thyrotropin-releasing hormone.
   (e) Triiodothyronine.

ANSWER: c

78. Thyrotropin-releasing hormone (TRH) stimulates the secretion of

   (a) TSH.
   (b) GH.
   (c) LH.
   (d) FSH.
   (e) ACTH.

ANSWER: a

79. Which of the following would **not** decrease thyroid hormone production?

    (a) A decrease in TSH production.
    (b) An iodine deficient diet.
    (c) An increase in TRH production.
    (d) Inhibition of the iodine pump.
    (e) Removal of the pituitary.

ANSWER: c

80. Which of the following is **not** a plasma protein to which circulating thyroid hormone is bound?

    (a) Albumin.
    (b) Thyroxine-binding prealbumin.
    (c) Thyroxine-binding globulin.
    (d) Thyroglobulin.
    (e) None of the above are correct.

ANSWER: d

81. Hyperthyroidism can be due to all of the following except

    (a) too much TRH.
    (b) too much TSH.
    (c) lack of iodine.
    (d) too much T_4 or T_3.
    (e) thyroid-stimulating immunoglobulin.

ANSWER: c

82. Thyroid-stimulating immunoglobulin

    (a) stimulates T_3 and T_4 secretion by the thyroid.
    (b) is inhibited by T_3 and T_4 in a negative-feedback fashion.
    (c) is found in all people but is present in excessive amounts in persons with Grave's disease.
    (d) Both (a) and (c) above are correct.
    (e) Both (a) and (b) above are correct.

ANSWER: a

83.   A goiter

    (a)   is an enlarged thyroid.
    (b)   always accompanies hypothyroidism.
    (c)   is present only with iodine deficient diets.
    (d)   occurs only when TSH levels are elevated.
    (e)   Both (a) and (d) above are correct.

ANSWER: a

84.   A goiter

    (a)   always secretes excess T_4 and T_3.
    (b)   refers to an enlarged thyroid gland.
    (c)   occurs only in the presence of thyroid-stimulating immunoglobulin.
    (d)   Both (a) and (b) above are correct.
    (e)   Both (b) and (c) above are correct.

ANSWER: b

85.   Hypothyroidism

    (a)   may occur secondary to anterior pituitary failure.
    (b)   may occur due to inadequate dietary supply of iodine.
    (c)   may be due to failure of the thyroid gland itself.
    (d)   Both (b) and (c) above are correct.
    (e)   All of the above are correct.

ANSWER: e

86.   Which of the following is associated with hyperthyroidism?

    (a)   poor resistance to cold
    (b)   myxedema
    (c)   weight gain
    (d)   slow speech, poor memory
    (e)   exophthalmos

ANSWER: e

87. Which of the following is **not** a function of thyroid hormone?

    (a) increases the overall metabolic rate
    (b) exerts a calorigenic effect
    (c) promotes absorption of dietary iodine by the intestine
    (d) exerts a sympathomimetic effort
    (e) is crucial in the normal development of the nervous system

ANSWER: c

88. Which of the following is **not** a possible cause of hypothyroidism?

    (a) lack of TRH
    (b) iodine-deficient diet
    (c) Grave's disease
    (d) lack of an enzyme necessary for one of the steps in the synthesis and release of thyroid hormone

ANSWER: c

89. Which of the following symptoms is **not** associated with hyperthyroidism?

    (a) Elevated basal metabolic rate.
    (b) Myxedema.
    (c) Weakness.
    (d) Excessive perspiration and poor tolerance of heat.
    (e) Palpitations.

ANSWER: b

90. A man is found to have the following symptoms: a large goiter, muscle weakness, excessively emotional and irritable disposition, extreme weight loss, a constant feeling of be- ing too warm in normal-temperature rooms, and bulging eyes. The probable diagnosis is

    (a) myxedema.
    (b) Cushing's disease.
    (c) Conn's syndrome.
    (d) Grave's disease.
    (e) Addison's disease.

ANSWER: d

91. Which of the following statements concerning adrenocortical hormones is **incorrect**?

(a) They are all derived from cholesterol.
(b) They are all steroids.
(c) They are all controlled primarily by ACTH.
(d) They all combine with intracellular receptors.
(e) Mineralocorticoids are essential for life.

ANSWER: c

92. The only adrenal sex hormone that has any biological importance is

(a) aldosterone.
(b) cortisol.
(c) dehydroepiandrosterone.
(d) estradiol.
(e) estriol.

ANSWER: c

93. The zona glomerulosa of the adrenal cortex secretes

(a) aldosterone.
(b) cortisol.
(c) androgens and estrogens.
(d) Both (b) and (c) above are correct.
(e) All of the above are correct.

ANSWER: a

94. Aldosterone

(a) conserves potassium by the kidney.
(b) is necessary for life.
(c) promotes gluconeogenesis.
(d) is regulated by ACTH.
(e) is secreted by the adrenal medulla.

ANSWER: b

95. Aldosterone

(a) enhances the ability of the kidneys to eliminate excess Na^+.
(b) directly promotes H_2O conservation by the kidneys.
(c) secretion is controlled primarily by ACTH.
(d) is a catecholamine.
(e) None of the above are correct.

ANSWER: e

96. Which of the following hormones is essential to life?

    (a) Thyroid hormone.
    (b) Aldosterone.
    (c) Cortisol.
    (d) Epinephrine.
    (e) Vasopressin.

ANSWER: b

97. Aldosterone

    (a) is the primary glucocorticoid.
    (b) enhances the kidney's ability to conserve sodium.
    (c) promotes urinary excretion of excess phosphate.
    (d) is secreted by the adrenal medulla.
    (e) None of the above are correct.

ANSWER: b

98. Mineralocorticoids

    (a) stimulate gluconeogenesis.
    (b) stimulate protein degradation.
    (c) act at the kidneys to promote sodium retention and enhance potassium elimination.
    (d) contribute to the pubertal growth spurt.
    (e) are important in maintaining proper plasma calcium levels.

ANSWER: c

99. Which of the following regulates aldosterone secretion?

    (a) ACTH is a major regulatory factor.
    (b) The renin-angiotensin system, which is activated by various factors related to a fall in plasma Na^+ concentration/ECF volume/arterial blood pressure.
    (c) A direct effect of plasma K^+ on the adrenal cortex.
    (d) Both (b) and (c) above are correct.
    (e) All of the above are correct.

ANSWER: d

100.   Increased renin levels would be expected to lead to

   (a)   increased plasma aldosterone levels.
   (b)   increased glucocorticoid levels.
   (c)   decreased plasma aldosterone levels.
   (d)   decreased glucocorticoid levels.
   (e)   None of the above are correct.

ANSWER: a

101.   Plasma sodium levels are high in a patient, but his plasma potassium levels are low. As an underlying cause of this condition, you might expect to find

   (a)   decreased plasma aldosterone levels.
   (b)   decreased plasma parathyroid hormone levels.
   (c)   increased plasma aldosterone levels.
   (d)   increased plasma parathyroid hormone levels.
   (e)   decreased insulin levels.

ANSWER: c

102.   Which of the following is characteristic of Conn's syndrome?

   (a) K^+ depletion.
   (b) Na^+ depletion.
   (c)   Hypertension.
   (d)   Both (a) and (c) above are correct.
   (e)   All of the above are correct.

ANSWER: d

103.   Which of the following is **not** an action of cortisol?

   (a)   Increases the conversion of glycogen to glucose.
   (b)   Stimulates gluconeogenesis in the liver.
   (c)   Increases protein degradation.
   (d)   Mobilizes fat from adipose tissue.
   (e)   Exerts permissive actions.

ANSWER: a

104. Both _____ and _____ are produced from
the same large precursor molecule, pro-opiomelanocortin.

(a) aldosterone, cortisol
(b) cortisol, androgen
(c) cortisol, MSH
(d) aldosterone, androgen
(e) aldosterone, MSH

ANSWER: c

105. An increase in plasma levels of ACTH leads to

(a) increased plasma cortisol levels.
(b) increased plasma glucagon levels.
(c) increased plasma vasopressin levels.
(d) increased plasma parathyroid hormone levels.
(e) increased plasma epinephrine levels.

ANSWER: a

106. Cortisol

(a) is the primary mineralocorticoid.
(b) excess is responsible for Cushing's syndrome.
(c) increases blood glucose, blood fatty acid, and blood
amino acid levels.
(d) Both (b) and (c) above are correct.
(e) All of the above are correct.

ANSWER: d

107. Which of the following hormones exhibits a marked diurnal
variation in secretion?

(a) Aldosterone.
(b) Cortisol.
(c) Thyroid hormone.
(d) Epinephrine.
(e) Calcitonin.

ANSWER: b

108. The actions of glucocorticoids include

   (a) increased gluconeogenesis and glycogenolysis.
   (b) increased fat mobilization.
   (c) increased breakdown of muscle proteins.
   (d) anti-inflammatory and immunosuppressive effects at
        pharmacological levels.
   (e) All of the above are correct.

ANSWER: e

109. The major factor that promotes increased secretion of
      cortisol from the adrenal cortex is

   (a) low Na$^+$ concentration in the extracellular fluid.
   (b) stress.
   (c) angiotensin II.
   (d) increased blood amino acid concentration.
   (e) increased blood glucose concentration.

ANSWER: b

110. Cortisol

   (a) exhibits a characteristic diurnal variation in
        secretion.
   (b) secretion increases in response to stress.
   (c) causes gluconeogenesis.
   (d) Both (a) and (b) above are correct.
   (e) All of the above are correct.

ANSWER: e

111. Diurnal variation in secretion

   (a) occurs with glucocorticoids.
   (b) is related to the sleep-awake cycle.
   (c) occurs as a result of stress.
   (d) Both (a) and (b) above are correct.
   (e) All of the above are correct.

ANSWER: d

112. Cortisol

   (a) secretion increases in response to stress.
   (b) is regulated via the renin-angiotensin-aldosterone mechanism.
   (c) blocks amino acid uptake by muscle cells, thus elevating blood amino acid levels.
   (d) promotes fat deposition.
   (e) is important in calcium homeostasis.

ANSWER: a

113. Adrenocorticotropic hormone

   (a) is a tropic hormone secreted by the adrenal cortex.
   (b) stimulates the production of androgens by the testes.
   (c) is controlled in part by CRH from the hypothalamus.
   (d) Both (a) and (c) above are correct.
   (e) All of the above are correct.

ANSWER: c

114. Glucocorticoids cause all of the following **except**

   (a) carbohydrate conservation.
   (b) protein degradation.
   (c) increased metabolic rate.
   (d) mobilization of fats for energy.
   (e) anti-inflammatory and immunosuppressive effects at pharmacological levels.

ANSWER: c

115. Which of the following is **not** characteristic of Cushing's syndrome?

   (a) Poor tolerance to heat.
   (b) High blood glucose.
   (c) Muscle weakness and fatigue.
   (d) Easily bruisablity.
   (e) "Moon-face" and "buffalo hump."

ANSWER: a

116. Which of the following is **not** seen in Addison's disease?

    (a) Marked Na^+ loss in the urine.
    (b) Lowered blood glucose levels.
    (c) K^+ retention.
    (d) Protein mobilization.
    (e) Poor response to stress.

ANSWER: d

117. Dehydroepiandrosterone

    (a) is the most abundant adrenal androgen.
    (b) is responsible for the development and maintenance of the female sex drive.
    (c) is controlled by the gonadotropic hormones.
    (d) Both (a) and (b) above are correct.
    (e) All of the above are correct.

ANSWER: d

118. Adrenal androgens

    (a) are normally secreted only in males, whereas adrenal estrogens are secreted in females.
    (b) are normally secreted in both males and females, but in insufficient amounts to cause masculinization.
    (c) are responsible for the female sex drive.
    (d) Both (b) and (c) above are correct.
    (e) All of the above are correct.

ANSWER: d

119. Which of the following is characteristic of the adreno-genital syndrome?

    (a) Precocious pseudopuberty in prepubertal boys.
    (b) Development of male-type external genitalia in female fetuses.
    (c) Hirsutism in adult females.
    (d) Both (a) and (c) above are correct.
    (e) All of the above are correct.

ANSWER: e

120.   The adrenogenital syndrome is associated with excess
        secretion of

    (a)   androgens from the adrenal cortex.
    (b)   glucocorticoids from the adrenal cortex.
    (c)   catecholamines from the adrenal medulla.
    (d)   renin from the kidney.
    (e)   testosterone from the testes.

ANSWER: a

121.   Catecholamines

    (a)   are secreted by the adrenal cortex.
    (b)   reinforce the parasympathetic nervous
        system.
    (c)   are important in the maintenance of
        blood pressure.
    (d)   promote glycogen storage.
    (e)   are secreted in response to hypothalamic stimula-
        tion.

ANSWER: c

122.   Epinephrine

    (a)   is secreted by the adrenal medulla.
    (b)   is essential for life.
    (c)   is a general reinforcer of the parasympathetic
        nervous system.
    (d)   Both (a) and (c) above are correct.
    (e)   All of the above are correct.

ANSWER: a

123.   Catecholamines are secreted from the adrenal medulla in
        response to

    (a)   increased secretion of ACTH from the anterior
        pituitary.
    (b)   stimulation of sympathetic postganglionic neurons
        leading to the adrenal medulla.
    (c)   decreased androgen secretion from the adrenal cortex.
    (d)   hyperglycemia.
    (e)   stimulation by chromaffin-releasing hormone.

ANSWER: b

124. Of the hormones secreted by the adrenal gland, those that promote an increase in the blood glucose level include

(a) aldosterone.
(b) cortisol.
(c) epinephrine.
(d) Both (b) and (c) above are correct.
(e) All of the above are correct.

ANSWER: d

125. Which of the following hormones elevates blood pressure?

(a) Cortisol.
(b) Epinephrine.
(c) Insulin.
(d) Glucagon.
(e) Parathyroid hormone.

ANSWER: b

126. Which of the following is **not** a characteristic of a tumor in the adrenal medulla that secretes large amounts of epinephrine and norepinephrine?

(a) High blood glucose.
(b) Rapid heart rate.
(c) Low blood pressure.
(d) Palpitations.
(e) Excessive sweating.

ANSWER

127. Which of the following hormones is **not** secreted in response to stress?

(a) CRH-ACTH-cortisol.
(b) Epinephrine.
(c) Vasopressin.
(d) Renin-angiotensin-aldosterone.
(e) Insulin.

ANSWER: e

128.   Excess circulating quantities of which of the following
        nutrient molecules can ultimately be stored in adipose
        tissue as triglyceride fat?

    (a)   Fatty acids.
    (b)   Glucose.
    (c)   Amino acids.
    (d)   Both (a) and (b) above are correct.
    (e)   All of the above are correct.

ANSWER: e

129.   Which of the following tissues is most dependent upon a
        constant blood supply of glucose?

    (a)   Liver.
    (b)   Brain.
    (c)   Working muscle.
    (d)   Non-working muscle.
    (e)   Adipose tissue.

ANSWER: b

130.   Gluconeogenesis

    (a)   refers to the conversion of amino acids into glucose.
    (b)   results in an increase in blood glucose.
    (c)   is stimulated by cortisol and glucagon.
    (d)   Both (a) and (b) above are correct.
    (e)   All of the above are correct.

ANSWER: e

131.   Glycogenesis

    (a)   refers to the conversion of glucose to glycogen.
    (b)   is stimulated by glucagon.
    (c)   is stimulated by insulin.
    (d)   Both (a) and (b) above are correct.
    (e)   Both (a) and (c) above are correct.

    ANSWER: e

132.   Which of the following acts to decrease blood glucose levels?

    (a)   Glucagon.
    (b)   Insulin.
    (c)   Cortisol.
    (d)   Epinephrine.
    (e)   Growth hormone.

ANSWER: b

133.   Which of the following does **not** characterize the postabsorptive state?

    (a)   Substantial reduction in blood glucose concentration compared to the absorptive state.
    (b)   Gluconeogenesis occurs.
    (c)   Glucose-sparing occurs.
    (d)   Insulin secretion is reduced.
    (e)   Glucagon secretion is increased.

ANSWER: a

134.   The pancreas secretes hormones that are important in the control of

    (a)   blood glucose levels.
    (b)   blood calcium levels.
    (c)   blood sodium levels.
    (d)   blood potassium levels.
    (e)   blood iron levels.

ANSWER: a

135.   Which of the following statements concerning somatostatin is **not** correct?   Somatostatin

    (a)   is produced by the hypothalamus
    (b)   is produced by the pancreatic D cells
    (c)   inhibits growth hormone secretion
    (d)   inhibits digestion of nutrients and decreases nutrient absorption
    (e)   is released in response to a fall in blood glucose and blood amino acids

ANSWER: e

136.   Insulin

    (a)   facilitates the transport of glucose into the
           glucose-dependent brain cells.
    (b)   increases blood glucose levels to assure adequate
           nourishment of the brain.
    (c)   promotes fat storage in the body.
    (d)   is stimulated by a lowered blood glucose.
    (e)   Both (a) and (c) above are correct.

ANSWER: c

137.   Which of the following tissues does **not** require insulin
        for glucose uptake?

    (a)   Working muscles.
    (b)   Kidneys.
    (c)   Stomach.
    (d)   Lungs.

ANSWER: a

138.   Which of the following tissues requires insulin for
        glucose uptake?

    (a)   Working muscles.
    (b)   Liver.
    (c)   Brain.
    (d)   Lungs.

ANSWER: d

139.   Insulin

    (a)   promotes the insertion of additional glucose trans-
           porters in the plasma membranes of insulin-dependent
           cells
    (b)   stimulates glycogenesis and inhibits glycogenolysis
    (c)   secretion is increased in response to a fall in blood
           glucose concentration
    (d)   Both (a) and (b) above are correct
    (e)   All of the above are correct

ANSWER: d

140. Which of the following is a metabolic effect of insulin?

(a) Increased glucose uptake by cells.
(b) Increased breakdown of fats.
(c) Decreased uptake of amino acids by cells.
(d) Both (a) and (b) above are correct.

ANSWER: a

141. Which of the following does **not** stimulate insulin secretion?

(a) Elevated blood amino acid concentration.
(b) Gastrointestinal hormones.
(c) Big Mac.
(d) Starvation.
(e) Elevated blood glucose concentration.

ANSWER: d

142. Increased levels of which of the following hormones would **not** result in increased blood fatty acid levels?

(a) Glucagon.
(b) Growth hormone.
(c) Insulin.
(d) Epinephrine.
(e) Cortisol.

ANSWER: c

143. Secretion of which of the following hormones is stimulated by an increase in blood glucose?

(a) Glucagon.
(b) Cortisol.
(c) Growth hormone.
(d) Insulin.
(e) Epinephrine.

ANSWER: d

144. Insulin

(a) facilitates the entry of glucose into brain tissue.
(b) promotes glucose output by the liver.
(c) lowers blood glucose levels.
(d) Both (a) and (c) above are correct.
(e) All of the above are correct.

ANSWER: c

145.   Which of the following does **not** characterize diabetes
       mellitus?

   (a)   Increased glucose utilization due to excessive
         glucose availability.
   (b)   Polyuria due to the osmotic effect of glucose in the
         urine.
   (c)   Acidosis due to the ketosis accompanying abnormal fat
         metabolism.
   (d)   Polydipsia due to dehydration.
   (e)   Hyperglycemia due to reduced glucose entry into the
         cells and increased hepatic output of glucose.

ANSWER: a

146.   Which of the following symptoms is **not** associated with
       insulin deficiency?

   (a)   Hypoglycemia.
   (b)   Polyuria, polydipsia, polyphagia.
   (c)   Metabolic acidosis.
   (d)   Glucosuria.
   (e)   Depression of the brain, leading to coma.

ANSWER: a

147.   In diabetes mellitus,

   (a)   too much glucose is transferred into the brain cells
         by an insulin excess.
   (b)   the brain cells do not receive an adequate supply of
         glucose, leading to symptoms of decreased CNS
         activity.
   (c)   too much glucose is being lost in the urine resulting
         in abnormally low blood glucose levels.
   (d)   the clinical abnormalities may include polyuria,
         polydipsia, polyphagia, ketosis, and acidosis.
   (e)   More than one of the above are correct.

ANSWER: d

148.   Which of the following characterizes Type I but not Type
       II diabetes mellitus?

   (a)   Hyperglycemia.
   (b)   Lack of insulin.
   (c)   Polyuria and polydipsia.

ANSWER: b

149. Coma (severely depressed CNS activity) may result from untreated

    (a) hyperthyroidism.
    (b) diabetes mellitus.
    (c) insulin excess.
    (d) Both (b) and (c) above are correct.
    (e) All of the above are correct.

ANSWER: d

150. The nervous manifestations occurring in diabetes mellitus

    (a) arise as a result of depression of the brain due to acidosis produced by excessive fat metabolism and ketone accumulation.
    (b) arise as a result of starvation of the brain tissue due to the inability of glucose to gain entry to the brain cells in the absence of insulin.
    (c) occur early in the course of the disease before other symptoms become obvious.
    (d) Both (a) and (c) above are correct.
    (e) Both (b) and (c) above are correct.

ANSWER: a

151. Untreated diabetes mellitus results in all of the following **except**

    (a) increased urinary excretion of glucose.
    (b) metabolic acidosis.
    (c) dehydration.
    (d) decreased levels of fatty acids in the blood.
    (e) increased levels of amino acids in the blood.

ANSWER: d

152. The symptoms of insulin excess result from

    (a) the effects of acidosis on the nervous system.
    (b) excessive glucose utilization by the brain.
    (c) reduced availability of glucose for the brain as a result of hypoglycemia.
    (d) excessive protein breakdown.
    (e) neuromuscular overexcitability as a result of hyperglycemia.

ANSWER: c

153.   In reactive hypoglycemia,

   (a)   too much glucose is transferred into the brain cells by an insulin excess.
   (b)   the brain cells do not receive an adequate supply of glucose, leading to symptoms of depressed CNS activity.
   (c)   an insulin deficiency exists.
   (d)   a glucagon excess exists.
   (e)   Both (b) and (d) above are correct.

ANSWER: b

154.   Which of the following hormones increases membrane transport of amino acids into many body cells?

   (a)   Cortisol.
   (b)   Growth hormone.
   (c)   Insulin.
   (d)   Both (b) and (c) above are correct.
   (e)   All of the above are correct.

ANSWER: d

155.   The hormone that, in general, is antagonistic to all the others in terms of metabolic effects is

   (a)   growth hormone.
   (b)   glucagon.
   (c)   epinephrine.
   (d)   insulin.
   (e)   cortisol.

ANSWER: d

156.   Glucagon

   (a)   is secreted by the beta cells of the islets of Langerhans.
   (b)   is secreted in response to a fall in blood glucose.
   (c)   is, in general, antagonistic to all other hormones in terms of metabolic effects.
   (d)   increases fat stores by inhibiting the enzyme that catalyzes triglyceride breakdown.
   (e)   None of the above are correct.

ANSWER: b

157. Which of the following hormones increases blood glucose?

(a) Growth hormone.
(b) Cortisol.
(c) Epinephrine.
(d) Both (a) and (b) above are correct.
(e) All of the above are correct.

ANSWER: e

158. Which of the following is an effect of glucagon?

(a) Decreased blood glucose levels.
(b) Increased breakdown of fats.
(c) Increased hepatic glucose producion.
(d) Increased amino acid uptake by cells.
(e) Increased Ca^{2+} reabsorption by the renal tubules.

ANSWER: b

159. In which of the following forms does Ca^{2+} exhibit profound effects on such things as neuromuscular excitability?

(a) Free, unbound diffusible Ca^{2+}.
(b) Intracellular Ca^{2+}.
(c) Calcium phosphate crystals impregnated in the organic matrix of bone.
(d) Calcium bound to plasma proteins.
(e) Insoluble Ca^{2+} salts.

ANSWER: a

160. Calcium is very important to the normal functioning of the body, so it is very important that the plasma Ca^{2+} concentration be well regulated. In which of the following ways does calcium play an important role?

(a) Calcium plays an important role in the absorption of Vitamin D from the digestive tract.
(b) Calcium is important for maintaining the proper excitability of nerves and muscles.
(c) Calcium stimulates osteoblasts to lay down bone.
(d) Both (a) and (b) above are correct.
(e) All of the above are correct.

ANSWER: b

161. Control of plasma calcium concentration is accomplished by the effect of several hormones on several different organs. Which of the following is **not** true concerning the control of calcium metabolism?

   (a) PTH (parathyroid hormone) causes an increase in plasma calcium by its actions on bone and the kidneys.
   (b) Vitamin D causes an increase in secretion of Ca^{2+} into the lumen of the digestive tract.
   (c) Calcitonin causes a decrease in plasma calcium by decreasing Ca^{2+} movement from the bone fluid into the plasma and by suppressing bone resorption.
   (d) When plasma calcium increases, PTH decreases and calcitonin increases.

ANSWER: b

162. Which of the following play(s) a role in Ca^{2+} metabolism?

   (a) Parathyroid hormone.
   (b) Calcitonin.
   (c) Vitamin D.
   (d) Both (a) and (b) above are correct.
   (e) All of the above are correct.

ANSWER: e

163. Which of the following is **incorrect** concerning PTH, calcitonin, and vitamin D?

   (a) Vitamin D deficiency is the cause of rickets.
   (b) PTH is the most important hormone in the control of calcium metabolism.
   (c) Both calcitonin and PTH are produced in the follicle cells of the thyroid gland.
   (d) Vitamin D is actually a hormone that increases calcium absorption in the intestine.
   (e) Parathyroid hormone is essential for life.

ANSWER: c

164.   Parathyroid hormone

    (a)   causes localized dissolution of bone.
    (b)   raises the renal threshold for Ca^{2+}.
    (c)   promotes absorption of vitamin D from the intestine.
    (d)   Both (a) and (b) above are correct.
    (e)   All of the above are correct.

ANSWER: d

165.   Which of the following statements concerning parathyroid hormone's actions is **incorrect**?

    (a)   An elevated plasma calcium acts directly on the parathyroid gland to stimulate PTH secretion.
    (b)   PTH promotes the rapid movement of Ca^{2+} from the bone fluid into the plasma.
    (c)   PTH promotes localized dissolution of bone by stimulating osteoclasts.
    (d)   PTH helps the kidneys remove excess phosphate from the body.
    (e)   PTH stimulates the activation of vitamin D.

ANSWER: a

166.   Which of the following statements concerning parathyroid hormone is **incorrect**?

    (a)   PTH causes localized dissolution of bone.
    (b)   PTH conserves Ca^{2+} by the kidney.
    (c)   PTH promotes urinary excretion of PO_4^{3-}.
    (d)   PTH directly stimulates Ca^{2+} absorption from the intestine.
    (e)   PTH is essential for life.

ANSWER: d

167.   PTH secretion is regulated by the plasma concentration of

    (a) Ca^{2+}.
    (b) Mg^{2+}.
    (c) PO_4^{3-}.
    (d)   glucose.
    (e) Na^+.

ANSWER: a

168.   Calcium reabsorption by the kidneys can be increased by

    (a)   calcitonin.
    (b)   aldosterone.
    (c)   active vitamin D.
    (d)   parathyroid hormone.
    (e)   vasopressin.

ANSWER: d

169.   Which of the following characterizes hypoparathyroidism?

    (a)   Hypocalcemia.
    (b)   Hypophosphatemia.
    (c)   Reduced neuromuscular excitability.
    (d)   Both (a) and (c) above are correct.
    (e)   All of the above are correct.

ANSWER: a

170.   Decreased levels of circulating parathyroid hormone may
result in

    (a)   increased plasma calcium levels.
    (b)   increased plasma thyroid hormone levels.
    (c)   decreased plasma calcium levels.
    (d)   decreased plasma thyroid hormone levels.

ANSWER: c

171.   Which of the following causes an elevation in plasma
calcium levels?

    (a)   Low levels of active vitamin D.
    (b)   High levels of parathyroid hormone.
    (c)   High calcitonin levels.
    (d)   High vasopressin levels.
    (e)   None of the above are correct.

ANSWER: b

172.   Calcitonin

    (a)   enhances the effect of parathyroid hormone on bone
and kidneys.
    (b)   is synthesized in the skin in the presence of
sunlight.
    (c)   deficiency produces diabetes insipidus.
    (d)   is secreted by the thyroid follicular cells.
    (e)   None of the above are correct.

ANSWER: e

173. Calcitonin

(a) is stimulated by TSH.
(b) is stimulated by TCSH.
(c) is secreted by the C-cells of the thyroid gland.
(d) is stored in the colloid of the thyroid follicles.
(e) Both (a) and (c) above are correct.

ANSWER: c

174. Which of the following statements concerning vitamin D is **incorrect**? Vitamin D

(a) can be synthesized by the skin on exposure to sunlight.
(b) must be modified by biochemical alterations within the liver and kidneys before it is biologically active.
(c) enhances the effect of calcitonin on bone.
(d) increases Ca^{2+} absorption in the intestine.
(e) deficiency in children results in rickets.

ANSWER: c

175. Which of the following hormones enhances the formation of the active form of vitamin D?

(a) Parathyroid hormone.
(b) Cortisol.
(c) Aldosterone.
(d) Calcitonin.

ANSWER: a

176. Which of the following does **not** characterize hypoparathyroidism?

(a) Hypocalcemia.
(b) Hypophosphatemia.
(c) Increased neuromuscular excitability.
(d) Death by asphyxiation as a result of spastic contraction of respiratory muscles in the complete absence of PTH.

ANSWER: b

177. Osteoporosis is characterized by

   (a) reduced bone mass as a result of diminished laying down of the organic matrix of bone.
   (b) abnormal bone calcification.
   (c) hypocalcemia.
   (d) Both (a) and (b) above are correct.
   (e) All of the above are correct.

ANSWER: a

178. Indicate which of the following are associated with growth hormone by circling the appropriate letters.

   (a) stimulates cell division
   (b) enhances breakdown of triglyceride fat
   (c) promotes glucose uptake by most cells
   (d) promotes amino acid uptake by most cells
   (e) stimulates osteoblast activity
   (f) stimulates protein synthesis and inhibits protein breakdown
   (g) causes the epiphyseal plate to thicken
   (h) regulated by GHRH and somatostatin
   (i) secretion markedly increases after onset of deep sleep
   (j) secretion increases in response to stress and exercise
   (k) secretion stimulated by a fall in blood glucose
   (l) secretion stimulated by a fall in blood amino acids
   (m) excess secretion commencing in childhood results in acromegaly
   (n) deficient secretion commencing in childhood results in dwarfism

ANSWERS: a, b, d, e, f, g, h, i, j, k, n

179.   Indicate which of the following are characteristic of insulin. (Circle all correct answers.)

(a)   secreted by pancreatic α cells
(b)   secretion stimulated by an increase in blood glucose concentration
(c)   lowers blood glucose levels
(d)   promotes glycogenesis
(e)   promotes gluconeogenesis
(f)   facilitates glucose transport into most cells
(g)   promotes triglyceride storage
(h)   secretion stimulated by an increase in blood amino acid levels
(i)   exerts a protein anabolic effect
(j)   is present in normal or even elevated levels in Type II diabetes mellitus
(k)   is under anterior pituitary control
(l)   secretion is stimulated by major gastrointestinal hormones
(m)   secretion is stimulated by the sympathetic nervous system
(n)   elevates blood amino acid levels

ANSWERS: b, c, d, f, g, h, i, j, l

180.   Indicate which of the following are associated with diabetes mellitus. (Circle all correct answers.)

(a)   hyperglycemia
(b)   metabolic acidosis
(c)   glucosuria
(d)   ketosis
(e)   brain starvation
(f)   polyuria
(g)   polydipsia
(h)   polyphagia
(i)   dehydration
(j)   coma
(k)   skeletal muscle weakness
(l)   deficient insulin activity
(m)   elevated glucagon secretion

ANSWERS: a, b, c, d, f, g, h, i, j, k, l, m

181.   Indicate which of the following are characteristics of PTH.   (Circle all correct answers.)

    (a)   increases plasma Ca^{2+} concentration
    (b)   secretion is increased in response to a rise in plasma Ca^{2+} concentration
    (c)   promotes rapid movement of Ca^{2+} into the plasma from the bone fluid.
    (d)   stimulates localized dissolution of bone
    (e)   increases renal reabsorption of Ca^{2+}
    (f)   increases renal reabsorption of PO_4^{3-}
    (g)   stimulates activation of vitamin D
    (h)   directly stimulates Ca^{2+} absorption in the intestine

ANSWERS: a, c, d, e, g

182.   Indicate which of the following characterize hypopar-athyroidism.   (Circle all correct answers.)

    (a)   osteomalacia
    (b)   osteoporosis
    (c)   rickets
    (d)   hypocalcemia
    (e)   hypophosphatemia
    (f)   overexcitability of the neuromuscular system
    (g)   kidney stones
    (h)   bone demineralization

ANSWERS: d, f

True/False

183.   The same chemical messenger may be either a hormone or a neurotransmitter, depending on its source and mode of delivery to the target tissue.

ANSWER: True

184.   Specialization of target-cell receptors explains the specificity of hormonal action.

ANSWER: True

185.   The nervous system exerts considerable control over the endocrine system, but hormones have no influence over the nervous system.

ANSWER: False

186. The hormones influence adjustments that require duration rather than speed, whereas the rapid coordinations of the body are controlled by the nervous system.

ANSWER: True

187. Endocrine responses occur more slowly and last longer than neural responses.

ANSWER: True

188. Minor differences in structure between hormones within each chemical category often result in profound differences in biological response.

ANSWER: True

189. Once a steroid hormone binds with its intracellular receptor, the hormone-receptor complex binds with a specific hormone response element on DNA, thereby activating a particular gene.

ANSWER: True

190. A tropic hormone acts primarily on nonendocrine tissues.

ANSWER: False

191. Hormones may be steroids, peptides or amines.

ANSWER: True

192. All hormones are synthesized by the endoplasmic reticulum/Golgi complex system.

ANSWER: False

193. Once synthesized, all hormones are stored within the endocrine cell until an appropriate signal for their release.

ANSWER: False

194. All amine hormones are hydrophilic.

ANSWER: False

195. Hydrophilic (lipophobic) hormones exert their effects primarily by activating second-messenger systems within their target cells.

ANSWER: True

196. Lipophilic (hydrophobic) hormones circulate in the blood largely bound to plasma proteins.

ANSWER: True

197. Peptide hormone receptors are located inside the target cell.

ANSWER: False

198. Steroid hormones act through the second-messenger system.

ANSWER: False

199. Each steroidogenic organ is capable of producing all of the steroid hormones.

ANSWER: False

200. Only hormones that are not bound to plasma proteins are biologically active.

ANSWER: True

201. Negative-feedback control tends to maintain hormone levels at a relatively constant set point, whereas neuroendocrine reflexes usually produce a sudden increase in hormone secretion in response to a specific stimulus.

ANSWER: True

202. The main control normally determining the plasma concentration of a particular hormone is its rate of inactivation and excretion.

ANSWER: False

203. Permissiveness refers to the conversion of inactive enzymes into active enzymes by hormones, thus permitting the enzymes to perform their function.

ANSWER: False

204. With down regulation, one hormone induces the loss of another hormone's receptors.

ANSWER: False

205. The hypothalamus synthesizes and regulates the release of hormones from the posterior pituitary.

ANSWER: True

206. Oxytocin and vasopressin are carried in the hypothalamic-hypophyseal portal system.

ANSWER: False

207. All hormones secreted by the hypothalamus and anterior pituitary gland are peptides.

ANSWER: True

208. Melanocyte-stimulating hormone plays a role in determining the different amount of melanin in the skin of various human races.

ANSWER: False

209. FSH and LH are collectively known as gonadotropins.

ANSWER: True

210. Each anterior pituitary hormone is controlled by a single hypophysiotropic hormone from the hypothalamus.

ANSWER: False

211. Growth hormone is controlled by both releasing and inhibiting hormones from the hypothalamus.

ANSWER: True

212. Transmission of nerve impulses from the hypothalamus to the anterior pituitary causes the stored hormones to be released.

ANSWER: False

213. Hypophysiotropic hormone secretion by the hypothalamus is regulated only by hormonal negative feedback.

ANSWER: False

214. Hypothalamic hypophysiotropic hormones cause the release of oxytocin and vasopressin from the posterior pituitary.

ANSWER: False

215. The hypothalamus is the highest integrative center in the hierarchical chain of command in endocrine control.

ANSWER: True

216.   The anterior pituitary is almost entirely nervous tissue.

ANSWER: False

217.   TSH controls the amount of testosterone secreted by the testes.

ANSWER: False

218.   The anterior pituitary is involved in the regulation of reproduction.

ANSWER: True

219.   Hypophysiotropic hormones are secreted into the systemic circulatory system.

ANSWER: False

220.   Growth hormone directly stimulates bone growth.

ANSWER: False

221.   Growth hormone exerts metabolic effects unrelated to growth.

ANSWER: True

222.   Growth hormone does not directly affect bone growth, but instead it stimulates the release of somatomedins from the liver, which in turn promote bone growth.

ANSWER: True

223.   Cellular hypertrophy is accomplished by increased cell division.

ANSWER: False

224.   Hypertrophy refers to an increase in cellular size.

ANSWER: True

225.   Dwarfism may be due to growth hormone deficiency in adults.

ANSWER: False

226.   Growth hormone is the only hormone that influences growth.

ANSWER: False

227. Growth hormone secretion increases markedly about an hour after the onset of deep sleep.

ANSWER: True

228. Growth hormone is the most abundant anterior pituitary hormone.

ANSWER: True

229. Somatomedins exert insulin-like activity.

ANSWER: True

230. Growth hormone promotes closure of the epiphyseal plate at adolescence

ANSWER: False

231. There are no known growth-related signals that influence growth hormone secretion.

ANSWER: True

232. Triiodothyronine and tetraiodothyronine are produced by the C-cells of the thyroid gland.

ANSWER: False

233. The "iodine pump" actively transports hormone-bound iodine from the thyroid gland into the circulation.

ANSWER: False

234. Thyroid-stimulating hormone is produced by the thyroid gland.

ANSWER: False

235. Monoiodotyrosine and diiodotyrosine are coupled within the colloid to form triiodothyronine.

ANSWER: True

236. Thyroglobulin is found in the cytosol of the thyroid follicular cells.

ANSWER: False

237. T_3 and T_4 are necessary for normal growth and nerve development.

ANSWER: True

238. The thyroid gland stores enough thyroid hormone to supply the body's needs for several months.

ANSWER: True

239. In the absence of TSH, the thyroid gland atrophies.

ANSWER: True

240. T_3 and T_4 are secreted into the blood by the process of exocytosis.

ANSWER: False

241. Thyroid hormone is stored within the colloid attached to thyroglobulin.

ANSWER: True

242. MIT and DIT are secreted along with T_3 and T_4.

ANSWER: False

243. Most of the secreted T_4 is converted into T_3 outside of the thyroid gland.

ANSWER: True

244. Over 99% of the circulating thyroid hormone is bound to plasma proteins.

ANSWER: True

245. Thyroid deficient children have stunted growth, which is reversible with thyroid hormone replacement therapy.

ANSWER: True

246. Thyroid deficiency from birth results in permanent mental retardation unless replacement therapy is commenced within a few months.

ANSWER: True

247. In the absence of TSH, the thyroid gland atrophies.

ANSWER: True

248. Hypothyroidism can occur even though the thyroid gland is perfectly normal.

ANSWER: True

249. Thyroid-stimulating immunoglobulin stimulates both the secretion and growth of the thyroid similar to TSH.

ANSWER: True

250. Because of the thyroid hormone's growth-promoting effects, excessive growth is one outcome of excess thyroid hormone secretion in children.

ANSWER: False

251. Exophthalmos accompanies some types of hypothyroidism.

ANSWER: False

252. Grave's disease is a type of hyperthyroidism.

ANSWER: True

253. Both hypothyroidism and hyperthyroidism may be accompanied by a goiter.

ANSWER: True

254. The presence of a goiter is always indicative of hyperthyroidism.

ANSWER: False

255. Myxedema is associated with hypersecretion of thyroid hormones.

ANSWER: False

256. ACTH stimulates cortisol secretion but not aldosterone secretion by the adrenal cortex.

ANSWER: True

257. Aldosterone is a mineralocorticoid that stimulates Na^+ and H_2O conservation.

ANSWER: True

258. ACTH stimulates cortisol but not aldosterone secretion by the adrenal cortex.

ANSWER: True

259. Cortisol is secreted by the zona glomerulosa, aldosterone by the zona fasciculata, and sex hormones by the zona reticularis.

ANSWER: False

260. Aldosterone circulates bound primarily to cortisteroid-binding globulin.

ANSWER: False

261. Cushing's syndrome is characterized by hyperglycemia, muscle weakness, "moon face" and "buffalo hump."

ANSWER: True

262. The symptoms of aldosterone hypersecretion include hypernatremia, hyperphosphatemia, and hypertension.

ANSWER: False

263. Stress is the primary stimulus for mineralocorticoid secretion.

ANSWER: False

264. Aldosterone and cortisol are both considered to be essential for life.

ANSWER: False

265. Cortisol is the primary mineralocorticoid.

ANSWER: False

266. The adrenocortical hormones cortisol and aldosterone are peptide hormones.

ANSWER: False

267. In people who work during the day, cortisol levels in the plasma are normally higher in the morning than at night.

ANSWER: True

268. One of the primary functions of cortisol secretion at normal physiological levels is its anti-inflammatory action.

ANSWER: False

269. Adrenal androgens are normally secreted only in males, whereas adrenal estrogens are secreted only in females.

ANSWER: False

270. Androgens and estrogens are secreted by the adrenal gland in both sexes.

ANSWER: True

271. The adrenal medulla is actually a modified part of the sympathetic nervous system.

ANSWER: True

272. Norepinephrine is released from sympathetic nerve terminals, whereas epinephrine is the most abundant secretory product of the adrenal medulla.

ANSWER: True

273. The stress response is believed to be more beneficial for coping with physical threats than psychosocial stressors.

ANSWER: True

274. Anabolism refers to the build-up or synthesis of larger organic macromolecules from the small organic molecular subunits.

ANSWER: True

275. The primary energy source for the body during the post-absorptive state is glucose.

ANSWER: False

276. Gluconeogenesis and glycogenolysis in the liver play a major role in maintaining a constant blood glucose level between meals.

ANSWER: True

277. The endocrine portion of the pancrecreas is known as the islets of Langerhans.

ANSWER: True

278. Insulin is secreted by the alpha cells of the islets of Langerhans.

ANSWER: False

279. The absorptive state is directed by an increase in insulin secretion.

ANSWER: True

280. Insulin increases glucose transport into all tissues.

ANSWER: False

281. Insulin enhances the entry of glucose into brain cells.

ANSWER: False

282. The blood glucose level is the primary controlling factor of insulin secretion.

ANSWER: True

283. Insulin secretion is decreased and glucagon secretion is increased in response to a fall in blood glucose concentration.

ANSWER: True

284. Blood glucose levels are always high in untreated diabetes insipidus.

ANSWER: False

285. Amino acids can be converted to glucose whereas fatty acids cannot.

ANSWER: True

286. All forms of diabetes mellitus are characterized by a lack of pancreatic insulin secretion.

ANSWER: False

287. Obesity can precipitate overt Type II diabetes mellitus in individuals genetically predisposed.

ANSWER: True

288. Both Type I and Type II diabetes must be treated by regular insulin injections.

ANSWER: False

289. Reactive hypoglycemia is best treated by a low carbohydrate diet.

ANSWER: True

290. Elevated blood amino acid levels stimulate the secretion of both insulin and glucagon even though they exert opposite effects on blood amino acid concentration.

ANSWER: True

291. Insulin promotes recruitment of glucose transporters in insulin-dependent cells.

ANSWER: True

292. Protein-bound Ca^{2+} is the form of calcium that is important in neuromuscular excitability.

ANSWER: False

293. The parathyroid gland secretes parathyroid hormone and calcitonin.

ANSWER: False

294. Plasma Ca^{2+} concentration is one of the most tightly controlled variables in the body.

ANSWER: True

295. Minor variations in plasma Ca^{2+} exert the most profound effects upon the blood clotting mechanisms compared to consequences on other body activities.

ANSWER: False

296. The greater the physical stress and compression to which a bone is subjected, the greater the rate of bone deposition.

ANSWER: True

297. An increase in plasma PO_4^{3-} concentration forces a reduction in plasma Ca^{2+} as a result of the inverse relationship between plasma PO_4^{3-} and Ca^{2+} levels.

ANSWER: True

298. Hyperparathyroidism is characterized by hypercalcemia and hyperphosphatemia.

ANSWER: False

299. Parathyroid hormone increases PO_4^{3-} reabsorption by the kidney tubules.

ANSWER: False

300. PTH increases plasma Ca^{2+} and decreases plasma PO_4^{3-}.

ANSWER: True

301. PTH enhances the rapid movement of calcium from the bone fluid into the plasma.

ANSWER: True

302. Calcitonin decreases plasma Ca^{2+}.

ANSWER: True

303. Calcitonin promotes localized dissolution of bone.

ANSWER: False

304. The presence of vitamin D is necessary for PTH to exert its effect on promoting intestinal Ca^{2+} absorption.

ANSWER: False

305. Vitamin D must be provided entirely by dietary sources.

ANSWER: False

306. Mineralocorticoids and parathyroid hormone are essential for life.

ANSWER: True

Fill-in-the-blanks

307. _____ are short-range chemical mediators released by neurons in response to action potentials.

   ANSWER: Neurotransmitters

308. _____ are long-range chemical mediators secreted by endocrine glands into the blood, which carries them to distant target organs.

ANSWER: Hormones

309. The specific site upon which a hormone exerts its effect is referred to as a _____ cell.

ANSWER: target

310. _____ refers to enhancement by one hormone of the responsiveness of a target organ to another hormone, for example by means of the first hormone increasing the number of receptors for the second hormone.

ANSWER: Permissiveness

311. _____ are hormones that consist of a chain of specific amino acids of varying length.

ANSWER: Peptide hormones

312. The majority of hormones fall into the class of _____.

ANSWER: peptide hormones

313. _____ are hormones derived from cholesterol.

ANSWER: Steroids

314. _____ are hormones derived from the amino acid tyrosine.

ANSWER: Amines

315. The _____ carries hypophysiotropic hormones from the hypothalamus to the anterior pituitary.

ANSWER: hypothalamic-hypophyseal portal system

316. _____ are the bone cell types that form bones.

ANSWER: Osteoblasts

317. _____ are the bone cell types that dissolve bone.

ANSWER: Osteoclasts

318. _____ are the bone cell types entombed in bone.

ANSWER: Osteocytes

319. The growth-promoting actions of growth hormone are directly exerted by peptide mediators known as
_____.

ANSWER: somatomedins

320. The _____ cells of the thyroid gland secrete the iodine-containing hormones _____ and _____, whereas the _____ cells of the thyroid secrete the Ca^{2+}-regulating hormone
_____.

ANSWERS: follicular, triiodothyronine (T_3), tetraiodothyro nine (T_4 or thyroxine), C, calcitonin

321. _____ and _____ are col-lectively referred to as thyroid hormone.

ANSWERS: Triiodothyronine (T_3), tetraiodothyronine (T_4 or thyroxine)

322. Thyroid hormone is a derivative of the amino acid
_____.

ANSWER: tyrosine

323. The active transport mechanism for the uptake of iodine from the blood by the thyroid is known as the
_____.

ANSWER: iodine pump (or iodine-trapping mechanism)

324. One I attached to tyrosine yields _____ whereas the addition of two I atoms to tyrosine forms
_____.

ANSWERS: monoiodotyrosine (MIT), diiodotyrosine (DIT)

325. Coupling of two DITs yields _____, whereas coupling of one DIT and one MIT results in the formation of _____.

ANSWERS: tetraiiodothyronine (T_4 or thyroxine), triiodothyronine (T_3)

326. The most abundant form of thyroid hormone secreted is _____, yet _____ is the most potent thyroid hormone.

ANSWERS: T_4, T_3

327. _____ is the most important physiological regulator of thyroid hormone secretion.

ANSWER: Thyroid-stimulating hormone (TSH)

328. An enlarged thyroid is called a _____.

ANSWER: goiter

329. The condition of being hypothyroid from birth is known as _____.

ANSWER: cretinism

330. The outer portion of the adrenal gland is known as the _____, which secretes hormones belonging to the chemical class of _____.

ANSWERS: adrenal cortex, steroids

331. The inner portion of the adrenal glands is known as the _____, which secretes hormones belonging to the chemical class of _____.

ANSWERS: adrena medulla, catecholamines

332. _____ refers to the generalized, nonspecific response of the body to any factor that threatens the maintenance of homeostasis.

ANSWER: Stress

333. The chemical reactions involving the three classes of energy-rich organic molecules are collectively known as _____.

ANSWER: intermediary (or fuel) metabolism

334. _____ refers to the synthesis of larger organic molecules from smaller organic molecules.

ANSWER: Anabolism

335. _____ refers to the degradation of large energy-rich molecules into smaller organic molecules or into CO_2, H_2O, and energy.

ANSWER: Catabolism

336. The _____ is normally dependent on the delivery of adequate blood glucose as its sole source of energy.

ANSWER: brain

337. The _____ is the principal site for metabolic interconversions of nutrient molecules.

ANSWER: liver

338. The three hormonal factors that influence Ca^{2+} metabolism are _____, _____, and _____.

ANSWERS: parathyroid hormone (PTH), calcitonin, vitamin D

339. Bone is a living tissue composed of an organic extra-cellular matrix impregnated with crystals consisting primarily of _____ salts.

ANSWERS: calcium phosphate

340. Calcitonin is produced by the _____ of the _____.

ANSWERS: C cells, thyroid gland

341. Vitamin D can be produced by the _____ upon exposure to sunlight.

ANSWER: skin

342. Vitamin D must be activated by the _____ and _____.

ANSWERS: liver, kidneys

Matching

343.   Indicate whether the following characteristics apply to
       the endocrine system or the nervous system by writing the
       appropriate letter in the blank using the answer code
       below.

       (a) = applies to the endocrine system
       (b) = applies to the nervous system
       (c) = applies to both the endocrine and nervous
             systems

       _____ Structural continuity in the system.
       _____ Releases hormones into blood.
       _____ Has an influence on other major control system.
       _____ Secretes chemical messengers that affect target
             cells.
       _____ Chemical messengers act at a long distance from
             their site of secretion.
       _____ Specificity is dependent on specificity of target-
             cell receptors.
       _____ Controls activities that require longer duration
             rather than speed.
       _____ Duration of action is brief (milliseconds).
       _____ Speed of response is long (minutes to days or
             longer).

ANSWERS: b, a, c, c, a, a, a, b, a

344.   Indicate which characteristics in the left column apply
       to the hormones in the right column by writing the
       appropriate letters in the blanks.

       _____ Synthesized by the endoplasmic   a. Steroids
             reticulum/Golgi complex system   b. Catecholamines
       _____ Synthesized by enzymatic modi-   c. Peptides
             fication of cholesterol.   d. Thyroid
       _____ Synthesized within colloid.   hormone
       _____ Once synthesized, actively
             transported into preformed
             vesicles for storage.

ANSWERS: c, a, d, b

345.   Indicate the solubility characteristics of each of the classes of hormones by writing the appropriate letter in the blank using the answer code below.

        (a) = Lipophilic (hydrophobic)
        (b) = Hydrophilic (lipophobic)

        _____ Steroids
        _____ Thyroid hormone
        _____ Peptides
        _____ Catecholamines

ANSWERS: a, a, b, b

346.   Use the following answer code to identify the characteristics of various types of hormones.

        (a) = applies only to peptides
        (b) = applies only to steroids
        (c) = applies only to catecholamines
        (d) = applies only to thyroid hormone
        (e) = applies to both peptides and catecholamines
        (f) = applies to both steroids and thyroid hormone
        (g) = applies to both catecholamines and thyroid hormone
        (h) = applies to peptides, catecholamines and thyroid hormone
        (i) = applies to some other combination of hormones
        (j) = applies to all hormones

_____   A. consist of a chain of specific amino acids of varying length
_____   B. included in the biochemical category of amines
_____   C. derived from cholesterol
_____   D. derived from the amino acid tyrosine
_____   E. hydrophilic
_____   F. lipophilic
_____   G. synthesized and packaged by the endoplasmic reticulum/Golgi complex mechanism
_____   H. released by exocytosis
_____   I. stored within the endocrine gland following synthesis
_____   J. transported entirely or to a large extent freely dissolved in the plasma
_____   K. transported primarily bound to plasma proteins
_____   L. bind directly with surface membrane receptors
_____   M. bind directly with intracellular receptors
_____   N. produce ultimate effect by altering specific protein activity within the target cell
_____   O. function by activating second messenger systems
_____   P. function by activating specific genes
_____   Q. cause the formation of new intracellular proteins

346. (cont.)

_____   R. alter the activity of preexisting proteins,
           usually enzymes
_____   S. regulate the rates of existing reactions rather
           than initiating new reactions
_____   T. secreted by the adrenal medulla
_____   U. secreted by the adrenal cortex, gonads, and
           placenta
_____   V. secreted by the hypothalamus, anterior pituitary,
           pancreas, parathyroid, gastrointestinal tract, and
           kidneys

ANSWERS: A.a; B.g; C.b; D.g; E.e; F.f; G.a; H.e;   I.h; J.e;
K.f; L.e; M.f; N.j; O.e; P.f, Q.f, R.e; S.j; T.c; U.b; V.a

347. Indicate which of the following features apply to the
      posterior and anterior pituitary by using the answer code
      below:

           (a) = applies to the posterior pituitary
           (b) = applies to the anterior pituitary
           (c) = applies to both the posterior and anterior
                 pituitary

_____ composed of glandular tissue
_____ composed of nervous tissue
_____ also known as adenohypophysis
_____ also known as neurohypophysis
_____ secretes MSH in humans
_____ stores hormones synthesized by the hypothalamus
_____ releases hormones into the general circulation
_____ its release of hormones is directly controlled by
       action potentials
_____ its release of hormones is directly controlled by
       hypothalamic hypophysiotropic hormones
_____ neurally connected to the hypothalamus
_____ connected to the hypothalamus by a vascular link
_____ synthesizes the hormones it secretes
_____ releases vasopressin and oxytocin into the blood
_____ releases primarily tropic hormones into the blood
_____ may be directly inhibited by negative feedback from its
       target organ

ANSWERS: b, a, b, a, b, a, c, a, b, a, b, b, a, b, b

348.   _____ stimulates somatomedin secretion   a. vasopressin
        by the liver   b. oxytocin
        _____ enhances H$_2$O retention   c. TSH
        by the kidneys   d. ACTH
        _____ responsible for ovulation   e. growth
        _____ stimulates cortisol secretion   hormone
        by the adrenal cortex   f. FSH
        _____ stimulates testosterone   g. LH
        secretion   h. prolactin
        _____ exerts a pressor effect on
        arterioles
        _____ stimulate growth of ovarian
        follicles and development of eggs
        _____ stimulates uterine contractions
        _____ regulates overall body growth
        _____ stimulates both estrogen and
        progesterone secretion
        _____ stimulates secretion of thyroid
        hormone
        _____ enhances breast development and
        milk production
        _____ promotes milk ejection from the
        mammary glands
        _____ also known as ICSH
        _____ important in organic metabolism
        _____ required for sperm production

ANSWERS: e, a, g, d, g, a, f, b, e, g, c, h, b, g, e, f

349.   Match the description in the left column with the types
       of bone cells in the right column by writing the appro-
       priate letters in the blanks.

        _____ Bone cells that form bone.   a. Osteocytes
        _____ Bone cells that are entombed   b. Osteoblasts
        in bone.   c. Osteoclasts
        _____ Bone cells that dissolve bone.
        _____ Stimulated by growth hormone.

ANSWERS: b, a, c, b

350. Indicate the source of each of the hormones by writing the appropriate letter in the blank.

_____ aldosterone
_____ insulin
_____ glucagon
_____ corticotropin-releasing
         hormone
_____ vitamin D
_____ cortisol
_____ adrenocorticotropic
         hormone
_____ tetraiiodothyronine
_____ parathyroid hormone
_____ calcitonin
_____ thyroid-stimulating
         hormone
_____ T$_3$
_____ epinephrine

a. alpha cells of
   islets of Langer-
   hans in the
   pancreas.
b. beta cells of
   islets of Langer-
   hans in the
   pancreas.
c. anterior pituitary
d. hypothalamus
e. adrenal cortex
f. adrenal medulla
g. parathyroid gland
h. thyroid gland
i. skin

ANSWERS: e, b, a, d, i, e, c, h, g, h, c, h, f

351. Match the hormone on the right to the disorder with which it is associated by writing the appropriate letter in the blank.

_____ Cushing's syndrome
_____ diabetes insipidus
_____ adrenogenital syndrome
_____ Grave's disease
_____ rickets
_____ diabetes mellitus
_____ Conn's syndrome
_____ pheochromocytoma

a. epinephrine
b. thyroid hormone
c. aldosterone
d. insulin
e. vitamin D
f. cortisol
g. adrenal sex
   hormones
h. vasopressin

ANSWERS: f, h, g, b, e, d, c, a

352. Indicate which stimulus in the right column increases the rate of secretion of the hormone in the left column by writing the appropriate letter in the blank. Each answer may be used more than once.

_____ epinephrine
_____ calcitonin
_____ insulin
_____ parathyroid hormone
_____ glucagon
_____ cortisol

a. increased blood glucose
b. decreased blood glucose
c. increased plasma calcium
d. decreased plasma calcium
e. stress

ANSWERS: e, c, a, d, b, e

353.   Indicate which hormone in the right column most closely
        matches the description in the left column by writing the
        appropriate letter in the blank.

_____   inhibits bone resorption.   a. Epinephrine
_____   increases renal tubular re-   b. Aldosterone
          absorption of Na⁺.   c. Parathyroid
_____   at highest blood concentra-   hormone
          tion in the morning and   d. Calcitonin
          lowest at night.   e. Vitamin D
_____   general reinforcer of   f. Cortisol
          sympathetic activity.   g. Insulin
_____   stimulates corisol   h. Glucagon
          secretion.   i. Thyroid hormone
_____   secreted by pancreatic   j. ACTH
          alpha cells.   k. Adrenal androgen
_____   stimulates osteoclast
          activity.
_____   iodine-containing tyrosine
          derivative.
_____   stimulates glycogenesis.
_____   directly promotes Ca^{2+} absorption
          from the small intestine.
_____   responsible for the female sex drive.

ANSWERS: d, b, f, a, j, h, c, i, g, e, k

354.   Identify the factors associated with each of the bio-
        chemical processes below by writing the appropriate letter
        in the blank preceding the statement.

        (a) = gluconeogenesis
        (b) = glycogenesis
        (c) = glycogenolysis
        (d) = both gluconeogenesis and glycogenolysis
        (e) = all of the above

_____   Conversion of amino acids into glucose.
_____   Conversion of glycogen into glucose.
_____   Conversion of glucose into glycogen.
_____   Stimulated by glucagon and cortisol.
_____   Stimulated by insulin.
_____   Increases the blood glucose concentration.
_____   Decreases the blood glucose concentration.

ANSWERS: a, c, b, d, b, d, b

355. Indicate what hormone abnormality in the right column would be responsible for the symptoms listed in the left column by writing the appropriate letter in the blank. There is only one correct answer per question. Not all answers in the right column will be used.

_____ high blood glucose, muscle weakness and fatigue, "moon-face", "buffalo hump"	a. Catecholamine excess
_____ female masculinization; hirsutism	b. Catecholamine deficiency
_____ deformed bones, especially weight-bearing bones	c. Mineralocorticoid excess
_____ hypernatremia, hypokalemia, high blood pressure	d. Glucocorticoid excess
_____ precocious pseudopuberty	e. Mineralocorticoid and glucocorticoid deficiency
_____ hypercalcemia, hypophos- phatemia, thinning of bone, Ca^{2+} -containing kidney stones, reduced excitability of neuromuscular system, cardiac disturbances	f. Adrenal androgen excess in adult women
	g. Adrenal androgen excess in pre- pubertal boys
_____ high blood pressure, rapid heart rate, excessive sweating, high blood glucose	h. Adrenal androgen excess before birth in female infants
_____ female pseudohermaphroditism	i. Parathyroid hor- mone deficiency
_____ hyponatremia, hyperkalemia, low blood pressure, low blood glucose, poor response to stress	j. Parathyroid hor- mone excess
	k. Vitamin D deficiency
_____ hyperglycemia, glucosuria, polyuria, polydipsia, poly- phagia, ketosis	l. Vitamin D excess
	m. Insulin deficiency
_____ extensive spasms of skeletal muscles, involving especially the extremities and larynx; fatal in severe cases	n. Insulin excess

ANSWERS: d, f, k, c, g, j, a, h, e, m, i

356.   Indicate the metabolic effects of each of the following
        hormones by writing the appropriate letter using the
        answer code below.

                    (a) = increases
                    (b) = decreases
                    (c) = has no effect on

Insulin   _____ blood glucose.
                    _____ blood fatty acids.
                    _____ blood amino acids.
                    _____ muscle protein.

Glucagon   _____ blood glucose.
                    _____ blood fatty acids.
                    _____ blood amino acids.
                    _____ muscle protein.

Epinephrine   _____ blood glucose.
                    _____ blood fatty acids.
                    _____ blood amino acids.
                    _____ muscle protein.

Cortisol   _____ blood glucose.
                    _____ blood fatty acids.
                    _____ blood amino acids.
                    _____ muscle protein.

Growth hormone   _____ blood glucose.
                    _____ blood fatty acids.
                    _____ blood amino acids.
                    _____ muscle protein.

ANSWERS: Insulin: b, b, b, a
            Glucagon: a, a, c, c
            Epinephrine: a, a, c, c
            Cortisol: a, a, a, b
            Growth hormone: a, a, b, a

357. Indicate the effect the item on the left has on the
secretion rate of the hormone on the right by circling the
appropriate letter using the answer code below.

(a) = increases
(b) = decreases
(c) = has little or no effect on

Increased TSH _____ thyroid hormone.
Increased TRH _____ TSH.
Increased thyroid hormone _____ TSH.
Decreased iodine in diet _____ thyroid hormone.
Increased ACTH _____ aldosterone.
Increased ACTH _____ cortisol.
Stress _____ cortisol.
Stress _____ epinephrine.
Increased renin-angiotensin _____ aldosterone.
Increased plasma K^+ _____ aldosterone.
Increased blood glucose _____ insulin.
Increased blood glucose _____ glucagon.
Increased plasma Ca^{2+} _____ parathyroid hormone.
Increased plasma Ca^{2+} _____ calcitonin.
Increased TSH _____ calcitonin.
Increased plasma PO_4^{3-} _____ parathyroid hormone.

ANSWERS: a, a, b, b, c, a, a, a, a, a, a, b, b, a, c, c

358. Indicate which characteristics apply to the following
hormones by using the answer code below. (Note - more
than one answer may apply).

(a) = applies to epinephrine
(b) = applies to cortisol
(c) = applies to aldosterone
(d) = applies to dehydroepiandrosterone

A. produced by the zona glomerulosa
B. produced by the zona fasciculata and zona reticularis
C. adrenal androgen
D. enhances K^+ elimination
E. stimulates protein degradation
F. stimulates lipolysis
G. essential for life
H. exerts a glucose-sparing effect by inhibiting glucose
uptake by many tissues but not the brain
I. important in the stress response
J. a catecholamine
K. a steroid
L. secretion is stimulated by the sympathetic nervous
system
M. stored in chromaffin granules

358. (cont.)

    N. promotes female sex drive
    O. secretion is stimulated via the renin-angiotensin
       system
    P. promotes Na^+ retention
    Q. stimulates hepatic gluconeogenesis
    R. stimulates breakdown of glycogen
    S. inhibits CRH and ACTH in negative-feedback fashion
    T. secretion is directly stimulated by an increase in
       plasma K^+
    U. increases blood glucose levels
    V. increases blood amino acid levels
    W. increases blood fatty acid levels
    X. exerts anti-inflammatory and immunosuppressive effects
       at pharmacological levels
    Y. secretion is largely controlled by ACTH
    Z. is secreted in excess in Conn's syndrome
   AA. is secreted in excess in Cushing's syndrome
   BB. is secreted in excess in adrenogenital syndrome
   CC. is secreted in excess by a pheochromocytoma
   DD. is deficient in Addison's disease
   EE. increases the heart rate
   FF. contributes to the "fight or flight" response
   GG. displays a marked diurnal rhythm
   HH. inhibits secretion of insulin

ANSWERS: A.c; B.b,d; C.d; D.c; E.b; F.a,b; G.c; H.b; I.a,b,c;
J.a; K.b,c,d; L.a; M.a; N.d; O.c; P.c; Q.b; R.a; S.b; T.c;
U.a,b; V.b; W.a,b; X.b; Y.b,d; Z.c; AA.b; BB.d; CC.a;
DD.b,c(and d); EE.a; FF.a; GG.b; HH.a

359. More than one answer may apply.

    _____ dissolves bone   a. osteoblast
    _____ secretes organic   b. osteocyte
           matrix of bone   c. osteoclast
    _____ stimulated by PTH
    _____ inhibited by PTH
    _____ inhibited by calcitonin
    _____ imprisoned bone cell

ANSWERS: c; a; a,b; c; a; c; b

AUDIOVISUAL AIDS

Films

A list of films available from West Publishing Company is presented in Appendix A. Following are other films that may be suitable. The sources for these films, which are coded by abbreviation, are provided in Appendix B.

Animal Hormones I: Principles and Functions, EI

Endocrine Glands, SEF, 14 min.

Animated Hormones I: Principles and Functions, EI

Diabetes: The Quiet Killer, FHS, 26 min.

Endocrine Glands: How They Affect You, MH, 15 min.

Endocrine System, UC, 20 min.

Growth Hormone: Use and Abuse, FHS, 26 min.

Hormones, MH, 28 min.

Hormones and the Endocrine System, IM, 45 min.

Hormones: Messengers (VCR), FM, 20 min.

Messengers, FM, 26 min.

Principles of Endocrine Activity, IU, 15 min.

So You Have Diabetes, MF, 10 min.

The Chemistry of Life: Hormones and the Endocrine System (VCR), HRM, 28 min.

The Endocrine Glands, EBE, 11 min.

The Endocrine Glands, IM, 29 min.

The Endocrine System, CFV, 16 min.

The Endocrine System, EBE, 20 min.

The Hormones: Small But Mighty, IU, 29 min.

The Human Body: Endocrine System, COR, 15 min.

The Living Body: Messengers (VCR), FM, 28 min.

<u>Understanding Diabetes</u>, COR, 35 min.

Software

<u>Biochemistry of Hormones</u>, EI. Emphasizes the basic principles of hormone action.

<u>Dynamics of Human Endocrine System</u>, EI. Describes important hormones, their sources and functions.

<u>Endocrine System</u>, CBS. Covers hormones and problems associated with the different hormones.

<u>Your Body: Series II</u>, SSS. Endocrine system is explored through interactive game format.

Chapter 16
Reproductive System

CONTENTS
(All page references are to the main text.)

-The end is a new beginning.   p.569

Chapter in Perspective: Focus on Homeostasis, p.569

Chapter Summary, p.570

LECTURE HINTS AND SUGGESTIONS

1. Use a torso or whole-body manikin to demonstrate the locations of the internal reproductive organs. This and other material suggested below are available from Carolina Biological Supply Company, Burlington, NC, and other supply houses.

2. Use models of male and female reproductive organs to illustrate their anatomy.

3. Use models of meiosis that show spermatogenesis and oogenesis.

4. Display various contraceptives and explain their functions and effectiveness. (These are available from family planning clinics.)

5. Microscope slides of human gonads are informative.

6. If available, living sperm from various animals can be used for an interesting demonstration.

7. Various animals (e.g., frogs, rats, pigeons) dissected to show the reproductive organs and relationship to the other organs are effective in illustrating reproductive anatomy.

8. Use models of birth to illustrate the major events in this process.

9. Display a collection of preserved vertebrate embryos or models of same.

CHAPTER TEST QUESTIONS

Multiple Choice

1. Which of the following is **not** part of the male reproductive
    system?

    (a)   Seminal vesicles.
    (b)   Prostate gland.
    (c)   Labia minora.
    (d)   Bulbourethral glands.
    (e)   Testes.

ANSWER: c

2. The primary reproductive organs in the male include the

    (a)   testes.
    (b)   prostate gland.
    (c)   seminal vesicles.
    (d)   bulbourethral glands.
    (e)   All of the above are correct.

ANSWER: a

3. The gonads

    (a)   consist of a pair of testes in males and
          ovaries in females.
    (b)   produce gametes and secrete sex hormones.
    (c)   refer to the externally visible genitalia in
          both sexes.
    (d)   Both (a) and (b) above are correct.
    (e)   All of the above are correct.

ANSWER: d

4. Which of the following hormones is responsible for the
    development and maintenance of the secondary sexual
    characteristics?

    (a)   Testosterone.
    (b)   Estrogen.
    (c)   Progesterone.
    (d)   Both (a) and (b) above are correct.
    (e)   All of the above are correct.

ANSWER: d

5. Which of the following statements concerning sex determi-
    nation and sex differentiation is correct?

    (a) An xy combination of sex chromosomes is a
         genetic male.
    (b) The secretion of testosterone by the fetal
         gonads induces the development of male external
         genitalia and reproductive tract.
    (c) The secretion of estrogen by the fetal gonads induces
         the development of female external genitalia and
         reproductive tract.
    (d) Both (a) and (b) above are correct.
    (e) All of the above are correct.

ANSWER: d

6. Which of the following statements concerning sex differ-
    entiation is <u>incorrect</u>?

    (a) A Y chromosome stimulates primitive gonadal cells
         to develop into testes.
    (b) Ovaries must be present for feminization of the
         reproductive tract and external genitalia to occur.
    (c) It is possible for a genetic male with xy sex
         chromosomes to develop an apparant anatomical female.
    (d) Secretion of testosterone and Müllerian-inhibiting
         factor by the fetal testes induces development of the
         reproductive tract and external genitalia along male
         lines.
    (e) Early in development, embryos of both sexes have the
         same indifferent reproductive tissues capable of
         differentiating into either a male or female repro-
         ductive system depending respectively on the presence
         or absence of masculinizing factors.

ANSWER: b

7. The factor responsible for differentiating the embryonic
    gonads into testes is

    (a) the sex-determining region of the X chromosome
    (b) the sex-determining region of the Y chromosome
    (c) autosomal chromosomes
    (d) male gonadal-determining factor
    (e) the Sertoli cells

ANSWER: b

8.   Testosterone

   (a)   is secreted by the Leydig cells of the testes.
   (b)   exerts a general protein anabolic effect.
   (c)   causes enlargement of the larynx and thickening of
         the vocal cords.
   (d)   Both (a) and (b) above are correct.
   (e)   All of the above are correct.

ANSWER: e

9.   Which of the following statements concerning testosterone
     is **incorrect**?   Testosterone

   (a)   secretion is stimulated by LH.
   (b)   is secreted by the seminiferous tubules.
   (c)   stimulates spermatogenesis.
   (d)   promotes closure of the epiphyseal plate.
   (e)   stimulates protein synthesis and promotes bone
         growth.

ANSWER: b

10.   Testosterone

   (a)   is responsible for the male secondary sexual char-
         acteristics.
   (b)   stimulates spermatogenesis.
   (c)   acts in negative-feedback fashion on the anterior
         pituitary and hypothalamus.
   (d)   secretion is stimulated by LH.
   (e)   All of the above are correct.

ANSWER: e

11.   Which of the following is not stimulated by testosterone?

   (a)   masculinization of the developing reproductive tract
         and external genitalia
   (b)   descent of the testes into the scrotum
   (c)   spermatid remodeling
   (d)   development and maintenance of male secondary sexual
         characteristics
   (e)   libido
   (f)   protein anabolism
   (g)   bone growth
   (h)   closure of the epiphyseal plates
   (i)   mitosis and meiosis of developing sperm cells

ANSWER: c

12.   The testes are located outside of the abdominal cavity in
      the scrotal sac

      (a)   to permit spermatogenesis.
      (b)   to protect the gonads against injury.
      (c)   to permit testosterone secretion.
      (d)   to maintain the testes at a higher than normal body
            temperature for normal testicular function.
      (e)   to permit capacitation of the sperm to take place.

ANSWER: a

13.   Spermatogenesis

      (a)   is accomplished by the seminiferous tubules.
      (b)   results in 16 spermatozoa for each spermatogonium
            that starts to divide and differentiate (if no
            developing sperm cells in the sequence are lost).
      (c)   is controlled by both testosterone and FSH.
      (d)   Both (a) and (b) above are correct.
      (e)   All of the above are correct.

ANSWER: e

14.   Spermatogenesis is **directly** controlled by

      (a)   LH.
      (b)   FSH.
      (c)   testosterone.
      (d)   Both (b) and (c) above are correct.
      (e)   All of the above are correct.

ANSWER: d

15.   During spermatogenesis,

      (a)   one spermatogonium containing 46 chromosomes yields
            16 spermatozoa each containing 23 chromosomes.
      (b)   one spermatogonium containing 46 chromosomes yields 1
            spermatozoon containing 23 chromosomes and a polar
            body containing the other 23 chromosomes.
      (c)   one spermatogonium containing 46 chromosomes yields 2
            spermatozoa each containing 23 chromosomes.
      (d)   one spermatogonium containing 46 chromosomes yields 1
            spermatozoon containing 46 chromosomes.
      (e)   one spermatogonium containing 23 chromosomes yields 1
            spermatozoon containing 23 chromosomes.

ANSWER: a

16. During spermatogenesis, the first meiotic division yields
     two _____ and the second meiotic division
     yields four _____.

     (a)   primary spermatocytes, secondary spermatocytes
     (b)   secondary spermatocytes, spermatids
     (c)   spermatids, spermatozoa
     (d)   spermatogonia, primary spermatocytes
     (e)   None of the above are correct.

ANSWER: b

17. Which of the following is **not** a function of Sertoli cells?

     (a)   form a blood-testes barrier
     (b)   phagocytize cytoplasm extruded from sperm during
           their remodeling
     (c)   secrete seminiferous tubule fluid
     (d)   secrete androgen-binding protein
     (e)   provide nourishment for developing sperm
     (f)   provide binding sites for LH
     (g)   secrete inhibin

ANSWER: f

18. The acrosome of the spermatozoon

     (a)   contains the sperm's genetic information.
     (b)   contains mitochondria for energy production.
     (c)   is a fructose-filled vesicle that provides energy for
           the spermatozoa.
     (d)   contains enzymes that enable the sperm to penetrate
           the ovum.
     (e)   contains microtubules that slide past each other to
           provide the sperm with motility.

ANSWER: d

19. Which of the following is **not** a function of the Sertoli
     cells?

     (a)   Secrete seminiferous tubule fluid.
     (b)   Phagocytize cytoplasm extruded from developing
           sperm and destroy defective sperm.
     (c)   Secrete melatonin.
     (d)   Secrete inhibin.
     (e)   Provide nourishment for developing sperm.

ANSWER: c

20. Which part of the spermatozoon contains the genetic information?

    (a) Head.
    (b) Acrosome.
    (c) Midpiece.
    (d) Tail.

ANSWER: a

21. GnRH

    (a) stimulates both FSH and LH secretion.
    (b) is inhibited by testosterone.
    (c) has low-level activity during the prepubertal period.
    (d) Both (a) and (b) above are correct.
    (e) All of the above are correct.

ANSWER: e

22. During spermatogenesis

    (a) FSH is required for spermatid remodeling.
    (b) LH is required for spermatid remodeling.
    (c) testosterone is essential for both mitosis and meiosis of the germ cells.
    (d) Both (a) and (c) above are correct.
    (e) Both (b) and (c) above are correct.

ANSWER: d

23. Inhibin

    (a) is produced by the Sertoli cells.
    (b) is produced by the developing sperm cells.
    (c) inhibits LH in negative-feedback fashion.
    (d) Both (a) and (c) above are correct.
    (e) Both (b) and (c) above are correct.

ANSWER: a

24. A reduction in the secretion of what hormone may serve as the trigger for the onset of puberty?

    (a) Inhibin.
    (b) Melatonin.
    (c) Adrenal androgens.
    (d) Gonadotropin-releasing hormone.
    (e) Anterior pituitary gonadotropic hormones.

ANSWER: b

25. The site for final maturation of the sperm for motility and fertility in the male is

    (a) the seminiferous tubules.
    (b) the epididymis and vas deferens.
    (c) the seminal vesicles.
    (d) the prostate gland.
    (e) the penis.

ANSWER: b

26. The prostate gland

    (a) secretes prostaglandins.
    (b) supplies fructose, which is utilized by the sperm for energy production.
    (c) secretes an alkaline medium that is important to neutralize acidic vaginal secretions.
    (d) Both (a) and (c) above are correct.
    (e) All of the above are correct.

ANSWER: c

27. The prostate gland

    (a) secretes an alkaline medium that neutralizes the acidic vaginal secretions.
    (b) stores sperm prior to ejaculation.
    (c) provides a site for final maturation for fertility and motility for the spermatozoa.
    (d) secretes directly into the urethra.
    (e) supplies fructose utilized by the sperm for energy.

ANSWER: a

28. The seminal vesicles

    (a) store sperm prior to ejaculation.
    (b) supply fructose to be utilized by the sperm for energy.
    (c) secrete prostaglandins.
    (d) Both (b) and (c) above are correct.
    (e) All of the above are correct.

ANSWER: d

29. Which of the following is **not** accomplished by the seminal vesicles?

    (a) Supply fructose, which serves as the primary energy source for ejaculated sperm.
    (b) Secrete prostaglandins.
    (c) Secrete fibrinogen.
    (d) Secrete an alkaline fluid that neutralizes the acidic vaginal secretions.
    (e) Provide more than half the semen.

ANSWER: d

30. Prostaglandins

    (a) present in the semen are secreted by the prostate gland.
    (b) may be involved in sperm transport within both the male and female reproductive tracts.
    (c) exert a powerful inhibitory effect on uterine musculature.
    (d) are all derivatives of essential amino acids.
    (e) exert influences only on the reproductive system.

ANSWER: b

31. Prostaglandins

    (a) are produced by most body tissues.
    (b) are derivatives of arachidonic acid.
    (c) act locally within or near their site of production.
    (d) Two of the above are correct.
    (e) All of the above are correct.

ANSWER: e

32. Erection

    (a) is caused by contraction of skeletal muscles within the penis.
    (b) occurs only upon stimulation of mechanoreceptors in the glans penis.
    (c) results in reflex closure of the sphincter at the neck of the bladder.
    (d) Both (b) and (c) above are correct.
    (e) All of the above are correct.

ANSWER: c

33. Erection

    (a) involves dilation of the arterioles supplying the spongelike vascular spaces of the penis.
    (b) occurs as a result of contraction of the skeletal muscles of the penis.
    (c) occurs when the seminiferous tubules of the penis become engorged with sperm.
    (d) occurs in response to sympathetic nervous stimulation of the penis.

ANSWER: a

34. Which of the following is **not** a component of the overall ejaculatory response?

    (a) Arterioles supplying the penis reflexly dilate, causing the erectile tissue to fill with blood and the penis to become erect.
    (b) The smooth muscles of the prostate, reprodutive ducts, and seminal vesicles contract, resulting in emission.
    (c) The sphincter at the neck of the bladder tightly closes.
    (d) Semen is expelled from the penis by a series of rapid contractions of skeletal muscles at the base of the penis.
    (e) Rhythmical contractions and accompanying systemic responses are associated with a pleasant sensation known as orgasm.

ANSWER: a

35. An average human ejaculate contains about _____ sperm.

    (a) 20-30 million
    (b) 100-120 million
    (c) 100-120 thousand
    (d) 300-400 million
    (e) None of the above are correct.

ANSWER: d

36. Which of the following is the proper sequence of phases in the sexual response cycle?

(a) Plateau, excitement, orgasmic, resolution.
(b) Excitement, plateau, orgasmic, resolution.
(c) Plateau, orgasmic, excitement, resolution.
(d) Resolution, plateau, orgasmic, excitement.
(e) Excitement, orgasmic, resolution, plateau.

ANSWER: b

37. Which of the following occurs in the female sexual response cycle?

(a) Erection.
(b) Tightening of the outer third of the vagina.
(c) "Tenting" of the upper two-thirds of the vagina.
(d) Both (b) and (c) above are correct.
(e) All of the above are correct.

ANSWER: e

38. The number of primary oocytes in a female

(a) is decreased continually throughout her reproductive life from puberty to menopause.
(b) is maintained constant during her reproductive life because those that are lost are continuously replaced by an equal number of new primary oocytes.
(c) become depleted at the time of menopause.
(d) Both (a) and (c) above are correct.
(e) Both (b) and (c) above are correct.

ANSWER: d

39. FSH

(a) is an anterior pituitary hormone that stimulates antrum formation in developing ovarian follicles.
(b) is produced by developing ovarian follicles.
(c) is sometimes referred to as ICSH in males.
(d) Both (a) and (c) above are correct.
(e) Both (b) and (c) above are correct.

ANSWER: a

40. During oogenesis

     (a)   there is a continual supply of primary oocytes
           through mitotic division.
     (b)   one primary oocyte yields 16 mature ova.
     (c)   one primary oocyte yields 1 mature ovum.
     (d)   Each ovum contains 46 chromosomes at the time of
           ovulation.
     (e)   Two of the above are correct.

ANSWER: c

41. One primary spermatocyte containing _____ chromosomes
     yields _____ spermatozoa containing _____ chromosomes,
     whereas one primary oocyte containing _____ chromosomes
     yields _____ ova (ovum) containing _____ chromosomes.

     (a)   46, 2, 23, 46, 2, 23
     (b)   46, 4, 23, 46, 1, 23
     (c)   46, 4, 23, 46, 4, 23
     (d)   23, 1, 23, 23, 1, 23
     (e)   None of the above are correct.

ANSWER: b

42. Which of the following statements concerning spermatoge-
     nesis and oogenesis is **incorrect**

     (a)   One primary spermatocyte or one primary oocyte
           containing 46 chromosomes respectively yield two
           spermatozoa or two ova, each containing 23 chro-
           mosomes.
     (b)   There is a continual supply of spermatogonia through
           mitotic activity.
     (c)   The first meiotic division involved in oogenesis is
           completed just prior to ovulation.
     (d)   It takes anywhere from about 11 to 50 years for the
           process of oogenesis to be completed.
     (e)   During oogenesis, there is unequal distribution of
           cytoplasm resulting in the production of polar bodies
           that disintegrate.

ANSWER: a

43. In what form is the "egg" when it is ovulated?

     (a)   Primary oocyte.
     (b)   Secondary oocyte.
     (c)   Mature ovum.

ANSWER: b

44. Which of the following statements concerning oogenesis is (are) correct?

  (a) The first meiotic division occurs just prior to ovulation and the second meiotic division is triggered by fertilization.
  (b) The process of oogenesis takes anywhere from 12 to 50 years to complete.
  (c) Oogonia proliferate mitotically throughout the reproductive life of a female.
  (d) Both (a) and (b) above are correct.
  (e) All of the above are correct.

ANSWER: d

45. LH is responsible for

  (a) reinitiation of meiosis in the oocytes of developing follicles.
  (b) halting estrogen synthesis by the follicular cells.
  (c) triggering ovulation.
  (d) formation of the corpus luteum.
  (e) All of the above are correct.

ANSWER: e

46. The corpus luteum

  (a) develops from the polar body after ovulation.
  (b) develops from the fertilized ovum through a process of division and differentiation.
  (c) develops from the ruptured follicle after ovulation.
  (d) of pregnancy is stimulated by estrogen and progesterone secretion from the placenta.
  (e) is sloughed during menstruation if fertilization does not occur.

ANSWER: c

47. A sharp burst in secretion of which of the following hormones is responsible for ovulation?

  (a) Estrogen.
  (b) Progesterone.
  (c) LH.
  (d) FSH.
  (e) Prolactin.

ANSWER: c

48. Which of the following does **not** occur during the follic-
     ular phase of the ovarian cycle?

     (a) The proliferative phase of the uterine cycle.
     (b) The menstrual phase of the uterine cycle.
     (c) Estrogen secretion.
     (d) Progesterone secretion.
     (e) FSH and LH secretion.

ANSWER: d

49. What ovarian hormone(s) is (are) secreted during the
     follicular phase of the ovarian cycle?

     (a) FSH.
     (b) Estrogen.
     (c) Progesterone.
     (d) LH.
     (e) Both estrogen and progesterone.

ANSWER: b

50. What hormone(s) is (are) secreted by the corpus luteum?

     (a) FSH.
     (b) Estrogen.
     (c) Progesterone.
     (d) LH.
     (e) Both estrogen and progesterone.

ANSWER: e

51. Which of the following statements concerning control of
     ovarian hormone secretion is **incorrect**?

     (a) Low levels of estrogen inhibit the hypothalamus and
          anterior pituitary in negative-feedback fashion.
     (b) Under the influence of estrogen from developing
          follicles, FSH and LH secretion both continue to
          decline throughout the follicular phase.
     (c) Both estrogen and progesterone are required to
          completely inhibit tonic LH secretion.
     (d) A high level of estrogen stimulates LH secretion and
          initiates the LH surge.
     (e) Progesterone powerfully inhibits both FSH and LH
          secretion.

ANSWER: b

52. Which of the following factors contributes to follicular development and estrogen secretion?

    (a) FSH.
    (b) LH.
    (c) Estrogen.
    (d) Both (a) and (b) above are correct.
    (e) All of the above are correct.

ANSWER: e

53. Which of the following is the proper sequence of the menstrual (uterine) cycle?

    (a) Menstrual phase, progestational phase, proliferative phase, ovulation.
    (b) Menstrual phase, proliferative phase, ovulation, progestational phase.
    (c) Proliferative phase, menstrual phase, ovulation, progestational phase.
    (d) Ovulation, menstrual phase, proliferative phase, progestational phase.
    (e) Ovulation, proliferative phase, progestational phase, menstrual phase.

ANSWER: b

54. The proliferative phase of the menstrual (uterine) cycle

    (a) occurs when the ovarian cycle is in the follicular phase.
    (b) lasts from menstruation to ovulation.
    (c) occurs when the endometrium is repairing itself and thickening under the influence of estrogen.
    (d) Two of the above are correct.
    (e) All of the above are correct.

ANSWER: e

55. During the menstrual phase of the uterine cycle,

    (a) a new ovarian follicular phase is beginning.
    (b) the highly vascular, nutrient-rich uterine lining is deprived of hormonal support.
    (c) vasoconstriction of the uterine vessels occurs in response to release of a uterine prostaglandin.
    (d) Both (b) and (c) above are correct.
    (e) All of the above are correct.

ANSWER: e

56. What hormone causes the endometrial glands to fill with glycogen and endometrial blood vessels to become more numerous?

   (a) Estrogen.
   (b) Progesterone.
   (c) FSH.
   (d) LH.
   (e) Chorionic gonadotropin.

ANSWER: b

57. During which phase(s) of the uterine cycle does progest-erone secretion occur?

   (a) Menstrual phase.
   (b) Proliferative phase.
   (c) Secretory, or progestational, phase.
   (d) Both (a) and (c) above are correct.
   (e) Both (b) and (c) above are correct.

ANSWER: c

58. The normal site of fertilization is the

   (a) ovary.
   (b) uterus.
   (c) oviduct.
   (d) vagina.
   (e) fimbria.

ANSWER: c

59. Implantation

   (a) is accomplished as the trophoblastic cells break down the endometrial tissue.
   (b) occurs during the secretory, or progestational, phase of the menstrual cycle.
   (c) occurs within 24 hours after ovulation.
   (d) Both (a) and (b) above are correct.
   (e) All of the above are correct.

ANSWER: d

60. Implantation normally occurs

    (a) in the oviduct.
    (b) about 3 days after fertilization.
    (c) during the secretory, or progestational, phase.
    (d) Both (b) and (c) above are correct.
    (e) All of the above are correct.

ANSWER: c

61. Which of the following statements concerning implantation
    is (are) correct?

    (a) Implantation is accomplished by enzymatic activity of
         the trophoblastic layer of the blastocyst.
    (b) The endometrium at the site of implantation is
         converted into the nutrient-rich decidua.
    (c) Implantation occurs within 24 hours after fertili-
         zation.
    (d) Both (a) and (b) above are correct.
    (e) All of the above are correct.

ANSWER: d

62. In the blastocyst

    (a) the trophoblast is destined to become the fetus.
    (b) the trophoblast is destined to become the fetal
         portion of the placenta.
    (c) the trophoblast is destined to become the inner cell
         mass.
    (d) the blastocoele serves the functions of the digestive
         system, lungs, and kidneys for the fetus.
    (e) the blastocoele is destined to become the fetus.

ANSWER: b

63. The trophoblast

    (a) is destined to become the fetus.
    (b) is responsible for accomplishing implantation.
    (c) is destined to become the fetal portion of the
         placenta.
    (d) Both (a) and (b) above are correct.
    (e) Both (b) and (c) above are correct.

ANSWER: e

64.   The trophoblast of the blastocyst is destined to become

(a)   the fetus.
(b)   the fetal portion of the placenta.
(c)   the inner cell mass.
(d)   the amniotic sac.
(e)   the corpus luteum of pregnancy.

ANSWER: b

65.   The placenta serves the functions of all of the following
systems for the fetus **except**

(a)   digestion.
(b)   respiration.
(c)   circulation.
(d)   kidneys.
(e)   The functions of all of these systems are served by
the placenta for the fetus.

ANSWER: c

66.   Which of the following statements concerning the placenta
is (are) correct?

(a)   The placenta secretes human chorionic gonadotropin,
estrogen, and progesterone.
(b)   The placenta serves the functions of the circulatory,
respiratory, and digestive systems for the fetus.
(c)   Maternal and fetal blood are mixed together within
the placenta.
(d)   Both (a) and (b) above are correct.
(e)   All of the above are correct.

ANSWER: a

67.   Human chorionic gonadotropin

(a)   is secreted by the corpus luteum of pregnancy.
(b)   in the urine is the basis of pregnancy diagnosis
tests.
(c)   stimulates placental secretion of estrogen and
progesterone.
(d)   Both (a) and (b) above are correct.
(e)   All of the above are correct.

ANSWER: b

68. What is the source of estrogen and progesterone during the first ten weeks of pregnancy?

    (a) Ovarian follicle.
    (b) Placenta.
    (c) Corpus luteum of pregnancy.
    (d) Anterior pituitary.
    (e) Trophoblast.

ANSWER: c

69. What is the source of estrogen and progesterone during the last seven months of pregnancy?

    (a) Ovarian follicle.
    (b) Placenta.
    (c) Corpus luteum of pregnancy.
    (d) Anterior pituitary.
    (e) Trophoblast.

ANSWER: b

70. The presence of what hormone in the urine forms the basis of pregnancy diagnosis tests?

    (a) Estrogen.
    (b) Progesterone.
    (c) Prolactin.
    (d) Human chorionic gonadotropin.
    (e) LH.

ANSWER: d

71. Human chorionic gonadotropin

    (a) is secreted by the ovary.
    (b) is secreted by the developing placenta.
    (c) stimulates and maintains the corpus luteum of pregnancy.
    (d) Both (a) and (c) above are correct.
    (e) Both (b) and (c) above are correct.

ANSWER: e

72. Which of the following statements concerning human chorionic gonadotropin is **incorrect**?

(a) It is secreted by the placenta.
(b) It maintains the corpus luteum of pregnancy.
(c) It is secreted by the corpus luteum of pregnancy.
(d) The presence of chorionic gonadotropin in the urine is the basis of pregnancy diagnosis tests.
(e) It is secreted primarily during the first ten weeks of gestation.

ANSWER: c

73. The third stage of labor

(a) involves dilation of the cervix to 10 cm.
(b) refers to the actual birth of the baby.
(c) occurs when the entire uterine contents shift downward and the fetus's head is positioned against the cervix.
(d) involves delivery of the placenta.
(e) is characterized by rupture of the membranes surrounding the amniotic sac.

ANSWER: d

74. According to the leading proposal, parturition is initiated by

(a) parasympathetic stimulation.
(b) an increase in uterine responsiveness to oxytocin as a result of an increased concentration of myometrial oxytocin receptors.
(c) a drop in oxytocin secretion.
(d) a negative-feedback loop established between progesterone and oxytocin.
(e) a rise in estrogen secretion.

ANSWER: b

75. Oxytocin

(a) is important in parturition by stimulating uterine contractions.
(b) causes contraction of the myoepithelial cells surrounding the alveoli of the breast.
(c) stimulates synthesis of milk by the milk glands.
(d) Both (a) and (b) above are correct.
(e) All of the above are correct.

ANSWER: d

76. Oxytocin

(a) is a powerful uterine muscle stimulant
(b) is involved in a positive feedback cycle during parturition
(c) stimulates production of milk by the mammary glands
(d) Both (a) and (b) above are correct.
(e) All of the above are correct.

ANSWER: d

77. Oxytocin

(a) is an extremely potent uterine muscle stimulant.
(b) causes milk ejection or "milk letdown".
(c) is secreted only in response to stimulation of mechanoreceptors in the nipple via suckling.
(d) Both (a) and (b) above are correct.
(e) All of the above are correct.

ANSWER: d

78. Which of the following stimulates uterine contractions?

(a) Oxytocin from the posterior pituitary.
(b) Prostaglandin from the decidua.
(c) Progesterone from the placenta.
(d) Both (a) and (b) above are correct.
(e) All of the above are correct.

ANSWER: d

79. Suckling

(a) stimulates prolactin secretion.
(b) stimulates oxytocin secretion.
(c) inhibits LH and FSH secretion.
(d) Both (a) and (b) above are correct.
(e) All of the above are correct.

ANSWER: e

80. Which of the following statements concerning estrogen is **incorrect**? Estrogen

   (a) promotes fat deposition.
   (b) promotes closure of the epiphyseal plates.
   (c) stimulates duct development in the breasts.
   (d) causes the cervical mucus to become thick and sticky.
   (e) enhances sperm transport to the site of fertilization by stimulating upward contractions of the uterus and oviduct.

ANSWER: d

81. Progesterone

   (a) exerts a strong inhibitory influence on the uterine musculature.
   (b) is responsible for the development and maintenance of female secondary sex characteristics.
   (c) promotes duct development in the breasts.
   (d) Both (a) and (c) above are correct.
   (e) All of the above are correct.

ANSWER: a

82. Birth control pills act as contraceptives by

   (a) preventing development of the endometrium into a suitable site for implantation.
   (b) preventing ovulation by inhibiting GnRH and thus FSH and LH secretion.
   (c) killing sperm.
   (d) precipitating in the cervical canal to act as a barrier to sperm entry.
   (e) increasing muscular contractions in the female reproductive tract so that ovulated eggs are flushed out before they have a chance to be fertilized.

ANSWER: b

True/False

83. Normal functioning of the reproductive system is not aimed toward homeostasis and is not necessary for survival of the individual.

ANSWER: True

84. Secondary sexual characteristics refer to the external characteristics not directly involved in reproduction that distinguish males and females.

ANSWER: True

85. Human cells have 23 pairs of sex chromosomes.

ANSWER: False

86. Each gamete contains 23 chromosomes.

ANSWER: True

87. In the absence of masculinizing factors, a female reproductive tract and external genitalia develop regardless of the genetic sex of the individual.

ANSWER: True

88. An xy combination of sex chromosomes is a genetic male.

ANSWER: True

89. An xx combination of sex chromosomes will always produce an anatomic female.

ANSWER: False

90. In an embryo with an xx combination of sex chromosomes, the presence of estrogen from the embryonic ovary induces the development of female external genitalia and reproductive tract.

ANSWER: False

91. The presence of the sex-determining region of the Y chromosome causes the embryonic gonad to differentiate into testes.

ANSWER: True

92. Fetal testes secrete testosterone and fetal ovaries secrete estrogen.

ANSWER: False

93. Testosterone in the male and progesterone in the female are responsible for the development and maintenance of secondary sexual characteristics.

ANSWER: False

94. In the male, the primary reproductive organs include the the testes, the prostate gland, the seminal vesicles, and the bulbourethral glands.

ANSWER: False

95. The significance of the scrotal location of the testes is to provide a warmer temperature for sperm production to occur.

ANSWER: False

96. The scrotal location of the testes provides the cooler. environment essential for spermatogenesis.

ANSWER: True

97. Failure of the testes to descend into the scrotal sac is known as cryptorchidism.

ANSWER: True

98. Testosterone promotes closure of the epiphyseal plate.

ANSWER: True

99. Development and maintenance of the male body configuration results from the general protein anabolic effect of testosterone.

ANSWER: True

100. Spermatogonia line the lumen of the seminiferous tubule.

ANSWER: False

101. Several hundred million sperm may reach maturity daily.

ANSWER: True

102. One spermatogonium containing 46 chromosomes yields two spermatozoa each containing 23 chromosomes.

ANSWER: False

103. Each spermatogonium gives rise to 16 spermatids through the process of spermatogenesis.

ANSWER: True

104. The human testis contains many Leydig cells (interstitial cells) at various stages of differentiation, some of which have only half the normal number of chromosomes.

ANSWER: False

105. The developing sperm cells arising from a single primary spermatocyte remain joined by cytoplasmic bridges until development is complete so that a Y-bearing sperm can be provided with essential products coded for by the X chromosome.

ANSWER: True

106. The sperm's genetic information is located in the head of the sperm.

ANSWER: True

107. The acrosome is an enzyme-filled vesicle at the tip of the head of the spermatozoon that enables the sperm to penetrate the ovum.

ANSWER: True

108. A spermatid and a spermatozoon each contain 23 chromosomes.

ANSWER: True

109. The Sertoli cells provide nourishment for the developing sperm cells.

ANSWER: True

110. A high local concentration of testosterone within the seminiferous tubules is essential for sustaining sperm production.

ANSWER: True

111. The Leydig cells secrete testosterone in response to stimulation by luteinizing hormone.

ANSWER: True

112. Inhibin is produced by the Sertoli cells and selectively inhibits the secretion of FSH from the anterior pituitary gland.

ANSWER: True

113. The pubertal process is initiated by an increase in GnRH activity.

ANSWER: True

114. In a sexually mature individual, pulses of GnRH are secreted once a day.

ANSWER: False

115. At puberty the hypothalamus becomes more sensitive to feedback inhibition by testosterone.

ANSWER: False

116. Testosterone is required for spermatid remodeling.

ANSWER: False

117. Spermatozoa comprise the largest bulk of the semen.

ANSWER: False

118. The seminal vesicles store sperm prior to ejaculation.

ANSWER: False

119. The prostate gland provides fructose to be utilized by the sperm for energy.

ANSWER: False

120. Vasectomy invariably results in a decrease in testosterone secretion.

ANSWER: False

121. Prostaglandins are secreted into the semen by the prostate gland.

ANSWER: False

122. Prostaglandins are found only in the semen.

ANSWER: False

123. Although discovered in the semen, prostaglandins are ubiquitous locally-acting chemical messengers that exert widespread effects throughout the body.

ANSWER: True

124. Erection is accomplished by contraction of skeletal muscles at the base of the penis.

ANSWER: False

125. Erection is a vascular phenomenon that involves decreased sympathetic and increased parasympathetic activity to the penile arterioles, resulting in arteriolar vasodilation and filling of the erectile tissue with blood.

ANSWER: True

126. Erection can occur only upon stimulation of the mechano-receptors in the glans penis.

ANSWER: False

127. Erection occurs as a result of reflex contraction of the skeletal muscles of the penis in response to stimulation of mechanoreceptors in the glans penis.

ANSWER: False

128. During ejaculation, the sphincter at the neck of the bladder reflexly opens to allow semen to enter the urethra.

ANSWER: False

129. Ejaculation is a two part reflex involving, first, contraction of the smooth muscle of the reproductive tract and accessory sex organs (emission) and, second, contraction of the skeletal muscles at the base of the penis (expulsion).

ANSWER: True

130. Orgasm is very similar in males and females with the exception of no ejaculation in females.

ANSWER: True

131. Erection and ejaculation are both spinal reflexes.

ANSWER: True

132.   During ejaculation the sphincter at the neck of the bladder is opened to permit entry of sperm into the urethra.

ANSWER: False

133.   Parasympathetic stimulation is required for erection whereas sympathetic stimulation is necessary for ejaculation.

ANSWER: True

134.   During the female sexual response, the lower third of the vagina expands to accommodate entry of the penis.

ANSWER: False

135.   Mucus secretions from the male provide the primary lubricant for intercourse.

ANSWER: False

136.   One primary oocyte containing 46 chromosomes yields 1 ovum containing 46 chromosomes.

ANSWER: False

137.   One primary oocyte containing 46 doubled chromosomes yields only one ovum containing 23 unpaired chromosomes.

ANSWER: True

138.   There is a limited lifetime supply of primary oocytes, which are present at the birth of a baby girl.

ANSWER: True

139.   Oogonia continually multiply to replenish the ovarian supply of gamete precursor cells.

ANSWER: False

140.   The first meiotic division of a primary oocyte occurs within a mature follicle just prior to ovulation.

ANSWER: True

141.   The process of oogenesis (from undifferentiated germ cell to released ovum) takes anywhere from 11 to 50 years to complete.

ANSWER: True

142. Developing follicles that fail to reach maturity to ovulate undergo atresia and form scar tissue.

ANSWER: True

143. If fertilization does not occur, the corpus luteum has a life span of about two weeks.

ANSWER: True

144. Low levels of estrogen inhibit the hypothalamus and anterior pituitary, whereas high levels of estrogen stimulate the hypothalamus and anterior pituitary.

ANSWER: True

145. High levels of estrogen directly stimulate the LH-secreting cells of the anterior pituitary.

ANSWER: True

146. The plasma concentration of estrogen reaches a higher level during the follicular phase than during the luteal phase, despite the fact that the follicle and corpus luteum both secrete estrogen.

ANSWER: True

147. The second meiotic division occurs within the ovary before ovulation takes place.

ANSWER: False

148. Luteinizing hormone and follicle-stimulating hormone are secreted by the gonads.

ANSWER: False

149. The corpus luteum develops from the polar body.

ANSWER: False

150. The endometrium is composed primarily of smooth muscle that thickens under the influence of estrogen.

ANSWER: False

151. The secretory phase of the uterine cycle lasts from menstruation to ovulation.

ANSWER: False

152.   The glycogen stored in the endometrial glands is broken down by the trophoblast to provide nourishment during the early stages of the developing embryo.

ANSWER: True

153.   There is an increase in estrogen secretion after menopause due to an increase in GnRH secretion.

ANSWER: False

154.   The normal site of fertilization is the uterus.

ANSWER: False

155.   The vagina is the site of fertilization.

ANSWER: False

156.   The fimbriae and cilia usually guide the egg into the oviduct following ovulation.

ANSWER: True

157.   If several sperm fertilize a single ovum as it is dividing, twins, or even triplets, may result.

ANSWER: False

158.   Progesterone causes the cervical mucus to become thick and sticky.

ANSWER: True

159.   The sperm's motility is the primary factor responsible for transporting it from the vagina to the site of fertilization.

ANSWER: False

160.   Implantation normally occurs within 24 hours after fertilization.

ANSWER: False

161.   The inner cell mass of the blastocyst is destined to become the fetus.

ANSWER: True

162.   Human chorionic gonadotropin in the urine is the basis of pregnancy diagnosis tests.

ANSWER: True

163.   Human chorionic gonadotropin is secreted by the corpus luteum of pregnancy.

ANSWER: ' False

164.   The placenta serves as the embryo's digestive tract, kidney, lungs, and circulatory system.

ANSWER: False

165.   Some of the precursors for secretion of hormones by the placenta come from the fetal adrenal cortex.

ANSWER: True

166.   The placenta provides a site for maternal and fetal blood to thoroughly mix to allow O_2 and nutrients to be delivered to the fetus and CO_2 and other waste products to be removed from the fetus.

ANSWER: False

167.   Blood is exchanged between the mother and fetus across the placenta.

ANSWER: False

168.   The placenta secretes hCG, which causes the ovaries to maintain cyclic follicular development (ovulations) during pregnancy.

ANSWER: False

169.   The third and final stage of labor involves the actual birth of the baby.

ANSWER: False

170.   Parasympathetic stimulation of the uterine muscle is involved in the process of parturition.

ANSWER: False

171.   Oxytocin is a powerful stimulant of uterine muscle contractility.

ANSWER: True

172. When the entire uterine contents shift downward during
      late gestation so that the baby's head is brought into
      contact with the cervix, this is often mistaken as the
      onset of labor, so-called "false labor."

ANSWER: False

173. As uterine contractions push the fetus against the cervix
      during parturition, oxytocin release from the posterior
      pituitary is reflexly increased, which further increases
      uterine contractions.

ANSWER: True

174. Estrogen stimulates duct development in the breasts.

ANSWER: True

175. Suckling stimulates oxytocin and prolactin secretion.

ANSWER: True

Fill-in-the-blanks

176. The _____ are the primary reproductive
      organs. In males they consist of a pair of
      _____ and in females a pair of
      _____.

ANSWERS: gonads, testes, ovaries

177. In both sexes the primary reproductive organs produce the
      reproductive cells or _____, which are
      _____ in the female and _____ in
      the male, as well secrete the sex hormones, which are
      _____ and _____ in the female and
      _____ in the male.

ANSWERS: gametes, ova (eggs), spermatozoa (sperm), estrogen,
          progesterone, testosterone

178. The reproductive tract includes a system of ducts plus
      _____ that secrete into these passageways.

ANSWER: accessory sex glands

179. The externally visible portions of the reproductive
      system are referred to as _____.

ANSWER: external genitalia

180.   The _____ refer to the many external characteristics not directly involved in reproduction that distinguish males and females. The hormone _____ in males and the hormone _____ in females are responsible for the development and maintenance of these characteristics.

ANSWERS: secondary sexual characteristics, testosterone, estrogen

181.   The single gene within the Y chromosome that is responsible for sex determination is the _____.

ANSWER: sex-determining region of the Y chromosome

182.   The three major stages of spermatogenesis are _____, _____, and _____.

ANSWERS: mitotic proliferation, meiosis, packaging

183.   The _____ of the testes secrete testosterone under the hormonal influence of _____.

ANSWERS: interstitial cells of Leydig, luteinizing hormone (LH)

184.   An undescended testis is known as a _____.

ANSWER: cryptorchid

185.   The _____ of a spermatozoon contains the sperm's genetic information; the _____ is an enzyme-filled vesicle for penetrating an ovum; power-generating mitochondria are concentrated in the sperm's _____; the _____ is a whiplike structure comprised of microtubules.

ANSWERS: head, acrosome, midpiece, tail

186.   The four phases of the sexual cycle in both sexes are _____, _____, _____ and _____ phases.

ANSWERS: excitement, plateau, orgasmic, resolution

187. The entire process of movement of the sperm and sex gland secretions out of the male reproductive tract is called _____; emptying of semen into the urethra is known as _____; forceful ejection of sperm from the penis is called _____.

ANSWERS: ejaculation, emission, expulsion

188. Prostaglandins are locally acting chemical messengers derived from the plasma-membrane component, _____.

ANSWER: arachidonic acid

189. A surge in _____ secretion from the anterior pituitary triggers ovulation.

ANSWER: luteinizing hormone (LH)

190. Following ovulation, the ruptured follicle is transformed into the _____.

ANSWER: corpus luteum

191. During gestation, the _____ produces dehydroepiandrosterone, which the _____ converts into estrogen.

ANSWERS: fetal adrenal cortex, placenta

192. The _____ of the blastocyst is destined to become the embryo/fetus.

ANSWER: inner cell mass

Matching

193. Match the three levels of sexual distinction between males and females by writing the appropriate letters in the blanks.

_____ genetic   a. Refers to the apparent anatomic
       sex   sex of the individual
_____ gonadal   b. Refers to the combination of sex
       sex   chromosomes at the time of
_____ phenotypic   conception.
       sex   c. Refers to the development of
                        testes or ovaries.

ANSWERS: b, c, a

194. Indicate the chromosomal composition of each of the
following stages of developing sperm by using the answer
code below:

(a) = contains a full set of 23 pairs of chromosomes
(b) = contains a full set of 23 pairs of doubled
      chromosomes
(c) = contains a half set of doubled chromosomes
(d) = contains a set of 23 single unpaired chro-
      mosomes

_____ spermatogonium
_____ primary spermatocyte
_____ secondary spermatocyte
_____ spermatid
_____ spermatozoan

ANSWERS: a, b, c, d, d

195. Indicate which description in the right column matches
the item in the left column by writing the appropriate
letter in the blank.

_____ chorion
_____ colostrum
_____ zona
       pellucida
_____ decidua
_____ placenta

a. Special milk produced during the
   first five days postpartum.
b. Evacuated from the uterus
   as "afterbirth."
c. Super-rich endometrial
   tissue at the implantation
   site.
d. The two-cell layered
   trophoblastic
   tissue that forms the fetal
   portion of the placenta.
e. The intervening membrane
   between
   the developing oocyte and
   surrounding granulosa
   cells.

ANSWERS: d, a, e, c, b

196.   Indicate whether the following functions are attributable
        to estrogen or progesterone using the answer code below:

> (a) = estrogen
> (b) = progesterone
> (c) = both estrogen and progesterone

_____ responsible for developing and maintaining female
        secondary sexual characteristics
_____ stimulates duct development in the breasts
_____ inhibits uterine contractility
_____ causes cervical mucus to become thick and sticky
_____ induces endometrial secretory capacity
_____ promotes thickening of the myometrium
_____ inhibits prolactin's ability to promote milk
        secretion

ANSWERS: a, a, b, b, b, a, c

197.   Indicate which item in the following answer code best
        matches the description in question by writing the
        appropriate letter in the blank.   There is only one
correct answer per question.   Each answer may be used   more
than once.   Some answers may not be used at all.

a. erection	l. prostate gland
b. acrosome	m. trophoblast
c. Leydig cells	n. corpus luteum
d. seminal vesicles	o. epididymis & ductus
e. oviduct	deferens
f. uterus	p. ovarian follicle
g. inner cell mass	q. ejaculation
h. seminiferous tubules	r. tail of sperm
i. midpiece of sperm	s. Sertoli cells
j. head of sperm	t. endometrium
k. vagina	u. placenta

_____ Formation is stimulated by LH after ovulation.
_____ Site of spermatogenesis.
_____ Stores sperm prior to ejaculation.
_____ Occurs as a result of vascular engorgement.
_____ Site of fertilization.
_____ Destined to become the fetus.
_____ Fills with glycogen and becomes richly vascularized
        under the influence of progesterone.
_____ Tissue that secretes testosterone.
_____ Contains enzymes utilized for penetration of ovum.
_____ Secretes human chorionic gonadotropin.
_____ Secretes prostaglandins into semen.
_____ Responsible for final maneuvering for
        penetration of ova.

197.   (cont.)

_____ Supplies fructose utilized by sperm for energy.

_____ Destined to become the fetal portion of the placenta.

_____ Semen expelled from penis.

_____ Consists primarily of the nucleus that contains the sperm's genetic information.

_____ Serves as a route by which nutrients reach developing sperm cells.

_____ Organ of exchange between mother and fetus.

_____ Secretes alkaline fluid to neutralize acidic vaginal secretions.

_____ Portion of blastocyst responsible for accomplishing implantation.

_____ Structure within which an ovum develops prior to ovulation.

_____ Site of final maturation of sperm for motility and fertility in the male.

_____ Contains mitochondria for energy production within sperm.

_____ Secretes estrogen but not progesterone.

_____ Secretes estrogen and progesterone during the first ten weeks of gestation.

_____ Secretes estrogen and progesterone during the last seven months of gestation.

ANSWERS: n, h, o, a, e, g, t, c, b, u, d, r, d, m, q, j, s, u, l, m, p, o, i, p, n, u

198. Write the appropriate letter in the blank by using the
following answer code to indicate the relative magnitude
of the two items in question.

>   (a) = A is greater than B.
>   (b) = B is greater than A.
>   (c) = A and B are approximately equal.

_____ A. The length of the luteal phase of the average
            menstrual cycle.
         B. The length of the follicular phase of the average
            menstrual cycle.

_____ A. The length of the luteal phase of the ovarian cycle.
         B. The length of the secretory phase of the menstrual
            cycle.

_____ A. The number of chromosomes in the ovulated secondary
            oocyte.
         B. The number of chromosomes in a primary oocyte.

_____ A. The number of primary follicles present in the ovary
            at any time during the menstrual cycle.
         B. The number of mature follicles just before ovulation.

_____ A. Plasma concentration of estrogen during the follicular
            phase of the ovarian cycle.
         B. Plasma concentration of estrogen during the luteal
            phase of the ovarian cycle.

_____ A. Plasma concentration of progesterone during the
            follicular phase of the ovarian cycle.
         B. Plasma concentration of progesterone during the luteal
            phase of the ovarian cycle.

ANSWERS: c, c, b, a, a, b

AUDIOVISUAL AIDS

Films

A list of films available from West Publishing Company is
presented in Appendix A. Following are other films that may be
suitable. The sources for these films, which are coded by
abbreviation, are provided in Appendix B.

>   Achieving Sexual Maturity, JW, 21 min.

>   A New Life, FM, 26 min.

Animal Hormones II: Regulation of the Human Menstrual Cycle (VCR), EI, 30 min.

A Woman's Body, FHS, 49 min.

Basic Nature of Sexual Reproduction, IU, 15 min.

Birth Control: The Choices, CH, 25 min.

Breast: Self-Examination, ACS, 16 min.

Cervical Cancer: A Warning to Women, FHS, 19 min.

Coming Together, FM, 26 min.

Contraception, JW, 23 min.

Contraceptive Methods, MF, 25 min.

Female Genitalia, JBL, 10 min.

Fertilization, MH, 28 min.

Herpes: The Forgotten Disease, FHS 28 min.

High-Speed Cinematography of Human Spermatozoa, NYU, 17 min.

Homosexuality, FHS, 26 min.

Hormone Control in Human Reproduction, MH, 16 min.

Human Body: Reproductive System, COR, 13 min.

Human Reproduction, CHM, 28 min.

Human Reproduction, MH, 20 min.

Into the World, FM, 26 min.

Male Genitalia, CHM, 28 min.

Ovulation, UI, 15 min.

Ovulation and Egg Transport in Mammals, UW, 14 min.

Patterns of Reproduction and Development, MH, 16 min.

Personal Decision, CG, 30 min.

Physiology of Conception, PS, 30 min.

<u>Physiology of Normal Menstruation</u>, SCH, 25 min.

<u>PMS and Endometriosis</u>, FHS, 19 min.

<u>Premenstrual Syndrome</u>, FHS, 26 min.

<u>Prostaglandins: Tomorrow's Physiology?</u>, UJ, 22 min.

<u>Reproduction</u>, MH, 28 min.

<u>Reproductive or Sexual Cycles in the Female</u>, TNF, 18 min.

<u>Sex Hormones and Sexual Density</u>, FHS, 26 min.

<u>Sperm Maturation in the Male Reproductive Tract: Development of Motility</u>, IF, 14 min.

<u>Steroids: Crossing the Line</u>, FHS, 54 min.

<u>Steroids: Shortcut to Make-Believe Muscles</u>, CBS, 32 min.

<u>Studies in Human Fertility</u>, SCH, 30 min.

<u>Sudden Changes: Post Hysterectomy Syndrome</u>, CG, 29 min.

<u>The Egg and Sperm</u>, MH, 15 min.

<u>The Female</u>, IM, 29 min.

<u>The Inguinal Canal and Scrotal Contents</u>, NFM, 25 min.

<u>The Living Body: Coming Together</u>, FM, 30 min.

<u>The Male</u>, IM, 29 min.

<u>The Male Sex Hormone</u>, SCH, 24 min.

<u>The Menopause Story</u>, CF, 30 min.

<u>The Menstrual Cycle</u>, EL, 12 min.

<u>The Menstrual Cycle</u>, LER, 21 min.

<u>The Physiology of Normal Menstruation</u>, LLU, 24 min.

<u>The Sexually Mature Adult</u>, JW, 16 min.

<u>The Ultimate Test Animal</u>, CG, 15 min.

<u>Vasectomy</u>, CH, 17 min.

<u>VD: A Newer Focus</u>, AEF, 20 min.

VD: A Plague on Our House, NBC

Venereal Diseases: The Hidden Epidemic, EBE, 23 min.

What Can a Guy Do?, CG, 15 min.

Where Spermatozoa Are Formed, UI, 9 min.

Software

Animal Reproduction, CBS. Covers gametogenesis and fertilization.

Contraception, EI. Describes how eight different contraceptive methods work.

Dynamics of the Human Reproductive System, EI. Describes reproductive structures and their functions.

Meiosis, SSS. Covers gamete formation, oogenesis, and spermatogenesis.

Reproduction, EI. Covers the entire reproductive process.

Sexually Transmitted Diseases, HRM. Discusses the implication of STD's, including AIDS.

Urinary System and Reproductive Systems, PLP. Covers organs and structures of both reproductive systems.

Venereal Disease, EI. Describes various diseases, treatments, causes, transmission, and prevention.

APPENDIX A
West's Life Science Video Library

The list of films below are available from West Publishing Company for use on VHS machines. Adopters may select films at no charge according to the following policy:

Adopters of 50 copies of a text may select one video at no charge.

Adopters of 100 copies of a text may select two videos at no charge.

Adopters of 200 copies of a text may select three videos at no charge.

Adopters of 300 copies of a text may select four videos at no charge.

Adopters of 400 copies or more of a text may select five videos at no charge.

Contact your West representative for further details.

Landscapes and Interiors. This program introduces students to Human Biology by examining a wide range of human activities such as how the body enables us to live in diverse climates and perform diverse functions. Extraordinary close-up filming of the body's exterior and interior enables viewers to see the immensely complex and interactive systems that constitute the living body. (26 minutes)

Muscle Power. This program demonstrates, on a microscopic level, what happens when a kung fu master is at work: how muscles work, how two types of molecules telescoping against each other produce enormous strength as they work in large numbers, how muscles of the heart and digestive tract move without conscious direction. (26 minutes)

Nerves at Work. This program looks at nerve signals and how they are transmitted. It examines the chemical and electrical activities of networks of nerve cells in contact, and the part played by nerve messages in reflex activities. (26 minutes)

Two Hearts that Beat as One. This program describes the structure and functioning of the heart. It analyzes the basic components of the heart-muscle, valves and pacemaker - and shows how each one contributes to the demands of daily life. (26 minutes)

Life under Pressure. This program follows the journey of a red blood cell through the circulatory system. It demonstrates the efficiency of the system as it delivers oxygen and food to all parts of the body and removes wastes before they can do harm. It shows how the veins and arteries are structured to perform their tasks, such as muscular arteries transmitting the force of the heart beat, and how veins with valves insure the blood's return to the heart. (26 minutes)

Internal Defenses. This program examines how the body responds when bacteria or viruses invade our system. With the common cold as the main example, it demonstrates the sequence of events from viral attack to recovery. Examined are the roles of the spleen, the lymphatic system, and the white blood cells. It also explains the body's production of antibodies.

Shares in the Future. This program looks at how the male and female bodies are prepared for reproduction. It demonstrates the characteristics of sperm and ova and shows how each contains a partial blueprint for future offspring. The mechanism of cell division is shown through exceptional microphotography and the mechanisms of heredity are carefully described. (26 minutes)

A new Life. A new Life follows the development of a fertilized egg through birth. With amazing photography of a fetus in the womb, the film examines how a baby is "sculpted" from basic cell mass, how the timing of various states of fetal development is controlled, and what life is like for a fetus. (26 minutes)

Messengers. The delicate interplay of hormones is responsible for all the events of reproduction. How many other body processes are controlled and coordinated by these chemical messengers becomes apparent in this program, which follows the role hormones play in response to a sudden emergency: the "flight or fight" reaction. (26 minutes)

Air Pollution: Outdoor. This program examines how fuels burn and how they can be made to burn more completely with fewer hazardous by-products, how pollutants can be filtered out before they escape into the environment and how they can be recycled or disposed of safely, and the status of research into new and cleaner fuels and combustion methods. (16 minutes)

Restoring the Environment. This program provides a look at how technology is being used to correct environmental problems that technology created. It shows the EPA's Oils and Hazardous Materials Spills branch where a mobile incinerator was developed for use in the destruction of PBC's, and a private electroplating business which has developed a pollution control system that may save an entire industry while protecting the environment. (26 minutes)

Heredity and Mutation. This program introduces the concepts of naturally-occurring and man-induced mutagens; demonstrates how X-radiation and chemical additives can produce genetic mutations; and shows how DNA is extracted and precipitated. Dr. Maclyn McCarty, one of three researchers who identified DNA as the substance that transformed one variety of Pneumococcus into another, is introduced. After viewing the program, students should understand why Drosophila melanogaster is so well-suited to genetic investigation, how mutation can be induced by chemicals, and how inherited variation is the result of a change in genetic code of DNA. (20 minutes)

The Evolution of Man. This program examines and analyzes a large 2.5 million-year-old fossil find in South Africa which includes fossils similar to man. It shows how measurements and comparisons are made between structures of these fossils and modern man. It also investigates the linkage between climatic change at the time and the formation of grasslands, as well as the apparent division in the evolutionary line. After viewing the program, students should have a basic understanding of the guideposts in human evolution. (20 minutes)

Available from the CNN Nutrition Videos Library:

Eating Healthy for Life. Take a special journey with Carolyn O'Neil as she explores good nutrition habits throughout the nation. Featured are people whose lives have been changed by good nutrition.

The following videos from **West's Health, Nutrition, and Fitness** video library are also available:

A Matter of Fat

Aids: Our Worst Fears

Alcohol Addiction

Beating the Depression Blues

Crack

Designer Bodies

Eating for Fitness

Here's to Your Health - Cancer: How to Detect and Prevent It

Here's to Your Health - Cancer: The Causes

Here's to Your Health - Cancer Treatment: A Success Story in the Making

Here's to Your Health - Sports Injuries

Here's to Your Health - Stress: Is Your Lifestyle Killing You?

Inheriting Alcoholism

Junk Food and Nutrition

My Heart, Your Heart

Sexually Transmitted Disease

Showdown on Tobacco Road

Starting and Sticking with Exercise

Stress to Your Advantage

Sweetness and Health

The New Sensible Workout

The Ten Most Asked Questions About Fat

The Ten Most Asked Questions About Food

ACC. . . Appleton-Century Crofts, Inc., 440 Park Avenue South, New York, NY 10016

ACS. . . American Cancer Society, 219 East 42nd Street, New York, NY 10017

AEF. . . American Educational Films, 132 Lasky Drive, Beverly Hills, CA 90212

AF . . . Academy Films, P.O. Box 1023, Venice, CA 90291

AHA. . . American Heart Association, 44 East 23rd Street, New York, NY 10010

AJN. . . American Journal of Nursing Film Library, 10 Columbus Circle, New York, NY 10019

AMA. . . American Medical Association, c/o Association-Sterling Films, 2221 South Live Street, Los Angeles, CA 90007

APS. . . American Physiological Society, 9650 Rockville Pike, Bethesda, MD 20814

ASF. . . Association-Sterling Films, 2221 South Live Street, Los Angeles, CA 90007

ASFT . . Association-Sterling, 8615 Directors Row, Dallas, TX 75240

AVC. . . A-V Corp., 2518 N. Boulevard, Houston, TX 77066

BARR . . Barr Films, P.O. Box 7878, 12 Schabarum Ave., Irwindale, CA 91706

BAX. . . Baxter Healthcare Corporation Creative Services, 1 Baxter Parkway, Deerfield, IL 60015

BFA. . A Educational Media, Division of CBS, Inc., 2211 Michigan Avenue, P.O. Box 1795, Santa Monica, CA 90404

BL . . . Bausch and Lomb, Inc., Film Distribution Service, 635 St. Paul St., Rochester, NY 14602

BTC. . . Bell Telephone Companies, c/o local offices

BNA. . . BNA Communications, 9401 Decoverly Hall Road, Rockville, Maryland 20850

BNF. . . Benchmark Films, Inc., 145 Scarborough Road, Briar-
cliff Manor, NY 10510

BYU. . . Brigham Young University, DMDP Media Business Services, W164 Stadium, Provo, UT 84602

CBS. . . Carolina Biological Supply Company, Burlington, NC
27215 -or- P.O. Box 187, Gladstone, OR 97027

CCM. . . CCM Films, Inc., 866 3rd Avenue, New York, NY 10022

CDL. . . Cambridge Development Laboratory, 100 5th Avenue,
Waltham, MA 02154

CF . . . Churchill Films, 12210 Nebraska Ave., Los Angeles, CA
90025

CFV. . . Coronet Film and Video, 108 Wilmot Rd., Deerfield, IL
60015

CG . . . Cinema Guild, 1697 Broadway, New York, NY 10019

CH . . . Churchill Films, 662 North Robertson Boulevard, Los
Angeles, 90069

CHM. . . Cleveland Health Museum, 8911 Euclid Ave., Cleveland,
OH 44106

CON. . . Conduir, P.O. Box 388, Iowa City, IA 52244

COR. . . Coronet Films, 65 East South Water Street, Chicago, IL
60601

CW . . . Communications World, 2316 2nd Avenue, Seattle, WA
98121

DUKE . . Duke University School of Medicine, Durham, NC 27702

EBC. . . Education Broadcasting Corporation, Distributed by
Films Incorporated, New York, NY

EBE. . . Encyclopedia Britannica Educational Corp., 425 North
Michigan Avenue, Chicago, IL 60611

EBF. . . Encyclopedia Britannica Education Corp., 425 N. Michigan Ave., Chicago, IL 60611

EFL. . . Edward Feil Productions, 4614 Prospect Avenue, Cleveland, OH 44103

EI . . . Educational Images, P.O. Box 367, Lyons Falls, NY 13368

EL... Eli Lilly and Co., Medical Division, Indianapolis, IN 46206

EUT. . . Emory University Television Network, Calhoun Medical Library, Atlanta, GA

FA . . . Film Associates of California, 6121 Sunset Boulevard, Los Angeles, CA 90028

FHS. . . Films for the Humanities and Sciences, Box 2053, Princeton, NJ 08543

FM . . . Films for the Humanities, Box 2053, Princeton, NJ 08540

FS . . . Florida State University Instructional Media Center, Tallahassee, FL 32206

HA . . . Hartley Productions, Cat Rock Road, Cos Cob, CN 06807

HR . . . Harper and Row College Media Department, 10 East 53rd Street, New York, NY 10022

HRM. . . Human Resources Media Software, 175 Tompkins Avenue, Pleasantville, NY 10570

HRW. . . Holt, Rinehart and Winston, 383 Madison Avenue, New York, NY 10017

ICI. . . Imperial Chemical Industries, Inc., P.O. Box 1274, 151 South St., Stamford, CT 06904

ICIA . . ICI American, Inc., Cowcord Pike and Murphy Road, Wilmington, DE 19899

IF . . . Iowa Films, AVC Media Library, University of Iowa Media Center, C-5 East Hall, Iowa City, IA 52240

IFB. . . International Film Bureau, 332 S. Michigan Ave., Chicago, IL 60604

IM . . . Insight Media, 121 West 85th St., New York, NY 10024

IOWA . . Film Productions Unit, Iowa State University, Ames, IA
50010

IP . . . Iwanami Productions, Inc., 22-2 Kanda Misakicho,
Chiyoda-Ku, Tokyo, Japan

ISC. . . Instructional Services Center, University of South
Carolina, Columbia, SC 29208

IU . . . Indiana University Audio-Visual Center, Bloomington,
IN 47405

JBL. . . J.B. Lippincott, East Washington Square, Philadelphia,
PA 19105

JF . . . Journal Films, 930 Pitner Avenue, Evanston, IL 60202

JW . . . John Wiley, Inc., 605 3rd Avenue, New York, NY 10016

KAL. . . Kalmia, Department C11, 21 West Circle, Concord, MA
01742

KSU. . . Kent State University Audiovisual Services, Kent, OH
44242

LER. . . Lilly Educational Resources Program, Department MC-
340, Eli Lilly and Company, P.O. Box 100B, Indianapolis, IN 46202

LL . . . Lederle Laboratories, Danbury, CT 06810

LLU. . . Loma Linda University Motion Picture Library, Loma
Linda, CA 90033

LPI. . . Lawren Productions, Inc., P.O. Box 666, Mendocino, CA
95460

MAC. . . The Macmillan Company, 866 3rd Avenue, New York, NY
10022

MG . . . Open University. The Media Guild, San Diego, CA
92112

MF . . . Milner-Fenwick, 2125 Greenspring Drive, Timonium, MD
21093

MGHT . . McGraw-Hill Films, 674 Via de la Valle, P.O. Box 641,
Del Mar, Ca 92014

MH . . . McGraw-Hill Book Company, Text-Film Division, 1221
Avenue of the Americas, New York, NY 10020

MI . . . Medcom, Inc., 1633 Broadway, New York, NY 10019

MIS. . . Moody Institute of Science Film Division, 1200 East Washington Boulevard, Whittier, CA 90606

MLA. . . Modern Learning Aids, P.O. Box 1717, Rochester, NY 14603

NAC. . . National Audio-Visual Center, National Archives, General Services Administration, Washington, DC 20409

NBC. . . NBC TV, Los Angeles, CA 90064 -or- 30 Rockefeller Plaza, New York, NY 10020

NET. . . NET Film Service, Indiana University, Bloomington, IN 47405

NF . . . National Foundation, 800 2nd Avenue, New York, NY 10019

NFM. . . National Foundation - March of Dimes, Professional Film Library, 600 Grand Avenue, Ridgefield, NY 07657

NG . . . National Geographic Society Education Services, Department 83, Washington, DC 20036

NIH. . . National Institutes of Health, 7500 Wisconsin Avenue, Bethesda, MD 20014

NM . . . National Medical Audiovisual Center, P.O. Box 13973, Station K, Atlanta, GA 30324

NYU. . . New York University, Film Library, 26 Washington Place, New York, NY 10030

OER. . . Office of Education Resources, University of Missouri, Kansas, MO

PAR. . . Paramount Communications, 5451 Marathon St., Hollywood, CA 90038

PE . . . Perennial Education, 477 Roger Williams, P.O. Box 855, Highland Park, IL 60035

PFP. . . Pyramid Films, P.O. Box 1048, Santa Monica, CA 90406

PH . . . Prentice-Hall Media, Inc., Service Code KB, 150 White Plains Road, Tarrytown, NY 10591

PHC. . . Phoenix Film Company, 468 Park Avenue South, New York, NY 10016

PLP. . . Projected Learning Programs, Inc., P.O. Box 2002, Chico, CA 95927

PMR. . . Peter M. Robeck and Co. Inc., Dist. by Time-Life Films Inc., 20 Biekman Place, New York, NY 10022

PRI. . . Professional Research, Inc., 461 North Labrea, Los Angeles, CA 90036

PS . . . Pennsylvania State University Audiovisual Services, University Park, PA 16802

PSP. . . Popular Science Publishing, 355 Lexington Avenue, New York, NY 10017

PYR. . . Pyramid Film Productions, P.O. Box 1048, Santa Monica, CA 90406

QP . . . Q-ED Productions, P.O. Box 1608, Burbank, CA 91507

RUF. . . Rockefeller University Film Service, P.O. Box 72, New York, NY 10021

SB . . . Senses Bureau, University of California at San Diego, P.O. Box 109, La Jolla, CA 92037

SCH. . . Schering Corp., 1011 Morris Avenue, Union, NJ 07083

SCI. . . Scientificom Audio Visual Distribution Center, 708 Dearborn St., Chicago, Il 60610

SEF. . . Sterling Educational Films, 241 East 34th Street, New York, NY 10016

SNM. . . Society of Nuclear Medicine, New York, NY

SOV. . . Southern Oregon Video Enterprises, P.O. Box 400, Ashland, OR 97520

SP . . . Stouffer Productions, P.O. Box 15057, Aspen, CO 81611

SRS. . . SRS Productions, 4224 Ellenita Ave., Tarzana, CA 91356

SSS. . . Science Software Systems, Inc., 11899 West Pico Boulevard, West Los Angeles, CA 90064

SU . . . Syracuse University Audiovisual Center, Syracuse, NY 13210

SV . . . L. Heimer. Springer-Verlog, New York, NY

SYN. . . Syntex Laboratories, 3401 Hillview Avenue, Palo Alto, CA 94304

TLV. . . Time Life Video Distribution Center, 100 Eisenhower Drive, P.O. Box 644, Paramus, NY 07652

TRA. . . Trainex Corp., P.O. Box 116, Garden Grove, CA 92642

UC . . . University of California Extension Media Center, 2223 Fulton St., Berkeley, CA 94702

UI . . . University of Illinois Film Center, 1325 South Oak Street, Champaign, IL 61820

UJ . . . Upjohn Professional Film Library, 7000 Portage Road, Kalamazoo, MI 49001

UM . . . University of Michigan, Michigan Media, 400 4th Street, Ann Arbor, MI 48109

UP . . . Upjohn Co., Film Library, 7000 Portage Rd., Kalamazoo, MI 94001

USC. . . University of Southern California, Department of Cinema, University Park, Los Angeles, CA 90007

USNAC. . U.S. National Audiovisual Center, General Services Administration, Washington, DC 20409

UT . . . University of Texas Medical Branch, Galveston, TX 77550

UW . . . United World Films, Inc., 221 Park Avenue South, New York, NY 10003

VA . . . VA, National Audiovisual Center, Capital Heights, MD

WARDS. . Ward's Natural History Establishment, P.O. Box 1712, Rochester, NY 14603

WAV. . . Western Audio Visual Enterprises, 826 North Cole Avenue, Hollywood, CA 90038

WAYNE. . Wayne State University, Media Services, 151 Purdy Library, Detroit, MI 48202

WFL. . . Wellcome Film Library, The Wellcome Building, 183-193 Euston Road, London N.W.1 England

WG . . . West Glen Films, Inc., 565 Fifth Avenue, New York, NY 10017

WHS. . . Wood Health Sciences Center, University of Texas,
Houston, TX

WNS. . . Wards Natural Science Establishment, 300 Ridge Road,
East Rochester, NY 14622

WSU. . . Wayne State University Center for Instructional
Technology, 77 West Canfield Avenue, Detroit, MI 48202

WX . . . Wexler Film Production, 801 North Seward Street, Los
Angeles, CA 91608

Biological Supply Houses

Carolina Biological Supply Company, 2700 York Road, Burlington,
NC 27215

Connecticut Valley Biological Supply Company, Inc., P.O. Box
326, Southampton, MA 01703

Delta Biologicals, P.O. Box 26666, Tucson, AZ 85726

Difco Laboratories, P.O. Box 1058A, Detroit, MI 48232

Fisher Scientific Company, 4901 West LeMoyne Street, Chicago,
IL 60651

Hubbard Scientific Company, 1946 Raymond Drive, Northbrook, IL
60062

International Biologics, Inc., 531 9th Street NW, New Brighton,
MN 55112

Nasco International, Inc., 901 Janesville Avenue, Fort Atkin-
son, WI 53538

Rand McNally Bio-Centre, P.O. Box 40, Somerset, WI 54025

Science Related Materials, Inc., P.O. Box 1368, Janesville, WI
53547

VWR Scientific, Inc., P.O. Box 1050, Rochester, NY 14603

Ward's Natural Science Establishment, 5100 West Henrietta Road,
P.O. Box 92912, Rochester, NY 14692

Waubun Laboratories, Inc., Drawer C, Schriever, LA 70395

Chapter 1, text page 13

1. The respiratory system eliminates internally produced CO_2 to the external environment. A decrease in CO_2 in the internal environment brings about a reduction in respiratory activity (that is, slower, shallower breathing) so that CO_2 produced within the body is allowed to accumulate instead of being blown off as rapidly as normal to the external environment. The extra CO_2 retained in the body increases the CO_2 levels in the internal environment to normal.

2. (b) below normal, (c) elevated, (b) be too acidic

3. immune defense system

4. b

5. widening

    The skin blood vessels widen when a person is engaged in strenuous exercise. As a result of this vessel widening, or vasodilation, increased blood flows through the skin, carrying the extra heat generated by increased muscle activity to the surface of the body. Loss of the extra heat from the skin surface to the surrounding environment helps maintain body temperature.

6. Loss of fluids threatens the maintenance of proper plasma volume and blood pressure. Loss of acidic digestive juices threatens the maintenance of the proper pH in the internal fluid environment. The urinary system will help restore the proper plasma volume and pH by reducing the amount of water and acid eliminated in the urine. The respiratory system will help restore the pH by adjusting the rate of removal of acid-forming CO_2. Adjustments will be made in the circulatory system to help maintain blood pressure despite fluid loss. Increased thirst will encourage increased fluid intake to help restore plasma volume. These compensatory changes in the urinary, respiratory, and circulatory systems as well as the sensation of thirst will all be regulated by the two control systems, the nervous and endocrine systems. Furthermore, the endocrine system will make internal adjustments to help maintain the concentration of nutrients in the internal environment despite the fact that no new nutrients are being absorbed from the digestive system.

1.   1000 gm/2.2 lb = 73,000 gm/x lb
      1000 x = 160,600
      x = approximately 160 pounds

2.   lysosomes

3.   When the body cells lose most of their ATP-producing
      capacity as a result of cyanide poisoning, they are
      unable to accomplish membrane transport, synthesis of
      new chemical compounds, and mechanical work. Death
      would occur as a result of the inability of the heart
      muscle to contract and pump blood and the respiratory
      muscles to contract to accomplish breathing. Death
      would occur before other ATP-dependent activities
      such as synthesis of secretory products or the
      membrane transport involved in urine formation would
      be seriously impaired.

4.   ATP is required for muscle contraction. Muscles are able
      to store limited supplies of nutrient fuel for use in the
      generation of ATP. During anaerobic exercise, muscles
      generate ATP from these nutrient stores by means of
      glycolysis, which yields two molecules of ATP per glucose
      molecule processed. During aerobic exercise, muscles can
      generate ATP by means of oxidative phosphorylation, which
      yields thirty-six molecules of ATP per glucose molecule
      processed. Because glycolysis inefficiently generates ATP
      from nutrient fuels, it rapidly depletes the muscle's
      limited stores of fuel and ATP can no longer be produced
      to sustain the muscle's contractile activity. Aerobic
      exercise, on the other hand, can be sustained for pro-
      longed periods. Not only does oxidative phosphorylation
      use far less nutrient fuel to generate ATP, but it can be
      supported by nutrients delivered to the muscle by means of
      the blood instead of relying on stored fuel in the muscle.
      Intense anaerobic exercise outpaces the ability to deliver
      supplies to the muscle by the blood, so the muscle must
      rely on stored fuel and inefficient glycolysis, thus
      limiting anaerobic exercise to brief periods of time
      before energy sources are depleted.

5.   skin.

      The mutant keratin weakens the skin cells of patients with
      epidermolysis bullosa so that the skin blisters in
      response to even a light touch.

6.   Some hereditary forms of male sterility involving
      nonmotile sperm have been traced to defects in the
      cytoskeletal components of the sperm's flagella. These

same individuals usually also have long histories of recurrent respiratory-tract disease because the same type of defects are present in their respiratory cilia, which are unable to clear mucus and inhaled particles from the respiratory system.

Chapter 3, text page 80

1.   c.

   As Na^+ moves from side 1 to side 2 down its concentration gradient, Cl^- remains on side 1, unable to permeate the membrane. The resultant separation of charges produces a membrane potential, negative on side 1 due to unbalanced chloride ions and positive on side 2 due to unbalanced sodium ions. Sodium does not continue to move to side 2 until its concentration gradient is dissipated because of the development of an opposing electrical gradient.

2.   d. active transport

   Leveling off of the curve designates saturation of a carrier molecule, so carrier-mediated transport is involved. The graph depicts that active transport is being utilized instead of facilitated diffusion because the concentration of the substance in the intracellular fluid is greater than the concentration in the extracellular fluid at all points until after the transport maximum is reached. Thus, the substance is being moved against a concentration gradient, so active transport must be the method of transport being used.

3.   c.

   The action potentials would stop as they met in the middle. As the two action potentials moving toward each other both reached the middle of the axon, the two adjacent patches of membrane in the middle would be in a refractory period so further propagation of either action potential would be impossible.

4.   A subthreshold stimulus would transiently depolarize the membrane but not sufficiently to bring the membrane to threshold, so no action potential would occur. Because a threshold stimulus would bring the membrane to threshold, an action potential would occur. An action potential of the same magnitude and duration would occur in response to a suprathreshold stimulus as to a threshold stimulus. Because of the all or none law, a stimulus larger than that necessary to bring the membrane to threshold would not produce a larger action potential. (The magnitude of the stimulus is coded in the frequency of action poten-

tials generated in the neuron, not the _size_ of the action potentials.)

5.   The hand could be pulled away from the hot stove by flexion of the elbow accomplished by summation of EPSPs at the cell bodies of the neurons controlling the biceps muscle, thus bringing these neurons to threshold. The subsequent action potentials generated in these neurons would stimulate contraction of the biceps. Simultaneous contraction of the triceps muscle, which would oppose the desired flexion of the elbow, could be prevented by generation of IPSPs at the cell bodies of the neurons controlling this muscle. These IPSPs would keep the triceps neurons from reaching threshold and firing so that the triceps would not be stimulated to contract.

6.   Initiation and propagation of action potentials would not occur in nerve fibers acted upon by local anesthetic because blockage of Na^+ channels by the local anesthetic would prevent the massive opening of voltage-gated Na^+ channels at threshold potential. As a result, pain impulses (action potentials in nerve fibers that carry pain signals) would not be initiated and propagated to the brain and reach the level of conscious awareness.

Chapter 4, text page 116

1.   Only the left hemisphere has language ability. When sharing of information between the two hemispheres is prevented as a result of severance of the corpus callosum, visual information presented only to the right hemisphere cannot be verbally identified by the left hemisphere, because the left hemisphere is unaware of the information. However, the information can be recognized by nonverbal means, of which the right hemisphere is capable.

2.   Insulin excess drives too much glucose into insulin-dependent cells so that the blood glucose falls below normal and insufficient glucose is delivered to the non-insulin-dependent brain. Therefore, the brain, which depends on glucose as its energy source, does not receive adequate nourishment.

3.   c.

      A severe blow to the back of the head is most likely to traumatize the visual cortex in the occipital lobe.

4.   Salivation when seeing or smelling food, striking the appropriate letter on the keyboard when typing, and many of the actions involved in driving a car are conditioned reflexes. The students will have many other examples.

5. Strokes occur when a portion of the brain is deprived of its vital O_2 and glucose supply either because the cerebral blood vessel supplying the area is blocked by a clot or has ruptured. Although a clot-dissolving drug could be helpful in restoring blood flow through a cerebral vessel blocked by a clot, such a drug would be detrimental in the case of a ruptured cerebral vessel sealed by a clot. Dissolution of a clot sealing a ruptured vessel would lead to renewed hemorrhage through the vessel and exacerbation of the problem.

6. The deficits following the stroke - numbness and partial paralysis on the upper right side of the body and inability to speak - are indicative of damage to the left somatosensory cortex and left primary motor cortex in the regions devoted to the upper part of the body plus Broca's area.

Chapter 5, text page 167

1. Pain is a conscious warning that tissue damage is occurring or about to occur. A patient unable to feel pain because of a nerve disorder does not consciously take measures to withdraw from painful stimuli and thus prevent more serious tissue damage.

2. The defect would be in the left optic tract or optic radiation.

3. Fluid accumulation in the middle ear in accompaniment with middle ear infections impedes the normal movement of the tympanic membrane, ossicles, and oval window in response to sound. All of these structures vibrate less vigorously in the presence of fluid, thereby causing temporary hearing impairment. Chronic fluid accumulation in the middle ear is sometimes relieved by surgical implantation of drainage tubes in the eardrum. Hearing is restored to normal as the fluid drains to the exterior. Usually the tubes "fall out" as the eardrum heals and pushes out the foreign object.

4. By promoting arteriolar constriction, epinephrine administered in conjunction with local anesthetics reduces blood flow to the region and thus helps keep the anesthetic in the region instead of being carried away by the blood.

5. By interfering with normal acetylcholine activity at the neuromuscular junction, α bungarotoxin leads to skeletal-muscle paralysis, with death ultimately occurring as a result of an inability to contract the diaphragm and breathe.

6. Syncope most frequently occurs as a result of inadequate delivery of blood carrying sufficient oxygen and glucose supplies to the brain. Possible causes include circulatory disorders such as impaired pumping of the heart or low blood pressure; respiratory disorders resulting in poorly oxygenated blood; anemia, in which the oxygen-carrying capacity of the blood is reduced; or low blood glucose resulting from improper endocrine management of blood glucose levels. Vertigo, on the other hand, typically results from a dysfunction of the vestibular apparatus, arising for example from viral infection or trauma, or abnormal neural processing of vestibular information, as for example with a brain tumor.

Chapter 6, text page 201

1. By placing increased demands on the heart to sustain increased delivery of O_2 and nutrients to working skeletal muscles, regular aerobic exercise induces changes in cardiac muscle that enable it to use O_2 more efficiently, such as increasing the number of capillaries supplying blood to the heart muscle. Intense exercise of short duration, such as weight training, in contrast, does not induce cardiac efficiency. Because this type of exercise relies on anaerobic glycolysis for ATP formation, there are no demands placed on the heart for increased delivery of blood to the working muscles.

2. The length of the thin filaments is represented by the distance between a Z line and the edge of the adjacent H zone. This distance remains the same in a relaxed and contracted myofibril, leading to the conclusion that the thin filaments do not change in length during muscle contraction.

3. Regular bouts of anaerobic, short-duration, high-intensity resistance training would be recommended for competitive downhill skiing. By promoting hypertrophy of the fast glycolytic fibers, such exercise better adapts the muscles to activities that require intense strength for brief periods, such as a swift, powerful descent downhill. In contrast, regular aerobic exercise would be more beneficial for competitive cross-country skiers. Aerobic exercise induces metabolic changes within the oxidative fibers that enable the muscles to use O_2 more efficiently. These changes, which include an increase in mitochondria and capillaries within the oxidative fibers, adapt the muscles to better endure the prolonged activity of cross-country skiing without fatiguing.

4. Botulinum toxin blocks the release of acetylcholine from the terminal button in response to an action potential in

the motor neuron. Dystonias are believed to occur as a result of an abnormality in the basal nuclei, leading to excessive release of acetylcholine from motor neuron terminals at the affected muscles. Injection of minute doses of botulinum toxin in the affected area can be used to reduce acetylcholine activity to normal levels so that the excessive, disruptive muscle-contracting activity can be curbed. Because the effect is temporary, patients require periodic injections. This treatment provides relief from the symptoms but does not address the underlying central nervous system disorder.

5. a.
Apparently, all of the muscle fibers within a single motor unit are of the same fiber type. This pattern usually is established early in life, but there is good evidence that the two types of fast-twitch fibers are interconvertible, depending on training efforts. Regular endurance activities can convert fast-glycolytic fibers to fast-oxidative fibers (capitalizing on the fast-oxidative fibers' resistance to fatigue during endurance activities),whereas fast-oxidative fibers can be shifted to fast-glycolytic fibers in response to power events such as weight training (captitalizing on the fast-glycolytic fibers' speed of contraction in power events). Although training can induce changes in muscle fibers' metabolic support systems, whether a fiber is fast- or slow-twitch is apparently established early in development by the fiber's nerve supply. Experimental switching of motor neurons supplying slow muscle fibers with those supplying fast fibers results in a gradual reversal of the speed at which these fibers contract.

6. The muscles in the immobilized leg have undergone disuse atrophy. The physician or physical therapist can prescribe regular resistance-type exercises that specifically use the atrophied muscles to help restore them to their normal size.

Chapter 7, text page 235

1. Because, at a given heart rate, the interval between a premature beat and the next normal beat is longer than the interval between two normal beats, the heart fills for a longer period of time following a premature beat before the next period of contraction and emptying begins. Because of the longer filling time, the end-diastolic volume is larger, and, according to the Frank-Starling law of the heart, the subsequent stroke volume will also be correspondingly larger.

2. Trained athletes' hearts are stronger and can pump blood more efficiently so that the resting stroke volume is larger than in an untrained person. For example, if the resting stroke volume of a strong-hearted athlete is 100 ml, a resting heart rate of only 50 beats/minute produces a normal resting cardiac output of 5000 ml/minute. An untrained individual with a resting stroke volume of 70 ml, in contrast, must have a heart rate of about 70 beats/minute to produce a comparable resting cardiac output.

3. The direction of flow through a patent ductus arteriosus is reverse of that which occurs through this vascular connection during fetal life. With a patent ductus arteriosis, some of the blood present in the aorta is shunted into the pulmonary artery because, after birth, the aortic pressure is greater than the pulmonary artery pressure. This abnormal blood flow produces a so-called "machinery murmur," which lasts throughout the cardiac cycle but is more intense during systole and less intense during diastole. Thus, the murmur waxes and wanes with each beat of the heart, sounding somewhat like a washing machine as the agitator rotates back and forth. The murmur is present throughout the cardiac cycle because a pressure differential between the aorta and pulmonary artery is present during both systole and diastole. The murmur is more intense during systole because more blood is diverted through the patent ductus arteriosus as a result of the greater pressure differential between the aorta and pulmonary artery during ventricular systole than during ventricular diastole. Typically, the systolic aortic pressure is 120 mmHg and the systolic pulmonary arterial pressure is 24 mmHg, for a pressure differential of 96 mmHg. By contrast, the diastolic aortic pressure is normally 80 mmHg and the diastolic pulmonary arterial pressure is 8 mmHg, for a pressure differential of 72 mmHg.

4. A transplanted heart that does not have any innervation adjusts the cardiac output to meet the body's changing needs by means of both intrinsic control (the Frank-Starling mechanism) and extrinsic hormonal influences, such as the effect of epinephrine on the rate and strength of cardiac contraction.

5. In left bundle-branch block, the right ventricle becomes completely depolarized more rapidly than the left ventricle. As a result, the right ventricle contracts before the left ventricle and the right AV valve is forced closed prior to closure of the left AV valve. Because the two AV valves do not close in unison, the first heart sound is "split;" that is, two distinct sounds in close succession

can be detected as closure of the left valve lags behind closure of the right valve.

6. Atrial fibrillation is characterized by rapid, irregular, uncoordinated depolarizations of the atria. Many of these depolarizations reach the AV node at a time when it is not in its refractory period, thus bringing about frequent ventricular depolarizations and a rapid heartbeat. However, since impulses reach the AV node erratically, the ventricular rhythm and thus the heart beat are also very irregular as well as being rapid.

Ventricular filling is only slightly reduced despite the fact that the fibrillating atria are unable to pump blood because most ventricular filling occurs during diastole prior to atrial contraction. Because of the erractic heart beat, variable lengths of time are available between ventricular beats for ventricular filling. However, the majority of ventricular filling occurs early in ventricular diastole after the AV valves first open, so even though the filling period may be shortened, the extent of filling may be near normal. Only when the ventricular filling period is very short is ventricular filling substantially reduced.

Cardiac output, which depends on stroke volume and heart rate, usually is not seriously impaired with atrial fibrillation. Because ventricular filling is only slightly reduced during most cardiac cycles, stroke volume, as determined by the Frank-Starling mechanism, is likewise only slightly reduced. Only when the ventricular filling period is very short and the cardiac-muscle fibers are operating on the lower end of their length-tension curve is the resultant ventricular contraction weak. When the ventricular contraction becomes too weak, the ventricles eject a small or no stroke volume. During most cardiac cycles, however, the slight reduction in stroke volume is often offset by the increased heart rate, so that cardiac output is usually near normal. Furthermore, if the mean arterial blood pressure falls because the cardiac output does decrease, increased sympathetic stimulation of the heart brought about by the baroreceptor reflex helps restore cardiac output to normal by shifting the Frank-Starling curve to the left.

On those cycles that ventricular contractions are too weak to eject enough blood to produce a palpable wrist pulse, if the heart rate is determined directly, either by the apex beat or via the ECG, and the pulse rate is taken concurrently at the wrist, the heart rate will exceed the pulse rate, producing a pulse deficit.

1. An elastic support stocking increases external pressure on the remaining veins in the limb to produce a favorable pressure gradient that promotes venous return to the heart and minimizes swelling that would result from fluid retention in the extremity.

2. a. 125 mm Hg
    b. 77 mm Hg
    c. 48 mm Hg; (125 mm Hg - 77 mm Hg = 48 mm Hg)
    d. 93 mm Hg; [77 + 1/3 (48) = 77 + 16 = 93 mm Hg]
    e. No; no blood would be able to get through the brachial artery, so no sound would be heard.
    f. Yes; blood would flow through the brachial artery when the arterial pressure was between 118 to 125 mm Hg and would not flow through when the arterial pressure fell below 118 mm Hg. The turbulence created by this intermittent blood flow would produce sounds.
    g. No; blood would flow continuously through the brachial artery in smooth, laminar fashion, so no sound would be heard.

3. The classmate has apparently fainted because of insufficient blood flow to the brain as a result of pooling of blood in the lower extremities brought about by prolonged standing still during the laboratory experiment. As the person faints and assumes a horizontal position, the pooled blood will quickly be returned to the heart, improving cardiac output and blood flow to his brain. Trying to get the person up would be counterproductive, so the classmate trying to get him up should be advised to let him remain lying down until he recovers on his own.

4. The drug is apparently causing the arteriolar smooth muscle to relax by means of causing the release of a local vasoactive chemical mediator from the endothelial cells that induces relaxation of the underlying smooth muscle.

5. a. Since activation of alpha-adrenergic receptors in vascular smooth muscle brings about vasoconstriction, blockage of alpha-adrenergic receptors reduces vasoconstrictor activity, thereby lowering the total peripheral resistance and arterial blood pressure.

    b. Drugs that directly relax arteriolar smooth muscle lower arterial blood pressure by promoting arteriolar vasodilation and reducing total peripheral resistance.

    c. Diuretic drugs reduce the plasma volume, thereby lowering arterial blood pressure, by increasing urinary output. Salt and water that normally would have been retained in the plasma are excreted in the urine.

d. Since sympathetic activity promotes generalized arteriolar vasoconstriction, thereby increasing total peripheral resistance and arterial blood pressure, drugs that block the release of norepinephrine from sympathetic endings lower blood pressure by preventing this sympathetic vasoconstrictor effect.

e. Similarly, drugs that act on the brain to reduce sympathetic output lower blood pressure by preventing the effect of sympathetic activity on promoting arteriolar vasoconstriction and the resultant increase in total peripheral resistance and arterial blood pressure.

f. Drugs that block Ca^{2+} channels reduce the entry of Ca^{2+} into the vascular smooth muscle cells from the ECF in response to excitatory input. Since the level of contractile activity in vascular smooth muscle cells depends on their cytosolic Ca^{2+} concentration, drugs that block Ca^{2+} channels reduce the contractile activity of these cells by reducing Ca^{2+} entry and lowering their cytosolic Ca^{2+} concentration. Total peripheral resistance and, accordingly, arterial blood pressure are decreased as a result of reduced arteriolar contractile activity.

g. Drugs that interfere with the production of angiotensin II block activation of the hormonal pathway that promotes salt and water conservation (the renin-angiotensin-aldosterone system). As a result, more salt and water are lost in the urine and less fluid is retained in the plasma. The resultant reduction in plasma volume lowers the arterial blood pressure.

6. The abnormally elevated levels of epinephrine found with a pheochromocytoma bring about secondary hypertension by (1) increasing the heart rate, (2) increasing cardiac contractility, which increases stroke volume, (3) causing venous vasoconstriction, which increases venous return and subsequently stroke volume by means of the Frank-Starling mechanism, and (4) causing arteriolar vasoconstriction, which increases total peripheral resistance. Increased heart rate and stroke volume both lead to increased cardiac output. Increased cardiac output and increased total peripheral resistance both lead to increased arterial blood pressure.

1. Because blood cells have a short life span, they must continuously be replaced through rapid multiplication of precursor stem cells. These rapidly multiplying stem cells may be destroyed inadvertently by chemotherapeutic drugs designed to destroy rapidly multiplying cancer cells. It is important, therefore, to closely monitor blood cell counts to ascertain that the number of functional precursor cells is still adequate to maintain satisfactory levels of circulating blood cells.

2. Most heart attack deaths are attributable to the formation of abnormal clots that prevent normal blood flow. The sought-after chemicals in the "saliva" of blood-sucking creatures are agents that break up or prevent the formation of these abnormal clots.

    Although genetically engineered tissue plasminogen activator (tPA) is already being used as a clot-busting drug, this agent brings about degradation of fibrinogen as well as fibrin.

    Thus, even though the life-threatening clot in the coronary circulation is dissolved, the fibrinogen supplies in the blood are depleted for up to 24 hours until new fibrinogen is synthesized by the liver. If the patient sustains a ruptured vessel in the interim, insufficient fibrinogen might be available to form a blood-staunching clot. For example, many patients treated with tPA suffer hemorrhagic strokes within 24 hours of treatment due to incomplete sealing of a ruptured cerebral vessel. Therefore, scientists are searching for better alternatives to combat abnormal clot formation by examining the naturally-occurring chemicals produced by blood-sucking creatures that permit them to suck a victim's blood without the blood clotting.

3. A vaccine against a particular microbe can be effective only if it induces formation of antibodies and/or activated T cells against a stable antigenic site that is present on all microbes of this type. Because HIV frequently mutates, it has not been possible to produce a vaccine against it. Specific immune responses induced by vaccination against one form of HIV may prove to be ineffective against a slightly modified version of the virus.

4. Failure of the thymus to develop embryonically would lead to an absence of T lymphocytes and no cell-mediated immunity after birth. This outcome would seriously compromise the individual's ability to defend against

viral invasion and cancer.

5. Researchers are currently working on ways to "teach" the
    immune system to view foreign tissue as "self" as a means
    of preventing the immune systems of organ-transplant
    patients from rejecting the foreign tissue while leaving
    the patients' immune defense capabilities fully intact.
    The immunosuppressive drugs currently being used to
    prevent transplant rejection cripple the recipients'
    immune defense systems and leave the patients more vul-
    nerable to microbial invasion.

6. Since the white blood cell count is within the normal
    range, the patient's pneumonia is most likely not caused
    by a bacterial infection. Bacterial infections are
    typically accompanied by an elevated total white blood
    cell count and an increase in percentage of neutrophils.
    Therefore, the pneumonia is probably caused by a virus.
    Because antibiotics are more useful in combating bacterial
    than viral infections, antibiotics are not likely to be
    useful in combating this patient's pneumonia.

Chapter 10, text page 360

1. Total atmospheric pressure decreases with increasing
    altitude, yet the percentage of O_2 in the air remains the
    same. At an altitude of 30,000 feet, the atmospheric
    pressure is only 226 mm Hg. Since 21% of atmospheric air
    consists of O_2, the P_{O_2} of inspired air at 30,000 feet is
    only 47.5 mm Hg, and alveolar P_{O_2} is even lower at about 20
    mm Hg. At this low P_{O_2}, hemoglobin is only about 30%
    saturated with O_2 -- much too low to sustain tissue needs
    for O_2.

    The P_{O_2} of inspired air can be increased by two means when
    flying at high altitude. First, by pressurizing the
    plane's interior to a pressure comparable to that of
    atmospheric pressure at sea level, the P_{O_2} of inspired air
    within the plane is 21% of 760 mm Hg, or the normal 160 mm
    Hg. Accordingly, alveolar and arterial P_{O_2} and percent
    hemoglobin saturation are likewise normal. In the
    emergency situation of failure to maintain internal cabin
    pressure, breathing pure O_2 can raise the P_{O_2} considerably
    above that accomplished by breathing normal air. When
    breathing pure O_2, the entire pressure of inspired air is
    attributable to O_2. For example, with a total atmospheric
    pressure of 226 mm Hg at an altitude of 30,000 feet, the
    P_{O_2} of inspired pure O_2 is 226 mm Hg, which is more than
    adequate to maintain normal arterial hemoglobin
    saturation.

2.   a. Hypercapnia would not accompany the hypoxia
        associated with cyanide poisoning. In
        fact, CO_2 levels decline because oxidative metabolism is
        blocked by the tissue poisons so that CO_2 is not being
        produced.

     b. Hypercapnia could but may not accompany the hypoxia
        associated with pulmonary edema. Pulmonary diffusing
        capacity is reduced in pulmonary edema but O_2 transfer
        suffers more than CO_2 transfer because the diffusion
        coefficient for CO_2 is twenty times that for O_2. As a
        result, hypoxia occurs much more readily than
        hypercapnia in these circumstances. Hypercapnia does
        occur, however, when pulmonary diffusing capacity is
        severely impaired.

     c. Hypercapnia would accompany the hypoxia associated with
        restrictive lung disease because ventilation is
        inadequate to meet the metabolic needs for both O_2
        delivery and CO_2 removal. Both O_2 and CO_2 exchange
        between the lungs and atmosphere are equally affected.

     d. Hypercapnia would not accompany the hypoxia associated
        with high altitude. In fact, arterial Pco_2 levels
        actually decrease. One of the compensatory responses
        in acclimatization to high altitudes is reflex stim-
        ulation of ventilation as a result of the reduction in
        arterial Po_2. This compensatory hyperventilation to
        obtain more O_2 blows off too much CO_2 in the process, so
        arterial Pco_2 levels decline below normal.

     e. Hypercapnia would not accompany the hypoxia associated
        with severe anemia. Reduced O_2-carrying capacity of the
        blood has no influence on blood CO_2 content, so arterial
        Pco_2 levels are normal.

     f. Hypercapnia would exist in accompaniment with circu-
        latory hypoxia associated with congestive heart
        failure. Just as the diminished blood flow fails to
        deliver adequate O_2 to the tissues, it also fails to
        remove sufficient CO_2.

     g. Hypercapnia would accompany the hypoxic hypoxia
        associated with obstructive lung disease because
        ventilation would be inadequate to meet the metabolic
        needs for both O_2 delivery and CO_2 removal. Both O_2 and
        CO_2 exchange between the lungs and atmosphere would be
        equally affected.

3. Po_2 = 122 mmHg

     .21 (atmospheric pressure - partial pressure of H_2O) =
     .21 (630 mm Hg - 47 mm Hg) = .21 (583 mm Hg) = 122 mm Hg

4.   Voluntarily hyperventilating before going underwater
     lowers the arterial Pco_2 but does not increase the O_2
     content in the blood. Because the Pco_2 is below normal,
     the person can hold his or her breath longer than usual
     before the arterial Pco_2 increases to the point that he or
     she is driven to surface for a breath. Therefore, the
     person can stay underwater longer. The risk, however, is
     that the O_2 content of the blood, which was normal, not
     increased, before going underwater, continues to fall.
     Therefore, the O_2 level in the blood can fall dangerously
     low before the CO_2 level builds to the point of driving the
     person to take a breath. Low arterial Po_2 does not
     stimulate respiratory activity until it has plummeted to
     60 mm Hg. Meanwhile, the person may lose consciousness
     and drown due to inadequate O_2 delivery to the brain. If
     the person does not hyperventilate so that both the
     arterial Pco_2 and O_2 content are normal before going
     underwater, the buildup of CO_2 will drive the person to the
     surface for a breath before the O_2 levels fall to a
     dangerous point.

5.   c.
     The arterial Po_2 will be less than the alveolar Po_2 and the
     arterial Pco_2 will be greater than the alveolar Pco_2.
     Because pulmonary diffusing capacity is reduced, arterial
     Po_2 and Pco_2 do not equilibrate with alveolar Po_2 and Pco_2.

     If the person is administered 100% O_2, the alveolar Po_2
     will increase and the arterial Po_2 will increase accord-
     ingly. Even though arterial Po_2 will not equilibrate with
     alveolar Po_2, it will be higher than when the person is
     breathing atmospheric air.

     The arterial Pco_2 will remain the same whether the person
     is administered 100% O_2 or is breathing atmospheric air.
     The alveolar Pco_2 and thus the blood-to-alveolar Pco_2
     gradient are not changed by breathing 100% O_2 because the
     Pco_2 in atmospheric air and 100% O_2 are both essentially
     zero (Pco_2 in atmospheric air = 0.3).

6.   Emphysema is characterized by a collapse of smaller
     respiratory airways and a breakdown of alveolar walls.
     Because of the collapse of smaller airways, airway
     resistance is increased with emphysema. As with other
     chronic obstructive pulmonary diseases, expiration is
     impaired to a greater extent than inspiration because
     airways are naturally dilated slightly more during

inspiration than expiration as a result of the greater
transmural pressure gradient during inspiration. Because
airway resistance is increased, a patient with emphysema
must produce larger-than-normal intra-alveolar pressure
changes to accomplish a normal tidal volume. Unlike quiet
breathing in a normal person, the accessory inspiratory
muscles (neck muscles) and the muscles of active
expiration (abdominal muscles and internal intercostal
muscles) must be brought into play to inspire and expire a
normal tidal volume of air.

The spirogram would be characteristic of chronic
obstructive pulmonary disease. Since the patient
experiences more difficulty emptying the lungs than
filling them, the total lung capacity would be essentially
normal, but the functional residual capacity and the
residual volume would be elevated as a result of the
additional air trapped in the lungs folowing expiration.
Because the residual volume is increased, the inspiratory
capacity and vital capacity will be reduced. Also, the
FEV_1 will be markedly reduced since the airflow rate is
decreased by the airway obstruction. The FEV_1 - to - vital
capacity ratio will be much lower than the normal 80%.

Because of the reduced surface area for exchange as a
result of a breakdown of alveolar walls, gas exchange
would be impaired. Therefore, arterial P_{CO_2} would be
elevated and arterial P_{O_2} reduced compared to normal.

Ironically, administering O_2 to this patient to relieve his
hypoxic condition would markedly depress his drive to
breathe by elevating the arterial P_{O_2} and removing the
primary driving stimulus for respiration. Because of this
danger, O_2 therapy should not be administered or
administered extremely cautiously.

Chapter 11, text page 395

1. The longer loops of Henle in desert rats (known as kangaroo rats) permits a greater magnitude of countercurrent
multiplication and thus a larger medullary vertical
osmotic gradient. As a result, these rodents are able to
produce urine that is concentrated up to an osmolarity of
almost 6000 mosm/l, which is five times more concentrated
than maximally concentrated human urine at 1200 mosm/l.
Because of this tremendous concentrating ability, kangaroo
rats never have to drink; the H_2O produced metabolically
within their cells during oxidation of foodstuff (food + O_2
yields CO_2 + H_2O + energy) is sufficient for their needs.

2. a. 250 mg/min filtered

    filtered load of substance = plasma concentration of substance x GFR

    filtered load of substance = 200 mg/100 ml x 125 ml/min

    filtered load of substance = 250 mg/min

    b. 200 mg/min reabsorbed

    A T_m's worth of the substance will be reabsorbed.

    c. 50 mg/min excreted

    amount of substance excreted = amount of substance filtered - amount of substance reabsorbed

    amount of substance excreted = 250 mg/min - 200 mg/min

    amount of substance excreted = 50 mg/min

3. Aldosterone stimulates Na^+ reabsorption and K^+ secretion by the renal tubules. Therefore, the most prominent features of Conn's syndrome (hypersecretion of aldosterone) are hypernatremia (elevated Na^+ levels in the blood) caused by excessive Na^+ reabsorption, hypophosphatemia (below normal K^+ levels in the blood) caused by excessive K^+ secretion, and hypertension (elevated blood pressure) caused by excessive salt and water retention.

4. Because the descending pathways between the brain and the motor neurons supplying the external urethral sphincter and pelvic diaphragm are no longer intact, the accident victim can no longer voluntarily control micturition. Therefore, bladder emptying in this individual will be governed entirely by the micturition reflex.

5. 75 ml/min

> clearance rate
> of a substance = urine concentration   urine flow
>   of the substance x   rate
>   plasma concentration ofthe
>   substance
>
>   = 7.5 mg/ml x 2 ml/min
>   0.2 mg/ml
>
>   = 75 ml/min

Since a clearance rate of 75 ml/min is less than the average GFR of 125 ml/min, the substance is being reabsorbed.

6. prostate enlargement

Chapter 12, text page 417

1. By inhibiting vasopressin secretion, alcohol promotes excessive free water excretion, thus increasing urine formation. Up to 20% of the filtered water that can be reabsorbed to a variable extent in the distal and collecting tubules subject to vasopressin control is lost in the urine in the absence of vasopressin. Thus, the person loses more fluid in the urine than consumed in the alcoholic beverage. Alochol-induced loss of free water leads to ECF hypertonicity. To compensate for the hypertonic condition, the person feels thirsty despite the excessive fluid consumption. Only a nonalcoholic beverage will relieve the hypertonic condition, however. Consumption of more alcoholic beverage will exacerbate the problem.

2. If a person loses 1500 ml of salt-rich sweat and drinks 1000 ml of water without replacing the salt during the same time period, there will still be a volume deficit of 500 ml and the body fluids will have become hypotonic (the remaining salt in the body will be diluted by the ingestion of 1000 ml of free H_2O). As a result, the hypothalamic osmoreceptors (the dominant input) will signal the vasopressin-secreting cells to decrease vasopressin secretion and thus increase urinary excretion of the extra free water that is making the body fluids too dilute. Simultaneously, the left atrial baroreceptors will signal the vasopressin-secreting cells to increase vasopressin secretion to conserve water during urine formation and thus help to relieve the volume deficit. These two conflicting inputs to the vasopressin-secreting cells are counterproductive. This is why it is important to replace both water and salt following heavy sweating or

abnormal loss of other salt-rich fluids. If salt is replaced along with water intake, the ECF osmolarity remains close to normal and the vasopressin-secreting cells receive signals only to increase vasopressin secretion to help restore the ECF volume to normal.

3. When a dextrose solution equal in concentration to that of normal body fluids is injected intravenously, the ECF volume is expanded but the ECF and ICF are still osmotically equal. Therefore, no net movement of water occurs between the ECF and ICF. However, when the dextrose enters the cell and is metabolized, the ECF becomes hypotonic as this solute leaves the plasma. If the excess free water is not excreted in the urine rapidly enough, water will move into the cells by osmosis.

4. Because baking soda ($NaHCO_3$) is readily absorbed from the digestive tract, treatment of gastric hyperacidity with baking soda can lead to metabolic alkalosis as too much HCO_3^- is absorbed. Treatment with antacids that are poorly absorbed is safer because these products remain in the digestive tract and do not produce an acid-base imbalance.

5. c.
    The hemoglobin buffer system buffers carbonic-acid-generated hydrogen ion. In the case of respiratory acidosis accompanying severe pneumonia, the $H^+ + Hb \rightarrow HHb$ reaction will be shifted toward the HHb side, thus removing some of the extra free H^+ from the blood.

6. The resultant prolonged diarrhea will lead to dehydration and metabolic acidosis due respectively to excessive loss in the feces of fluid and $NaHCO_3$ that normally would have been absorbed into the blood.

    Compensatory measures for dehydration have included increased vasopressin secretion, resulting in increased water reabsorption by the distal and collecting tubules and a subsequent reduction in urine output. Simultaneously, fluid intake has been encouraged by increased thirst. The metabolic acidosis has been combatted by removal of excess H^+ from the ECF by the HCO_3^- member of the H_2CO_3:HCO_3^- buffer system, by increased ventilation to reduce the amount of acid-forming CO_2 in the body fluids, and by the kidneys excreting extra H^+ and conserving HCO_3^-.

Chapter 13, text page 461

1. Patients who have had their stomachs removed must eat small quantities of food frequently instead of consuming the typical three meals a day because they have lost the

ability to store food in the stomach and meter it into the small intestine at an optimal rate. If a person without a stomach consumed a large meal that entered the small intestine all at once, the luminal contents would quickly become too hypertonic as digestion of the large nutrient molecules into a multitude of small, osmotically active, absorbable units outpaced the more slowly acting process of absorption of these units. As a consequence of this increased luminal osmolarity, water would enter the small intestine lumen from the plasma by osmosis, resulting in circulatory disturbances as well as intestinal distention. To prevent this "dumping syndrome" from occurring, the patient must "feed" the small intestine only small amounts of food at a time so that absorption of the digestive end-products can keep pace with their rate of production. The person has to consciously take over metering the delivery of food into the small intestine because the stomach is no longer present to assume this responsibility.

2. Pernicious anemia occurs when insufficient vitamin B_{12} is absorbed. When the stomach is removed, pernicious anemia occurs because of a lack of intrinsic factor, which is produced by the parietal cells of the stomach and must be in combination with vitamin B_{12} for the vitamin to be absorbed. It occurs when the terminal ileum is removed because this region is the only site where vitamin B_{12} in combination with intrinsic factor can be absorbed by pinocytosis.

3. Defecation would be accomplished entirely by the defecation reflex in a patient paralyzed from the waist down because of lower spinal cord injury. Voluntary control of the external anal sphincter would be impossible because of interruption in the descending pathway between the primary motor cortex and the motor neuron supplying this sphincter.

4. When insufficient glucuronyl transferase is available in the neonate to conjugate all of the bilirubin produced during erythrocyte degradation with glycuronic acid, the extra unconjugated bilirubin cannot be excreted into the bile. Therefore, this extra bilirubin remains in the body, giving rise to mild jaundice in the newborn.

5. The large number of immune cells in the gut-associated lymphoid tissue is adaptive as a first line of defense against foreign invasion when considering that the surface area of the digestive tract lining represents the largest interface between the body proper and the external environment.

6.   A person whose bile duct is blocked by a gallstone ex-
     periences a painful "gallbladder attack" after eating a
     high-fat meal because the ingested fat triggers the
     release of cholecystokinin, which stimulates gallbladder
     contraction. As the gallbladder contracts and bile is
     squeezed into the blocked bile duct, the duct becomes
     distended prior to the blockage. This distention is
     painful.

     The feces are grayish white because no bilirubin-
     containing bile enters the digestive tract when the bile
     duct is blocked. Bilirubin, when acted on by bacterial
     enzymes, is responsible for the brown color of feces,
     which are grayish white in the absence of bilirubin.

Chapter 14, text page 477

1.   Evidence suggests that CCK serves as a satiety signal. It
     is believed to serve as a signal to stop eating when
     enough food has been consumed to meet the body's energy
     needs, even though the food is still in the digestive
     tract. Therefore, when drugs that inhibit CCK release are
     administered to experimental animals, the animals overeat
     because this satiety signal is not released.

2.   Don't go on a "crash diet". Be sure to eat a nutrition-
     ally balanced diet so that all essential nutrients are
     provided but reduce total caloric intake, especially
     cutting down on high-fat foods. Spread consumption of the
     food out throughout the day instead of just eating several
     large meals. Avoid bedtime snacks. Burn more calories
     through a regular exercise program.

3.   Engaging in heavy exercise on a hot day is dangerous be-
     cause of problems arising from trying to eliminate the
     extra heat generated by the exercising muscles. First,
     there will be conflicting demands for distribution of the
     cardiac output -- temperature-regulating mechanisms will
     trigger skin vasodilation to promote heat loss from the
     skin surface, whereas metabolic changes within the exer-
     cising muscles will induce local vasodilation in the
     muscles to match the increased metabolic needs with
     increased blood flow. Further exacerbating the problem of
     conflicting demands for blood flow is the loss of
     effective circulating plasma volume resulting from the
     loss of a large volume of fluid through another important
     cooling mechanism, sweating. Therefore, it is difficult
     to maintain an effective plasma volume and blood pressure
     and simultaneously keep the body from overheating when
     engaging in heavy exercise in the heat, so heat exhaustion
     is likely to ensue.

4. When a person is soaking in a hot bath, loss of heat by radiation, conduction, convection, and evaporation are limited to the small surface area of the body exposed to the cooler air. Heat is being gained by conduction at the larger skin surface area exposed to the hotter water.

5. Thermoconformers would not run a fever when they have a systemic infection because they have no mechanisms for regulating internal heat production or for controlling heat exchange with their environment. Their body temperature varies capriciously with the external environment no matter whether they have a systemic infection or not. They are not able to maintain body temperature at a "normal" set point or an elevated set point (i.e., a fever).

6. Cooled tissues need less nourishment than they do at normal body temperature because of their prounounced reduction in metabolic activity. The lower O_2 need of cooled tissues accounts for the occasional survival of drowning victims who have been submerged in icy water considerably longer than one could normally survive without O_2.

Chapter 15, text page 530

1. It is not advisable to rotate the nursing staff on different shifts every week because such a practice would disrupt the individuals' natural circadian rhythms. Such disruption can affect physical and psychological health and have a negative impact on work performance.

2. The concentration of hypothalamic releasing and inhibiting hormones would be considerably lower (in fact, almost nonexistent) in a systemic venous blood sample compared to the concentration of these hormones in a sample of hypothalamic-hypophyseal portal blood. These hormones are secreted into the portal blood for local delivery between the hypothalamus and anterior pituitary. Any portion of these hormones picked up by the systemic blood at the anterior pituitary capillary level is greatly diluted by the much larger total volume of systemic blood compared to the small volume of blood within the portal vessel.

3. If CRH and/or ACTH are elevated in accompaniment with the excess cortisol secretion, the condition is secondary to a defect at the hypothalamic/anterior pituitary level. If CRH and ACTH levels are below normal in accompaniment with the excess cortisol secretion, the condition is due to a primary defect at the adrenal cortex level, with the excess cortisol inhibiting the hypothalamus and anterior pituitary in negative-feedback fashion.

4. An infection elicits the stress response, which brings about increased secretion of cortisol and epinephrine, both of which increase the blood glucose level. This can become a problem in managing the blood glucose level of a diabetic patient. When the blood glucose is elevated too high, the patient can reduce it by injecting additional insulin or, preferably, by reducing carbohydrate intake and/or exercising to use up some of the extra blood glucose. In a normal individual, the check-and- balance system between insulin and the other hormones that oppose insulin's actions helps to maintain the blood glucose within reasonable limits during the stress response.

5. The presence of Chvostek's sign is due to increased neuromuscular excitability caused by moderate hyposecretion of parathyroid hormone.

6. "Diabetes of bearded ladies" is descriptive of both excess cortisol and excess adrenal androgen secretion. Excess cortisol secretion causes hyperglycemia and glucosuria, symptoms which mimic diabetes mellitus. Excess adrenal androgen secretion in females promotes masculinizing characteristics, such as beard growth. Simultaneous hypersecretion of both cortisol and adrenal androgen most likely occurs secondary to excess CRH/ACTH secretion, because ACTH stimulates both cortisol and androgen production by the adrenal cortex.

Chapter 16, text page 572

1. The anterior pituitary responds only to the normal pulsatile pattern of GnRH and does not secrete gonadotropins in response to continuous exposure to GnRH. In the absence of FSH and LH secretion, ovulation and other events of the ovarian cycle do not ensue, so continuous GnRH administration may find use as a contraceptive technique.

2. Testosterone hypersecretion in a young boy causes premature closure of the epiphyseal plates so that he stops growing before he reaches his genetic potential for height. The child would also display signs of precocious pseudopuberty, characterized by premature development of secondary sexual characteristics, such as deep voice, beard, enlarged penis, and sex drive.

3. A potentially troublesome side effect of drugs that inhibit sympathetic nervous system activity as part of the treatment for high blood pressure is the inability to carry out the sex act in males. Both divisions of the autonomic nervous system are required for the male sex act. Parasympathetic activity is essential for accom-

plishing erection and sympathetic activity is important for ejaculation.

4. Posterior pituitary extract contains an abundance of stored oxytocin, which can be administered to induce or facilitate labor by increasing uterine contractility. Exogenous oxytocin is most successful in inducing labor if the woman is near term, presumably because of the increasing concentration of myometrial oxytocin receptors at that time.

5. GnRH or FSH and LH are not effective in treating the symptoms of menopause because the ovaries are no longer responsive to the gonadotropins. Thus, treatment with these hormones would not cause estrogen and progesterone secretion. In fact, GnRH, FSH and LH levels are already elevated in postmenopausal women because of lack of negative feedback by the ovarian hormones.

6. The first warning of a tubal pregnancy is pain caused by stretching of the oviduct by the growing embryo. A tubal pregnancy must be surgically terminated because the oviduct cannot expand as the uterus does to accommodate the growing embryo. If not removed, the enlarging embryo will rupture the oviduct, causing possibly lethal hemorrhage.

Appendix D

List of Colored Acetate Transparencies to Accompany
Fundamentals of Physiology: A Human Perspective
Second Edition

Acetate Number	Figure Number	Title
1.	Fig. 1-3	Interdependent Relationship of Cells, Body Systems, and Homeostasis
2.	Fig. 1-5	Negative Feedback
3.	Fig. 2-1	Schematic Three-Dimensional Illustration of Cell Structures Visible Under Electron Microscope
4.	Fig. 2-3	Transport Vesicles Moving from the Endoplasmic Reticulum to the Golgi Complex and Release of Secretory Vesicles from the Golgi Complex after Further Processing
5.	Fig. 2-6	Endocytosis
6.	Fig. 2-18	Microtrabecular Lattice in Relation to Other Cytoskeletal Structures and Organelles
7.	Fig. 3-3	Fluid Mosaic Model of Plasma Membrane Structure
8.	Fig. 3-4	Postreceptor Event: Channel Regulation
9.	Fig. 3-5	Postreceptor Event: Cyclic AMP Second-Messenger System
10.	Fig. 3-6	Spot Desmosome
11.	Fig. 3-7	Tight Junction
12.	Fig. 3-8	Gap Junction
13.	Fig. 3-10	Diffusion through a Membrane
14.	Fig. 3-13	Osmosis
15.	Fig. 3-16	Osmosis When Pure Water is Separated from a Solution Containing a Nonpenetrating Solute
16.	Fig. 3-17	Carrier-Mediated Transport: Facilitated